INTERNATIONAL DIMENSIONS OF ORGANIZATIONAL BEHAVIOR

FIFTH EDITION

NANCY J. ADLER
McGill University

with

ALLISON GUNDERSEN
Case Western Reserve University

THOMSON
SOUTH-WESTERN

Australia · Brazil · Canada · Mexico · Singapore · Spain · United Kingdom · United States

THOMSON
™
SOUTH-WESTERN

International Dimensions of Organizational Behavior, Fifth Edition
by Nancy J. Adler with Allison Gundersen

VP/Editorial Director:
Jack W. Calhoun

Editor-in-Chief:
Melissa S. Acuña

Senior Acquisitions Editor:
Michele Rhoades

Marketing Manager:
Clint Kernen

Senior Marketing Manager:
Kimberly Kanakes

Senior Marketing Communications Manager:
Jim Overly

Manager, Editorial Media:
John Barans

Technology Project Manager:
Kristen Meere

Associate Content Project Manager:
Joanna Grote

Senior Frontlist Buyer:
Doug Wilke

Production House:
Graphic World Inc.

Senior Art Director:
Tippy McIntosh

Internal Design:
Patti Hudepohl

Cover Art:
Global Rose
Nancy J. Adler

Printer:
West
Eagan, MN

Library of Congress Control
Number: 2007928990

For more information about
our products, contact us at:
**Thomson Learning
Academic Resource Center**
1-800-423-0563

Thomson Higher Education
5191 Natorp Boulevard
Mason, OH 45040
USA

To my mother, Liselotte Adler, who brought together two worlds and two very different cultures in creating the home in which I grew up.
—Nancy J. Adler

To my nieces, Stephanie and Melissa Merakis, who give me hope and inspiration for the future.
—Allison Gundersen

Preface

The world of organizations is no longer defined by national boundaries. *International Dimensions of Organizational Behavior* breaks down the conceptual, theoretical, and practical boundaries that limit our ability to understand and work with people in countries and cultures around the world. Prior to the 21st century, a disproportionate amount of the published material on management came from the United States. American managers and American-trained researchers observed the behavior of people in U.S.-based organizations. From their observations and research, they developed models and theories to explain the behavior of people and organizations. The problem was in their implicit assumption: most scholars assumed that what was true for Americans working in the United States was also true for people from other countries working worldwide. Both managers and researchers assumed that Americans' work behavior was universal. They were wrong. *International Dimensions of Organizational Behavior* challenges us to transcend our parochialism—no matter which country we grew up in—and to see the world from a global perspective.

Today, managers no longer have the luxury of reducing global complexity to the simplicity of assumed universality; they no longer have the luxury of assuming that there is only one best way to manage. Luckily, we have learned that global complexity is neither unpredictable nor random. Variations across cultures and their impact on organizations follow systematic, predictable patterns. Starting with a core of traditional, primarily U.S.-based understandings of the behavior of people in organizations, *International Dimensions* becomes a guide for modifying our attitudes, thinking patterns, and behavior. Far from ignoring the historical body of managerial knowledge, *International Dimensions* expands our understanding of people's behavior at work to include the diversity and complexity of today's global environment.

International Dimensions of Organizational Behavior is divided into three parts. Part 1, "The Impact of Culture on Organizations," describes the ways in which cultures vary, how that variance systematically affects organizations, and how people can recognize, manage, and effectively use cultural variance within their own work environments. Chapter 1 provides a broad context for understanding the global nature of today's business environment. Chapter 2 focuses on the nature of cultural differences worldwide and how they impact organizations. Chapter 3 provides a framework for understanding how to effectively communicate across cultures. Part 2, "Leveraging Cultural Diversity," presents an integrated approach to managing in multicultural work environments. Chapter 4 investigates cross-cultural problem solving and organizational development; Chapter 5 presents the dynamics of multicultural teams; Chapter 6 reviews approaches to global leadership; Chapter 7 focuses on the best approaches for inspiring and motivating people from around the world; Chapter 8 reviews decision making from a global perspective; and Chapter 9 summarizes global approaches to negotiating and resolving conflict.

Part 3, "Managing Global Managers," presents a series of issues that are unique to managing people in a global environment. It addresses the human resource management dilemmas involved in managing one's life and career while moving across international borders. Chapter 10 describes the cross-cultural entry and re-entry transitions from the employee's perspective and addresses such questions as: What is culture shock? How does one adjust to a new culture? How can employees who have worked abroad successfully navigate re-entry back into their home countries and home organizations? Chapter 11 also presents global transition issues, but from the perspective of the spouse. Chapter 12 introduces the challenges of managing a global career. How do the routes to the top of major companies vary from one country to another? What do managers see as the most important benefits and drawbacks of pursuing global careers? Given its focus on global managers, this section goes far beyond the scope of domestically oriented books on both management and organizational behavior.

International Dimensions of Organizational Behavior is used by executives, managers, and college students in a number of ways. First, it is frequently used as a basis for cross-cultural management seminars in which each chapter of the book forms the core of a course module. When used in this way, the book is often supplemented with current readings that provide a more in-depth look at specific areas of the world, as well as with news articles on contemporary world business events. After being introduced to each module with a chapter from *International Dimensions*, seminar participants often expand on the material in the book, based on their current interests and experience, by looking at how it applies, for instance, to e-commerce in Eastern Europe or to China's and India's rapidly expanding economies.

Alternatively, the book is used as a supplement to core organizational behavior courses. In this case, professors first use their standard introduction to the study of people's behavior in organizations. Using Chapters 1 and 2, they then introduce the international dimensions of organizational behavior. Following this introduction, they pair a chapter from *International Dimensions of Organizational Behavior* with each of the modules of their standard course. They pair Chapter 3, for example, with their perception and/or communications module; Chapter 4 with their problem solving and/or organizational development and change module; Chapter 5 with their module on group dynamics and team building; Chapters 6, 7, and 8 with their discussions of leadership, motivation, and decision making; and Chapter 9 with material they present on conflict management and negotiation. In addition, in combination with a module on human resource management or managing careers, or as a completely independent module, professors present Part 3 of *International Dimensions,* which deals with issues related to managing global managers. Participants complete the course with an in-depth understanding of organizational behavior issues from a global, rather than simply a domestic, perspective.

As a third alternative, *International Dimensions of Organizational Behavior* is sometimes used as a self-contained part of a more traditional organizational behavior, management, human resource management, or international business course. Professors selecting this option often present their more domestically oriented material first, and then add a section on international dimensions. As the economy becomes more globally integrated, this third option is preferred less frequently.

Because a substantial amount of the traditional management literature is based on the behavior of Americans working in the United States, and many practicing managers as well as students of management are familiar with U.S. patterns, *International Dimensions* often uses the United States as a reference point and as a point of comparison. Readers in the United States will recognize the familiar ways in which organizational behavior is usually described and be able to add a more global perspective to their knowledge and skills. Readers from all countries will gain a better understanding of their own culture's practices and ways of conducting business, both relative to traditional U.S.-based descriptions and, more importantly, relative to a wide variety of countries and cultures worldwide. No country's system or perspective is any better or worse—any more or less effective—than any other country's; rather, each is distinct and therefore must not be understood as a replica of any other nation.

Cross-cultural management (i.e., studying the international dimensions of people's behavior in organizations) is a relatively new field compared to the traditional study of management. *International Dimensions of Organizational Behavior* integrates the best of what is known in the field as of the first decade of the 21st century. Our knowledge will continue to grow far beyond today's understandings. Even though the limits of our understandings at times restrict us, they also define the expanding boundaries and excitement of an important and rapidly growing field of knowledge. Far from leaving with a sense of knowing all there is to know, it is hoped that readers will finish the book with a sophisticated awareness of the world beyond their own national borders, an understanding of the limits of their own knowledge, and a set of frameworks and questions to guide their managerial decisions and future inquiry.

ACKNOWLEDGMENTS

The process of understanding the human dynamics in global management has brought together some of the best thinking and insights from executives, consultants, managers, and scholars worldwide. The process is evolving. What we know today is so much more than what we understood yesterday, and yet so much less than what we will need for tomorrow. The excitement and passion in the search is predicated on our need to understand ourselves in a world in which no part of humanity is very far away, a world in which our success as well as our survival depends on our understanding and respect for each other.

We would like to thank the many people who have contributed to this book, each from his or her unique perspective and expertise. The quality of this book is shared by all; the errors and limitations are ours alone. Our thanks to: Liselotte Adler (USA), Arshad Ahmad (Pakistan), Nakiye Boyacigiller (Turkey), Jill deVillafranca (Canada), Joseph J. DiStefano (Switzerland), Angela Dowson (Canada), Paul Evans (England), John Graham (USA), Jon Hartwick (Canada), Mary Hess (USA), Maryann Jelinek (USA), André Laurent (France), Phyllis Lefohn (USA), Robert T. Moran (USA), Eileen Newmark (USA), Pri Notowidigdo (Indonesia), Roger Putzel (USA), Vijit Ramchandani (India), Indrei Ratiu (Britain/Romania), George Renwick (USA), Stephen Rhinesmith (USA), David Ricks (Austria), Karlene Roberts (USA), Anita Salustro (USA), Frances Westley (Canada), and Rola Zoayter (Lebanon). In addition, we would like to thank the Organizational Behavior departments at Case Western Reserve and McGill Universities for their support, and the faculty and staff of the Summer Institute for Intercultural Communication for their commitment to the field and research assistance.

A very special thank you goes to Troy Anderson at McGill University for his always extremely helpful research, insights, and editing assistance, and to Darlene Fowler for her patient and conscientious organizing and typing of each new revision until the chapters you see here became the fifth edition. The current fifth edition of the book *International Dimensions of Organizational Behavior* would not be possible without the work contributed by many dedicated colleagues on prior editions, including Louise Dubreil, without whose help, encouragement, and insight, the first edition of this book would have never become a reality; Robine Andrau for her excellent editing of the second and third editions; and John Szilagyi for his professionalism and enthusiasm in managing the fourth edition and the initiation of the current fifth edition.

About the Authors

NANCY J. ADLER

Nancy J. Adler is a Professor of Organizational Behavior and International Management at McGill University's Faculty of Management in Montreal, Canada. She received her B.A. in economics, M.B.A. and Ph.D. in management from the University of California at Los Angeles (UCLA).

Dr. Adler conducts research and consults on global leadership, cross-cultural management, women as global managers and leaders, and the arts and leadership. She has authored over 100 articles, produced the film *A Portable Life*, and, in addition to *International Dimensions of Organizational Behavior*, published the books *Women in Management Worldwide, Competitive Frontiers: Women Managers in a Global Economy*, and *From Boston to Beijing: Managing with a Worldview*.

Dr. Adler consults to private corporations and government organizations on projects in Asia, Africa, Europe, North and South America, and the Middle East. She has taught Chinese executives in the People's Republic of China, held the Citicorp Visiting Doctoral Professorship at the University of Hong Kong, and taught executive seminars worldwide, including at INSEAD in France, Oxford University in England, and Bocconi University in Italy. She received McGill University's first Distinguished Teaching Award in Management and is one of only a few professors to have received it a second time. Honoring her as one of Canada's preeminent university professors, she was selected as a 3M Teaching Fellow.

Dr. Adler has served on the Board of Governors of the American Society for Training and Development (ASTD); the Canadian Social Science Advisory Committee to UNESCO; the Strategic Grants Committee of the Social Sciences and Humanities Research Council; the Executive Committees of the Pacific Asian Consortium for International Business, Education and Research; the International Personnel Association; and the Society for Human Resource Management's International Institute, as well as having held leadership positions in the Academy of International Business (AIB); the Society for Intercultural Education, Training, and Research (SIETAR); and the Academy of Management. Dr. Adler received ASTD's International Leadership Award, SIETAR's Outstanding Senior Interculturalist Award, the YWCA's Femme de Mérite (Woman of Distinction) Award, and the Sage Award for scholarly contributions to management. She was elected to both the Fellows of the Academy of International Business and the Academy of Management Fellows, as well as being inducted into the Royal Society of Canada. In addition to her role as a global manager professor and consultant, Dr. Adler is an artist, working primarily in water color and Asian ink traditions.

ALLISON GUNDERSEN

Allison Gundersen received her A.B. from Cornell University and her M.A. in Intercultural Relations from Lesley University. She has extensive experience managing and consulting in information technology and investment banking in Asia and North America, having been based in both Tokyo and New York City. Her global management work has focused on diverse teams, global responsibilities, and expatriation. Allison is currently conducting research on global leadership, international management, and cross-cultural teams as part of the Department of Organizational Behavior at Case Western Reserve University's Weatherhead School of Management (repeatedly rated as the number one Organizational Behavior department in the world by the *Financial Times*), where she is pursuing her doctoral degree.

Contents

INTERNATIONAL DIMENSIONS OF
ORGANIZATIONAL BEHAVIOR

PART 1

The Impact of Culture on Organizations

Chapter 1

Culture and Management

Verité en-deçà des Pyrénées, erreur au-delà.

("There are truths on this side of the Pyrenees
which are falsehoods on the other.")[1]

—Blaise Pascal

---

*Capital raised in London in the Eurodollar market by a Belgium-
based corporation may finance the acquisition of machinery by a
subsidiary located in Australia. A management team from French
Renault may take over an American-built automotive complex
in the Argentine. Clothing for dolls, sewn in Korea on Japanese-
supplied sewing machines according to U.S. specifications, may be
shipped to Northern Mexico for assembly with other components
into dolls being manufactured by a U.S. firm for sale in New York
and London during the Christmas season. A California-manufac-
tured [plane] . . . is powered by British . . . engines, while a competing [aircraft] . . . flies on Canadian wing assemblies. A
Frenchman is appointed president of [a] U.S. domiciled . . . corporation, while an American establishes . . . a Swiss-based international mutual fund (28:1-2).*

Managing the global enterprise and modern business management have
become synonymous. The terms *international, multinational, transnational,* and *global* can no longer be relegated to a subset of organizations
or to a division within the organization. Definitions of success now transcend national boundaries. In fact, the very concept of domestic business
may have become anachronistic. Today "the modern business enterprise
has no place to hide. It has no place to go but everywhere" (56:xiii).

Executives no longer question the increasing importance of global
business. As indicated in the 21st Century Report (38), more than two-
thirds of the world's CEOs view foreign competition as a key factor in
their firms' business success. Similarly, two-thirds of the world's CEOs

expect to generate employment and revenues increasingly from outside their firms' home countries (38:30,31). These same executives believe that effectively managing human resources is critical to global success (38:2). The post–World War II years saw a major expansion of world trade. From 1948 through 1972 world exports grew from $51 billion to $415 billion, representing a sevenfold increase in monetary terms and a four-fold increase in volume (22:23).[2] By 1980 international trade volume exceeded $1 trillion as compared with $800 billion in 1975 (48). In the 1990s, world exports grew from $4.3 trillion in 1990 to $7.1 trillion in 1999, an increase of 65 percent (27), and by 2005 they had grown to $12.6 trillion, an increase of an additional 77 percent (47). By the 1990s, Coca-Cola, for example, earned higher profits selling soda to the Japanese than to Americans (82:5). By 2006, Coca-Cola produced nearly 400 prod-ucts in over 200 countries, with more than 70 percent of its income coming from outside the United States (21). Mexicans, not Americans, lead the world in the consumption of Coca Cola's beverages, consum-ing, on average, 533 8-oz. beverages per year (21). Today's world trade dwarfs all prior statistics.

By the mid-1980s, the U.S. Commerce Department estimated that some 70 percent of U.S. firms faced "significant foreign competition" in their domestic markets, up from only 25 percent a decade earlier (67:11). By the end of the 1980s, the chairman of the Foreign Trade Council estimated the figure to be 80 percent. Companies are increas-ingly looking outside their domestic markets for revenue. In a study of U.S. companies with revenues over $1 billion, Accenture found that, on average, executives expect sales revenue generated abroad to reach 42 percent of their overall earnings by 2009, compared with 26 percent in 2002 (14). Ninety-seven "percent report that their organization is upgrading its global operations" (14). Today, in the early years of the twenty-first century, global competition is serious, pervasive, and here to stay (49).

What does the future portend? According to *The Economist,* between 1995 and 2020, "the world will see the biggest shift in economic strength in more than a century" (33:3). Emerging economic giants will dwarf developed industrial economies, and "within a generation, China will overtake . . . [the United States] as the world's biggest economy" (33:4). Since 2000, the average annual percentage change in total output in devel-oping countries was more than twice that of advanced economies (9.5% versus only 4.1% [47]). Moreover, many of the top 15 economic perform-ers this century will be from today's rapidly developing economies, with countries such as Thailand and Taiwan overtaking Britain (33:4). In fact, the five fastest growing economies from 1990-2004 were Albania, Bosnia and Herzegovina, China, Ireland, and Vietnam (96:1). The developing world's share of world exports of manufactured goods jumped more than 400 percent in the last quarter of the twentieth century (33:4). Developing countries are playing a greater role in the global marketplace, with low- and middle-income economies accounting for 28.5 percent of world trade, up from 22.3 percent in 1999 (96:3).

Will today's economically developed countries continue to prosper or will they lose out to the gains forecast for developing economies?[3] Experts differ in their predictions. Pessimists from economically developed countries argue that with increasing access to advanced technology, jobs are shifting from workers in rich countries to cheaper, educated labor in economically developing countries. They see free trade with developing countries as a recipe for increasing unemployment in previously economically developed countries, huge wage inequalities, and a massive migration of firms to countries with high skills and low wages. In a dramatic role reversal, economically developing countries that historically were considered victims of multinational exploitation are viewed as villains, stealing capital and jobs and, ironically, creating inequities by destroying the wealth of developed economies.

On the surface this pessimistic scenario appears likely, especially when comparing the hourly wages of production workers. Midway through the first decade of the twenty-first century, it cost $33 an hour to employ a production worker in Germany, $23 an hour in the United States, and $22 an hour in Japan; but only $5.50 in Hong Kong, $2.50 in Mexico, and 50 cents in Sri Lanka (94). According to the president of the World Economic Forum, it has become possible for countries to simultaneously have high productivity, advanced technology, and low wages (81). A major French consumer electronics group, for example, employs three times as many highly skilled workers in Asia as it does in France. Similarly, the Italian sportswear maker Fila produces only 10 percent of its sportswear in Italy; it subcontracts the rest in lower-wage Asian economies. Thomas Friedman, author and *New York Times* editorial columnist, accurately depicts the complex reality of today's global business environment by tracing the supply chain for his Dell notebook from his telephone order through delivery to his home in Maryland. It "involved about four hundred companies in North America, Europe, and primarily Asia, but with 30 key players"; even with a delay, this just-in-time process took only 17 days (32:515-520).

Optimists from economically developed countries, however, predict a different scenario. According to optimists, advanced economies, far from losing out to the growing prosperity of economically developing countries, are benefiting from it. Billions of new consumers in the developing world are markedly increasing demand for exports from the advanced economies. In just the past decade, exports from high-income to low- and middle-income countries have already more than doubled. India's middle class, estimated to grow to over 350 million by 2010, is an example of growing markets, "clamoring for the latest in flavored tooth-paste and flat-panel TVs" (85). In addition, the optimists contend that both advanced and developing economies benefit from increased competition. Greater economies of scale and better allocation of resources resulting from increased competition and financial diversification are improving expected rates of return for all major players. The proportion of foreign direct investment into developing countries increased from 12 to 41 percent of the total over the 1990s (97). In absolute terms, the flow of foreign direct investment into economically developing countries is even more impressive, increasing nearly sevenfold from $36 billion to $233 billion from 1990 to 2005 (93). Over the same period, foreign direct investment in the world's richest economies increased from $172 billion to $380 billion over the same period (93), indicating that investment in emerging economies has not occurred to the detriment of developed economies.

Although international businesses have existed for centuries, the world has clearly entered an era of unprecedented global economic activity that includes worldwide production and distribution, as well as increasingly large numbers of international joint ventures, multinational mergers and acquisitions, and global strategic alliances. Examples of new global operations and alliances abound, with almost every major firm earning more from their global than from their domestic operations. Global companies such as ABB (Asea Brown Boveri), Honda, BP, Siemens, and Tata each do business in more than 100 countries (1;13;83;87). The economic integration of the European Union and the introduction of the common European currency, the Euro, focused the world's attention on transborder business activity and the importance of trading blocs. India and China, with their large populations and expanding economies, are rapidly becoming powerful forces in world markets. Although the U.S. and Canadian economies have been inextricably linked to the world economy for years, the signing of the North American Free Trade Agreement refocused Canadian, Mexican, and U.S. attention on international business.

As Professor Ian Mitroff observes, "For all practical purposes, all business today is global. Those individual businesses, firms, industries, and whole societies that clearly understand the new rules of doing business in a world economy will prosper; those that do not will perish" (64:ix). Mitroff challenges us to realize that "It is no longer business as usual. Global competition has forced . . . [executives] to recognize that if they and their organizations are to survive, let alone prosper, they will have to learn to manage and to think very differently" (64:x).

GLOBAL STRATEGY AND CULTURE

To succeed, corporations must develop global strategies (98).[4] The final decades of the twentieth century made the importance of such recognition commonplace, at least among leading firms and management scholars; the twenty-first century has made it imperative. Incorporating today's global realities, new time- and quality-sensitive approaches to managing research and development, production, marketing, and finance have evolved rapidly. More recently an equivalent evolution in the understanding of international organizational behavior and management of global human resource systems has developed. Although other functional areas have increasingly been using global financial, production, and marketing strategies that were largely unheard of—or would have been deemed inappropriate—only one or two decades ago, many firms are continuing to conduct the worldwide management of people as if neither the strategic challenges presented by the external economic and technological environment nor the internal structure and organization of the firm have changed.

Focusing on global strategies and management approaches from the perspective of people and culture allows us to understand the influence of national and ethnic cultures on organizational functioning. Rather than becoming trapped within the commonly asked (and unfortunately misleading) question of whether organizational dynamics are universal or culturally specific, this book focuses on the crucially important questions of *when* and *how* to be sensitive to culture.

GOING GLOBAL: PHASES OF DEVELOPMENT

As we investigate the influence of cultural diversity on multinational and global firms, it becomes clear that national cultural differences are indeed important, but that their relative impact depends on the stage of development of the firm, industry, and world economy. Using the model shown in Table 1-1, which traces the development of global enterprises, we can distinguish distinct variations in the relative importance of cultural diversity and, consequently, equally distinct variations in the most appropriate approaches to managing people worldwide (4;5;95). Whereas historically the order of the phases has varied, depending primarily on the organization's age and origin as an Asian, European, or North American firm, the order presented here reflects the most common evolution for North American firms. Today, as transnational dynamics increasingly define global business competitiveness, firms frequently skip phases in order to more rapidly position themselves to maximize their global competitive advantage.

DOMESTIC PHASE

As shown in Tables 1-1 and 1-2, historically, most firms initially operated from a domestic, or ethnocentric, perspective. Firms produced
unique products and services that they offered almost exclusively to the
domestic market. The uniqueness of the product or service and the lack
of international competition negated the firm's need to demonstrate
sensitivity to national cultural differences. When firms exported products, they often did so without altering them for foreign consumption.
Foreign buyers, rather than the home country product-design, manufacturing, or marketing teams, absorbed the inconvenience of inherent
cultural differences. In this phase, products from English-speaking
countries, for example, were sent to non-English speaking countries
without translating the packaging into the local language. In some ways
the implicit message sent to people outside the home country was "We
will *allow* you to buy our product"; and, of course, the assumption was
that foreigners would want to buy. During this initial phase, people,
assumptions, and strategies from the headquarter's country dominated
management: firms in the domestic phase regarded cross-cultural management and global human resource systems as largely irrelevant.

MULTIDOMESTIC PHASE

Domestic competition ushered in the second phase, and with it the initial need to market and produce abroad. Irrelevant during the initial
domestic phase, sensitivity to cultural differences became critical to
implementing effective corporate strategy in the multidomestic phase.
The domestic phase's product orientation shifted to a market orientation, with companies now needing to address each foreign market separately and differently.

Whereas the unique technology of, and single market for, the domestic
phase's products and services fit well with an ethnocentric "one-best-way"
approach, during the multidomestic phase firms began to assume there
were "many good ways" to manage, each dependent on the particular
country involved. Successful companies no longer expected foreigners to
absorb cultural mismatches between buyers and sellers. Rather, home-
country representatives modified their style to fit with that of their clients
and colleagues in foreign markets. Although cultural differences became
important in the design and marketing of culturally appropriate products
and services, they became *critical* in worldwide production. Managers had
to learn culturally appropriate approaches to managing people in each
country in which the company operated.

MULTINATIONAL PHASE

By the 1980s many industries had entered the multinational phase. The
competitive environment for these industries had changed again, giving

TABLE 1-1   Global Corporate Evolution

	Domestic Phase	Multidomestic Phase	Multinational Phase	Global Phase
Competitive strategy	Domestic	Multidomestic	Multinational	Global
Importance of world business	Marginal	Important	Extremely important	Dominant
Primary orientation	Product/Service	Market	Price/Cost	Strategy
Product/service	New, unique	More standardized	Completely standardized (commodity)	Mass-customized
Type of development emphasized	Product engineering	Process engineering	Engineering not emphasized	Product and process engineering
Technology	Proprietary	Limited sharing	Widely shared	Almost instantly and extensively shared
R&D/ Sales	High	Decreasing	Very low	Very high
Profit margin	High	Decreasing	Very low	Initially high, yet immediately decreasing
Competitors	None	Few	Many	Significant (few or many)
Market	Small and domestic	Large and multidomestic	Larger and multinational	Largest and global
Production location	Domestic	Domestic and primary foreign markets	Multinational, based on least cost	Global, least cost and best quality
Exports	None	Growing, high potential	Large, saturated	Imports, exports, and "transports"
Structure	Functional divisions	Functional with inter-national division	Multinational lines of business	Global alliances, flattened "heterarchy"
	Centralized	Decentralized	Centralized	Coordinated and decentralized

Source: Adapted by Adler, 2007; based on Adler and Ghadar (5); with *phases* I-III based on Vernon (95).

TABLE 1-2   Corporate Cross-Cultural Evolution

	Domestic Phase	Multidomestic Phase	Multinational Phase	Global Phase
Strategy	Domestic	Multidomestic	Multinational	Global
Primary orientation	Product/ Service	Market	Price/Cost	Strategy
Perspective	Ethnocentric	Polycentric or Regiocentric	Multinational	Global/ Multicentric
Cultural sensitivity	Marginally important	Very important	Somewhat important	Critically important
With whom	No one	Clients	Employees	Employees and clients
Level	No one	Employees and clients	Managers	Executives, managers, employees and clients
Strategic assumption	"One way" or "One best way"	"Many good ways" Equifinality	"One least-cost way" Simultaneously	"Many good ways"

Source: Adapted by Adler, 2007; based on Adler and Ghadar (5).

rise to demands for culturally sensitive management practices within each firm. In multinational industries, a number of companies produce almost indifferentiable products (practically commodities), with price defining their only potentially significant competitive advantage. From this global price-sensitive—and therefore cost-sensitive—perspective, cultural awareness, vis-à-vis clients, declines in importance. Price competition among almost identical products and services produced by various multinational companies negates the importance of most cultural differences and almost all advantages gained by cultural sensitivity when marketing to customers worldwide.

As shown in Table 1-2, the primary product design and marketing assumption is no longer the domestic phase's "one best way" or even the multidomestic phase's "many good ways," but rather "one least-cost way." The primary market becomes global, with almost no geography-based market segmentation. Firms can gain competitive advantage only through process engineering, sourcing critical factors on a worldwide basis, and benefiting from economies of scale. Price competition significantly reduces the influence of cultural differences.

GLOBAL PHASE
Many managers believed that the multinational phase would be the ultimate phase for all industries. Their assumption proved to be false. Although some industries today continue to operate under the norms of the multinational phase, a fourth phase has emerged for firms in globally

competitive industries. In this global (or transnational) phase, top quality, least possible-cost products become the baseline, the minimally acceptable standard. Competitive advantage comes from strategic thinking, mass customization, and outlearning one's competitors. Product and service ideas are drawn from worldwide sources, as are the factors and locations of production. Companies, however, tailor final products and services and their marketing to discrete market niches. Critical components of this type of market segmentation are nationality and ethnicity. Culture, once again, becomes a critical competitive factor.

Successful global firms competing under transnational dynamics need to understand their potential clients' needs, no matter where in the world the clients live. They need to be able to quickly translate these worldwide client needs into products and services, produce those products and services on a timely and least-cost basis, and then deliver them to clients in a culturally acceptable fashion for each of the national and ethnic communities involved.

In the global phase, the exclusive product, sales, or price orientation of past phases almost completely disappears. Companies replace these individual orientations with a culturally responsive design orientation, accompanied by a rapid, worldwide, least-cost production function. The company that designs and brings to market the next new-best-thing wins. Needless to say, culture is critically important at this most advanced stage. Similarly, the ability to manage cross-cultural interaction, multinational teams, and global alliances becomes fundamental to overall business success. Whereas effective global human resource strategies varied from irrelevant to helpful in past phases, in the global phase they have become essential, a minimum requirement for organizational survival and success.

CROSS-CULTURAL MANAGEMENT

The importance of world business has created a demand for managers sophisticated in global management and skilled at working with people from countries other than their own (80). Cross-cultural management explains the behavior of people in organizations around the world and shows people how to work in organizations with employee and client populations from many different cultures (24;41;71). Cross-cultural management *describes* organizational behavior within countries and cultures; *compares* organizational behavior across countries and cultures; and, most important, seeks to understand and improve the *interaction* of co-workers, managers, executives, clients, suppliers, and alliance partners from countries and cultures around the world. Cross-cultural management thus expands the scope of domestic management to encompass international and multicultural dynamics. Rather than global management being a subset of traditional domestic approaches, single-culture/domestic management is now recognized as a limited subset of global, cross-cultural management.

PAROCHIALISM

Parochialism means viewing the world solely through one's own eyes and perspective. A person with a parochial perspective neither recognizes other people's different ways of living and working nor appreciates that such differences can offer significant opportunities or create serious consequences. People in all cultures are, to a certain extent, parochial. Journalists, politicians, and managers alike, for example, have frequently decried Americans' parochialism.[5] Americans speak fewer foreign languages, demonstrate less interest in other cultures, and are more naïve in global business situations than most of their trading partners. In *The Tongue-Tied American* (84), U.S. Congressman Paul Simon deplored the shocking state of foreign language illiteracy in the United States and emphasized the heavy price Americans pay for it diplomatically, commercially, economically, and culturally. His message was a "shocking indictment of the complacent, potentially catastrophic monolingual arrogance of . . . [Americans], from top government leaders to the . . . [person] in the street" (90). Echoing Simon's sentiments in reference to South America, former U.S. Congressman James Symington explained the problem as Americans'

> *fundamental, dogged, appalling ignorance of the Latin mind and culture. Foreign students and statesmen refresh their perceptions of the United States by reading our poets, essayists, novelists and humorists. But our approach is like that of the man who, when asked which hurts most, ignorance or apathy, replied, "I don't know and I don't care." Such indifference cannot be justified by our otherwise commendable concern for what people do rather than what they think. . . . Preoccupied with acting, we seldom miss opportunities to ignore thought. [Perhaps, in the future] . . . diplomats—possibly even presidents—might know something of the cultural lessons that stir our neighbors' hearts* (86).

Fortune magazine reports that "A 'Copernican revolution' must take place in the attitudes of American CEOs as the international economy no longer revolves around the U.S., and the world market is shared by many strong players" (54:157). Lester Thurow, former dean of MIT's Sloan School of Management, asserts that CEOs "must have an understanding of how to manage in an international environment. . . . To be trained as an *American* manager is to be trained for a world that is no longer there" (34:50). Similarly, Harvard management professor Rosabeth Moss Kanter asserts that "Global thinking is what's important for companies today,

not [simply] international operations" (50; also see 7;8;9;36;57;65;70;74;75;76).
"The task is not to build a sophisticated structure, but to build a
matrix in the minds of managers" (7:212). Many business leaders predict
that the next generation of top executives will have to perform well on
multiple global assignments to reach the top (15:B18;20). Royal Dutch Shell,
for example, requires four expatriate assignments before it considers a
manager for promotion into senior management. Yet in the United
States such global exposure and experience has neither been the norm in
the past nor, unfortunately, is it as common as it should be today (11).

In the closing decades of the twentieth century, a Dun & Bradstreet
survey found that only a handful of the 87 chairmen and presidents of
the 50 largest U.S. multinational corporations could be considered
career internationalists. Of the 87 top executives, 80 percent had had no
international experience at all, except for inspection tours (25). Today,
executive recognition of the importance of global experience has
increased, but not as rapidly in the United States as in many other parts
of the world. For example, whereas almost two-thirds of today's U.S.
executives see "emphasizing an international outlook" as very important for twenty-first century CEOs, only a third consider experience
outside of the United States as equally important, and fewer than one in
five consider foreign language training as very important (54:158). By
comparison, more than eighty percent of non-U.S. executives consider
an international outlook as very important for future CEOs, twice as
many (70% versus 35%) consider experience outside of their home
country as very important, and more than three times as many (64% versus 19%) consider foreign language training as very important (38;54:158).

Why have many Americans ignored the need to think and to act
globally? Americans' historic parochialism is understandable and at the
same time unfortunate. Because the United States has such a large domestic market (over 300 million people) and English has become the world's
business language, many Americans continue to assume that they neither need to speak other languages nor to go to other countries to succeed in business. Few young Brazilians, Israelis, Swedes, or Thais remain
trapped in this parochial and privileged assumption.

Historical U.S. political and technological dominance also led many
Americans to believe that they could conduct business strictly from an
American perspective. In many fields in which for years U.S. technology
was the only advanced technology available, potential clients and trading
partners from around the world had no option but to "buy American."
Global business expertise was unnecessary because the product sold
itself (domestic phase). In the public sector, projects transferring technology from the United States to economically developing countries
further encouraged Americans to view the world from an American
perspective (multidomestic phase). An Indonesian's comments about

Americans' views of people from economically developing countries capture this technologically based parochialism:

> *The questions Americans ask me are sometimes very embarrassing, like whether I have ever seen a camera. Most of them consider themselves the most highly civilized people. Why? Because they are accustomed to technical inventions? Consequently, they think that people living in bamboo houses or having customs different from their own are primitive and backward (79).*

The academic community further reinforced U.S. managers' tendency toward parochialism. Most management schools are in the United States, the vast majority of management professors and researchers are U.S. educated, and the majority of management research has focused on U.S. companies. In a survey conducted in the 1980s of more than 11,000 articles published in 24 management journals, approximately 80 percent reported on studies focusing on U.S. companies conducted by American researchers (2). Fewer than 5 percent of research articles describing the behavior of people in organizations included the concept of culture (2). Less than 1 percent focused on people from two or more cultures working together, a crucial area to understand for global business success (2). The publishing of cross-cultural management articles is increasing much more slowly than the rate at which business has gone global (35;58;60;66).

Even in the last decade, only 6.5 percent of organizational behavior and human resource management (HRM) articles published in leading U.S. management journals were international; however, almost three times as many (17.5%) organizational behavior and HRM articles in leading management journals published outside of North America were international (4). Among these international articles, almost every study (96%) found that culture had a significant impact on managerial styles and organizational success (4). The manager about to negotiate a major contract with a client from another country, the executive about to become director of Asian, European, or Latin American operations, and the newly promoted vice president for global marketing all receive less guidance than they need from the available management literature. Cultural misunderstandings persist at the most sophisticated levels of intercultural interaction. In September 2005, for example:

> *[U.S.] Deputy Secretary of State Robert Zoellick gave a speech to the National Committee on United States-China Relations in which he repeatedly urged China to become a responsible 'stakeholder' in the international system. It turns out that there is no word in Chinese for 'stakeholder,' and the initial Chinese reaction was puzzlement and reaching for a dictionary. Did Mr. Zoellick mean 'steak holder?'*

After all, he was speaking at a dinner. Maybe this was some Texas slang for telling China it had to buy more U.S. beef? Well, eventually the Chinese got a correct interpretation (32).

The United States will continue to have a large domestic market, English will continue to be the language of international business, and technological excellence will continue to typify many U.S. companies. Nonetheless, the domain of business has rapidly moved beyond national boundaries; the limitations of monolingualism have become more apparent; and sustained technological superiority in many industries has become a cherished memory. The intense global competition of the past decade renders parochialism self-defeating. No nation can afford to act as if it is alone in the world (parochialism) or as if it is superior to other nations (ethnocentrism). The U.S. economy, like that of all other countries, is inextricably linked to the health of the world's economy. Like businesspeople the world over, Americans must now compete on a global scale and contribute based on world-class standards.

GLOBAL VERSUS DOMESTIC ORGANIZATIONS

Two fundamental differences between global and domestic organizations are geographic dispersion and multiculturalism. The term *geographic dispersion* refers to the spread of global organizations' operations over vast distances worldwide (51). Whether organizations produce in multiple countries or only export to them, whether employees work as expatriates or only travel abroad, whether legal ownership involves joint ventures, wholly owned subsidiaries, or strategic alliances, global firms must manage despite the added complexity of working in many countries simultaneously. Geographic dispersion confronts organizations with political risk, fluctuations in exchange rates, substantial transportation and communication costs, varying regulatory structures, and many other complexities determined by greater distances and national borders.

Multiculturalism, the second fundamental dimension of global firms, means that people from many countries and/or cultures interact regularly. Domestic firms can be multicultural if their employees or clients come from more than one culture.[6] Many organizations in Québec, for example, employ Anglophones (English speakers) and Francophones (French speakers) to work within the same organization. Similarly, many companies in California hire Hispanic and Asian as well as Anglo-Saxon employees. Multiculturalism adds to the complexity of global firms by increasing the number of perspectives, approaches, and business methods represented within the organization.

To successfully manage the geographical dispersion and multiculturalism of multinational organizations, managers must develop a global mindset (7;9;17;18;36;53;57;65;74;88). In fact, it is the mindsets of key managers that shape business strategy and ultimately determine the success of the firm. Managers with a global mindset address strategic business decisions as cosmopolitans, always considering the broader world picture rather than just the local situation (9 based on 63;42). Similarly, using their highly developed cognitive complexity, managers with a global mindset simultaneously consider the complex multicultural situations facing the firm, and consistently make appropriate trade-offs among competing multinational options (9).

Whereas most books on global management have focused on understanding and managing geographical dispersion, this book focuses primarily on managing multiculturalism and raises such questions as: How do people vary across cultures? How do cultural differences affect organizations? When do global managers recognize cultural differences? What are the best strategies for managing multiculturalism? How can companies best leverage cultural diversity, using it as a competitive advantage rather than viewing it as a source of problems?

WHAT IS CULTURE?

To understand the differences between domestic and global management, it is necessary to understand the primary ways in which cultures around the world vary. Anthropology has produced a literature rich in descriptions of a full range of cultural systems, containing profound implications for managers working outside their native countries. Anthropologists view culture in many ways. *Culture* is seen as "that complex whole which includes knowledge, belief, art, law, morals, customs and any capabilities and habits acquired by a . . . [person] as a member of society" (86:1). Alternatively, it is viewed as "a way of life of a group of people, the configuration of all the more or less stereotyped patterns of learned behavior, which are handed down from one generation to the next through the means of language and imitation" (6:4). After cataloging more than 100 different definitions of culture, anthropologists Kroeber and Kluckhohn (55:181) offered one of the most comprehensive and generally accepted definitions:

> *Culture consists of patterns, explicit and implicit, of and for behavior acquired and transmitted by symbols, constituting the distinctive achievement of human groups, including their embodiment in artifacts; the essential core of culture consists of traditional (i.e., historically derived and selected) ideas and especially their attached values; culture systems may, on the one hand, be considered as products of action, on the other, as conditioning elements of future action.*

Culture is therefore (19:19)

- Something shared by all or almost all members of a given social group
- Something older members of a group pass on to younger members
- Something (as in the case of morals, laws, and customs) that shapes behavior, or . . . structures one's perception of the world

Managers frequently see culture as "the collective programming of the mind which distinguishes the members of one human group from another . . . the interactive aggregate of common characteristics that influence a human group's response to its environment" (45:25). In general, we see people as being from different cultures if their ways of life as a group differ significantly.

Cultural Orientations The cultural orientation of a society reflects the complex interaction of values, attitudes, and behaviors displayed by its members (43). As shown in Figure 1-1, individuals express culture and its normative qualities through the values they hold about life and the

FIGURE 1-1   Influence of Culture on Behavior and Behavior on Culture

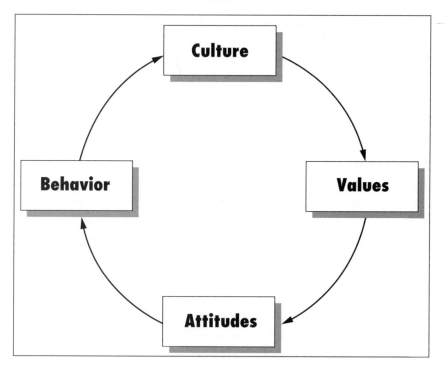

world around them. These values in turn affect their attitudes about the form of behavior considered most appropriate and effective in any given situation. The continually changing patterns of individual and group behavior eventually influence the society's culture, and the cycle begins again. What are the differences among values, attitudes, and behavior?

Values   A value is that which is explicitly or implicitly desirable to an individual or group and which influences the selection from available modes, means, and ends of action. Values can be both consciously and unconsciously held (52). Values therefore reflect relatively general beliefs that either define what is right and wrong or specify general preferences (16:23). Research has shown that personal values affect corporate strategy (12;30;37;39;44;73;75;78;92) and that managerial values affect all forms of organizational behavior (7;29;68;69), including selection and reward systems (16), superior/subordinate relationships (61), group behavior, communication, leadership, conflict management styles (56), and approaches to negotiating. Latin American managers, for example, consider loyalty to the family to be highly important—a value that leads them to hire competent members of their own family whenever possible. U.S. managers strongly believe in individual achievement—a value that leads them to emphasize a candidate's track record and performance on qualifying exams rather than family membership. In both cases a strongly held value influences managerial behavior.

Attitudes   An attitude expresses values and disposes a person to act or to react in a certain way toward something. Attitudes are present in the relationship between a person and some kind of object. Initial market research, for example, showed that French Canadians have a positive attitude toward pleasant or sweet smells, whereas English Canadians prefer smells with efficient or clean connotations. The first advertisements for Irish Spring soap directed at French Canadians therefore stressed the pleasant smell, whereas the ads directed at English Canadians stressed the inclusion of effective deodorants.[7]

Behavior   Behavior is any form of human action. For example, based on their culture, Middle Easterners stand closer together (a behavior) than do North Americans, whereas Japanese stand farther apart than do either North Americans or Middle Easterners. Latin Americans touch each other more frequently during business negotiations than do North Americans, and both touch more frequently than do Japanese. People's behavior is defined by their culture.

CULTURAL DIVERSITY

Diversity exists both within and among cultures; however, within a single culture certain behaviors are favored and others repressed. The norm for a society is the most common and most generally accepted pattern of values, attitudes, and behavior. In global business, for example, a man wearing a dark gray business suit reflects the norm through a favored behavior, whereas a man wearing a green business suit would violate the norm. A cultural orientation describes the attitudes of most people most of the time, never of all people all of the time. Accurate stereotypes reflect societal or cultural norms.

Societies enforce norms by communicating disapproval toward transgressors—people who engage in prohibited behavior. Some norms, such as laws, may be highly significant; whereas other norms, such as customs and habits, may be less important. A norm's importance is measured by how severely society condemns those who violate it. In the United States, for example, an important norm proscribes bribery. Companies caught using bribery to increase their business are publicly prosecuted and fined; both punishments reflect severe cultural sanctions. A less important norm in the United States is the tradition of saying "Good morning" when greeting colleagues at the beginning of the day. If I fail to say "Good morning" one day, it is unlikely that society will punish me severely. At worst, my colleagues may assume that I am preoccupied or perhaps tired.

Anthropologists Kluckhohn and Strodtbeck (52) discuss a set of assumptions that allows us to understand the cultural orientations of a society without doing an injustice to the diversity within the society.[8] The six assumptions (73) are as follows:

1. "There are a limited number of common human problems for which all peoples at all times must find some solutions." Each society, for example, must decide how to clothe, feed, and house its people. Each society must decide on systems of justice, communication, education, health, commerce, transportation, and government.
2. "There are a limited number of alternatives which exist for dealing with these problems." People, for example, may house themselves in tents, caves, igloos, single-family dwellings, or apartment buildings, but they cannot survive the winter without some form of housing.
3. "All alternatives are present in all societies at all times, but some are preferred over others."
4. "Each society has a dominant profile or values orientation and, in addition, has numerous variations or alternative profiles." People may cure disease, for example, with chemotherapy, surgery, acupuncture, acupressure, prayer, or nutrition. Many Chinese prefer acupressure and acupuncture; many British prefer chemotherapy and surgery; many Indians prefer ayurvedic medicine and many Christian Scientists prefer prayer.

5. "In both the dominant profile and the variations, there is a rank ordering of preference for alternatives."

6. "In societies undergoing change, the ordering of preferences will not be clearcut." As the cyber revolution changes society, for example, organizations' preferences to communicate using the Internet, fax, telephone, e-mail, courier, or postal system become unclear; different organizations make different choices. These assumptions emphasize that cultural descriptions always refer to the norm or stereotype; they never refer to the behavior of all people in the culture, nor do they predict the behavior of any particular person.

HOW DO CULTURES VARY?

As shown in Table 1-3, six basic dimensions describe the cultural orientations of societies: people's qualities as individuals, their relationship to nature and the world, their relationship to other people, their primary type of activity, and their orientation in space and time (52;56). The six dimensions answer the questions: Who am I? How do I see the world? How do I relate to other people? What do I do? How do I use space and time? Each orientation reflects a value and each value has behavioral and attitudinal implications. As summarized in Table 1-4, this section introduces the six value dimensions and gives managerial examples for each. Because many people are familiar with U.S. business customs, the examples highlight differences between the managerial practices in the United States and those in a number of other countries.

HOW PEOPLE SEE THEMSELVES What is the nature of the individual: good or evil? Americans traditionally see people as a mixture of good and evil, capable of choosing one over the other. They believe in the possibility of improvement through change. Some other cultures see

TABLE 1-3   Values Orientation Dimensions

Perception of		Dimensions	
Individual	Good	Good and evil	Evil
World	Dominant	Harmony	Subjugation
Human Relations	Individual	Laterally extended groups	Hierarchical groups
Activity	Doing	Controlling	Being
Time	Future	Present	Past
Space	Private	Mixed	Public

Source: Based on Kluckhohn and Strodtbeck (52), as adapted by Lane and DiStefano (56).

TABLE 1-4   Cultural Orientations and Their Implications for Management

Cultural Dimensions	U.S. Cultural Orientation	Contrasting Cultural Orientation
What is the nature of people?	**Mixture of good and evil** **Change is possible.**	**Good** **(Evil)** **Change is impossible.**
Example:	Emphasize training and development; give people the opportunity to learn on the job.	Emphasize selection and fit; select the right person for the job; do not expect employees to change once hired.
What is a person's relationship to the external environment, including nature?	**People dominant over nature and other aspects of the external environment.**	**Harmony (Subjugation)**
Example:	Policy decisions made to alter nature to fulfill people's needs—i.e., building dams and roads.	Policy decisions made to protect nature while meeting people needs—i.e., sustainable development.
What is a person's relationship to other people?	**Individualistic**	**Group (Hierarchical or Lateral)**
Example:	Personnel director reviews academic and employment records of each candidate to select the best person for the job.	Personnel director selects the closest relative of the chief executive as the best person for the job.
Example:	Individuals make decisions	Groups make decisions
What is the primary mode of activity?	**Doing**	**Being (Controlling)**
Example:	Employees work hard to achieve goals; employees maximize their time at work.	Employees work only as much as needed to earn enough to live; employees minimize their time at work.
How do people see space?	**Private**	**Public**
Example:	Executives hold important meetings in large offices behind closed doors with a secretary screening out interruptions.	Executives hold important meetings in open areas, with open doors and many interruptions from employees and visitors.
What is a person's temporal orientation?	**Future/Present**	**Past (Present)**
Example:	Mission statement refers to 5- and 10-year goals while focus is kept on this year's bottom line and quarterly reports; innovation and flexibility to meet a dynamic, changing future are emphasized.	Mission statement this year reflects policy statements 10 years ago; the company strives to use tradition to perform in the future as it has in the past.

Source: Adapted by Adler (3:411) updated 2007; based on Kluckhohn and Strodtbeck (52) and DiStefano (23); also see Lane and DiStefano (56).

people as basically evil—as reflected in the Puritans' orientation. Others see people as basically good—as reflected in utopian societies throughout the ages. Societies that consider people good tend to trust them a great deal, whereas societies that consider people evil tend to suspect or mistrust them. In high-trust societies, for example, people leave doors unlocked and do not fear being robbed or assaulted. In low-trust societies, people bolt their doors. After making a purchase on the internet, people in high-trust societies expect to receive the merchandise and to have their credit card appropriately debited; they do not expect to be cheated. In low-trust societies, *caveat emptor* ("let the buyer beware") rules the marketplace; one can trust only oneself. In many countries people are more trusting in rural communities than in urban centers. Today's web-mediated e-business challenges buyers to trust unseen sellers, and sellers to assess their confidence levels in unseen buyers.

Today many citizens of the United States and Canada lament that their fellow citizens cannot be trusted the way they used to be. A Toronto hotel, for example, posts a sign reminding guests that "Love is leaving the towels." Los Angeles gas stations, to assure that motorists will not drive away without paying, require motorists to pay twenty dollars or sign a credit card slip before filling their gas tanks. A Minneapolis firm, National Credential Verification Service, makes a profitable business of exploiting the lack of trust among corporate recruiters and job candidates by exposing résumé deception. Out of 233 personnel officers responding to a survey of *Fortune 500* companies, only one said that deception by applicants for executive positions was diminishing (59:85). To add to this mistrust, many people find it more difficult to trust foreigners than citizens of their own country.

Managers in the People's Republic of China describe their approach as combining the extremes of good (Confucian tradition) with evil (the tradition of Lao Tzu)—a marriage of opposites. They also describe their belief that peasants are good while rich people are not so good, as reflected in a story told among people living in Tianjin, the fourth largest city in China:

> At the Franco-Chinese joint venture winery in Tianjin between France's Rémy Martin and China's Dynasty, a French director left his wallet filled with French francs in a ped-a-cab. The ped-a-cab driver, a peasant, waited all day outside the winery to return the wallet to the Frenchman.

Perhaps because people fear the unknown, they frequently tend to assume that evil intentions motivate foreigners' behavior. Canadian government officials, for example, thought the Inuits, a native people, were evil when they burned down the doors in their Canadian-built public

PERCEPTION OF THE INDIVIDUAL
Good Versus Evil

Can a Bosnian Trust a Canadian Working in Sweden?[9]

A young Canadian in Sweden found summer employment working in a restaurant owned by Bosnians. As the Canadian explained, "I arrived at the restaurant and was greeted by an effusive Bosnian man who set me to work at once washing dishes and preparing the restaurant for the June opening.

"At the end of the first day, I was brought to the backroom. The owner took an old cash box out of a large desk. The Bosnian owner counted out my wages for the day and was about to return the box to the desk when his private phone rang in the front room. The owner hesitated: should he leave me sitting in the room with the money or take it with him? Quite simply, could he trust me?

"After a moment, the man got up to answer the phone, leaving me with the open money box. I sat there in amazement: how could he trust me, someone he had known for less than a day, a person whose last name and address he didn't even know?"

This incident contrasts perceptions of individuals as good or evil. The Bosnian manager saw individuals as good and inherently trustworthy. For this reason, he could leave his new employee alone with the money without worrying that the Canadian would steal it before he returned. The Canadian employee's surprise that this stranger trusted him with the money is a reflection of a North American's values orientations toward individuals. Believing that people are capable of both good and evil, most North Americans would proceed more cautiously than did the Bosnian. If the Canadian had been in the owner's shoes, he probably would have taken the cash box with him to the other room to answer the telephone, fearing that the money might be stolen.

---

housing projects. The officials misinterpreted the Inuits' behavior as vandalism and therefore judged it to be evil, whereas the Inuits had actually altered the houses to fit their normal more collective—and therefore doorless—lifestyle. The Canadian government condemns the destruction of property, whereas the Inuits condemn closed doors that separate people from family members and neighbors.

Apart from their tendencies toward good or evil, can human beings improve themselves? Societies and organizations vary in the extent to which they believe that adults can change or improve. Organizations that believe people can change, for example, emphasize training and development, whereas organizations that believe people are incapable of change emphasize selection systems. With today's Internet and information systems revolution, some organizations have chosen to replace many of their current administrative-support personnel with e-technology and information systems experts. Other companies have retrained their current

employees to use the new state-of-the-art technologies. The first strategy—
primarily hiring new employees—assumes that change is not possible,
whereas the second strategy of training present employees implies
that change is possible. North Americans' emphasis on MBA education
and executive development seminars strongly reflects their belief
that change is possible. The Chinese saying that the "Chinese . . . strive
to become better and, when better, to become perfect" also reflects a
strong belief in the ability of adults to change. As one Shanghai executive exclaimed, applying the belief to his own career path, "I was
trained as an engineer and now I am an export/import manager. I
changed!"

PEOPLE'S RELATIONSHIP TO THE WORLD

What is a person's relationship to the world? Are people dominant over their
environment, in harmony with it, or subjugated by it? North Americans
generally see themselves as dominant over nature. Other societies, such as
traditional Chinese and Navaho, attempt to live in harmony with nature.
They see no real separation between people and their natural environment,
and their beliefs allowed them to live for many generations at peace with the
environment. In contrast to both of these orientations, a few remote tribal
societies see people as subjugated by nature. In these cultures people accept
and honor, rather than interfere with, the inevitable forces of nature.

How does an organization see its environment? Are the relevant
external environments—cultural, economic, legal, political, social, and
technological—seen as stable and predictable or as chaotic, turbulent,
and unpredictable? Does an organization assume that it can control its
environment, that it must harmonize with it, or that it will be dominated by it?

North Americans' approach to agriculture exemplifies the dominance
orientation. By assuming, for instance, that people can and ethically
should modify nature to enhance their own well-being, dominance-
oriented agribusiness executives use fertilizers, pesticides, and genetically
modified seeds to increase crop yields. By contrast, harmony-oriented
farmers attempt only to plant the "right" crops in the "right" places at the
"right" time of the year in order to maintain the soil in good condition.
Farmers subjugated by nature hope that sufficient rain will fall, but
they do not construct irrigation systems to assure sufficient water for
their crops. Although they hope or pray that pests will not attack their
crops, they refuse to use insecticides. Other examples of North
Americans' dominance orientation include astronauts' conquest
(dominance) of space, economists' structuring of markets, sales representatives' attempts to influence buyers' decisions, and, perhaps most con-
troversial today, the attempts by biotechnology and genetic engineering

HOW DO I RELATE TO THE WORLD?
Dominance Versus Harmony

Given the rapid expansion of their Asian practice, an American law firm chose to add a newly promoted American partner to its Asian headquarters in Shanghai. The Shanghai lawyers gave the new expatriate American partner a prominent office and encouraged her to decorate it herself. Having studied Chinese culture in the months prior to leaving the United States, the American expatriate chose to place a large, particularly artistically rendered Chinese painting of a fish in her office, immediately to the left of the door. She had learned that a fish symbolizes lasting prosperity, as the pronunciation in Chinese of the word "fish" suggests that "You will make a profit and the profit will stay with you."

The partner was therefore very surprised to watch one Chinese client after another become uncomfortable upon entering her office; with many choosing not to meet with her a second time. Within a week, she grew frustrated and increasingly upset by her potential clients' behavior.

Luckily, she sought the help of the local *Feng shui* master. *Feng shui*, or "wind water," are earth forces which many traditional Chinese believe can cause success or failure. *Feng shui* reflects the belief that people and their activities are affected by the orientation and layout of buildings, rooms, and objects, including in offices and homes. The goal of *feng shui* is for people to remain in harmony with the environment.

The *feng shui* master explained that the problem was the placement of the painting. The head of the fish, which faced the door, symbolized that profit would flow away from the client and out the door. The expatriate executive had been right about the overall symbolism of the fish. However, based on Chinese cultural tradition, the closeness of the fish painting to the door, and the fact that the fish's head faced the door, had created exactly the opposite message of the one the American lawyer had tried to convey. With the guidance of the *feng shui* master, the fish painting was re-located above the lawyer's desk, far away from the door. Chinese clients immediately stopped reacting negatively to the American lawyer's office. Her Asian practice grew steadily, with more than an average amount of success. In the ensuing months, there were no business failures or other dire business consequences. The expatriate's clients were comfortable with her new office and ultimately chose to bring her their most important legal work.

Chinese and North American perceptions of the world clearly differ. Traditional Chinese desire to be in harmony with nature, whereas most North Americans want to control nature. The American expatriate partner did not yet know enough about Chinese culture to create harmony with nature. From a North American dominance perspective, the fish painting, and its placement in her office would be irrelevant. But to traditional Chinese, her choice to hang a fish painting close to the door, and with the head of the fish pointing toward the door, appeared irrational; from the Chinese perspective, the American had failed to achieve harmony with nature and was unnecessarily bringing a lack of luck

HOW DO I RELATE TO THE WORLD?
Dominance Versus Harmony (continued)

to herself and her clients. By consulting the *feng shui* master and changing the location of the painting, the expatriate American exhibited a more profound sensitivity to the local culture and demonstrated true respect for her clients' beliefs and traditions.[10]

to alter the nature of life itself. The contrasting relationships become clearer in the sayings of three societies:

Saying	Culture	Reflected Meaning
Ayorama: "It can't be helped"	Inuit—Canada	Subjugation
En Shah Allah: "If God is willing"	Moslem—Arab	Harmony with nature and submission to God
Can Do: "I will do it"	American—U.S.	Dominance

A society's orientation toward the world is pervasive. When Sir Edmund Hillary reached the top of Mt. Everest, for example, the Western dominance-oriented press reported the story as "Man conquers mountain"; in contrast, the Chinese harmony-oriented press reported the same story as "Man befriends mountain." Religious writings similarly reflect a people's cultural orientation. The *Bible*, for example, states in Genesis, "Let them have dominion over the earth"; whereas the *Tao Te Ching* states, "Those who would take over the earth and shape it to their will, I notice, never succeed"— a dominance orientation contrasting with one of harmony.

PERSONAL RELATIONSHIPS: INDIVIDUALISM OR COLLECTIVISM[11]
Americans are individualists; they use personal characteristics and achievements to define themselves, and they value individual welfare over that of the group. By contrast, in group-oriented societies people define themselves as members of clans or communities and consider common goals and the group's welfare most important. Lateral group membership includes all who are currently members of a particular family, community, or organization. Hierarchical group membership has a temporal definition; it includes current members of the particular group and members from prior generations.

The United States is strongly individualistic and weak in loyalty to groups, teams, and communities. Americans, for example, praise their sports heroes by singling out individual excellence: "Mark Smith and the

PERSONAL RELATIONSHIPS
Individualism Versus Collectivism

The German Won't Hire the Serbian's Daughter[12]

Rade, an engineer who had immigrated to western Germany from the former Yugoslavia, worked for a highly respected German engineering firm. His daughter Lana had recently graduated as one of the top students from a prestigious German university. Rade considered it his duty to find his daughter a job, and he wanted his German boss to hire Lana. Although the boss felt Lana was extremely well qualified for the open position, he refused to have a father and daughter working in the same office. The very suggestion of hiring family members was repugnant to him. Rade believed that his boss was acting unfairly—he saw no problem in his daughter working with him in the same office.

The unfortunate outcome was that Lana was neither considered nor hired; the boss lost respect for Rade; and Rade became so upset that he requested a transfer to a new department. Neither Rade nor his boss understood that the conflict was caused by the fundamental difference in their values orientations.

team trounced the opposition." They praise corporate performance by singling out and rewarding the chief executive officer (CEO). General Electric's outstanding financial performance over the past 20 years has been most frequently attributed to former CEO Jack Welch, as in the subtitle of the book *Control Your Destiny or Someone Else Will: How Jack Welch Is Making General Electric the World's Most Competitive Company* (89).

Compared with people in more group-oriented societies, Americans are more geographically mobile and their relationships, especially with co-workers, are less permanent. Due to its individualistic orientation, the United States has been described as a temporary society with temporary systems, uprootedness, disconnectedness, nonpermanent relationships, and mobility (10). More group-oriented societies, such as Japan, China, and the Israeli kibbutzim, emphasize group harmony, unity, and loyalty. Individuals in these societies frequently fear being personally ostracized or bringing shame to their family or group for behavior that deviates from the norm.

Personnel policies can follow more individual or more group orientations. Individual-oriented personnel directors tend to hire those best qualified to do the job based on personal skills and expertise. Individualistic applicants will therefore submit résumés listing personal, educational, and professional achievements. Group-oriented personnel directors also tend to hire those most qualified, but the prime qualifications they seek are trustworthiness, loyalty, and compatibility with co-workers. They hire people who are well known to them, including friends and relatives of people already working for the organization. Therefore, rather than sending well-prepared résumés listing individual achievements, applicants seek introductions to the personnel director through a mutual friend or relative; and initial discussions center on mutual friends, family, or community members. The managing director of one group-oriented company in Ghana expressed his belief that only people who are known by other employees in the company can possibly be trusted to act responsibly.

These personnel managers' actions can appear biased, illogical, and unfair when viewed from the perspective of a contrasting culture. Many individualistic North Americans see group-oriented hiring practices as nepotism because they see these practices only from their own culture's perspective. Many more group-oriented Latin Americans question the ethics of North American managers, who choose not to be loyal to their friends and family (92).

The organization of firms in individualistic and collectivist societies differs. In individualistic societies, such as those of Canada and the United States, organization charts generally specify individual positions, each with a detailed job description listing formal duties and responsibilities. By contrast, organization charts in more group-oriented societies, such as Hong Kong, Indonesia, and Malaysia, tend to specify only sections, departments, and divisions, except for the top one or two positions (72). Group-oriented societies describe assignments, responsibilities, and reporting relationships in collective terms.

The individual versus group orientation also influences decision making. In North America, individuals make decisions. North Americans, therefore, make decisions relatively quickly, although implementation frequently gets delayed while the decision maker explains the decision and gains concurrence from other members of the organization. By contrast, in Japan, a group-oriented culture, many people make the decision rather than just one. The process of group decision making is less flexible and more time-consuming than the individualistic system because concurrence must be achieved prior to making the decision. However, because all parties already understand and concur, the Japanese are able to implement a decision almost immediately after it is made.

ACTIVITY: DOING OR BEING
Americans' dominant mode of activity is *doing,* or action. They stress achieving outcomes that they can measure by objective standards; that is, standards believed to be external to the particular individual and capable of being consistently applied to other situations and outcomes. Managers in doing-oriented cultures often motivate employees with promises of promotions, raises, bonuses, and other forms of public recognition. The contrasting orientations are *being* and *controlling.* In the *being* orientation, people, events, and ideas flow spontaneously;

ACTIVITY
Doing Versus Being

Kashmir Versus Sweden[13]

The United Nations appointed a Swedish army officer as an observer in Kashmir. His job was to travel around the turbulent province situated between Pakistan and India looking for troop movements on each side. The officer and his family moved into a houseboat on the river in Srinagar, the capital of the province. As has been customary for Europeans working in Kashmir, the family employed a local "boy"—a servant—to perform all the family's household services during their stay. The servant was always very polite and pleasant, cooked delicious meals, and kept the houseboat neat and clean.

The family was very pleased with his work, and after a short time decided to give him a raise. Surprisingly, the servant did not turn up for work the next day, and his little brother arrived in his place. On his new higher salary, the servant had employed his younger brother to work for the family. With the raise he could maintain his own desired standard of living and help his younger brother without personally having to work.

Consistent with the Kashmiri servant being a Hindu, he did not believe that he could improve his standard of living in his lifetime. So by being good and not disturbing the harmony of his circumstances (i.e., by simply *being*), he believed he could be reincarnated into a higher position in his next life. This natural tendency to accept life with no expectations for either improvement or material goods contrasts sharply with the Swedish family's notion of working hard to achieve personal goals and improve one's material lot in this life (i.e., their *doing* orientation). The Swede's surprise at seeing the younger Kashmiri brother arrive for work reflects this contrast.

---

people stress release, indulgence of existing desires, and living and working for the moment. If managers in *being*-oriented cultures do not enjoy their colleagues and current projects, they quit; they will not work strictly for future rewards. The doer is more active; the person focused on being is more relaxed. The doer actively tries to achieve the most in life; the person focused on being wants to experience life as it is.

The doing and being orientations affect planning quite differently. *Being-oriented* managers view time as generational, and therefore believe that planning should allow for the extended time needed for true change to occur. Major projects often need a generation, or certainly a decade, to achieve significant results. Managers are focused on allowing change to occur at its own, often slow, pace. They do not push or rush things to achieve short-term results. By contrast, doers believe that planning can speed up the change process if plans are carefully

TIME
The Long Term Versus The Short Term

A Question of Contracts[14]

The directors of a Japanese firm and a Canadian firm met in Vancouver to negotiate the sale of coal shipments from British Columbia to Japan. The companies
arrived at a stalemate over the length of the contract. The Japanese, ostensibly to
reduce the uncertainty in their coal supply and to assure continuous, stable production in Japan, wanted the Canadians to sign a 10-year contract. The Canadians,
on the other hand, did not wish to commit themselves to such a lengthy agreement
in the event that they could find a more lucrative offer in the interim. Whereas the
Japanese wanted to reduce the level of risk in their coal supply, the Canadians
revealed their willingness to risk losing a steady buyer in exchange for the flexibility
needed to remain open to future, potentially more profitable future clients.

   The negotiations had hit a snag. Unless the culturally based time frame of the
contract could be resolved, no contract would be signed. A deal that would benefit both parties had a distinct possibility of remaining unconsummated.

thought out, specific target dates set, and progress frequently reported
(77). Be-ers believe that this type of planning is possible but unwise,
because it rarely works immediately and is fruitless in the long run.

   The activity orientation also explains why people work. To achieve
goals, doers maximize work; to live fully, be-ers minimize work.
Increasing the salaries of doers and be-ers has opposite effects. Salary
increases motivate most doers to work more hours because the rewards
are greater; they motivate most be-ers to work fewer hours because
they can earn enough money in less time and still enjoy life. U.S. expatriate managers (doers), using salary as a motivational tool, made a
costly mistake when they raised the salaries of a group of rural Mexican
workers (be-ers), only to discover that by doing so they had decreased
the total hours that these particular Mexicans wanted to work.
Similarly, Canadians working in Malaysia found that workers were
more interested in spending extra time with their family and friends
than in earning overtime pay bonuses. Americans who want a more
balanced life, with more time at home, are in effect questioning one of
their culture's core values.

TIME: PAST, PRESENT, OR FUTURE
What is the temporal focus of human life? What relationship does a
given society have toward time? Is the society oriented toward the past,
present, or future? Past-oriented cultures believe that plans should
be evaluated in terms of their fit with the customs, traditions, and the

TIME
A Past Orientation

The People's Republic of China

Whereas odysseys to outer space lure more future-oriented Americans to movie houses, historical dramas have traditionally led box-office sales in China, and the more ancient the story, the better. Chinese children, so far, have no space-age superman to emulate. Even at play, they pretend to be the Monkey King, the supernatural hero of a famous medieval epic (62:12).

Similarly, Chinese scientists look to the past for inspiration. In the national archives, teams of Chinese meteorologists comb voluminous weather records of the last 300 years in an effort to discover patterns that might help them predict the droughts and floods that still plague the country. Seismologists in charge of improving China's earthquake prediction methods use similar long-term, past-oriented approaches (62).

---

historic wisdom of society and that innovation and change are justified only to the extent that they fit with past experience. By contrast, future-oriented cultures believe that they should evaluate plans in terms of their projected future benefits. Future-oriented cultures justify innovation and change mostly in terms of future economic benefits; they have less regard for past social, cultural or organizational customs and traditions.

In contrast with most North Americans, many Europeans are more past-oriented. Many Europeans believe that preserving history and conserving past traditions remain important, whereas North Americans give tradition less importance. North American business-people focus on the present and near future; they may talk about achieving five- or 10-year plans, but they work toward achieving this quarter's results while keeping a daily focus on share-price. North American employment practices also reflect a short-term orientation. Employees who do not perform well during their first year with an organization are fired or at best not promoted. U.S. companies do not give new employees 10 years to demonstrate their worth. Japan by contrast, has traditionally had a more long-term, future-oriented time horizon. Traditionally, when large Japanese firms hired employees, both parties made a commitment for life. Major Japanese firms invested in years of training for each employee because they could expect the employee to work with the firm for 30 to 40 years. North American firms have normally invested far less in training because a lifetime commitment between the company and the employee was neither given nor expected.

Societies use different standards of temporal precision. Culture defines when people are considered to have arrived late and when they are judged to be on time for work, meetings, or business lunches. The amount of leeway depends on the particular culture. How long managers expect scheduled appointments to last—five minutes or two hours—also depends on the cultures involved.

What is the typical length of a project assignment—one week or three years? A U.S. engineer working in Bahrain expressed surprise at his Arab client's response to his apologetic explanation that, "Unfortunately, due to unforeseen delays, the new plant would not be ready to open until six months after the originally planned date." The Bahrainian responded, "We have lived for thousands of years without this plant; we easily can wait another six months or a year. This is no problem."

Diversity exists within societies as well as between societies. Past-, present-, and future-oriented people exist within every society. Comparing lawyers and economists in the United States highlights this temporal diversity. U.S. lawyers use a past orientation in citing precedent to adjudicate the outcome of cases, whereas economists use a future orientation in conducting cost-benefit analyses to predict the possible risks and revenues of alternative corporate and governmental strategies over the next five to 10 years.

SPACE: PUBLIC OR PRIVATE

How do people use physical space? Is a conference room, an office, or a building seen as public or private space? When can I enter an office directly, and when must I wait outside until granted permission to enter? The public versus private dimension defines the arrangement of organizational space. North Americans give private offices to more important employees, and even separate open-plan offices with partitions between desks. They hold important meetings behind closed doors, usually in the executive's large, private office, and generally allow minimal interruptions.

The Japanese, by contrast, use no partitions to divide desks; bosses often sit together with their employees in the same large room. Middle Easterners often have numerous people present during important meetings—some related, and some not related, to the issues being discussed. Both Middle Easterners and Japanese have a more public orientation to space than do most North Americans. By contrast, German and British businesspeople typically exhibit an even more private orientation than do most North Americans. When visitors meet a German manager for the first time, the German's secretary must generally announce the guests before the German manager's closed office door will be opened to admit them.

SUMMARY

Cultures vary in distinct, significant, and predictable ways. Our ways of thinking, feeling, and behaving as human beings are neither random nor haphazard but rather are profoundly influenced by our cultural heritage. Until we leave our community, we often remain oblivious to the dynamics of our own culture. As we come in contact with people from other cultures, we become aware of our uniqueness and begin to appreciate our differences. In interacting with foreigners, we learn to recognize and value our fundamental humanity—our cultural similarities and dissimilarities. For years, many managers chose to believe that organizational functioning was beyond the influence of culture; they operated as if organizational outcomes were determined only by task and technology. Today we know that neither work nor success is simply a mechanistic outgrowth of either technology or task. At every level, culture profoundly influences the behavior of organizations as well as the behavior of people within organizations.

QUESTIONS FOR REFLECTION

1. **Individual Cultural Self-Awareness.** As summarized in Table 1-4, which values do you think best reflect your personal orientation on each of the six dimensions? Why? Think of an example of your own behavior that fits each values orientation.

2. **National Cultural Self-Awareness.** Describe your country's dominant culture on each of the six values orientations. What concrete evidence do you have supporting the position of your country's culture on each dimension? If managers from a foreign country were observing your culture for the first time, what would they observe that would convince them of your culture's position on each of the values orientations?

3. **Cross-Cultural Awareness.** Think about a cross-cultural situation you have been in—a situation in which you are working or negotiating with people from another culture. Describe their values orientations on each of the six dimensions. Where do your own values and their values orientations differ? What problems have been caused or might be caused by the differences in your values orientations? What benefits could you potentially gain by using the differences between your two cultures to your advantage?

4. **Cross-Cultural Interaction Skills.** Select a situation reported in the international press involving people from more than one culture (such as Russians negotiating a trade agreement with Indians). Analyze the situation using one or more of the values dimensions. In what ways do the values differences increase the probability of a successful outcome? In what ways might the values differences decrease the chances of success?

5. **Parochialism and Ethnocentrism.** In what ways is your culture parochial? In what ways is it ethnocentric? Give concrete examples from situations that you have observed or that you have read about in the press. As a consultant, how might you help the managers from your culture to act in a less parochial way? How might you assist them to act in a less ethnocentric way?

FILM NOTE

The British Broadcasting Corporation video program "World Without Borders" documents the evolution of a multinational firm, Cable and Wireless, from its domestic origins through the multidomestic stage, and into its current multinational and planned transnational strategies. European and North American professors comment on Cable and Wireless's strategy and competitive environment, while presenting frameworks for understanding and managing the evolution of global firms. (Director: Steve Wilkinson, The British Broadcasting Corporation, Open University Production Centre, Walton Hall, Milton Keynes, England MK7 68H; Tel: 44-1908-655-343; Fax: 44-1908-655-300)

NOTES

1. Blaise Pascal's *Pensées,* 60 (294), as cited in Hofstede's *Culture's Consequences* (45; 46).
2. Unless otherwise stated, all dollar figures are in U.S. dollars.
3. Arguments for both the pessimistic and optimistic appreciations of shifting world business dynamics summarized by Professor Arshad Ahmad, Concordia University, Montreal, Canada.
4. Adapted from material originally appearing in the "Preface" by Nancy J. Adler of Lane, DiStefano and Maznevski's *International Management Behavior* (56:xii–xvi).
5. Although the term *American* literally refers to all peoples from North and South America, it is used in this book as a shorthand way to refer to citizens of the United States of America.
6. Domestic multiculturalism refers to multiple cultures within a particular country. Multi-culturalism, as it is used in this book, refers to international multiculturalism; that is, many cultures represented from multiple countries.
7. As conducted and cited by Jim Cornell et al., "Cultural Aspects Influencing Advertising Messages Aimed at French Canadians" (Working Paper, McGill University), interview with Jacques Grenier of Publi Plus, Inc., March 10, 1982.
8. Kluckhohn and Strodtbeck (52) reflect a North American perspective in their work. Their framework is therefore most accurate in describing Western cultures.
9. Stig-Eric Gruman, BCom, McGill University.

10. Mr. Lew Yung-Chien born in China and founder of the Montreal-based communication design studio Hablutzel & Young.

11. For an excellent review of the literature on individualism and collectivisim, see Earley and Gibson (26), and Triandis (91).

12. Ismail Elkholy, MBA, McGill University.

13. Matts Franck, MBA, McGill University.

14. John Clancy, BCom, McGill University.

REFERENCES

1. ABB (2006), www.abb.com

2. Adler, N. J. "Cross-Cultural Management Research: The Ostrich and the Trend," *Academy of Management Review*, vol. 8, no. 2 (1983), pp. 226–232.

3. Adler, N. J. "Women as Androgynous Managers: A Conceptualization of the Potential for American Women in International Management." *International Journal of Intercultural Relations*, vol. 3, no. 6 (1979), pp. 407–435. Page 411 reprinted with permission.

4. Adler, N. J.; & Bartholomew, Susan. "Academic and Professional Communities of Discourse: Generating Knowledge on Transnational Human Resource Management," *Journal of International Business Studies*, vol. 23, no. 3 (1992), pp. 551–569.

5. Adler, N. J.; & Ghadar, Fariborz. "International Strategy from the Perspective of People and Culture: The North American Context," in A. M. Rugman, ed., *Research in Global Strategic Management: Intercultural Business Research for the Twenty-First Century: Canada's New Research Agenda*, vol. 1 (Greenwich, Conn.: JAI Press, 1990), pp. 179–205.

6. Barnouw, V. *Culture and Personality* (Homewood, Ill.: Dorsey Press, 1963).

7. Bartlett, Chris A.; & Ghoshal, Sumantra. *Managing Across Borders: The Transnational Solution*, 2nd ed. (Boston: Harvard Business School Press, 1998).

8. Bartlett, Chris A.; & Ghoshal, Sumantra. "Matrix Management: Not a Structure, a Frame of Mind," *Harvard Business Review*, (July–August, 1990), pp. 138–145.

9. Beechler, Schon; Taylor, Sully; Boyacigiller, Nakiye A.; & Levy, Orly. "Building Global Mindset for Competitive Advantage: A Conceptual Integration of Global Mindset, International Human Resource Management, and Organizational Performance in Multinational Corporations," paper presented at the Academy of Management Annual Meeting, Chicago (August 1999).

10. Bennis, Warren; & Slater, P. *The Temporary Society* (New York: Harper & Row, 1968), p. 124.

11. Black, Stuart; Gregersen, Hal; & Mendenhall, Mark. *Global Assignments* (San Francisco: Jossey-Bass, 1992).

12. Boyacigiller, Nakiye; Kleinberg, M. Jill; Phillips, Margaret E.; & Sackman, Sonja. "Conceptualizing Culture" in B. J. Punnett and O. Shenkar, eds., *Handbook for International Management Research* (Cambridge: Blackwell, 1996), pp. 157–208.

13. BP (2006), http://www.bp.com/subsection.do?categoryId=4&contentId=2006741.

14. Brannen, Laurie; & Cummings, John. "U.S. Companies Bullish on Global Sales," *Business Finance,* December 2005, p. 10.

15. Brown, L. K. "For Women in Business, No Room in the Middle," *New York Times* (December 28, 1981), p. B18.

16. Brown, M. A. "Values—A Necessary but Neglected Ingredient of Motivation on the Job," *Academy of Management Review,* vol. 1 (1976), pp. 15–23.

17. Calori, R.; Johnson, G.; & Sarnin, P. "CEO's Cognitive Maps and the Scope of the Organization," *Strategic Management Journal,* vol. 15 (1994) pp. 435–457.

18. Caproni, P. J.; Lenway, S. A.; & Murtha, T. P. "Multinational Mind Sets: Sense Making Capabilities as Strategic Resources in Multinational Firms," Working paper #679, Division of Research, School of Business Administration, The University of Michigan (1992).

19. Carrol, M. P. "Culture," in J. Freedman, ed., *Introduction to Sociology: A Canadian Focus* (Scarborough, Ontario: Prentice-Hall, 1982), pp. 19–40.

20. Chandler, C. H., as quoted in C. H. Deutsch, "Losing Innocence Abroad: American Companies Are Trying to Shake Their Provincialism by Shipping Executives Overseas," *New York Times* (July 10, l988), Business, pp. 1, 2.

21. *The Coca Cola Company* (2006), http://www2.coca-cola.com/our-company/aroundworld.html.

22. Daniels, J. D.; Ogram, E. W.; & Radebaugh, L. H. *International Business Environments and Operations,* 3rd ed. (Reading, Mass.: Addison-Wesley, 1982).

23. DiStefano, Joseph J. "A Conceptual Framework for Understanding Cross-Cultural Management Problems" (London, Ontario: School of Business Administration, University of Western Ontario, 1972). Also see H. W. Lane and J. DiStefano, *International Management Behavior,* 4th ed. (Cambridge: Blackwell, 2000).

24. Dowling, Peter; Welch, D.; & Schuler, Randall, *International Human Resource Management,* 3rd ed. (Cincinnati, Ohio: South-Western, 1999).

25. Dun & Bradstreet, Canada, Ltd. *Canadian Book of Corporate Management, 1980* (Toronto: Dun & Bradstreet, Canada, Ltd., 1980).

26. Earley, Christopher; & Gibson, Christina. "Taking Stock in Our Progress on Individualism-Collectivism: 100 Years of Solidarity and Community," *Journal of Management,* vol. 24, no. 3 (1998), pp. 265–304.

27. *Economic Outlook* (Washington, DC: International Monetary Fund, October 1998).

28. Eiteman, David K.; & Stonehill, Art I. *Multinational Business Finance,* 2nd ed. (Reading, Mass.: Addison-Wesley, 1979).

29. England, G. W. *The Manager and His Values: An International Perspective* (Cambridge, Mass.: Ballinger, 1975).

30. Erez, Miriam; & Earley, P. Christopher. *Culture, Self-Identity, & Work* (New York: Oxford University Press, 1993).

31. Friedman, Thomas L. "The Axis of Order?" *New York Times,* January 13, 2001, p. A21.

32. Friedman, Thomas L. *The World is Flat: A Brief History of the Twenty-First Century* (New York: Farrar, Straus and Giroux, 2006), pp. 515–520.

33. "The Global Economy," *The Economist* (October 1, 1994), pp. 3–4, 14.

34. "Global Strategist," *U.S. News & World Report* (March 7, 1988), p. 50.

35. Godkin, L.; Braye, C. E.; & Caunch, C. L. "U.S.-Based Cross-Cultural Management Research in the Eighties," *Journal of Business and Economic Perspectives,* vol. 15, no. 2 (1989), pp. 37–45.

36. Govindarajan, V.; & Gupta, A. "Success Is All in the Mindset," *Financial Times* (London, February 27, 1998), pp. 2–3.

37. Guth, W. D.; & Taguiri, R. "Personal Values and Corporate Strategies," *Harvard Business Review,* vol. 43 (1965), pp. 123–132.

38. Hambrick, D. C.; Korn, L. B; Frederickson, J. W.; & Ferry, R. M. *21st Century Report: Reinventing the CEO* (New York: Korn/Ferry and Columbia University's Graduate School of Business, 1989), pp. 1–94.

39. Hampden-Turner, Charles; & Trompenaars, Fons. *The Seven Cultures of Capitalism: Value Systems for Creating Wealth in the United States, Britain, Japan, Germany, France, Sweden, and the Netherlands* (New York: Doubleday, 1993).

40. Hamrin, R. D. *Managing Growth in the 1980s* (New York: Praeger, l980).

41. Hannerz, U. "Cosmopolitans and Locals in World Culture," in U. Hannerz, ed., *Transnational Connections: Culture, People, Places* (London: Routlege, 1996), pp. 102–111; originally published in *Theory, Culture and Society,* vol. 7 (1991), pp. 237–251.

42. Hannerz, U. *Transnational Connections: Culture, People, Places* (London: Routlege, 1996).

43. Hofstede, Geert. "Attitudes, Values and Organizational Culture: Disentangling the Concepts," *Organizational Studies,* vol. 19, no. 3 (1998), pp. 477–492.

44. Hofstede, Geert. *Cultures and Organizations: Software of the Mind* (London: McGraw-Hill, 1991).

45. Hofstede, Geert. *Culture's Consequences: International Differences in Work-Related Values* (Beverly Hills, Calif.: Sage, 1980), p. 25.

46. Hofstede, Geert. *Culture's Consequences: Comparing Values, Behaviors, Institutions, and Organizations across Nations* (Thousand Oaks, Calif.: Sage, 2001).

47. International Monetary Fund, *World Economic Outlook Database* (April 2006), http://www.imf.org/external/pubs/ft/weo/2006/01/data/index.htm.

48. International Monetary Fund and ACLI International, Inc. *Wall Street Journal* (May 28, 1981), p. 50.

49. Jelinek, Mariann; & Adler, N. J. "Women: World Class Managers for Global Competition," *Academy of Management Executive,* vol. 2, no. 1 (1988), pp. 11–19.

50. Kanter, Rosabeth Moss. "Afterward: What 'Thinking Globally' Really Means," in R. S. Barnwik and R. M. Kanter, eds., *Global Strategies* (Boston: Harvard Business School Press, 1994), pp. 227–232.

51. Kanter, Rosabeth Moss. *World Class: Thriving Locally in the Global Economy* (New York: Simon and Schuster, 1995).

52. Kluckhohn, F.; & Strodtbeck, F. L. *Variations in Value Orientations* (Evanston, Ill.: Row, Peterson, 1961).

53. Kobrin, Steve J. "Is There a Relationship Between a Geocentric Mind-Set and Multinational Strategy?" *Journal of International Business Studies* (Third Quarter 1994), pp. 493–511.

54. Korn, L. B. "How the Next CEO Will Be Different," *Fortune* (May 22, 1989), pp. 157–158.

55. Kroeber, A. L.; & Kluckhohn, F. *Culture: A Critical Review of Concepts and Definitions, Peabody Museum Papers,* vol. 47, no. 1 (Cambridge, Mass.: Harvard University, 1952), p. 181. Reprinted with permission of the Peabody Museum of Archaeology and Ethnology, Harvard University.

56. Lane, Harry W.; DiStefano, Joseph J.; & Maznevski, Martha L. *International Management Behavior,* 5th ed. (Malden, Mass.: Blackwell, 2006).

57. Levy, Orly; Beechler, Schon; Taylor, Sully; & Boyacigiller, Nakiye. "What We Talk About When We Talk About 'Global Mindset,'" paper presented at the Academy of Management Annual Meeting (Chicago, August 1999).

58. Lyles, Marjorie. "A Research Agenda for Strategic Management in the 1990s," *Journal of Management,* vol. 27, no. 4 (1990), pp. 363–375.

59. McCain, M. "Résumés: Separating Fact from Fiction," *American Way* (December 1983), p. 85.

60. McEvoy, G. M.; & Buller, P. F. *International Human Resource Management Publications: Even in the Eighties and Needs for the Nineties,* Utah State University (1992), pp. 1–21.

61. Mankoff, A. W. "Values—Not Attitudes—Are the Real Key to Motivation," *Management Review,* vol. 63, no. 12 (1979), pp. 23–29.

62. Mathews, J.; & Mathews, L. *One Billion: A China Chronicle* (New York: Ballantine Books, 1983).

63. Merton, R. K. "Patterns of Influence: Local and Cosmopolitan Influentials" in R. K. Merton, *Social Theory and Social Structure* (Glencoe, Ill.: Free Press, 1957), pp. 368–380.

64. Mitroff, Ian I. *Business Not As Usual* (San Francisco: Jossey-Bass, 1987).

65. Murtha, Thomas P; Lenway, Stephanie A.; & Bagozzi, Rick P. "Global Mind-Sets and Cognitive Shift in a Complex Multinational Corporation," *Strategic Management Journal,* vol. 19, no. 2 (1998), pp. 97–114.

66. Peng, T. K.; Peterson, Mark F.; & Shri, Y. P. "Quantitative Methods in Cross-National Management Research: Trends and Equivalence Issues," *Journal of Organization Behavior,* vol. 12, no. 1 (1990), pp. 87–107.

67. Peters, T. "Competition and Compassion," *California Management Review,* vol. 28, no. 4 (1986), pp. 11–26.

68. Porter, Michael E. *The Competitive Advantage of Nations* (New York: The Free Press, 1990).

69. Posner, Barry Z.; & Munson, J. M. "The Importance of Values in Understanding Organizational Behavior," *Human Resource Management,* vol. 18 (1979), pp. 9–14.

70. Prahalad, C. K.; & Doz, Yves L. *The Multinational Mission: Balancing Local Demands and Global Vision* (New York: The Free Press, 1987).

71. Pucik, Vladimir. "Globalization and Human Resource Management," in V. Pucik, N. Tichy, and C. Barnett, eds., *Globalization Management: Creating and Leading the Competitive Organization.* (New York: John Wiley & Sons, 1992), pp. 61–84.

72. Redding, S. Gordon; & Martyn-Johns, T. A. "Paradigm Differences and their Relation to Management with Reference to South-East Asia," in G. W. England, A. R. Negandhi, and B. Wilpert, eds., *Organizational Functioning in a Cross-Cultural Perspective* (Kent, Ohio: Kent State University Press, 1979).

73. Rhinesmith, Stephen H. *Cultural Organizational Analysis: The Interrelationship of Value Orientations and Managerial Behavior* (Cambridge, Mass.: McBer Publication Series Number 5, 1970).

74. Rhinesmith, Stephen H. "Global Mindsets for Global Managers," *Training and Development,* vol. 46, no. 10 (1992), pp. 63–69.

75. Rhinesmith, Stephen H. *A Manager's Guide to Globalization: Six Keys to Success in a Changing World* (Homewood, Ill.: Business One Irwin, 1993).

76. Rhinesmith, Stephen H. "Open the Door to a Global Mindset," *Training and Development,* vol. 49, no. 5 (1995), pp. 35–43.

77. Rhinesmith, Stephen H.; & Renwick, George W. *Cultural Managerial Analysis Questionnaire* (New York: Moran, Stahl and Boyer, 1982).

78. Sackman, Sonja. *Cultural Knowledge in Organizations: Exploring the Collective Mind* (Newbury Park, Calif.: Sage, 1991).

79. Scarangello, A., ed., *American Education Through Foreign Eyes* (New York: Hobbs, Dorman, 1967). Examples contributed by Robert Kohls.

80. Schneider, Susan C.; & Barsoux, Jean-Louis. *Managing Across Cultures* (New York: Prentice Hall, 1997).

81. Schwab, K.; & Smadja, C. "The New Rules of the Game in a World of Many Players," *Harvard Business Review* (July–August 1994), pp. 40–44, 46, 50.

82. Shapiro, A. C. *Multicultural Financial Management,* 4th ed. (Needham Heights, Mass.: Allyn & Bacon, 1992), p. 5.

83. *Siemens AG* (2006), http://www.siemens.com/index.jsp?sdc_p=ft4mls7uo1336680i1032511pcz3&sdc_bcpath=1327885.s_0,&.

84. Simon, P. *The Tongue-Tied American: Confronting the Foreign Language Crisis* (New York: Continuum Publishing Corp., 1980).

85. Singh, Abhay; & Sharma, Subramaniam, "Shop Till You Really Drop in India: Battle for Middle Class Buyers Is Not for the Faint-of-Heart," *International Herald Tribune* (Business Asia by Bloomberg), April 5, 2006, p. 21.

86. Symington, J. W. "Learn Latin America's Culture," *New York Times* (September 23, 1983). Copyright © 1983/94 by The New York Times Company. Reprinted by permission.

87. Tata Group Profile, *The Tata Group* (2006), http://www.tata.com/0_about_us/group_profile.htm.

88. Tichy, Noel M.; Brimm, Michael Ian; Charan, R.; & Takeuchi, H. "Leadership Development as a Lever for Global Transformation," in V. Pucik, N. M, Tichy, and C. K. Barnett, eds., *Globalizing Management: Creating and Leading the Competitive Organization* (New York: John Wiley, 1992), pp. 47–60.

89. Tichy, Noel; & Sherman, S. *Control Your Destiny or Someone Else Will: How Jack Welch Is Making General Electric the World's Most Competitive Company* (New York: Currency/Doubleday, 1993).

90. Tinsley, R. L., as quoted in V. V. Merchant's book review of *The Tongue-Tied American: Confronting the Foreign Language Crisis,* in *International Psychologist,* vol. 25, no. 1 (1983).

91. Triandis, Harry C. *Individualism and Collectivism* (Boulder, Colo.: Westview Press, 1995).

92. Trompenaars, Fons; & Hampden-Turner, Charles. *Riding the Waves of Culture: Understanding Cultural Diversity in Business,* 2nd ed. (New York: McGraw-Hill, 1998).

93. United Nations Conference on Trade and Development, "Major FDI indicators" (2006), http://stats.unctad.org/FDI/TableViewer/tableView.aspx? ReportId=5.

94. U.S. Department of Labor, Bureau of Labor Statistics, "Hourly Compensation Costs For Production Workers in Manufacturing" (February 2006), ftp://ftp.bls.gov/pub/special.requests/Foreign Labor/industrynaics.txt.

95. Vernon, Raymond. "International Investment and International Trade in the Product Cycle," *Quarterly Journal of Economics*, vol. 8, no. 2 (1966), pp. 129–144.

96. The World Bank, 06 *World Development Indicators* (2006), http://devdata.worldbank.org/wdi2006/contents/Section6_1.htm.

97. *1999 World Development Indicators* (Washington, DC: The World Bank, 1999).

98. Yip, George S.; Johnansson, Johny K.; & Roos, Johan. "Effects of Nationality on Global Strategy," *Management International Review,* vol. 37, no. 4 (1997), pp. 365–385.

Chapter 2

How Cultural Differences
Affect Organizations

*Deep cultural undercurrents structure life in subtle but highly
consistent ways that are not consciously formulated. Like the
invisible jet streams in the skies that determine the course of a
storm, these currents shape our lives; yet their influence is only
beginning to be identified.*

—Edward T. Hall (7:12)

People eat different foods, celebrate different holidays, and dress differently in countries around the world. But do those differences affect the ways in which people work together? Do people organize, manage, and work differently from culture to culture?

WORK BEHAVIOR VARIES ACROSS CULTURES

In what ways does the behavior of people in organizations vary across cultures? Researchers have observed systematic and culturally based differences in managers' values, attitudes, and behaviors.

Each of us has a set of attitudes and beliefs—filters through which we see management situations. Figure 2-1 shows how managers' beliefs, attitudes, and values affect behavior. To a certain extent, beliefs, attitudes, and values cause both vicious and benevolent cycles of behavior. Douglas McGregor, an early American management theorist, gave us prototypical examples of this pattern in his classic "Theory X" and "Theory Y" managerial styles (17). According to McGregor, Theory X managers do not trust their subordinates and believe that employees will not do a good job unless closely supervised. These managers establish tight control systems—such as time clocks and frequent employee observation—to reassure themselves that employees are working. The employees, realizing that management does not trust them, start behaving irresponsibly—they arrive on time only when the time clock is working and only work when the manager is watching. The manager, observing this behavior,

**FIGURE 2-1   Influence of Managers' Attitudes on Employees'
Behavior: A Self-Fulfilling Prophecy**

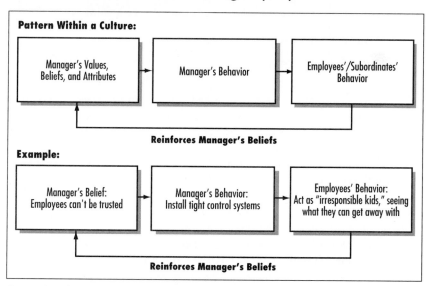

Source: Based on McGregor (17); adapted by Adler, 2007.

becomes more distrustful of the employees and installs even tighter control systems. According to McGregor, the manager's belief that employees cannot be trusted leads to the employees' irresponsible behavior, which in turn reinforces the manager's belief that employees cannot be trusted—a vicious cycle and a counterproductive, yet self-fulfilling, prophecy.

McGregor's Theory Y describes a more benevolent cycle. Managers who trust their employees give them overall goals and tasks without instituting tight control systems or close supervision. The employees, believing that management trusts them, do their best work whether or not their manager is watching them. The manager, seeing that the employees are present and working, becomes more convinced that they can be trusted. Managers' attitudes influence their own behavior, which in turn influences their employees' attitudes and behavior, which then reinforce the managers' original attitudes and behavior.

Managers communicate respect for and trust in their employees in different ways, depending on their cultural background. Managers from more *specific cultures,* for example, tend to focus only on behavior that takes place at work, whereas managers from more *diffuse cultures* focus on a wider range of behavior, including behavior taking place in employees' private and professional lives. As a part of a major cross-cultural management study, Fons Trompenaars and Charles Hampden-Turner (21), a world-renowned Dutch and British management

MANAGEMENT
Trusting or Naive

Canadian Employees and Filipino Management[1]

A Canadian bank employee described his Filipino boss's low-trust approach to management:

> While working at the Royal Bank, I had a most unbearable and suspicious manager who had authority over all administrative employees, including me. The problem was that he seemed to totally distrust his subordinates. He constantly looked over our shoulders, checking our work, attitudes, and punctuality. Although most of his employees resented this treatment, they recognized that he was an extremely conscientious supervisor who honestly believed in what he called "old-style" management. He really thought that employees are lazy by nature. He therefore believed that he must pressure them into working. As the manager, he felt justified in treating his employees severely.
>
> I found his attitude condescending and counterproductive. As a group, the employees thought of themselves as basically trustworthy. However, we decided that since our boss showed no respect for us, we would give him the same treatment in return. This resulted in a work environment filled with mistrust and hostility. The atmosphere affected everyone's work: employees became less and less willing to work, and the manager increasingly believed that his employees were lazy and that he needed to be severe with them. Luckily, the situation caught the eye of a senior manager, who resolved it after lengthy discussions. Only then did it become clear that we were not seeing the situation in the same way. From the manager's perspective, he was simply showing his caring and involvement with his subordinates. As he explained, Filipino employees who were not treated like this might have felt neglected and unimportant. Unfortunately, we were not Filipinos and, as Canadians, we did not respond as many Filipinos might have responded.

research and consulting team, asked managers from around the world if their companies should provide employees with housing. Whereas most managers from such diffuse cultures as the former Yugoslavia (89%), Hungary (83%), China (82%), and Russia (78%) believe that the company should provide housing, managers from more specific cultures reject the idea as interfering with employees' private lives (21:86). Less than 20 percent of managers from such specific cultures as Australia, Denmark, France, the Netherlands, Sweden, Switzerland, the United Kingdom, and the United States believe that providing housing is a good idea (21:86). Managers from diffuse cultures communicate their respect by showing concern for an employee's whole life. By contrast, managers from specific cultures demonstrate their respect by not intruding in employees' private lives. It is easy to see how misunderstanding and mistrust can grow between managers from one culture and employees from another culture.

WORLDWIDE DIFFERENCES IN MANAGERIAL STYLE

André Laurent (15), a highly acclaimed professor at INSEAD, (a leading international management school located in France), studied the philosophies and behaviors of managers in nine Western European countries, the United States, and three Asian countries (Indonesia, Japan, and China). Laurent asked managers from each country to describe their approaches to more than 60 common work situations. He found distinctly different patterns for managers in each of the countries.

Task and Relationship In response to the statement, "The main reason for a hierarchical structure is so that everybody knows who has authority over whom," for example, managers from some countries strongly agreed, whereas managers from other countries strongly disagreed. As shown in Table 2-1, most U.S. managers disagree with the statement; they believe that the main reason for a hierarchical structure is to organize tasks and facilitate problem solving around those tasks. Coming from an extremely task-oriented culture, many Americans believe that a flat organization with few hierarchical levels—in which most employees work as colleagues rather than bosses and subordinates—can function effectively. They believe that such minimal hierarchy is possible if tasks and roles are clearly defined and the organization is not too large.

By contrast, many managers from more relationship-oriented cultures, such as most Asians, Latin Americans, Middle Easterners, and Southern Europeans, strongly agree with Laurent's statement. Eighty-three percent of Indonesian managers reported that the main reason for a hierarchical structure was to have everyone know who has authority over whom. They did not believe that even a small organization could exist, let alone succeed, without a formal hierarchy.

TABLE 2-1   **"The Main Reason for a Hierarchical Structure Is So That Everybody Knows Who Has Authority Over Whom."**

More Task Oriented   More Relationship Oriented

Agreement Rate Across Countries										
United States	Germany	Sweden	Netherlands	Great Britain	Spain	Italy	France	Japan	China	Indonesia
17%	26%	30%	31%	34%	34%	42%	43%	50%	70%	83%

Source: Laurent (15), updated and expanded, 2007.[2]

Perhaps these different beliefs explain some problems that can occur when Americans work, for example, with Indonesians. Americans typically approach a project by outlining the overall goal, designating each of the major steps, and then addressing staffing needs. Their approach goes from task to people. Indonesians, on the other hand, typically want to first know who will manage the project and who will work on it. Once they know who the leader will be and the hierarchy of people involved, they can assess the project's feasibility. The Indonesians' approach goes from people to task. Both cultures need to understand the project's goals and staffing arrangements, but the importance of each is reversed. An American would rarely discuss candidates for project director before at least broadly defining the project, whereas Indonesians would rarely discuss project feasibility before knowing who would be leading the project.

Similarly, in response to the statement, "In order to have efficient work relationships it is often necessary to bypass the hierarchical line," Laurent found large and consistent differences across cultures. As shown in Table 2-2, Swedish managers see the least problem with bypassing. They are task oriented and value getting the job done; to Swedes, solving problems means going directly to the person most likely to have the needed information and expertise, and not necessarily to their boss. Most Swedish managers believe that a perfect hierarchy—in which their boss would know everything—is impossible; they therefore view bypassing as a natural, logical, and appropriate way for employees to work efficiently in today's complex and rapidly changing organizations.

By contrast, most Italians, being more relationship oriented than the Swedes, consider bypassing the boss as an act of insubordination. Most Italian managers believe that frequent bypassing indicates a poorly designed organization. Italians therefore respond to bypassing by reprimanding the employee or redesigning the hierarchical reporting structure. Imagine the frustration and potential for failure when Swedes form joint ventures and strategic alliances with Italians. When Swedish employees

TABLE 2-2   "In Order to Have Efficient Work Relationships, It Is Often Necessary to Bypass the Hierarchical Line."

More Task Oriented   More Relationship Oriented

					Disagreement Rate Across Countries				
Sweden	United States	Great Britain	France	Nether-lands	Germany	Indonesia	Italy	China	Spain
26%	32%	35%	43%	44%	45%	51%	56%	59%	74%

Source: Laurent (15), updated and expanded, 2007.[2]

begin working in a typical Italian organization, they will attempt to accomplish their work goals responsibly by continually bypassing hierarchical lines and going directly to the people in the organization whom they believe have the needed information and expertise. Because the Swedes do not first consult their new Italian boss, the Italian will assume that the Swedes are insubordinate and hence a threat to both the alliance and the project. In the reverse situation, the Swedish boss will rapidly become frustrated with her Italian subordinates' constant communication and seemingly endless requests for information and permission. Before long, the Swedish boss will assume that Italian employees lack initiative and are neither willing to use their personal judgment nor to take risks. Why else, asks the Swedish manager, would the Italians always consult me, the boss, before acting on matters for which the boss need not be consulted? Is either side right? No, they are just different.

Managers: Experts or Problem Solvers? Laurent found little agreement across national borders on the nature of the managerial role. As shown in Figure 2-2, more than four times as many Indonesian and Japanese managers as U.S. managers agreed with the statement, "It is important for managers to have at hand precise answers to most questions their

FIGURE 2-2   The Manager's Role Varies Across Cultures

Source: Laurent, (15), updated and expanded, 2007.[2]

subordinates may raise about their work." Most U.S. managers believe that the role of the manager is to be a problem solver: managers should help their employees discover ways to solve problems, rather than simply answering their questions directly. Furthermore, U.S. managers believe that merely providing answers discourages subordinates' initiative and creativity and ultimately diminishes their productivity. By contrast, the French generally see the manager as an expert. Most French managers believe that they should give precise answers to subordinates' questions in order to maintain their credibility as experts and as managers. They believe that their subordinates' sense of security depends on receiving precise answers. Most French believe that people should not hold managerial positions unless they can give precise answers to most work-related questions. (See page 83, the Iranian's view, for another example of the expert perspective.)

Is a manager primarily an expert or a problem solver? Again, the question has no single right answer because organizations from different cultures maintain different beliefs. Problems, however, arise when managers from one culture interact with managers and employees from other cultures. When an American manager tells French employees, "I don't know the answer, but maybe if you talk to Simon in marketing he will know," the French employees do not assume that they have received appropriate problem-solving help but rather assume that their American boss is incompetent. Similarly misunderstanding the situation, American employees who receive specific answers from their French boss may consider the boss egotistical rather than competent: "Why didn't the French boss tell us that Simon in marketing is the expert and has the most up-to-date answer?"

Laurent concludes that the national origin of Asian, European, and North American managers significantly affects their views on how effective managers should manage (15:77). Overall, the extent to which managers see organizations as primarily political, authoritarian, role-formalizing, or hierarchical-relationship systems varies according to their country of origin (15).

DIMENSIONS OF DIFFERENCE

Differences in work-related attitudes exist across a wide range of cultures. Geert Hofstede, an eminent Dutch management researcher, corroborated and integrated the results of Laurent's and others' research. In a 40-country study (11), which was later expanded to more than 60 countries worldwide (5;9;10;12;13), 160,000 managers and employees working for a U.S. multinational corporation were surveyed twice. Hofstede, like Laurent, found highly significant differences in the behavior and attitudes of employees and managers from each country even though they worked within the same multinational corporation— differences that did not change over time. Hofstede found that national culture explained more of the differences in work-related values and attitudes than did position within the organization, profession, age, or gender. In summarizing the most important differences, Hofstede initially found that managers and employees varied on four primary dimensions: individualism/collectivism, power distance, uncertainty avoidance, and career success/quality of life.[3] Later, Hofstede and his colleagues identified a fifth dimension, Confucian dynamism (5;13).

Individualism and Collectivism *Individualism* exists when people define themselves primarily as separate individuals and make their main commitments to themselves. Individualism implies loosely knit social networks in which people focus primarily on taking care of themselves and their immediate families. *Collectivism* is characterized by tight social networks in which people strongly distinguish between their own groups (in-groups, such as relatives, clans, and organizations) and other groups. Collectivists hold common goals and objectives, not individual goals that focus primarily on self-interest. People in collective cultures expect members of their particular in-groups to look after them, protect them, and give them security in exchange for their loyalty to the group. Two-thirds of all surveyed Arab executives, for example, thought employee loyalty was more important than efficiency (18). This dimension reflects values similar to those of the individual/group values orientation discussed in Chapter 1 (6).

Collectivism characterizes such cultures as the Japanese, in which people believe that the will of the group should determine members' beliefs and behavior. This belief is reflected in the Japanese saying, "The nail that sticks out will be pounded down." By contrast, free will and self-determination characterize individualistic cultures such as that of the United States, where individuals believe that each person should determine his or her own beliefs and behavior. In each nation, cultural beliefs become self-fulfilling. People from individualistic cultures also often believe that certain universal values should be shared by all. People from collectivist cultures, on the other hand, accept that different groups hold different values. Being individualistic, most North Americans believe that democracy—especially North American–style democracy—ideally should be shared by all countries worldwide. Many people from collectivist cultures find such a view both hard to understand and unacceptable.

Collectivist cultures control their members more through external societal pressure (shame), whereas individualistic cultures control their members more through internal pressure (guilt). Members of collectivist cultures place more importance on fitting in harmoniously

and saving face. Members of individualistic cultures place more emphasis on individual self-respect. In many ways the two orientations trade
off individual freedom against collective protection: Do I do what is best
for me or what is best for the group? Do I take care only of myself or
does the group take care of me? Do I expect the boss to hire me because
I have the right education and work experience (individual) or because I
come from the right family or social class (group)? Do I expect to be
promoted on the basis of my performance in the company or on the
basis of my seniority with the company? In times of economic recession, do I expect that the least productive workers will be laid off or that
every employee will take a pay cut? Figure 2-3 shows the ranking of

**FIGURE 2-3   Position of 60 Countries on Power Distance
and Individualism/Collectivism**

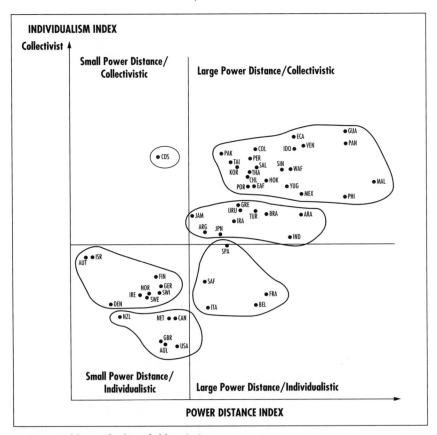

Note: See Table 2-3 for list of abbreviations.

Source: Geert Hofstede, *Culture's Consequences: Comparing Values, Behaviors,
Institutions, and Organizations Across Nations,* 2d ed. (Thousand Oaks, CA: Sage
Publications, 2001), 217. Copyright © Geert Hofstede.

**TABLE 2-3   Country Abbreviations as Used in
Figures 2-3, 2-4, and 2-5**

ARA	Arab countries	FRA	France	JPN	Japan	SAL	El Salvador
ARG	Argentina	GBR	Great Britain	KOR	Korea (S.)	SIN	Singapore
AUL	Australia	GER	Germany (W.)	MAL	Malaysia	SPA	Spain
AUT	Austria	GRE	Greece	MEX	Mexico	SWE	Sweden
BEL	Belgium	GUA	Guatemala	NET	Netherlands	SWI	Switzerland
BRA	Brazil	HOK	Hong Kong	NOR	Norway	TAI	Taiwan
CAN	Canada	IDO	Indonesia	NZL	New Zealand	THA	Thailand
CHL	Chile	IND	India	PAK	Pakistan	TUR	Turkey
COL	Columbia	IRA	Iran	PAN	Panama	URU	Uruguay
COS	Costa Rica	IRE	Ireland	PER	Peru	USA	United States
DEN	Denmark	ISR	Israel	PHI	Philippines	VEN	Venezuela
EAF	East Africa	ITA	Italy	POR	Portugal	WAF	West Africa
ECA	Ecuador	JAM	Jamaica	SAF	South Africa	YUG	Yugoslavia
FIN	Finland						

Source: Based on Hofstede (10:70); adapted by Adler and Gundersen, 2007.[4]

countries on the individualism/collectivism dimension, and Table 2-3 shows the abbreviations used in Figures 2-3, 2-4, and 2-5.

The Dutch-British management research team of Fons Trompenaars and Charles Hampden-Turner also found that managers worldwide vary markedly in their orientation toward individualism and collectivism (21). Among other questions, they asked managers which of the following two options would be most likely to improve the quality of life (21:47):

1.   Giving individuals the maximum opportunity to develop themselves; or

2.   Having individuals continuously taking care of their fellow human beings

The vast majority of American (79%), Canadian (79%), and Norwegian managers (76%), for example, selected the first option stressing individual freedom, whereas most managers in Nepal (69%), Kuwait (61%) and Egypt (59%) selected the second option stressing collective responsibility (21:48).

Which is better, individualism or collectivism? The answer is neither and both. In complex societies and organizations, however, forming a synthesis between opposites has become increasingly necessary (8). Individualism and collectivism complement each other, with their relationship being "essentially circular with two starting points" (21:55). Individualistic and collectivist cultures

> go through . . . [the same] cycles, but starting at different points [with each reversing what the other considers to be ends and means]. The individualistic culture sees the individual as "the end" and improvements

to collective arrangements as the means to achieve it. The collectivist culture sees the group as its end and improvements to individual capacities as a means to that end (21:55).

Power Distance The second cultural dimension, *power distance,* reflects the extent to which less powerful members of organizations accept an unequal distribution of power. How willing are employees to accept that their boss has more power than they have? Is the boss right because he or she is the boss (high power distance) or only when he or she knows the correct answer (low power distance)? Do employees do their work in a particular way because the boss wants it that way (high power distance) or because they personally believe that it is the best way to do it (low power distance)?

INDIVIDUALISM AND COLLECTIVISM

The Pacific Area Travel Association[5]

A global market research firm in Tokyo conducted a survey of travel market potential for the Pacific Area Travel Association (PATA), an organization of national tourist offices from various Pacific Rim nations. Although they conducted the survey through a standard questionnaire, each nation was invited to submit a few of its own open-ended questions.

All countries responded promptly. Of the ten countries surveyed, the U.S. Department of Commerce was the first to send in its questions. The same individual's name was always attached to each letter from the United States.

Shortly after completing the PATA survey, the company received a contract for a similar study for the Association of Southeast Asian Nations (ASEAN). Due to the similar content, the researchers attempted to conduct the ASEAN study in an almost identical fashion to the PATA survey. They requested open-ended questions from the national tourism offices of Indonesia, Malaysia, the Philippines, Singapore, and Thailand. Because they had completed the collection of questions in a little over a month for PATA, the company assumed six weeks would be more than sufficient for the ASEAN nations. They were wrong! The ASEAN nations required considerably more time than did the PATA countries. The market research firm had to exchange many letters and faxes with the Philippines and Tokyo before it received their final responses. Moreover, every communication from the Philippines bore a different individual's name on it as its sender.

In thinking over these responses, the researchers concluded that the contrast between the Americans' and the Filipinos' responses to the same task stemmed from the relative emphasis on the individual versus the group. Whereas the U.S. office gave sole responsibility to an individual, the more group-oriented Filipinos delegated the task to a whole department. Since the Philippines office involved everyone in the task, it naturally took longer.

POWER DISTANCE

An American Executive in London[6]

An American executive moved to London to manage his company's British head-quarters. Although the initial few weeks passed relatively uneventfully, it bothered the executive that visitors were never sent directly to his office. A visitor first had to speak with the receptionist, then the secretary, and then the office manager. Finally the office manager would escort the visitor to see the American executive. The American became annoyed with this practice, which he considered a total waste of time. When he finally spoke with his British employees and urged them to be less formal and to send visitors directly to him, they were chagrined.

After a number of delicate conversations, the American executive began to understand the greater emphasis on formality and hierarchy in England. He slowly learned to ignore his impatience when the British greeted guests using their more formal, multistep approach. Visitors to the British headquarters continued to see the receptionist, secretary, and office manager before being sent to meet the American.

In high power-distance countries, such as India, the Philippines, Poland, and Venezuela, managers and employees consider bypassing to be insubordination; whereas in low power-distance countries, such as Israel and Denmark, employees expect, and are expected, to bypass their bosses frequently in order to get their work done (19). When negotiating in high power-distance countries, companies find it important to send representatives with titles equivalent to or higher than those of their counterparts from the other organization. Titles, status, and formality command less importance in low power-distance countries. As shown in Figures 2-3 and 2-4, the United States ranks relatively low on power distance.

Uncertainty Avoidance The third cultural dimension, *uncertainty avoidance,* reflects the extent to which people in a society feel threatened by ambiguity and therefore try to avoid ambiguous situations by providing greater certainty and predictability. Organizations reduce uncertainty by establishing more formal rules, rejecting deviant ideas and behavior, accepting the possibility of identifying absolute truths and attaining unquestionable expertise, and providing their employees with greater career stability. Offering lifetime employment, for example, is more common in high uncertainty-avoidance countries such as Greece, Japan, and Portugal; whereas high job mobility occurs more commonly in

**FIGURE 2-4   Position of 60 Countries on Power Distance
and Uncertainty Avoidance**

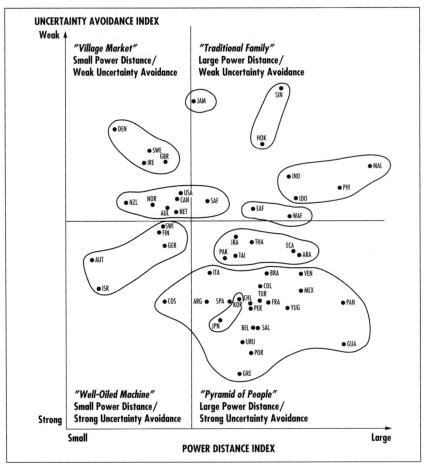

Note: See Table 2-3 for list of abbreviations.

Source: Geert Hofstede, *Culture's Consequences: Comparing Values, Behaviors,
Institutions, and Organizations Across Nations,* 2d ed. (Thousand Oaks,
CA: Sage Publications, 2001), 152. Copyright © Geert Hofstede. Adapted by
Adler, 2007.

low uncertainty-avoidance countries such as Denmark and Singapore.
The United States, with its very high job mobility, ranks relatively low on
uncertainty avoidance.

As shown in Figure 2-4, common images of organizations vary
markedly depending on a country's orientation in terms of power
distance and uncertainty avoidance. People in countries such as
Denmark that rank low on both dimensions see organizations as

resembling village markets: the organizations have little hierarchy, everyone talks with everyone else, and risk taking is both expected and encouraged.

Employees in high power-distance/low uncertainty-avoidance countries, such as Singapore and the Philippines, tend to view their organizations as traditional families. As the traditional head of the family, the father protects family members physically and economically. In exchange, the family expects loyalty from its members. Reflecting the same dynamics, bosses in Singapore expect to take care of their employees in exchange for the employees' loyalty.

Employees in countries such as the former Yugoslavia and Mexico, which are high on both dimensions, tend to view their organizations as pyramids of people rather than traditional families. Everyone in the organization knows who reports to whom, and formal lines of communication run vertically, never horizontally, up and down the organization. In pyramid organizations, management reduces uncertainty by emphasizing who has authority over whom. Pyramid organizations resemble a fire department: not only is it clear who is chief, but the fire chief's word becomes law (high power distance). The department clearly defines all procedures and tolerates little or no questioning or deviance—little or no ambiguity. When the alarm rings, firefighters do not stop to discuss who will drive the pumper or who will ride on the hook and ladder, because management has previously clearly defined each role and task.

In high uncertainty-avoidance/low power-distance countries such as Israel and Austria, organizations tend to resemble well-oiled machines: they operate highly predictably without needing a strong hierarchy. Most North American post offices provide excellent examples of this type of organization: they reduce uncertainty by clearly defining roles and procedures.

Career Success and Quality of Life The fourth cultural dimension contrasts societies focused more narrowly on career success with those more broadly emphasizing quality of life.[7] *Career-success* societies emphasize assertiveness and the acquisition of money and things (materialism), while not showing particular concern for people. By contrast, *quality-of-life* societies emphasize relationships among people, concern for others, and the overall quality of life.

Societies that stress career success usually define women's and men's roles more rigidly and narrowly than do quality-of-life societies. For example, women may drive trucks or practice law and men may become preschool teachers, nurses, or house husbands more easily in societies emphasizing quality of life than in those stressing traditional career success.

FIGURE 2-5 **Position of 40 Countries on Uncertainty Avoidance and Career Success/Quality of Life**

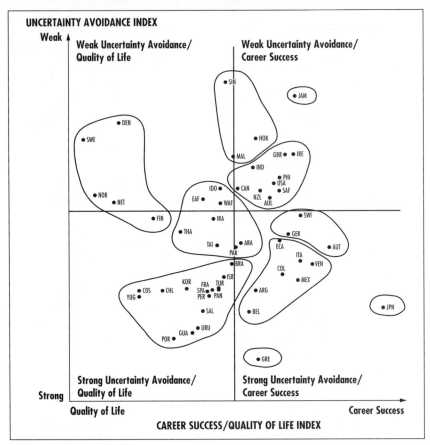

Note: See Table 2-3 for list of abbreviations.

Source: Geert Hofstede, *Culture's Consequences: Comparing Values, Behaviors, Institutions, and Organizations Across Nations, 2d ed.* (Thousand Oaks, CA: Sage Publications, 2001), 334. Copyright © Geert Hofstede. Adapted by Adler, 2007.

As shown in Figure 2-5, the Scandinavian countries strongly emphasize quality of life, the United States emphasizes career success more than quality of life, and Japan and Austria strongly emphasize career success. Japanese and Austrians generally expect women to stay home and to care for children without following a career outside the home. The United States encourages women to work, but offers them only a limited amount of support for company-sponsored maternity leaves and child care. The Swedes expect women to work outside the home; Sweden offers parents the option of paternity or maternity leave to take care of newborn children and the state provides day-mothers to care for older children.

CAREER SUCCESS AND QUALITY OF LIFE

Swedish Managers' Supposedly Inadequate Business Commitment[8]

Swedish policy allows parents to take paternity or maternity leave at their discretion. When Sweden first initiated the policy, the managing director of the Swedish Postal Service created an uproar by announcing his intention to take paternity leave for a number of months to stay home with his newborn child. At a press conference, he explained that executives do not differ from other employees: everyone wants and needs to balance work with family life. He also explained that he believed that any organization that cannot function for a period of time without its managing director had no *raison d'être*.

Swedish expatriate managers often do not have the opportunity to explain their desire for balancing their professional and private life to their colleagues from other countries. Swedes frequently surprise their international clients when they end the work week on Friday at 5 p.m. or announce their intention to fly home at the end of the day because they want to spend more time with their families. Swedish businesspeople describe many of their international colleagues, especially Americans, as willing to work all evening and all weekend just to finish an important project. Americans, on the other hand, frequently resent the Swedes' behavior, judging it to reflect an inadequate commitment to work. In actuality, the Swedes' choices simply demonstrate their strong commitment to quality of life, whereas the Americans and other similar foreigners behave according to their equally strong commitment to the particular project (career-success orientation).

The career-success/quality-of-life dimension strongly affects workplace motivation. Japanese *quality circles,* for example, primarily strive to achieve maximum quality (career success/high uncertainty avoidance); whereas the innovative Swedish work groups—originally used at Volvo—attempt to enhance job satisfaction and flexibility (high quality of life/low uncertainty avoidance). Because societies emphasizing quality of life also often create high-tax environments, extra income frequently fails to strongly motivate employees (in Sweden, for example). Conversely, societies emphasizing career success often develop into lower-tax environments in which extra income and other visible signs of career success effectively reward achievement (in the United States, for example).

Confucian Dynamism After identifying the first four dimensions, Hofstede and his Hong Kong-based colleague, the eminent cross-cultural psychologist Michael Bond, conducted the first global management survey ever developed with Chinese managers and employees. Based on this survey, Hofstede and Bond identified a fifth dimension, *Confucian* *dynamism,* which measures employees' devotion to the work ethic and their respect for tradition (5;13). Many observers attribute the rapid economic growth in the 1990s of Asia's "Four Tigers"—Hong Kong, Singapore, South Korea, and Taiwan—to their extremely strong work ethic and commitment to traditional Confucian values (13;10).

Rules and Relationships Building on the work of Laurent and Hofstede, Trompenaars and Hampden-Turner (21) conducted a major survey of more than 15,000 managers in 40 countries. In addition to results that corroborate those of their colleagues, they went beyond the prior work to document additional dimensions and to highlight some of the ethical issues posed by managers misinterpreting conflicting cultural signals.

Trompenaars and Hampden-Turner (21:34), for example, asked managers from around the world to consider what they would do in the following situation:

> *You are riding in a car driven by a close friend. He hits a pedestrian. You know he was going at least 35 miles per hour in an area of the city where the maximum allowed speed is 20 miles per hour. There are no witnesses. His lawyer says that if you testify under oath that he was only driving 20 miles per hour it may save him from serious consequences. What right has your friend to expect you to protect him?*
>
> *a. My friend has a definite right as a friend to expect me to testify to the lower figure.*
> *b. He has some right as a friend to expect me to testify to the lower figure.*
> *c. He has no right as a friend to expect me to testify to the lower figure.*
>
> *What do you think you would do in view of the obligations of a sworn witness and the obligation to your friend?*
>
> *1. Testify that he was going 20 miles an hour.*
> *2. Not testify that he was going 20 miles an hour.*

In response to this situation, managers expressed a wide range of opinions. More than 90 percent of managers in Canada (96%), the United States (95%), Switzerland (94%), Australia (93%), Sweden (93%), Norway (93%), and Western Germany (91%) said that society's rules were made for everyone and that, therefore, their friend had no right to expect them to testify falsely (21:35). They consequently would not testify that their friend was driving at 20 miles per hour when the truth was that he was driving faster (21:35). By contrast, fewer than half the managers in South Korea (26%), Venezuela (34%), Russia (42%), Indonesia

(47%), and China (48%) would refuse to support their friend and would therefore testify for him (21:35).

Why do such extreme differences characterize the managers' responses? The underlying dimension separating those who would and would not testify falsely is whether the society believes more in universalism or particularism. Managers who refuse to testify adhere to more universalistic values. Universalistic societies, such as Canada and the United States, believe that laws apply to everyone and that they therefore must be upheld by everyone at all times. The general (or universalistic) principle of what is legal, or illegal, takes precedence over the particular details of who is involved in the specific situation. By contrast, in particularist societies, such as South Korea and Venezuela, the nature of the relationship determines how someone will act in a particular situation. To a person from a particularist culture, it makes a difference if someone is a best friend or family member. For a person from a universalistic culture, it makes no difference what my relationship is to a particular person; rules are seen as applying equally to everyone. Ask yourself what you would do in the situation. Then ask yourself, if it had been your mother or daughter driving the car, would you be more or less likely to testify than you would be for a friend? How much difference does relationship make for you? When is loyalty more important than truth? When is truth more important than loyalty?

Although firms tend to become more universalistic as they operate more globally, clashes between universalistic and particularistic cultures remain legendary. Universalistic cultures, for example, rely on extensive and specific contracts to document the "rules" of doing business together, whereas particularistic cultures use much more loosely written agreements and rely on the strength of their personal relationships to maintain the commitment. Particularists view detailed contracts, and especially penalty clauses, as a sign that they are not trusted and that therefore no relationship exists. They consequently feel little need to adhere to the contract. Interestingly, as many Asian, Middle Eastern, and Latin cultures have shown, personal relationships can, at times, be more durable than contracts, as well as more flexible.

Clearly, joint ventures, strategic alliances, and overall business negotiations between universalists and particularists raise ethical questions, from both cultures' perspectives:

> *Businesspeople from both societies . . . tend to think [of] each other [as] corrupt. A universalist will say of particularists, "they cannot be trusted because they will always help their friends"; a particularist, conversely, will say of universalists, "you cannot trust them: they would not even help a friend"* (21:32).

Coming from a particularistic culture, a team of Brazilian negotiators explained to us that they only tell the truth once they have gotten to know the other party; that is, once they have developed a personal relationship. They described American and Canadian negotiators, who often accused Brazilians of lying, as naïve for not understanding how negotiating really works. The Americans, for whom truth is an absolute—a "universal" that is unrelated to the particular negotiation or the particular people involved—accused Brazilians of acting deceitfully. Americans tell the same "truth" to everyone, without regard for the nature or depth of the relationship. Brazilians tailor their comments, their "truth," to the particular individuals involved. Both sides consider truth and relationship to be important, however the relative emphasis on truth telling versus loyalty causes marked differences in behavior.

ARE ORGANIZATIONS BECOMING MORE SIMILAR?

Are organizations becoming more similar worldwide or are they maintaining their cultural dissimilarities? Is the world gradually creating one way to conduct business or is the world maintaining a set of distinct markets defined by equally distinct national boundaries, each with its own culturally distinct approach to business?

The question of convergence versus divergence has puzzled global managers for years. If people around the world are becoming more similar, then understanding cross-cultural differences should become less important. If people are remaining dissimilar, then understanding cross-cultural differences in organizations will become increasingly important.

To clarify this dilemma, John Child (4), a leading British management scholar, compared research on organizations across cultures. Reviewing a myriad of cross-cultural studies, he found one group of highly reputable management scholars repeatedly concluding that the world is becoming more similar and another equally reputable group of scholars concluding the opposite—that the world's organizations are maintaining their dissimilarity. Looking more closely, Child discovered that most studies concluding convergence focused on macro-level issues— such as the organization's structure and its technology—whereas most studies concluding divergence focused on micro-level issues—in particular, the behavior of people within organizations. We can therefore conclude that organizations worldwide are growing more similar, while the behavior of people within them is maintaining its cultural uniqueness. Organizational structures and strategies in Canada and Germany may look increasingly similar from the outside, but Canadians and Germans continue to behave in their own culturally distinct fashion within each organization. Although both Germans and Canadians, for example, install robotics in their factories, each culture interacts differently with the robotics.

ORGANIZATIONAL CULTURE AND NATIONAL CULTURE

Over the last decade, managers and researchers have increasingly recognized the importance of organizational culture as a socializing influence and climate creator [2;3;10;14;22]. Unfortunately, rather than enhancing our understanding of national cultures [1;20], our understanding of organizational culture has often tended to limit it. Many managers believe that organizational culture moderates or erases the influence of national culture. They assume that employees working for the same organization—even if they come from different countries—will behave more similarly than differently. They implicitly believe that national cultural differences only become important in working with foreign clients, not in working with international colleagues within their own organization.

Does organizational culture erase or at least diminish national culture? Surprisingly, the answer is no [16]. Employees and managers bring their cultural background and ethnicity to the workplace. As described earlier, Hofstede found striking cultural differences within a single multinational corporation. In his study, national culture explained 50 percent of the differences in employees' attitudes and behaviors. National culture explained more of the differences than did professional role, age, gender, or race [11].[9]

Even more strikingly, Laurent found more pronounced cultural differences among employees from around the world working within the same multinational company than among those working for organizations in their native lands. After observing managers from nine Western European countries and the United States who were working for companies in their native countries (e.g., Swedish managers working for Swedish companies, Italian managers working for Italian companies), Laurent replicated his research in a single multinational corporation with subsidiaries in each of the ten original countries. He assumed that managers working for the same multinational corporation would behave more similarly than their domestically employed colleagues. Instead, as shown in Figure 2-6, he found the managers employed by the multinational maintaining and even strengthening

**FIGURE 2-6   Organization Culture Magnifies
Cross-Cultural Differences**

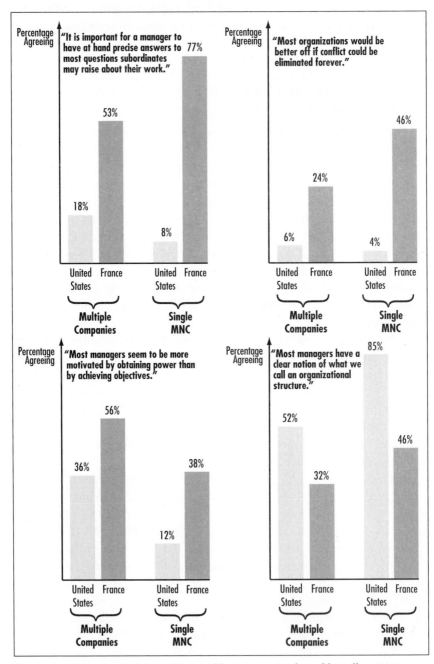

Source: André Laurent, INSEAD. Fontainebleau, France. Adapted by Adler, 2007.

their cultural differences. The cultural differences were significantly greater among managers working within the same multinational corporation than they were among managers working for companies in their own native countries. When working for multinational companies, Germans seemingly became more German, Americans more American, Swedes more Swedish, and so on. Surprised by these results, Laurent replicated his research in two additional multinational corporations, each with subsidiaries in the same nine Western European countries and the United States. Similar to the results from the first company, corporate culture did not reduce or eliminate national differences in the second and third corporations. Far from reducing national differences, organizational culture maintains and enhances them.

Why might organizational culture enhance national cultural differences? Neither managers nor researchers know the answer with certainty. Perhaps pressure to conform to the organizational culture of a foreign-owned company brings out employees' resistance, causing them to cling more firmly to their own national identities. Perhaps our ethnic culture is so deeply ingrained in us by the time we reach adulthood that a company's organizational culture cannot erase it. Perhaps other as-yet unexplained forces are operating. The unambiguous conclusion remains, however, that employees maintain or enhance their culturally specific ways of working when employed by multinational or global organizations.

SUMMARY

Laurent's research documents a wide range of cultural differences in work-related values, attitudes, and behavior. Hofstede's five dimensions—individualism/collectivism, power distance, uncertainty avoidance, career success/quality of life, and Confucian dynamism—along with Trompenaars and Hampden-Turner's additional dimensions, highlight the most important cultural differences influencing organizations. To manage effectively in either a global or a domestic multicultural environment, we must recognize which differences are operating and learn to use them to our advantage, rather than either attempting to ignore the differences or simply allowing them to cause problems. Chapter 3 presents various ways in which we perceive, describe, interpret, and evaluate cultural differences. Chapter 4 then explores approaches organizations can take to benefit from the diversity of cultural backgrounds among their employees. The myth that organizations can operate "beyond nationality" remains, in reality, a myth.

QUESTIONS FOR REFLECTION

1. **Cultural Self-Awareness.** Where is your culture located on Hofstede's original four dimensions and on universalism/particularism? How does your organizational culture differ from your national culture on each dimension?

2. **Cross-Cultural Awareness.** Select a culture with which you have had contact. How does it differ from your own culture on Hofstede's original four dimensions and on universalism/particularism? How might these differences show up in negotiations or ongoing business relationships?

3. **Cultural Self-Identity.** In which ways are you a product of the culture in which you grew up? How does your personal cultural background affect your values, attitudes, thinking, and behavior? How does your cultural background make it easier for you to work internationally? How does your cultural background hinder your effectiveness in working internationally?

4. **Cross-Cultural Interpretation.** Select a situation described in the international press involving two or more cultures. Analyze the situation using Hofstede's original four dimensions, plus the universalism/particularism and task/relationship dimensions. How does your cultural analysis help to explain the situation? Given your understanding of the cultural similarities and differences, what would you recommend each side do (or avoid doing) to resolve the situation?

5. **Cross-Cultural Analysis and Action.** Ask a colleague to describe a cross-cultural situation in which he or she is currently involved. Analyze it from a cross-cultural perspective using any relevant dimension discussed in Chapters 1 and 2. Based on your cross-cultural analysis, what would you recommend your colleague do? What would you recommend your colleague avoid doing?

NOTES

1. Ken Dang, MBA, McGill University.

2. Reprinted with permission of M.E. Sharpe, Inc., Armonk, N.Y.

3. Hofstede (11) originally labeled this dimension as masculinity/femininity. Since the dimension does not correspond with contemporary understandings of masculinity and femininity, however, Adler changed the labels to more accurately reflect their underlying meanings. It should be noted that Hofstede never intended to suggest that today's male and female students or managers possess or lack certain attributes that would make one a better manager than the other.

4. Although there is large cultural variance among Arab-speaking and West African countries, due to a limited number of respondents, Hofstede

combined Ghana, Nigeria and Sierra Leone into a composite West African score (WAF); Ethiopia, Kenya, Tanzania, and Zambia into a composite East African score (EAF); and Egypt, Iraq, Kuwait, Lebanon, Libya, Saudi Arabia, and the United Arab Emirates into a composite score for Arab speaking countries (ARA).

5. Shigeki Iwashita, MBA, McGill University.

6. Jennifer Oakes, BCOMM, McGill University.

7. See Note 3.

8. Matts Franck, MBA, McGill University.

9. Hofstede (10:373) posits that national cultures differ primarily in their values, while organizational cultures differ mainly in their practices. See Hofstede (10) for a chapter devoted to variance in organizational cultures.

REFERENCES

1. Adler, N. J.; & Jelinek, S. "Is 'Organization Culture' Culture Bound?" *Human Resource Management,* vol. 25, no. 1 (1986), pp. 73–90.

2. Boyacigiller, Nayike; Kleinberg, M. Jill; Phillips, Margaret E.; & Sackman, Sonja. "Conceptualizing Culture" in B. J. Punnett & O. Shenkar, eds., *Handbook for International Management Research* (Cambridge: Blackwell, 1996), pp. 157–208.

3. Burke, Warner, ed., "Special Issue on Organizational Culture," *Organizational Dynamics* (Autumn 1983).

4. Child, John. "Culture, Contingency & Capitalism in the Cross-National Study of Organizations," in L. L. Cummings & B. M. Staw, eds., *Research in Organizational Behavior,* vol. 3 (Greenwich, Conn.: JAI Press, 1981), pp. 303–356.

5. Chinese Culture Connection. "Chinese Values and the Search for Culture-Free Dimensions of Culture," *Journal of Cross-Cultural Psychology,* vol. 18, no. 2 (1987), pp. 143–164.

6. Earley, Christopher; & Gibson, Christina. "Taking Stock in Our Progress on Individualism/Collectivism: 100 Years of Solidarity and Community," *Journal of Management,* vol. 24, no. 3 (1998), pp. 265–305.

7. Hall, Edward T. *Beyond Culture.* Copyright © 1976, 1981 by Edward T. Hall. Used by permission of Doubleday, a division of Bantam Doubleday Dell Publishing Group, Inc., New York.

8. Hampden-Turner, Charles. *Charting the Corporate Mind* (Oxford, England: Blackwell, 1991).

9. Hofstede, Geert. *Cultures and Organizations: Software of the Mind* (London: McGraw-Hill, 1991).

10. Hofstede, Geert. *Culture's Consequences: Comparing Values, Behaviors, Institutions, and Organizations Across Nations,* 2nd ed. (Thousand Oaks, Calif.: Sage Publications, 2001).

11. Hofstede, Geert. *Culture's Consequences: International Differences in Work-Related Values* (Beverly Hills, Calif.: Sage, 1980).

12. Hofstede, Geert. "Motivation, Leadership, and Organizations: Do American Theories Apply Abroad?" *Organizational Dynamics* (Summer 1980), pp. 42–63.

13. Hofstede, Geert; & Bond, Michael H. "The Confucius Connection: From Cultural Roots to Economic Growth," *Organizational Dynamics,* vol. 16, no. 4 (1988), pp. 4–21.

14. Jelinek, Mariann; Smircich, Linda; & Hirsch, Paul, eds., "Organizational Culture" (Special Issue), *Administrative Science Quarterly,* vol. 28 (September 1983), p. 3.

15. Laurent, André. "The Cultural Diversity of Western Conceptions of Management," *International Studies of Management and Organization,* vol. 13, no. 1–2 (1983), pp. 75–96.

16. Lubatkin, M.; Calori, R.; Very, Philippe; & Veiga, J. "Managing Mergers Across Borders: A Two-Nation Exploration of a Nationally Bound Administrative Heritage," *Organization Science,* vol. 9, no. 6 (1998), pp. 670–684.

17. McGregor, Douglas M. *The Human Side of Enterprise,* 25th anniversary edition (New York: McGraw-Hill, 1985).

18. Muna, F. A. *The Arab Executive* (New York: Macmillan, 1980), Table 6.2.

19. Nasierowski, Wojcieck; & Mikula, Bogusz. "Culture Dimensions of Polish Managers: Hofstede's Indices," *Organizational Studies,* vol. 19, no. 3 (1998), pp. 495–509.

20. Schneider, Susan. "National vs. Corporate Culture: Implications for Human Resource Management," *Human Resource Management,* vol. 27, no. 2 (1988), pp. 231–246.

21. Trompenaars, Fons; & Hampden-Turner, Charles. *Riding the Waves of Culture: Understanding Cultural Diversity in Business,* 2d ed. (New York: McGraw-Hill, 1998).

22. Uttal, B. "The Corporate Culture Vultures," *Fortune,* vol. 108, no. 8 (1983), pp. 66–72.

Chapter 3

Communicating Across Cultures

If we seek to understand a people, we have to try to put our-selves, as far as we can, in that particular historical and cultural background. . . . It is not easy for a person of one country to enter into the background of another country. So there is great irritation, because one fact that seems obvious to us is not immediately accepted by the other party or does not seem obvious to him at all. . . . But that extreme irritation will go when we think . . . that he is just differently conditioned and simply can't get out of that condition. One has to recognize that whatever the future may hold, countries and people differ . . . in their approach to life and their ways of living and thinking. In order to understand them, we have to understand their way of life and approach. If we wish to convince them, we have to use their language as far as we can, not language in the narrow sense of the word, but the language of the mind. That is one necessity. Something that goes even further than that is not the appeal to logic and reason, but some kind of emotional awareness of other people.

—Jawaharlal Nehru, *Visit to America*

All business activity involves communicating. Within global businesses, activities such as leading, motivating, negotiating, decision making, problem solving, and exchanging information and ideas are all based on the ability of managers and employees from one culture to communicate successfully with colleagues, clients, and suppliers from other cultures. Communicating effectively challenges managers even when they are working domestically with a culturally homogeneous workforce. When colleagues speak a variety of languages and come from an array of cultural backgrounds, communicating effectively becomes considerably more difficult (13:3–5,121–128;18:1).

COMMUNICATING CROSS-CULTURALLY

Communication involves the exchange of meaning: it is my attempt to let you know what I mean. Communication includes any behavior another person perceives and interprets: it is your understanding of what I mean. Communication includes sending both verbal messages (words) and nonverbal messages (tone of voice, facial expression, behavior, physical setting, etc.). It includes consciously sent messages as well as messages that the sender is totally unaware of having sent. Whatever I say and do, I cannot *not* communicate. Communication therefore involves a complex, multilayered, dynamic process through which we exchange meaning.

Every communication has a message sender and a message receiver. As shown in Figure 3-1, the sent message is never identical to the received message. Why? Communication is not direct, but rather indirect; it is a symbolic behavior. I cannot communicate my ideas, feelings, or information directly; rather, I must externalize or symbolize them before they can be communicated. *Encoding* describes the producing of a symbol message. *Decoding* describes the receiving of a meaning from a symbol message. Message senders must encode their meaning into a form that the receiver will recognize; that is, into words and behavior. Receivers must then decode the words and behavior—the symbols—back into messages that have meaning for them.

FIGURE 3-1   Communicating Across Cultures

For example, because the Cantonese word for *eight* sounds like *faat,* which means prosperity, Hong Kong textile manufacturer Lau Ting-Pong paid $5 million for car registration number 8. A year later, a European millionaire paid $4.8 million at Hong Kong's Lunar New Year auction for vehicle registration number 7, a decision that mystified the Chinese, since the number 7 has little significance in the Chinese calculation of fortune (17).

Similarly, the members of Hong Kong's prestigious Legislative Council refrained from using numbers ending in 4 to identify their newly installed lockers. Some Chinese consider numbers ending with the digit 4 to be jinxed, because the sound of the Cantonese word *sei* is the same for *four* and *death.* The number 24, for instance, sounds like *yee sei,* or *death-prone* in Cantonese (12).

The process of translating meanings into words and behaviors, that is, into symbols, and back again into meanings is based on a person's cultural background and differs accordingly for each person. The greater the difference between senders' and receivers' backgrounds, the greater the difference in the meanings they attach to particular words and behaviors. For example:

> *A British boss asked a new, young American employee if he would like to have an early lunch at 11 A.M. each day. The employee answered, "Yeah, that would be great!" The boss, hearing the word yeah instead of the word yes, assumed that the employee was rude, ill-mannered, and disrespectful. The boss responded curtly, "With that kind of attitude, you may as well forget about lunch!" The employee was bewildered. What had gone wrong? In the process of encoding agreement (the intended meaning) by the employee into yeah (a word symbol) and then the boss's decoding of that same sym- bol, the boss received a message entirely different from the message the employee had meant to send. Unfortunately, as is the case in most miscommunication, neither the sender nor the receiver was fully aware of what had gone wrong and why.*

Cross-cultural communication occurs when a person from one cul- ture sends a message to a person from another culture. Cross-cultural miscommunication occurs when the person from the second culture does not receive the sender's intended message. The greater the differ- ence between the sender's and the receiver's cultures, the greater is the chance for cross-cultural miscommunication. For example:

> *A Japanese businessman wants to signal his Norwegian client that he is uninterested in a particular sale. To be polite, the Japanese says, "That will be very difficult." The Norwegian interprets*

the statement to mean that unresolved problems remain, not that the deal is off. The Norwegian responds by asking how her company can help solve the problems. The Japanese, believing he has sent a message indicating no sale, is mystified by the Norwegian's response.

Communication does not necessarily result in understanding. Cross-cultural communication continually involves misunderstandings caused by misperception, misinterpretation, and misevaluation. When the sender of a message comes from one culture and the receiver from another, the chances of accurately transmitting the message are reduced. People from different countries see, interpret, and evaluate events differently, and consequently act upon them differently. In approaching cross-cultural situations, effective businesspeople therefore assume difference until similarity is proven. They recognize that all behavior makes sense from the perspective of the person behaving and that logic and rationale are culturally relative. In cross-cultural business situations, labeling others' behavior as bizarre usually reflects culturally based misperception, misinterpretation, or misevaluation; rarely does the behavior reflect intentional malice or pathological motivation. See the Box "Culturally 'Bizarre' Behavior" for an example of culturally based misperception.

CULTURALLY "BIZARRE" BEHAVIOR

Only in the Eyes of the Beholder[1]

While in Bangkok's notoriously congested traffic, a Canadian executive's car was hit by a Thai motorist who had crossed over the double line while passing another vehicle. After failing to establish that the fault lay with the Thai driver, the Canadian flagged down a policeman. After several minutes of seemingly futile discussion, the Canadian pointed to the double line in the middle of the road and asked the policeman directly, "What do these lines signify?" The policeman replied, "They indicate the center of the road and are there so I can establish just how far from the center the accident occurred." The startled Canadian became silent. It had never occurred to him that the double line might not mean "no passing allowed."

Unwritten rules reflect a culture's interpretation of its surroundings. A foreign columnist for the English-language Bangkok Post once proclaimed that the unwritten traffic rule in Thailand is: "When there are more than three cars in front of you at a stop sign or intersection, start your own line!" This contravenes the Western stay-in-line ethic, of course, but it effectively portrays, albeit in slightly exaggerated fashion, a fairly consistent form of behavior at intersections in Thailand. And it drives non-Thais crazy!

CROSS-CULTURAL MISPERCEPTION

Do the French and the Chinese see the world in the same way? No. Do Venezuelans and Ghanaians see the world in the same way? Again, no. No two national groups *see* the world in exactly the same way. Perception is the process by which individuals select, organize, and evaluate stimuli from the external environment to provide meaningful experiences for themselves (4;15;18;22). When Mexican children, for example, view simultaneous tachistoscopic pictures of a bullfight and a baseball game, they generally only remember seeing the bullfight. Looking through the same tachistoscope, American children only remember seeing the baseball game (5). Similarly, when researchers show adult card players altered playing cards, they fail to see what they don't expect to see—in this case, that the hearts are black and the clubs are red.

Why do the children not see both pictures? Why do the adults fail to correctly see the unexpected playing card colors? The answer lies in the nature of perception. Perceptual patterns are neither innate nor absolute. They are selective, learned, culturally determined, consistent, and inaccurate.

- Perception is **selective.** At all times the environment contains too many stimuli for us to observe at one time. We therefore screen out most of what we see, hear, taste, and feel. We screen out the overload and allow only selected information through our perceptual filter to our conscious mind (6).

- Perceptual patterns are **learned.** We are not born seeing the world in a particular way; rather, experience teaches us to perceive the world in specific ways.

- Perception is **culturally determined.** We learn to see the world in a particular way based on our cultural background.

- Perception is **consistent.** Once we see something in a particular way, we tend to continue to see it that way.

- Perception is **inaccurate.** We see things that do not exist and do not see things that do exist. Our background, values, interests, and culture act as filters and lead us to distort, block, and even create what we choose to see and to hear. We perceive what we expect to perceive. We perceive things according to what we have been trained to see, according to our cultural map.

For example, read the following sentence and quickly count the number of *F*s:

FINISHED FILES ARE THE RESULT OF YEARS OF SCIENTIFIC STUDY COMBINED WITH THE EXPERIENCE OF YEARS.

Most people who do not speak English see all six *Fs*. By contrast, many English speakers only see three *Fs*; they do not see the *Fs* in the word *of*. Why? Because people automatically revert to their habitual and natural behavior; that is, they do what they always do. People who can read English will automatically *read* the sentence (a natural behavior), even when asked to *count* the *Fs* (an unusual behavior). Because the word *of* is not important for understanding the sentence's meaning, they simply do not see either the *ofs* or the *Fs* in *of*. We selectively see those words that are important according to our cultural conditioning (in this case, our linguistic conditioning). Once we see a phenomenon in a particular way, we usually continue to see it in that way. Once we stop seeing *ofs*, we do not see them again (even when we look for them); we do not see things that do exist. One particularly astute manager at Canadian National Railways makes daily use of perceptual filters to her firm's advantage. She gives reports written in English to bilingual Francophones to proofread and those written in French to bilingual Anglophones. She uses the fact that the native English-speakers "see" more errors—especially small errors—in French and native French-speakers "see" more errors in English.

The distorting impact of perceptual filters causes us to see things that do not exist. In an executive development program, for example, U.S. executives were asked to study the picture shown in Figure 3-2 and then to

FIGURE 3-2   Perceptual Filters Change the Story

Source: Rumor Clinic of the Anti-Defamation League. Reprinted by permission. Projected picture from an experiment on the accuracy of communication from the Anti-Defamation League of the B'nai B'rith Rumor Clinic.[2]

describe it to a second colleague who had not seen the picture.[2] The second colleague then attempted to describe the picture to a third colleague who had not seen the picture, and so on. Finally, the fifth colleague described his perception of the picture to the group of executives and compared it with the original picture. Among the numerous distortions, the executives, similar to other groups, consistently described the black and the white man as fighting; the knife as being in the hand of the black man; the white man as wearing a business suit; and the black man as wearing laborer's overalls. Clearly the stereotype of blacks (as poorer, working class, and more likely to commit crimes) and of whites (as richer, upper class, and less likely to perpetrate violent crime) altered the observers' perceptions, thus totally changing the meaning of the picture (3). The executives' personal and cultural experiences, and therefore their perceptual filters, allowed them to see things that did not exist and to miss seeing things that did exist.

CROSS-CULTURAL MISINTERPRETATION

Interpretation occurs when an individual assigns meaning to observations and their relationships; it is the process of making sense out of perceptions. Interpretation organizes our experience to guide our behavior. Based on our experience, we make assumptions about what we perceive so we will not have to rediscover meanings each time we encounter similar situations. We make assumptions, for example, about how doors work, based on our experience of entering and leaving rooms; thus we do not have to relearn how to open a door each time we encounter a new door. Similarly, when we smell smoke, we generally assume it is the result of a fire. We do not have to stop and wonder if the smoke indicates a fire or a flood. Consistent patterns of interpretation help us to act appropriately and quickly within our day-to-day world.

CATEGORIES

Because we are constantly bombarded with more stimuli than we can absorb and more perceptions than we can keep distinct or interpret, we only perceive those images that may be meaningful to us. We group perceived images into familiar categories that help us to simplify our environment, become the basis for our interpretations, and allow us to function in an otherwise overly complex world. As a driver approaching an intersection, for example, I may or may not notice the number of children in the back seat of the car next to me, but I will notice whether the traffic light is red or green (selective perception). If the light is red, I automatically place it in the category of all red traffic signals (categorization).

This time, like prior times, I stop (behavior based on interpretation). Although people are capable of distinguishing thousands of subtly different colors, I do not take time to notice if the red light in Istanbul is brighter or duller than the one in Singapore or more orange or purple than the one in Nairobi; I simply stop. Categorizing helps me to distinguish what is most important in my environment and to behave accordingly.

Categories become counterproductive when we place people and things in the wrong groups. Cross-cultural miscategorization occurs when I use home-country categories to make sense of situations abroad. A Korean businessman, for example, entered a client's office in Stockholm and encountered a woman sitting behind the desk. Assuming she was a secretary, he announced that he wanted to see Mr. Silferbrand. The woman responded by saying that the secretary would be happy to help him. The Korean became confused. In assuming that most women work as secretaries rather than managers, he misinterpreted the situation and acted inappropriately. His categorization made sense to him because most women in Korean offices are secretaries, but it proved inaccurate and counterproductive here, because this particular Swedish woman was an executive, not a secretary.

STEREOTYPES

Stereotyping involves a form of categorization that organizes our experience and guides our behavior toward various groups within society. Stereotypes never accurately describe individual behavior; rather, they describe the behavioral norm for members of a particular group (2;8). The Paris-based Intercultural Management Associates, for example, describes stereotypes of English and French businesspeople as follows:

> We have found that for every set of negative stereotypes distinguishing the British and French there corresponds a particular values divergence that, when recognized, can prove an extraordinary resource. To illustrate: The French, in describing the British as "perfidious," "hypocritical," and "vague," are in fact describing English . . . [managers'] typical lack of a general model or theory and . . . their preference for a more pragmatic, evolutionary approach. This fact is hard for the French . . . to believe, let alone accept as a viable alternative, until, working alongside one another, the French . . . come to see that there is usually no ulterior motive behind . . . English . . . [managers'] vagueness but rather a capacity to think aloud and adapt to circumstances. For [their] part, the English . . . come to see that, far from being "distant," "superior," or "out of touch with reality," . . . [French managers'] concern for a general model or theory is what lends vision, focus, and cohesion to an enterprise or project, as well as leadership and much needed authority (9).

Stereotypes, like other forms of categories, can be helpful or harmful depending on how we use them. Effective stereotyping allows people to understand and act appropriately in new situations. A stereotype becomes helpful when it is

- *Consciously held.* People should be aware they are describing a group norm rather than the characteristics of a specific individual.
- *Descriptive rather than evaluative.* The stereotype should describe what people from this group will probably be like and not evaluate the people as good or bad.
- *Accurate.* The stereotype should accurately describe the norm for the group to which the person belongs.
- *The first best guess* about a group prior to acquiring information about the specific person or persons involved.
- *Modified*, based on continuing observation and experience with the actual people and situations.

Because we believe stereotypes reflect reality, subconsciously held stereotypes are difficult to modify or discard even after we acquire real information about a person. If a subconscious stereotype also inaccurately evaluates a person or situation, we are likely to maintain an inappropriate, ineffective, and frequently harmful guide to reality. Assume, for example, that I subconsciously hold the stereotype that Anglophone Québecois[3] refuse to learn French and therefore believe they should have no rights within the predominantly French-speaking province of Quebec (an inaccurate, evaluative stereotype). I then meet a monolingual Anglophone and say, "See, I told you that Anglophones aren't willing to speak French! They don't deserve to have rights here." I next meet a bilingual Anglophone and conclude, "He must be an American because Canadian Anglophones always refuse to learn French." Instead of questioning, modifying, or discarding my stereotype ("Some Anglophone Canadians speak French"), I alter reality to fit the stereotype ("He must be American"). Stereotypes increase effectiveness only when used as a first best guess about a person or situation prior to acquiring direct information. Stereotypes never help when adhered to rigidly.

Indrei Ratiu (19), in his work with INSEAD, a leading international business school in France, and the London Business School, found that managers identified as "most internationally effective" by their colleagues altered their stereotypes to fit the actual people involved, whereas managers identified as "least internationally effective" maintained their stereotypes even in the face of contradictory information. For example, internationally effective managers, prior to their first visit to Germany, might consciously stereotype Germans as being extremely task oriented.

Upon arriving in Frankfurt and meeting a very friendly and lazy Herr Schmidt, they would alter their description to say that most Germans appear extremely task oriented, but Herr Schmidt seems friendly and lazy. Months later, the most internationally effective managers are only able to say that some Germans appear very task oriented, whereas others seem quite relationship oriented (friendly); it all depends on the person and the situation. In this instance, the highly effective managers use the stereotype as a first best guess about the group's behavior prior to meeting any individuals from the group. As time goes on, they modify or discard the stereotype entirely; information about a particular individual always supersedes the group stereotype. By contrast, the least internationally effective managers maintain their stereotypes. They would assume, for example, that the contradictory evidence in Herr Schmidt's case represents an exception, and would continue to believe that Germans are highly task oriented. In drawing conclusions too quickly on the basis of insufficient information—premature closure (15)—their stereotypes become self-fulfilling (23).

In his classic studies, Canadian psychologist Donald Taylor (6;24) found that most people maintain their stereotypes even in the face of contradictory evidence. Malcolm Gladwell, in his popular research-based book, *Blink: The Power Of Thinking Without Thinking* (9), demonstrated that people today continue to stereotype, often in the most complex, consequential, and stressful situations. Taylor, for example, asked English and French Canadians to listen to one of three tape recordings of a French Canadian describing himself. In the first version, the French Canadian used the Francophone stereotype and described himself as religious, proud, sensitive, and expressive. In the second version, he used neutral terms to describe himself. In the third version, he used terms to describe himself that contradicted the stereotype, such as not religious, humble, unexpressive, and conservative. After having listened to one of the three versions, each person was asked to describe the Francophone on the tape (not Francophones in general). Surprisingly, people who listened to each of the three versions used the same stereotypic terms—religious, proud, sensitive, and expressive—even when the voice on the tape had conveyed the opposite information. People evidently maintain stereotypes even in the face of contradictory information.

Given that stereotyping is useful as an initial guide to reality, why do people malign it? Why do parents and teachers admonish children not to stereotype? Why do sophisticated managers rarely admit to stereotyping, even though each of us stereotypes every day? The answer is that we have failed to accept stereotyping as a natural process and have consequently failed to learn to use it to our advantage. For years we have viewed stereotyping as a form of primitive thinking, as an unnecessary simplification of reality. We have also viewed stereotyping as unethical: stereotypes can be inappropriate judgments of individuals based on inaccurate descriptions of groups. It is true that labeling people from a certain ethnic group as "bad" is not ethical, but grouping individuals into categories is neither good nor bad—it simply reduces complexity to manageable proportions. Negative views of stereotyping simply cloud our ability to understand people's actual behavior and impair our awareness of our own stereotypes. *Everyone* stereotypes. Rather than pretending not to stereotype, effective global managers need to become aware of their cultural stereotypes and learn to set them aside when faced with contradictory evidence.

In conclusion, some people stereotype effectively and others do not. Stereotyping becomes counterproductive when we place people in the wrong group, when we incorrectly describe group norms, when we evaluate the group rather than simply describing it, when we confuse the stereotype with the description of a particular individual, and when we fail to modify the stereotype based on our actual observations and experience.

SOURCES OF MISINTERPRETATION

Misinterpretation can be caused by inaccurately perceiving a person or situation. It can be caused by inaccurately interpreting what is seen; that is, by using my meanings to make sense out of your reality. An example of this type of misinterpretation (or misattribution) is reflected in the following encounter between an Austrian and a North American businessperson.

> *I meet an Austrian client for the sixth time in as many months. He greets me as Herr Smith. Using my North American perspective, I interpret his very formal greeting as a warning that he either dislikes me or is uninterested in developing a closer business relationship with me. However, I have misinterpreted the situation. I have inappropriately used the norms for North American business behavior, which are more informal and demonstrative (by the sixth meeting, I would say "Good morning, Fritz," not "Good morning, Herr Ranschburg"), to interpret the Austrian's more formal behavior ("Good morning, Herr Smith"). Based on a North American interpretation, businesspeople would only maintain formal behavior after the first few meetings if they either disliked or distrusted their associates. Such misinterpretation could jeopardize both the business transaction and the relationship.*

Culture strongly influences, and in many situations determines, how we interpret situations. Our cultural background determines both the categories we use and the meanings we attach to them. Sources of cross-cultural misinterpretation include subconscious cultural "blinders," a lack of cultural self-awareness, projected similarity, and parochialism.

Subconscious Cultural Blinders Because most interpretation goes on at a subconscious level, we are often unaware of the assumptions we make and their cultural basis. Our home-culture reality never forces us to examine our assumptions or the extent to which they are culturally based, because we share them with most other citizens of our country. All we know is that things do not work as smoothly or logically when we work outside our own culture as when we work with people more similar to ourselves. For example:

> *Canadians conducting business in Kuwait were surprised when their meeting with a high-ranking official was not held in a closed office and was constantly interrupted. Using Canadian-based cultural assumptions—that important people have large private offices with secretaries monitoring the flow of people into the office, and because important business takes precedence over less important business, it is not interrupted—the Canadians interpreted the Kuwaiti's open office and constant interruptions to mean that the official was neither as high ranking nor as interested in conducting business with them as they had previously thought. The Canadians' misinterpretation of the Kuwaiti's office environment led them to lose interest in working with the Kuwaiti.*

The problem is that the Canadians' interpretation derives from their own North American cultural norms, not from the norms of Middle Eastern culture. The Kuwaiti may well have been a high-ranking official who was very interested in doing business. The Canadians will never know.

Cases of subconscious cross-cultural misinterpretation occur frequently. In the 1980s, for example, a Soviet Russian poet, after lecturing at U.S. universities for two months, observed that "Attempts to please an American audience are doomed in advance, because out of twenty listeners five may hold one point of view, seven another, and eight may have none at all" (2). The Soviet poet confused Americans' freedom of thought and speech with his ability to please them. He assumed that one can only please an audience if all members hold the same opinion. Another example of well-meant misinterpretation comes from the U.S. Office of Education's advice to U.S. teachers working with newly arrived Vietnamese refugee students (25):

> *Students' participation was discouraged in Vietnamese schools by liberal doses of corporal punishment, and students were conditioned to sit rigidly and speak out only when spoken to. This background . . . makes*

speaking freely in class hard for a Vietnamese student. Therefore, don't mistake shyness for apathy.

Perhaps the extent to which this interpretation is culturally based becomes clearer when we imagine the opposite advice that the Vietnamese Ministry of Education might have given to Vietnamese teachers planning to instruct American children for the first time:

> *Students' proper respect for teachers was discouraged by a loose order and students were conditioned to chat all the time and to behave in other disorderly ways. This background makes proper and respectful behavior in class hard for an American student. Therefore, do not mistake rudeness for lack of reverence.*

Lack of Cultural Self-Awareness Although we may think that the biggest obstacle to conducting business around the world is understanding foreigners, the greater difficulty actually involves becoming aware of our own cultural conditioning. As anthropologist Edward Hall explains, "What is known least well, and is therefore in the poorest position to be studied, is what is closest to oneself" (11:45). We are generally least aware of our own cultural characteristics and express surprise when we hear foreigners describe us. Many Americans, for example, are surprised to discover that foreigners see them as hurried, overly law-abiding, very hard working, extremely explicit, and overly inquisitive (see the box "Cross-Cultural Awareness: Americans as Others See Them"). Many American businesspeople were equally surprised by a *Newsweek* survey reporting the characteristics most and least frequently associated with them (see Table 3-1). Asking foreigners to describe businesspeople from your country is a powerful way to see yourself as others see you.

Another revealing way to understand the norms and values of a culture is to listen to their common sayings and proverbs. What does a society encourage, and what does it prohibit? The box on page 84, "North American Values: Proverbs," lists some common North American proverbs and the values each teaches.

To the extent that we can begin to see ourselves through the eyes of people from other cultures, we can begin to modify our behavior, emphasizing our most appropriate and effective characteristics and minimizing those that are least helpful. The more culturally self-aware we are, the more able we are to predict the effect our behavior will have on others.

Projected Similarity Projected similarity refers to the assumption that people are more similar to you than they actually are or that

Table 3-1   How Others See Americans

Characteristics Most Commonly Associated with Americans*

France	Japan	Western Germany	Great Britain	Brazil	Mexico
Industrious	Nationalistic	Energetic	Friendly	Intelligent	Industrious
Energetic	Friendly	Inventive	Self-indulgent	Inventive	Intelligent
Inventive	Decisive	Friendly	Energetic	Energetic	Inventive
Decisive	Rude	Sophisticated	Industrious	Industrious	Decisive
Friendly	Self-indulgent	Intelligent	Nationalistic	Nationalistic	Greedy

Characteristics Least Commonly Associated with Americans*

France	Japan	Western Germany	Great Britain	Brazil	Mexico
Lazy	Industrious	Lazy	Lazy	Lazy	Lazy
Rude	Lazy	Sexy	Sophisticated	Self-indulgent	Honest
Honest	Honest	Greedy	Sexy	Sexy	Rude
Sophisticated	Sexy	Rude	Decisive	Sophisticated	Sexy

*From a list of 14 characteristics.
Source: Newsweek.[4]

another person's situation is more similar to your own situation than it in fact is. Projecting similarity is both a natural and a common process. Managers from 14 countries, for example, described the work and life goals of a foreign colleague in their work team (7). As shown in Figure 3-3, in every case the managers assumed their foreign colleagues were more like themselves than they actually were. Projected similarity involves assuming, imagining, and actually perceiving similarity when differences exist. Projected similarity particularly handicaps people in cross-cultural situations. As a South African, I assume that my

FIGURE 3-3   Projected Similarity: People from Other Cultures Appear More Similar to Me Than They Are

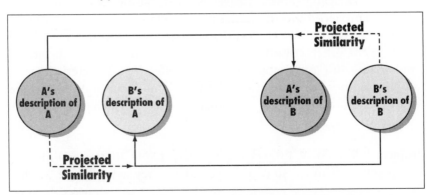

CROSS-CULTURAL AWARENESS
Americans As Others See Them

People from many countries often become puzzled and intrigued by the intricacies and enigmas of American culture. The following quotations report actual observations made by people from around the world who visited the United States. As you read their observations, ask yourself in each case if the observer is accurate. How would you explain the trait in question?

India. "Americans seem to be in a perpetual hurry. Just watch the way they walk down the street. They never allow themselves the leisure to enjoy life; there are too many things to do."

Australia. "I am impressed by the fact that American teachers never seem to stop going to school themselves."

Turkey. "Once we were out in a rural area in the middle of nowhere and saw an American come to a stop sign. Though he could see in both directions for miles and no traffic was coming, he still stopped!"

Colombia. "The tendency in the U.S. to think that life is only work hits you in the face. Work seems to be their one type of motivation."

Japan. "Americans seem to feel that they have to say something instead of having silence—even when what they say is so well known that it sounds stupid. They say things that are so obvious. Japanese people realize that we have all observed these things so that it is unnecessary to talk about them."

Vietnam. "Americans are handy people. They do almost everything in the house by themselves, from painting walls and doors to putting glass in their windows. Most of them showed me the pretty tables and bookshelves they made by themselves in their spare time."

Iran. "The first time . . . my [American] professor told me, 'I don't know the answer, I will have to look it up,' I was shocked. I asked myself, 'Why is he teaching me?' In my country a professor would give the wrong answer rather than ever admitting ignorance."

Japan. "Unfortunately, I was given a bad impression by some American students who speak of their own country very poorly, especially of its foreign policy. I knew all of the foreign policy of America wasn't good, but I did not want to be told so by a native. I hate people who speak badly of their own land, even if they speak the truth."

Colombia. "I was surprised to see so many young people who were not living with their parents, although they were not yet married. Also, I was surprised to see so many single people of all ages living alone, eating alone, and walking the streets alone. The United States must be the loneliest country in the world."

The Netherlands. "Imagine my astonishment when I went to the supermarket and looked at eggs. You know, there are no small eggs in America; they just don't exist. They tend to be jumbo, extra large, large or medium. It doesn't matter that the medium are little. Small eggs don't exist [in America] because, I guess, that might be bad or denigrating."

Source: L. R. Kohls Survival Kit for Overseas Living: For Americans Planning to Live and Work Abroad, 4th ed. (London: Nicholas Brealey Publishing in association with Intercultural Press, Yarmouth, Maine, 2001) pp. 47–49. Based on Kohls (15:47–49); adapted by Adler, 2007.

NORTH AMERICAN VALUES
Proverbs

It is much more potent in teaching practicality to say "Don't cry over spilt milk" than "You'd better learn to be practical." North Americans have heard this proverb hundreds of times, and it has made its point. Consider the following North American proverbs and the values each teaches.

Proverb	*Value*
Cleanliness is next to godliness.	Cleanliness
A penny saved is a penny earned.	Thriftiness
Time is money.	Time thriftiness
Don't cry over spilt milk.	Practicality
Waste not; want not.	Frugality
Early to bed, early to rise, makes one healthy, wealthy, and wise.	Diligence; Work ethic
God helps those who help themselves.	Initiative
It's not whether you win or lose, but how you play the game.	Good sportsmanship
A person's home is his castle.	Privacy, Value of personal property
No rest for the wicked.	Guilt, Work ethic
You've made your bed, now sleep in it.	Responsibility
Don't count your chickens before they hatch.	Practicality
A bird in the hand is worth two in the bush.	Practicality
The squeaky wheel gets the grease.	Aggressiveness
Might makes right.	Superiority of physical power
There's more than one way to skin a cat.	Originality, Determination
A stitch in time saves nine.	Timeliness of action
All that glitters is not gold.	Wariness
Clothes make the man.	Appearance
If at first you don't succeed, try, try again.	Persistence, Work ethic
Take care of today, and tomorrow will take care of itself.	Preparation for future
Laugh, and the world laughs with you; weep and you weep alone.	Pleasant outward appearance

Source: L. R. Kohls, Survival Kit for Overseas Living: For Americans Planning to Live and Work Abroad, 4th ed. (London: Nicholas Brealey Publishing in association with Intercultural Press, Yarmouth, Maine, 2001) pp. 41–42. Based on Kohls (15:41–42); adapted by Adler, 2007.

Greek colleague is more South African than he actually is. As an Egyptian, I assume that my Chilean colleague behaves more similarly to me than she actually does. When I act based on this assumed similarity, I often find that I have acted inappropriately and thus ineffectively.

With the accelerated use of global communication tools—such as the Internet, e-mail, and all forms of e-commerce—the probability of inappropriately projecting similarity has increased markedly (10;20;21).

Why? Because the probability that people from different cultures who do not know each other will communicate with one another is higher, while the amount of contextual information they have about each other is much lower when communicating through these new media than it is in face-to-face meetings. Parties contacting each other electronically simply do not notice that they need to adjust their ways of communicating and interpreting meaning to fit the cultures involved.

เกี่ยวกับทัศนคติของวัฒนธรรม

Parochialism Underlying projected similarity is subconscious parochialism. I assume that the only way to be is my way. I assume that the only way to see the world is my way. I therefore view other people in reference to me and to my way of viewing the world. People may fall into an

> *illusion of understanding while being unaware of . . . [their] misunderstandings. "I understand you perfectly but you don't understand me" is an expression typical of such situations. Or all communicating parties may fall into a collective illusion of mutual understanding. In such a situation, each party may wonder later why other parties do not live up to the "agreement" they had reached* (16:3).

Most global managers do not think of themselves as parochial. They believe that as world travelers they are able to appreciate foreigners' perspectives, which is not always true. The following are two examples of managers' projected similarity and their consequent culturally based misinterpretation:

> *Danish managers working with a Saudi executive reacted with concern when the Saudi explained that the plant would be completed on time, "En shah allah" ("If God is willing"). The Danes didn't believe that God's will would influence the progress of construction. They continued to see the world from their parochial Danish perspective and assumed that "En shah allah" was either an excuse for not getting the work done, or was altogether meaningless.*
>
> *Similarly, when Balinese workers' families refused to use birth control methods, explaining that it would break the cycle of reincarnation, few Western managers considered the possibility that they too might be reborn a number of times. Instead, they pejoratively assumed that the Balinese either were superstitious, or simply did not understand, or feared, Western medical approaches.*

While it is important to understand and respect the other culture's point of view, it is not necessary to either accept or adopt it.

Understanding and respect do not imply acceptance. Rigid adherence to one's own belief system, however, reflects parochialism, and parochialism underlies projected similarity.

One of the best exercises for developing empathy and reducing both parochialism and projected similarity is role reversal (see the box "How Well Do You Know Your International Colleagues?"). Imagine, for example, that you are a businessperson from a culture other than your own. Imagine the type of family you come from, the number of brothers and sisters you have, the social and economic conditions you grew up with, the type of education you received, the ways in which you chose your profession and position, the manner in which you were introduced to your spouse, your goals in working for your organization, and your life goals. Asking these questions forces you to see other people as they really are, and not as mere reflections of yourself. It forces you to see the similarities and differences, and not simply to imagine similarities when differences actually exist. Moreover, role reversal encourages highly task-oriented businesspeople, such as Americans, to see the person from another culture as a whole person rather than merely as someone with a position and a set of skills needed to succeed on a particular project.

CROSS-CULTURAL MISEVALUATION

Even more than perception and interpretation, cultural conditioning strongly affects evaluation. Evaluation involves judging whether someone or something is good or bad. Cross-culturally, we use our own culture as a standard of measurement, judging that which is like our own culture as normal and good and that which is different as abnormal and bad. Our own culture becomes a self-reference criterion: because no other culture is identical to our own, we tend to judge all other cultures as inferior. Evaluation rarely helps in our efforts to understand, communicate with, or conduct business with people from another culture. The following example highlights the potentially negative consequences of misevaluation:

> *A Swiss executive waits more than an hour past the appointed time for his Spanish colleague to arrive to sign a major supply contract. In his impatience he concludes that Spaniards must be lazy and totally unconcerned about business. The Swiss executive has misevaluated his colleague by negatively comparing the colleague's behavior to his own culture's standards for business punctuality. Implicitly, he has labeled his own culture's behavior as good ("The Swiss arrive on time, especially for important meetings, and that is good") and the other culture's behavior as bad ("The Spanish do not arrive on time and that is bad").*

HOW WELL DO YOU KNOW YOUR INTERNATIONAL COLLEAGUES?

Think about a colleague from another culture with whom you are currently working or have worked in the past. See how many of the following questions about
him or her you can answer, how many you think you know the answer to, but are
not certain of (and therefore run a risk of *projected-similarity error*), and how
many you do not know at all (and therefore run a high risk of *selective-perception
error*). If you are still in contact with the colleague, you may want to check the
accuracy of your perceptions with him or her after having completed the exercise.
Note that the exercise is written as if your international colleague is a woman. If
your colleague is a man, just imagine the following questions are about him
(instead of about *her*).

Family Background

- How large a family does she come from? How many brothers and sisters does
  she have? Is she the oldest? Youngest?
- From what socioeconomic status is her family? Are they among the richest
  in the country? The poorest? Did her parents earn the family wealth or
  was it inherited? Is the family highly respected in the community? Why?
  Why not?
- What is her religion? How important is religion to her? Can you ask her about
  her religion? Does she want to tell you about her spiritual beliefs? How does
  her religion or spiritual beliefs affect the way she works? How does it affect the
  way she works with you?
- What type of education did she receive? Did she attend private schools?
  Public schools? Religious schools? What proportion of people in her country
  has attained the same level of education? Did she gain entrance into the
  highest levels of education primarily through performance (tests), money, or
  personal connections? Did she receive all of her education in her home country? Does she consider her education to be superior or inferior to your own
  education?
- Is she married? Whom did she marry? Was it an arranged marriage? Does her
  husband's family influence where she works? Is her closest relationship with
  her husband? Her mother? Her children?
- Does she have children? How many? What type of relationship does she have
  with her children? How much time does she spend with her children each
  day? Would she consider sending her children away to boarding school?
  What does she see as her responsibility to her children?
- What type of home does she live in? Is it in an elite neighborhood? Is she satisfied with it? Does she live with her extended family (parents, grandparents, aunts,
  uncles) or her nuclear family?
- As a person, what is most important to her? What are some of her most deeply
  held values?

HOW WELL DO YOU KNOW YOUR INTERNATIONAL COLLEAGUES? (continued)

Career Background

- Why did she choose the career or profession she did? Is it what her father did? Is it what her mother did? Is it considered a high-status profession?
- Why does she work? For the money? Prestige? Loyalty? Responsibility? Personal satisfaction? Does she have to work to survive economically? Does she come from a culture that "works to live" or "lives to work"?
- What does she need to do to get ahead in her career? How important to her career is the success of her work with you?
- In her culture, how are people viewed who work with foreigners? Who travel internationally? Who have foreigners as friends?
- Do high-potential managers in her company (and culture) or just average performers usually get sent abroad to work?

Culture

- What does she think about your culture? What does she see as your culture's strengths? What would she like to learn from your culture? What does she want to learn from you?
- What totally annoys her about your culture? What does she see as your culture's weaknesses? How does she see your culture as getting in the way of working with you?
- In which ways does she see your culture as being ahead of her culture? In which ways does she see her culture as being ahead of your culture? Does she believe in cultural synergy; that is, that you can combine your two cultures to develop new and innovative approaches to business, including to managerial and organizational challenges?

COMMUNICATION: GETTING THEIR MEANING, NOT JUST THEIR WORDS

Effective cross-cultural communication is possible; however, global managers cannot approach communication in the same way as domestic managers. First, effective global managers "know that they don't know." They assume difference until similarity is proven rather than assuming similarity until difference is proven.

Second, in attempting to understand their colleagues from other cultures, effective global managers emphasize description by observing what is actually said and done, rather than interpreting or evaluating it. Describing a situation is the most accurate way to gather information about it. Interpretation and evaluation, unlike description, are based more on the observer's own culture and background than on the observed situation. My interpretations and evaluations therefore tell me more about myself than about the actual situation. Although managers, as decision makers, must evaluate people (e.g., performance appraisal) and situations (e.g., project evaluation) based on their organization's standards and objectives, effective global managers delay judgment until they have taken sufficient time to observe the situation from the perspectives of all cultures involved.

Third, when attempting to understand or interpret an international situation, effective global managers try to see it through the eyes of their colleagues from other cultures. This role reversal reduces the myopia of viewing situations strictly from one's own perspective.

Fourth, once effective global managers develop an explanation for a situation, they treat the explanation as a guess (as a hypothesis to be tested) rather than a certainty. They systematically check with colleagues from both home and abroad to make certain that their guesses—their initial interpretations—are plausible. This checking process allows them to converge meanings—to delay accepting their interpretations of the situation until they have confirmed them with others.

UNDERSTANDING: CONVERGING MEANINGS

A variety of methods can increase the chances that we will accurately understand businesspeople from other cultures. The set of recommendations in the box "What Do I Do If They Do Not Speak My Language?" suggests what to do when business colleagues are not native speakers of your language. Each technique involves presenting the message through multiple channels (for example, stating your position and showing a graph to summarize the same position), paraphrasing to check that colleagues from other cultures have understood your meaning (and not just your words), and converging meanings (always double-checking with the other person to verify that you have communicated what you had intended to communicate).

STANDING BACK FROM YOURSELF

Perhaps the most difficult skill in communicating across cultures involves standing back from yourself; becoming aware that you do not know everything, that a situation may not make sense, that your guesses may be wrong, and that the ambiguity in the situation may continue. In this sense the ancient Roman dictum "knowledge is power" becomes true. In knowing yourself, you gain power over your perceptions and reactions; you can control your own behavior and your reactions to others' behavior. Cross-cultural awareness complements in-depth self-awareness. A lack of self-awareness negates the usefulness of cross-cultural awareness.

A very poignant example of the powerful interplay between description, interpretation, evaluation, and empathy involved a Scottish

WHAT DO I DO IF THEY DO NOT SPEAK MY LANGUAGE?

Verbal Behavior

- *Clear, slow speech.* Enunciate each word. Do not use colloquial expressions.
- *Repetition.* Repeat each important idea using different words to explain the same concept.
- *Simple sentences.* Avoid compound, long sentences.
- *Active verbs.* Avoid passive verbs.

Nonverbal Behavior

- *Visual restatements.* Use as many visual restatements as possible, such as pictures, graphs, tables, and slides.
- *Gestures.* Use appropriate facial and hand gestures to emphasize the meaning of words.
- *Demonstration.* Act out as many themes as possible.
- *Pauses.* Pause more frequently.
- *Summaries.* Distribute written summaries of your verbal presentation.

Accurate Interpretation

- *Silence.* When the other person is silent, wait. Do not jump in to fill the silence. The other person is probably just thinking more slowly in the non-native language, translating, or greater use of silence may be a cultural norm.
- *Intelligence.* Do not equate poor grammar and mispronunciation with lack of intelligence; it is usually a sign of non-native language use.
- *Differences.* If unsure, assume difference, not similarity.

Comprehension

- *Understanding.* Do not just assume they understand; assume they do not understand.
- *Checking comprehension.* Have colleagues paraphrase their understanding of your presentation back to you. Do not simply ask whether they understand. Let them explain what they understood.

Design

- *Breaks.* Take more frequent breaks. Second language comprehension is exhausting.
- *Small modules.* Divide the material you are presenting into smaller modules.
- *Longer time frame.* Allocate more time for each module than you usually need for presenting the same material to native speakers of your language.

Motivation

- *Encouragement.* Verbally and nonverbally encourage speaking by non-native language participants.
- *Drawing out.* Encourage marginal and passive participants to contribute.
- *Reinforcement.* Do not embarrass novice speakers.[5]

COMMUNICATING ACROSS CULTURES
Japanese Pickles and Mattresses, Incorporated

It was my first visit to Japan. As a gastronomic adventurer, and because I believe cuisine is one route that is freely available and highly effective as a first step towards a closer understanding of another country, I felt disappointed on my first evening when the Japanese offered me a Western meal.

As tactfully as possible, I suggested that sometime during my stay I would like to try a Japanese menu, if it could be arranged without inconvenience. The small reluctance evident on the part of my hosts was due, I assumed, to their thought that I was just being polite asking for Japanese food, but that I didn't really like it. So to be good hosts, the Japanese had to politely find a way to not serve it to me! But eventually, by an elegantly progressive route starting with Western food with a slightly Japanese bias through to genuine Japanese food, my hosts were convinced that I really wanted to eat Japanese style and was not simply "posing."

From then on they became progressively more enthusiastic in suggesting the more exotic Japanese dishes, and I guess I graduated when, after an excellent meal one night (apart from the Japanese pickles) on which I had lavished praise, they said, "Do you like Japanese pickles?" To this, without preamble, I said, "No!" With great laughter all around, they responded, "Nor do we!"

During this gastronomic getting-together week, I had also been trying to persuade them that I really did wish to stay in traditional Japanese hotels rather than the very Westernized ones my hosts had selected because they thought I would prefer my "normal" lifestyle. I should add that, at this time, traditional Japanese hotels were still available and often cheaper than, say, the Osaka Hilton.

Anyway, after the pickles joke, it was suddenly announced that Japanese hotels could be arranged. For my remaining two weeks in Japan, as I toured the major cities, on most occasions a traditional Japanese hotel was substituted for the Western one on my original itinerary.

As you know, a traditional Japanese room has no furniture except a low table and a flower arrangement. The "bed" is a mattress produced from a concealed cupboard just before you retire, accompanied by a cereal-packed pillow.

One memorable evening my host and I had finished our meal together in my room. I was expecting him to shortly say goodnight and retire to his own room, as he had been doing all week.

However, he stayed unusually long and was obviously in some sort of emotional crisis. Finally, he blurted out, with great embarrassment, "Can I sleep with you?!"

As they say in the novels, at this point I went very still! My mind was racing through all the sexual taboos and prejudices my own upbringing had instilled, and I can still very clearly recall how I analyzed: "I'm bigger than he is so I can fight him off, but then he's probably an expert in the martial arts, but on the other hand he has shown no signs of being gay up until now and he is my host and there is a lot of business at risk and there's no such thing as rape, et cetera . . . !"

COMMUNICATING ACROSS CULTURES
Japanese Pickles and Mattresses, Incorporated (continued)

It seemed a hundred years, though it was only a few seconds, before I said, feeling as if I was pulling the trigger in Russian roulette, "Yes, sure."

Who said that the Orientals are inscrutable? The look of relief that followed my reply was obvious. Then he looked worried and concerned again, and said, "Are you sure?"

I reassured him and he called in the maid, who fetched his mattress from his room and laid it on the floor alongside mine. We both went to bed and slept all night without any physical interaction.

Later I learned that for the traditional Japanese one of the greatest compliments you can be paid is for the host to ask, "Can I sleep with you?" This goes back to the ancient feudal times, when life was cheap, and what the invitation was really saying was, "I trust you with my life. I do not think that you will kill me while I sleep. You are my true friend."

To have said "No" to the invitation would have been an insult—"I don't trust you not to kill me while I sleep"—or, at the very least, my host would have been acutely embarrassed because he had taken the initiative. If I refused because I had failed to perceive the invitation as a compliment, he would have been out of countenance on two grounds: the insult to him in the traditional context and the embarrassment he would have caused me by "forcing" a negative, uncomprehending response from me.

As it turned out, the outcome was superb. He and I were now "blood brothers," as it were. His assessment of me as being "ready for Japanization" had been correct and his obligations under ancient Japanese custom had been fulfilled. Through my own cultural conditioning, I had initially totally misinterpreted his intentions. It was sheer luck, or luck plus a gut feeling that I'd gotten it wrong, that caused me to respond correctly to his extremely complimentary and committed invitation.[6]

---

businessman's relationship with a Japanese colleague. The box "Communicating Across Cultures: Japanese Pickles and Mattresses, Incorporated" recounts the Scottish businessman's experience.

SUMMARY

Cross-cultural communication confronts us with our limited ability to perceive, interpret, and evaluate people and situations. Our culturally based perspectives render everything relative and slightly uncertain. Entering a culture that is foreign to us is tantamount to knowing the words without knowing the music, or knowing the music without knowing the dance. Our natural tendencies lead us back to our prior experience: our default option becomes the familiarity of our own culture, thus precluding our accurate understanding of others' cultures.

Strategies to overcome our natural parochial tendencies exist. With care, we can avoid our ethnocentric default options. We can learn to see, understand, and transcend our cultural conditioning. When working in other cultures, we can emphasize description rather than interpretation or evaluation, and thus minimize self-fulfilling stereotypes and premature judgments. We can recognize and use our initial stereotypes as guides rather than rejecting them as unsophisticated simplifications. Effective cross-cultural communication presupposes the interplay of alternative realities. It rejects the actual or potential domination of one reality over another.

QUESTIONS FOR REFLECTION

1. **Stereotyping.** The most effective global managers use stereotypes. In what ways can you use stereotypes to your advantage when working with people from other cultures?

2. **Using Stereotyping.** What stereotypes do you have about lawyers? About South Africans? If you had an appointment with two South African lawyers, how would you expect them to act? How would you prepare for the meeting?

3. **Communicating Across Cultures.** Today many managers work with people from other cultures, both at home and when traveling abroad. What are some of the ways in which your organization could train managers to communicate more effectively with people from other cultures?

4. **Communicating Nonverbally: Cultural Self-Awareness.** In seeking to understand the importance of nonverbal communication, we must start by examining ourselves. Describe four examples of nonverbal communication that you commonly use and what each means to you. Then indicate how each might be misinterpreted by someone from another culture.

5. **Communicating Nonverbally: Cross-Cultural Awareness.** Describe four examples of nonverbal communication that managers in other parts of the world use but managers from your own country do not. Indicate how each might be misinterpreted by colleagues from your own country.

NOTES

1. From Michael Miles, *Adaptation to a Foreign Government*, Canadian International Development Agency.

2. The Anti-Defamation League Rumor Clinic designed the sessions to show how rumors operate and how to distinguish rumors from gossip. This image is from a filmstrip consisting of four frames that demonstrate how rumors and stories become changed and distorted when told and retold (3).

3. Anglophone Québecois are native English speakers living in the predominantly French-speaking province of Quebec, Canada.
4. From *Newsweek*, July 11, 1983, p. 50. Copyright © by *Newsweek*, Inc. All rights reserved. Reprinted by permission.
5. From Adler and Kiggundu (1).
6. This example recounts the actual experience of a Scottish executive as described to his colleagues in the *Managerial Skills for International Business* executive seminar at INSEAD, in Fontainebleau, France.

REFERENCES

1. Adler, Nancy J.; & Kiggundu, Moses N. "Awareness at the Crossroad: Designing Translator Based Training Programs" in Dan Landis and Richard Brislin, eds., *Handbook of Intercultural Training: Issues in Training Methodology*, vol. II. (New York: Pergamon Press, 1983) pp. 124–150.
2. Aksenova, Olga; & Beadle, Mary. "America and Russia in International Communication," *Journal of Language for International Business*, vol. 10, no. 1 (1999), pp. 8–23.
3. Anti-Defamation League Rumor Clinic. Reprinted with permission.
4. Asch, Solomon. "Forming Impressions of Persons," *Journal of Abnormal and Social Psychology*, vol. 40 (1946), pp. 258–290.
5. Bagby, J. W. "Dominance in Binocular Rivalry in Mexico and the United States," in I. Al-Issa & W. Dennis, eds., *Cross-Cultural Studies of Behavior* (New York: Holt, Rinehart & Winston, 1970), pp. 49–56. Originally in *Journal of Abnormal and Social Psychology*, vol. 54 (1957), pp. 331–334.
6. Berry, John; Kalin, R.; & Taylor, Donald. *Multiculturalism and Ethnic Attitudes in Canada* (Ottawa: Minister of Supply and Services, 1977).
7. Burger, P.; & Bass, Bernard M. *Assessment of Managers: An International Comparison* (New York: Free Press, 1979).
8. Carney, Carmen V.; & Franciulli, Matilde. "Stereotypes of Latin Americans Among Graduate Students of International Management: Determining Cultural Needs of the U.S.-Trained Business Professional," *Journal of Language for International Business*, vol. 10, no. 2 (1999), pp. 29–45.
9. Gladwell, Malcolm. *Blink: The Power of Thinking without Thinking* (Boston: Little, Brown and Company, 2005).
10. Gundling, Ernest. "How to Communicate Globally," *Training and Development Journal*, vol. 53, no. 6 (1999), pp. 28–31.
11. Hall, Edward T. *Beyond Culture* (Garden City, N.Y.: Anchor Press/Doubleday, 1976). Also see Edward T. Hall's *The Silent Language* (Doubleday, 1959, and Anchor Books, 1973); and *The Hidden Dimension* (Doubleday, 1966, and Anchor Books, 1969).
12. Ho, A. "Unlucky Numbers Are Locked out of the Chamber," *South China Morning Post* (December 26, 1988), p. 1.

13. Kanungo, Rabindra N. *Biculturalism and Management* (Ontario: Butterworth, 1980).

14. Kohls, L. R. *Survival Kit for Overseas Living: For Americans Planning to Live and Work Abroad,* 4th ed. (London: Nicholas Brealey Publishing in association with Intercultural Press, Yarmouth, Maine, 2001).

15. Lau, J. B.; & Jelinek, Mariann. "Perception and Management," in *Behavior in Organizations: An Experiential Approach* (Homewood, Ill.: Irwin, 1984), pp. 213–220.

16. Maruyama, M. "Paradigms and Communication," *Technological Forecasting and Social Change,* vol. 6 (1974), pp. 3–32.

17. "Mystery Man Gives a Fortune for Lucky '7,'" *South China Morning Post* (January 22, 1989), p. 3; and "Lucky '7' to Go on Sale" (January 4, 1989), p. 4.

18. Prekel, Truda. "Multi-Cultural Communication: A Challenge to Managers," paper delivered at the International Convention of the American Business Communication Association, N.Y., November 21, 1983.

19. Ratiu, Indre. "Thinking Internationally: A Comparison of How International Executives Learn," *International Studies of Management and Organization,* vol. 13, nos. 1–2 (1983), pp. 139–150. Reprinted by permission of publisher, M. E. Sharpe, Inc., Armonk, N.Y.

20. Reeder, Kenneth; Macfadyen, Leah P.; Roche, Joerg; & Chase, Mackie. "Negotiating Cultures in Cyberspace: Participation Patterns and Problematics," *Language Learning and Technology,* vol. 8, no. 2 (2004), pp. 88–105.

21. Setlock, Leslie D.; Fussell, Susan R.; & Neuwirth, Christine. "Taking It Out of Context: Collaborating Within and Across Cultures in Face-to-Face Settings and via Instant Messaging," paper presented at the Association for Computing Machinery conference on Computer Supported Cooperative Work (CSCW '04), Chicago, Illinois, November 6–10, 2004.

22. Singer, Marshall. "Culture: A Perceptual Approach," in L. A. Samovar & R. E. Porter, eds., *Intercultural Communication: A Reader* (Belmont, Calif.: Wadsworth, 1976), pp. 110–119.

23. Snyder, M. "Self-Fulfilling Stereotypes," *Psychology Today* (July 1982), pp. 60–68.

24. Taylor, Donald. "American Tradition," in R. G. Gardner & R. Kalin, eds., *A Canadian Social Psychology of Ethnic Relations* (Toronto: Methuen Press, 1980).

25. U.S. Office of Education. *On Teaching the Vietnamese* (Washington, DC: General Printing Office, 1976).

PART 2

Leveraging Cultural Diversity

Chapter 4

Creating Cultural Synergy

Bhinneka Tunggal Ika

("Unity Through Diversity")

—National Motto of Indonesia

E Pluribus Unum

("Out of Many One")

—Motto on all coins in the United States of America

Is culture visible? Does cultural diversity have an impact on organizations? If so, is its impact positive or negative, helpful or harmful to organizations? How should businesspeople manage cultural diversity? Should they ignore it, minimize it, or leverage it? This chapter investigates the invisibility of culture and our own cultural blindness. It describes the advantages and disadvantages of working in culturally diverse environments, and presents alternative strategies for managing and potentially benefitting from cultural diversity and its outcomes.

CULTURAL INVISIBILITY: STRATEGIES FOR RECOGNIZING CULTURE

CULTURAL INVISIBILITY

Do managers see culture? No. Few managers believe that culture significantly affects the day-to-day operations of organizations. Often today, global managers see themselves as beyond passport, and global organizations as beyond nationality.

To better understand the impact of cultural diversity on organizations, we conducted a series of studies (5). We selected Montreal as an ideal location to study cultural diversity because, beyond having a population with representatives from many cultures, it has the largest English-speaking population in the predominantly French-Canadian province of Quebec. In the initial study, 60 organizational development consultants described the positive and negative impacts of cultural diversity on the organizations they were working with. Two-thirds of the consultants said they saw no impact whatsoever. Of the remaining one-third, only one consultant reported observing a positive impact. Interestingly, although television, radio, Internet, and newspaper reports daily attest to Montrealers' recognition of the influence of bilingualism and biculturalism on the social, political, and economic environment of Quebec, most organizational development consultants reported seeing no influence of culture on the world of work.

The consultants are not alone. Management scholars also display an equivalent cultural blindness (2;6;7;9;10). In the 1970s, less than 5 percent of management research published in the most prominent academic and professional journals considered the notion of either international or domestic multiculturalism (2). Given the dramatic increase in international business activity in the closing decades of the twentieth century, one would have expected a significant increase in the proportion of international and multicultural articles published (6:552). Trends similar to those in the 1970s, however, continued in the 1980s and the 1990s (11;14;21;24). Not until 1990 did the number of articles that included an international and multicultural perspective begin to increase, and even then the proportion remained less than 10 percent (6). Moreover, even by 2004, the majority (87%) of editors of top journals were still from North America and Europe, and more than half (55%) were from the United States (23). American scholars have conducted the vast majority of management studies, with most focusing on U.S. organizations, and yet most continue to assume their findings apply universally (7;9;10).[1] Given that the United States is culturally distinct on a number of dimensions— most prominently, Americans' extreme individualism—their tendency to overgeneralize is particularly problematic. Management researchers, perhaps to an even greater extent than their business colleagues, have ignored the influence of culture on organizations.

CULTURAL BLINDNESS: IS SEEING CULTURE ILLEGITIMATE?
Cultural diversity, whether international or domestic, does exist and does affect the ways in which we operate within organizations (for examples, see Chapters 1 and 2). As one Swiss executive recognized, "Local culture affects virtually every aspect of our business." Yet, according to two South African executives, "Interest in cultural differences is offensive" (25).

People very often associate recognizing cultural differences with simplistic, primitive, and sometimes even immoral ways of thinking. They label managers who recognize the diversity within their organizations as prejudiced, racist, sexist, ethnocentric, and unprofessional. North American cultural norms, for example, encourage managers to blind themselves to gender, race, and ethnicity; that is, to attempt to see people only as individuals and therefore to judge them based solely on their professional skills. This culture-blind approach causes problems by confusing the recognition of culturally based differences with the judging of those same differences. Managers recognize cultural differences when they realize that people from different cultures behave differently and that those differences affect the ways in which their organizations function. Recognition, however, is not the same as judging people from one culture to be better or worse than those from other cultures; it is simply an acknowledgment that they differ. No cultural group inherently manages any better or worse than any other group. Judging colleagues and clients based on their membership in particular groups fosters prejudice—a prejudgment based on group, rather than individual, characteristics—not productivity. Far from increasing organizational effectiveness, judging cultural differences as good or bad usually leads to inappropriate, offensive, racist, sexist, and ethnocentric attitudes and behaviors. Recognizing differences has the opposite effect. In fact, ignoring cultural differences can be unproductive. *Cultural blindness*—choosing not to see cultural differences—limits our ability to benefit from diversity; that is, it precludes our ability to minimize the problems caused by cultural diversity and to maximize the potential advantages it offers.

When we blind ourselves to cultural diversity, people from other cultures become mere projections of ourselves. As described in Chapter 3, we frequently see similarity even when difference exists; we project similarity. As one Canadian manager inaccurately observed, "It is very easy to work with people from other cultures. People are basically the same and have the same needs and aspirations" (8). Although people are not the same, we often inaccurately perceive them to be the same—to have the same needs and aspirations. Cultural blindness is therefore both perceptual and conceptual: we neither see nor want to see differences. To effectively manage cross-culturally, a concentrated effort must be made to recognize cultural diversity without judging it—to see difference where difference exists.

DIVERSITY CAUSES PROBLEMS

Culture is generally invisible and, when visible, we usually see it as causing problems. People rarely believe cultural diversity benefits organizations. Global executives attending management seminars at INSEAD, the leading international management school in France, for example, described the advantages and disadvantages of cultural diversity to their organizations. Whereas every executive could describe disadvantages, fewer than a third could list even one advantage (8;20). As one French executive summarized, "I have been involved in many situations over the years, but I can't think of one made easier because it involved more than one culture." His Danish colleague agreed, "I can think of no situation in my experience where managing ordinary business became easier or more effective because it involved people from more than one culture."

In the Montreal study described earlier (5), only one of the 60 organizational development consultants mentioned an advantage accruing to the organization from cultural diversity. Similarly, the 52 corporate and academic experts from around the world who participated in the McGill International Symposium on Cross-Cultural Management were able to identify a number of diversity-related problems, but had a considerably harder time identifying potential benefits (1).

What types of problems does diversity cause? As shown in Table 4-1, diversity most frequently causes problems in convergent processes, at times when the organization needs employees to think or to act in similar ways. Diversity renders communication (converging on similar meanings) and integration (converging on similar actions) more difficult. People from different cultures may fail to understand one another; they may not work in the same ways or at the same pace. The potential for increased ambiguity, complexity, and confusion becomes

TABLE 4-1   Potential Advantages and Disadvantages of Diversity

Advantages	Disadvantages

Synergistic Advantages:
   Organizational Benefits Derived
      from Cultural Diversity
	Disadvantages:
	   Organizational Costs
	      Caused by Cultural Diversity

Expanding meanings
   Greater openness to new ideas
   Multiple perspectives
   Multiple interpretations
	Diversity increases
	   Ambiguity
	   Complexity
	   Confusion

Expanding alternatives
   Increasing creativity
   Increasing flexibility
   Increasing problem-solving skills
	Difficulty converging meanings
	   Miscommunication
	   Harder to reach agreement
	Difficulty converging actions
	   Harder to agree on specific actions

Culture-Specific Advantages:
   Benefits from Working with
      a Particular Culture
	Culture-Specific Disadvantages:
	   Costs Inherent in Working with
	      a Particular Culture

Better understanding of local employees
Better able to work effectively with
   local clients
Better able to market effectively to
   local customers
Increased understanding of local
   political, social, legal, economic,
   and cultural environment
	Overgeneralizing
	   Organizational policies
	   Organizational strategies
	   Organizational practices
	   Organizational procedures
	Ethnocentrism

highest when an organization or project requires direction and clarity—convergence.

Diversity causes problems when managers and employees overgeneralize organizational practices and processes from one culture to dissimilar countries and cultures. Problems result, for example, when managers export marketing campaigns developed in one country without adapting them to destination countries:

> **Africa/United States** *An American multinational tried to sell baby food in Africa by using its regular label showing a smiling baby and stating the type of baby food in the jar. Unfortunately, the local population took one look at the labels and interpreted them to mean the jars contained ground-up babies! Sales, of course, were terrible* (26:31).

Cultural diversity can also cause problems when a culturally diverse group must reach a single agreement, whether formal or informal:

> **Japan/Switzerland** *Settlement of a licensing agreement between a Japanese and a Swiss company became much more difficult due to big differences in the decision-making and legal systems between the two countries, the inability of the Swiss to understand the Japanese language, the long distances, and the lack of spontaneity. In one's own country, these difficulties would not exist or could easily be overcome* (14).

Cultural diversity increases the complexity and difficulty of developing company-wide policies procedures:

> **Personnel Records in Europe** *In line with the American parent company's policies, European subsidiaries attempted to design a common system for developing historical medical records on all employees. Human resource managers from Germany, Italy, Luxembourg, the Netherlands, Spain, Sweden, and the United Kingdom convened a meeting to agree on what could be accomplished and how. Despite procedures that worked well in the United States, the American parent company found that the variety of national legislation, cultural concerns, and requirements to consult with work councils and trade unions prior to reaching agreement imposed severe limitations on the scope of usable information that could be gathered. In a domestic setting, the variety of constraints would have been minimal and those remaining clearly understood by the people developing the system. An effective personnel records system would have been much easier to develop if only one country had been involved* (8).

DIVERSITY MAKES POTENTIAL ADVANTAGES POSSIBLE

Whereas diversity causes the most problems in convergent processes, it leads to potential advantages in divergent processes. Diversity becomes most advantageous when the organization wants to expand its perspective, strategy, tactics, or approach. Diversity can become an advantage when attempting to reposition the organization, reposition strategy from a bricks-and-mortar to an e-commerce environment, launch a new project, create a new idea, develop a new marketing plan, design a new operation, or assess emerging trends from a new perspective.

If diversity is well managed, organizations can benefit from both synergistic and culture-specific advantages, including enhanced creativity, flexibility, and problem-solving skills (especially in regard to complex problems involving many qualitative factors), improved effectiveness in working with culturally distinct clients and colleagues, and an enhanced understanding of the dynamics and communication patterns within the organization (15;30). As outlined in Table 4-1, some managers focus on the synergistic advantages of multicultural organizations, in particular on their ability to operate more flexibly and to stay open to new ideas. They note the advantages that multiple perspectives bring to problem solving and to avoiding *groupthink*.[2] Others stress culture-specific advantages, including the ability of multicultural organizations to better understand customers' needs worldwide; for example, in tailoring their marketing campaigns to the national and cultural preferences of clients in each country.

When managers use cultural diversity as a resource, rather than treat it as a liability, they benefit from its potential advantages. Global managers reap the benefits of cultural diversity in strategic alliances, joint ventures, global projects, and all types of multinational business. Executives describe the following benefits to their companies from diversity (8):

> ***New Product Development***   *A U.S. pharmaceutical firm developed a new, lucrative anticancer drug by combining an initial discovery made in its Italian subsidiary with research conducted in conjunction with the U.S.-based National Cancer Institute (the best-equipped institute for therapeutic research in the world), new Swedish creativity techniques, new Japanese and Chinese therapy indications, and major financing from Germany and the United States.*

> ***Accepting New Ideas***   *New ideas that seem threatening or absurd when mentioned by someone from one's own country are often easier to "hear" when suggested by people from another culture. During a particularly serious global energy crisis, for example, American and*

British workers initially complained that low thermostat settings in production facilities were restrictive. When a British team subsequently went to Korea to design the Pony car, they were amazed to discover that the Koreans sometimes had to break ice before they could wash their products. Thereafter, the low thermostat settings no longer seemed so restrictive.

New Perspectives, Better Communication, and Cooperation *A European firm involved all its European subsidiaries in creating a Technical and Field Support Center. By including all countries in defining the "where, how, and why" of operations, the Center avoided any one nation's dictatorial decisions, which, in the past, had caused continuous conflicts between countries.*

New Perspectives—Neutrality *A Franco-American joint venture required an outside audit of their Algerian subsidiary. The American partner unsuccessfully proposed an American accounting firm. The French partner similarly proposed a French accounting firm, but failed to gain agreement from the American partner. The two finally agreed on a French-affiliated office of an American accounting firm that agreed to assign two French-speaking British citizens to do the job. Everybody was happy.*

RECOGNIZING AND BENEFITING FROM THE ADVANTAGES OF DIVERSITY

Culture is not one of the concepts easily recognized or readily used by managers to explain the behavior of individuals, teams, or organizations. Unless given an explicit model indicating the impact of cultural diversity, managers often fail to consider it as a possible explanation for variations in organizational functioning. They see individual and organizational behavior as influenced by factors other than culture. The follow-up to the Montreal organizational development study highlighted the value of giving managers a model demonstrating cultural diversity's ability to both generate advantages and cause problems for an organization (5). The value of the model became evident when the follow-up study did not replicate the results of the original interviews. Following the initial 60 interviews in the original study, a similar group of 75 Canadian organizational development consultants received questionnaires asking them to describe the positive and negative impacts of cultural diversity on their organizations. Unlike the open-ended interviews, the structured questionnaire specifically gave the consultants a model highlighting the potentially positive and negative consequences of cultural diversity. Most consultants responding to the questionnaire, unlike their interviewed counterparts, reported seeing an impact of cultural diversity on their organization, with almost half identifying positive impacts.

As shown in Figure 4-1, the original interviewees had viewed the impact of cultural diversity in one of three ways. Most had considered it nonexistent, as having no impact whatsoever. Some had seen it as being primarily negative. Only a very few had viewed the impact of cultural diversity as being potentially either negative or positive, but not both. In the interviews, the consultants had failed to see the possibility of cultural diversity simultaneously offering advantages and disadvantages to the organization. By contrast, most questionnaire respondents recognized the possibility of cultural diversity leading simultaneously to both highly positive and highly negative outcomes within the same organization. They did not see positive impacts (advantages) as necessarily related to a lack of negative impacts (problems) (5).

The two parts of the research project differed in that the first group included in the study, the interviewees, were not given a definition of the word culture nor a model suggesting culture's potential positive and negative impacts, whereas the second group—those responding to the questionnaire—were explicitly given both. Although they rarely do so naturally, managers are able to "see" cultural diversity and appreciate its positive and negative impacts when given a model to guide them. If culture is not explicitly pointed out to them, managers often remain culture blind.

FIGURE 4-1   What Impact Does Cultural Diversity Have on Organizations? Positive? Negative? Both? Neither?

DIMENSIONS:	No Impact; No Dimension	Only Negative Impacts	Either Positive or Negative Impacts	Both Positive and Negative Impacts	
High			↑	↑↑	Positive Impacts
Low	■	↓	↓	↓	No Impact
High					Negative Impacts
IMPACTS:	Cultural diversity has no impact on organizations.	Cultural diversity only causes problems for organizations.	Cultural diversity either causes problems or leads to advantages for organizations, not both.	Cultural diversity simultaneously causes problems and leads to advantages for organizations.	

Source: Adapted by Adler, 2007; based on Adler (5).[3]

STRATEGIES FOR MANAGING CULTURAL DIVERSITY

Managers' ability to recognize cultural diversity and its potential advantages and disadvantages defines an organization's approach to managing that diversity (5). As shown in Table 4-2, managers' most common response to cultural diversity is *parochial*—they choose not to recognize cultural diversity or its impact on the organization. In parochial organizations, managers believe that "our way is the only way" to organize and manage. The second most common response is *ethnocentric*—managers recognize diversity, but only as a source of problems. In ethnocentric organizations, managers believe that "our way is the best way" to organize and work; they view all other ways as inferior. Only when managers explicitly recognize the concept of culture—and see cultural diversity as potentially leading to both advantages and disadvantages—can their response to cultural diversity be *synergistic*. Employees and managers using synergistic approaches believe that "our way and their way differ, but neither is inherently superior to the other." They believe that creative combinations of our way and their way produce the best approaches to organizing and working.

Each of these three categories of assumptions and perceptions has different implications for organizations' approaches to managing diversity. If managers assume the impact of cultural diversity is negligible, as is the case in parochial organizations, they will select a strategy that ignores diversity. As one parochial manager stated, "Cultural diversity is just not important enough to consider; it is irrelevant." This strategy precludes the possibility of effectively managing diversity. It precludes the possibility of enhancing its positive impacts and minimizing its negative impacts.

Alternatively, if managers assume that the only impacts of cultural diversity are negative, as is the case in ethnocentric organizations, then they will select a strategy that minimizes the sources and impacts of cultural diversity within the organization. Ethnocentric managers implement minimizing strategies in one of two ways: either by attempting to select a culturally homogeneous workforce, or by attempting to socialize all employees into the behavioral patterns of the dominant culture. Ethnocentric organizations, by minimizing diversity, preclude all possibility of benefiting from the many cultures of their employees and clients.

Managers who see the impacts of cultural diversity as potentially both positive and negative attempt to *manage the impacts of cultural diversity rather than manage the diversity itself.* Managers using this synergistic approach attempt to minimize potential problems posed by diversity, rather than minimize the diversity itself. Similarly, they maximize potential advantages of diversity by managing its impacts, rather

TABLE 4-2   Which Organizations Benefit from Cultural Diversity?

Type of Organization	Perception	Strategy	Most Likely Consequences	Frequency
	What is the perceived impact of cultural diversity on organizations?	*How should the impact of cultural diversity on organizations be managed?*	*What consequences can managers expect when using perception and strategy?*	*How common are these perceptions and strategies?*
Parochial Our way is the only way.	**No impact:** Cultural diversity has no impact on organizations.	**Ignore differences:** Ignore the impact of cultural diversity on organizations.	**Problems:** Problems occur but they are not attributed to cultural diversity.	Very common
Ethnocentric Our way is best.	**Negative impact:** Cultural diversity causes problems for organizations.	**Minimize differences:** Minimize the sources and impact of cultural diversity on organizations. If possible, select a monocultural workforce.	**Some problems and few advantages:** Managers reduce problems by reducing diversity; they ignore or eliminate potential advantages.	Common
Synergistic Leveraging our ways and their ways may work best.	**Potential negative and positive impacts:** Cultural diversity leads to both problems and advantages for organizations.	**Manage differences:** Train managers to recognize and use cultural differences to create advantages for the organization.	**Some problems and many advantages:** Managers recognize and benefit from cultural diversity. Some problems continue to occur and need to be managed.	Less Common

Source: Adapted by Adler, 2007; based on Adler (5).[3]

than by ignoring it. Organizations using a synergistic approach train their members to recognize cultural differences and to leverage them to create advantages for the organization.

The first two strategies—ignoring and minimizing cultural differences—occur naturally and are therefore quite common. Only when managers recognize both the existence of cultural diversity and its potential advantages to the organization does it become probable that they will choose to manage the diversity rather than attempt to ignore or minimize it. Cultural diversity has both potential advantageous and disadvantageous impacts; the organization's approach to diversity, not the diversity itself, determines its ultimate costs and benefits.

CULTURAL SYNERGY

According to Buckminster Fuller, synergy involves "a new way of thinking . . . which helps to free one from outdated patterns and can break the shell of permitted ignorance" (13). Synergy is "the behavior of whole systems that cannot be predicted by the behavior of any parts taken separately. . . . In order to really understand what is going on, we have to abandon starting with parts, and we must work instead from whole to particular" (13). The book *Managing Cultural Synergy* by Robert Moran and Philip Harris emphasizes that "the very differences in the world's people can lead to mutual growth and accomplishment that is more than the single contribution of each party to the intercultural transaction" (22). It suggests that we can

> *go beyond awareness of our own cultural heritage to produce something greater by cooperation and collaboration. Cultural synergy builds upon similarities and fuses differences resulting in more effective human activities and systems. The very diversity of people can be utilized to enhance problem solving by combined action. Those in international management have unique opportunities to foster synergy on a global basis* (22).

Cultural synergy, as an approach to managing the impact of cultural diversity, involves a process in which managers form organizational strategies, structures, and practices based on, but not limited to, the cultural patterns of individual organization members and clients. Culturally synergistic organizations create new forms of management and organization that transcend the distinct cultures of their members (3:172). This approach recognizes both the similarities and differences among the cultures that compose a global organization and suggests that we neither ignore nor minimize cultural diversity, but rather view it as a resource in designing and developing organizational systems (3:172).

From a synergistic perspective, cultural diversity is a key resource in all global learning organizations.

As summarized in Table 4-3, a set of assumptions that differs from those most commonly held about cross-cultural interaction within work settings forms the basis of the cultural synergy approach (4). The first commonly held, and yet misleading, assumption is *homogeneity*, the belief that all people are basically the same. Believing that a culture is homogeneous is a very common assumption—especially in countries such as the United States, where it forms the basis of the national "melting pot" myth. Cultural synergy, by contrast, assumes *heterogeneity*, what Canadians refer to as the cultural mosaic. Synergy is based on the assumption that we are not all the same—that the various groups within society differ, with each maintaining its cultural distinctness. Appreciating a pluralistic, rather than a homogeneous, society underlies the synergy approach. In addition, rather than assuming that the similarities among people are most important, cultural synergy assumes that similarities and differences share equal importance. Moreover, whereas the most commonly held assumption posits that "our way is the only way" of living, working, and reaching business goals (parochialism), cultural synergy assumes *equifinality*—that many equivalent ways (*equi*) to live, to work, and to reach goals (*finality*) exist, and that no culture's way is inherently superior. Furthermore, whereas most people are, to some extent, *ethnocentric* (believing that theirs is the best way to live and to work), the synergy approach assumes *cultural contingency*—that the best way depends on the situation and the particular cultures of the people involved.

In a survey of 145 executives from around the world, 83 percent preferred the synergy approach, yet only a third described their organizations as using a synergistic approach to solve multinational and multicultural problems (8). Although global managers clearly recognize the value of approaching problem solving from a synergistic perspective, they also appreciate that the approach is neither easy nor traditional. The following section describes a three-step process for creating synergistic solutions to dilemmas faced by culturally diverse organizations.

CULTURALLY SYNERGISTIC PROBLEM SOLVING

Culturally synergistic organizations reflect the best aspects of all members' cultures in their strategy, structure, and process without violating the norms of any single culture. Managers in synergistic organizations regularly use diversity as a key resource in solving problems. As outlined in Figure 4-2, the process of developing culturally synergistic solutions to organizational problems involves describing the situation from each

TABLE 4-3 Cultural Assumptions and their Implications for Management

Common, but Misleading, Assumptions		Less Common, but More Appropriate, Assumptions	
Homogeneity	*Belief in the melting pot:* We are all the same.	**Heterogeneity**	*Belief in cultural pluralism; in the cultural mosaic:* We are not all the same; groups within society differ.
Similarity	*Similarity myth:* "They" are all just like me.	**Similarity and Difference**	*They are not just like me:* Many people differ from me culturally. Most people exhibit both cultural similarities and differences when compared to me.
Parochialism	*Only-one-way myth:* Our way is the only way. We do not recognize any other way of living or working.	**Equifinality**	*Multiple ways:* Many culturally distinct ways of living one's life, working, and reaching one's goals exist.
Ethnocentrism	*One-best-way myth:* Our way is the best way; all other approaches are inferior.	**Cultural Contingency**	*Our way is one possible way:* Many different and equally good ways can be used to reach the same goal. The best way depends on the cultures of the people involved.

Source: Adler (4): Adapted by Adler, 2007.[4]

FIGURE 4-2   Creating Cultural Synergy

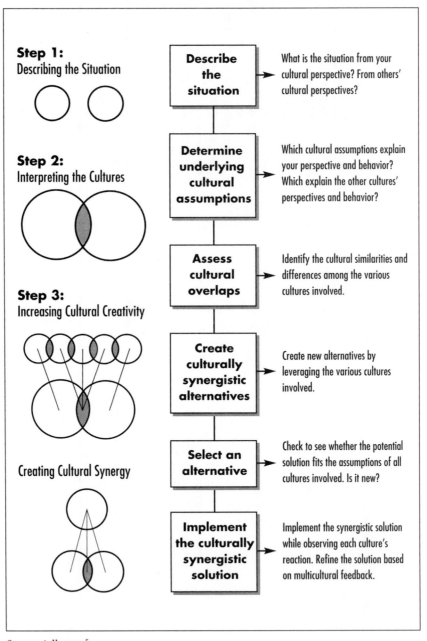

Source: Adler (3).[5]

culture's perspective, culturally interpreting the situation, and developing new culturally creative solutions (3:173).

Step 1: Describing the Situation What cross-cultural dilemmas does the organization face? What cross-cultural conflicts do managers face? Going beyond their own perspective, can managers describe conflicts from the perspectives of each of the various cultures involved? Describing the situation involves one of the most difficult and critical steps in finding solutions to complex multicultural problems. Across cultures, people's divergent values, perceptions, attitudes, and behaviors magnify the challenges faced in understanding and resolving organizational problems. In each of the following examples, conflict arises because each culture views the situation exclusively from its own perspective (3:178):

> **Japan**   *An American sales manager expressed his growing frustration with his Japanese employees: "I'm an 'open-door manager.' I expect my employees to come to me when they have a problem. But these Japanese never come until there's a crisis . . . until it's too late to do anything." When questioned later about his behavior, the Japanese sales representatives explained that "Americans see everything as a problem!" In analyzing the situation, it became clear that people's cultural perspectives determine when they see a situation as a problem. Westerners often see life as a series of problems to be resolved, whereas non-Westerners frequently view life as a series of situations to be accepted (27). Americans, therefore, define more situations as problems than do the Japanese. Americans also define a situation as a problem much earlier than do the Japanese* (3:178).

> **Egypt**   *An Egyptian executive, after entertaining his Canadian guest, offered him joint partnership in a new business venture. The Canadian, delighted with the offer, suggested that they meet again the next morning with their respective lawyers to finalize the details. The Egyptian never showed up. The surprised and disappointed Canadian tried to understand what had gone wrong: Did Egyptians lack punctuality? Was the Egyptian expecting a counter-offer? Were lawyers unavailable in Cairo? None of these explanations proved to be correct; rather, the problem was caused by the different meaning Canadians and Egyptians attach to inviting lawyers. The Canadian foresaw the lawyers' presence as facilitating the successful completion of the negotiation; the Egyptian interpreted it as signaling the Canadian's mistrust of his verbal commitment (3:178). Canadians often use the impersonal formality of a lawyer's services to finalize*

agreements. Egyptians, by contrast, more frequently depend on the personal relationship between bargaining partners to accomplish the same purpose.

The first step in the process of creating cultural synergy involves recognizing that a problem situation exists. Global managers recognize that a conflict may develop even when it does not make sense from their own cultural perspective (3:178). They then describe the situation from each culture's perspective (not just from their own perspective), while refraining from interpreting or evaluating the situation from any culture's point of view.

Step 2: Culturally Interpreting the Situation Why do members of different cultures think, feel, and act the way they do? What historical and cultural assumptions must we make to understand the present situation? Once global managers recognize that a problem exists, they can use the synergistic approach to analyze it from each culture's perspective. The second step in the process of creating cultural synergy, therefore, involves identifying and interpreting the similarities and differences in thoughts, feelings, and actions among the cultures involved (3:178). All behavior is rational and understandable from the perspective of the person behaving; however, our culturally based perspectives and biases often lead us to misunderstand the logic of other cultures' behavioral patterns (3:179). Whereas a single-culture perspective limits managers' flexibility in global situations, multiple perspectives enhance their understanding and options.

Changing perspectives is achieved through role reversal. During cultural interpretation, managers from each culture attempt to understand the underlying assumptions that lead people from other cultures to behave as they do. During this process, managers identify similarities and differences between their own culture's assumptions and behaviors and those of other cultures. The following example illustrates Americans' and Iranians' misinterpretations of each other's culture:

> *Iran   An American engineer who was teaching Persians to use a particularly complex technology became disappointed in his trainees' progress and therefore decided to give them poor performance reviews. One Persian came to the American and queried, "But I thought you were my friend. Why don't you give me a better review?" The American became furious. Only later, in analyzing and interpreting the underlying cultural assumptions, did the American come to understand the importance Persians place on friendship relative to task accomplishment. Similarly, the Persian came to recognize that Americans often base their system of equity solely on competence rather than on competence and relationship (27;28).*

CREATING CULTURAL SYNERGY
Uruguay and the Philippines

Situation Description

A Uruguayan doctor on staff at a major California hospital expressed concern upon realizing that a Filipino nurse was improperly using a particular machine to treat a patient. He instructed the nurse on the proper procedure and asked if she understood. She said she did. Two hours later the patient's condition deteriorated because the nurse had continued to administer the treatment improperly. The doctor more sharply queried the nurse, and she again affirmed her understanding of the procedure. What went wrong?

In analyzing the situation, the doctor came to understand that many Filipinos will not contradict people in respected positions. To the Filipino nurse, the doctor's status was clearly above hers. He was older; she was younger. He was a doctor; she was a nurse. He was a man; she was a woman. Based on her cultural assumptions, she could not tell the doctor that she did not understand without implying that he had given her poor instructions and thus cause him to lose face. The doctor, based on his cultural assumptions, expected "open communication"; he expected the nurse to say whether she understood his instructions and to ask questions if she did not. He considered it a sign of incompetence to assume responsibility for a patient's care without fully understanding the treatment procedure.

Synergistic Solution

After analyzing the situation, the hospital administrator suggested a culturally synergistic solution. Upon giving his initial instructions, the doctor was to ask the nurse to describe the procedure that she would follow. As the doctor listened, he could assess the accuracy of the nurse's understanding and identify areas that needed further explanation. The nurse, never having been asked directly if she understood, would not be forced to say "no" to a superior. The hospital administrator solved the problem without violating either culture's assumptions (3:179-180). The hospital could achieve its goal—the delivery of excellent medical care—without violating the norms of either culture.

Both cultures value friendship and achievement; they simply differ in the relative importance they attach to each in a business context (3:179).

Step 3: Increasing Cultural Creativity Organizations create synergistic alternatives by searching for culturally appropriate ways to solve problems involving people from multiple cultures. The initial question—"What can people from one culture learn from people of another culture to enhance their effectiveness and productivity?"—focuses on learning transfer. The second, and more important, question—"How

CREATING CULTURAL SYNERGY
Japanese and American Scheduling

Situation Description

American sales representatives of a U.S.–based air freight company with extensive Asian operations generally promised customers specific dates and hours for flight arrivals of freight shipments. Shipments, however, often arrived late. American customers would usually expect, understand, and forgive these delays if given an adequate explanation, whereas Japanese customers expected the company to keep its promises and lost faith in the company when it failed to adhere to the promised arrival times. Unlike the Americans, the Japanese sales representatives often refused to promise delivery times until, as one American sarcastically explained, "the plane had already arrived on the runway" or, as the Japanese explained, "they could be certain that their promises would be kept." The Japanese sales representatives' lack of promising, however, did not work with American clients, who expected definite timetables; when they were not given scheduled arrival times, the American clients began to distrust the company's ability to deliver its services.

Interpretation

The air freight company needed to design a uniform "promising" system that would be culturally appropriate for both American and Japanese employees and clients. From the American perspective, the system had to be precise enough to engender credibility with American customers. From the Japanese perspective, promises to customers had to sufficiently conform to reality so that no one would lose face.

Synergistic Solution

After analyzing the underlying cultural dynamics in both systems, the sales representatives agreed that they should begin promising delivery within a range of time, rather than at specific times. For instance, they would promise clients delivery "late morning Thursday," rather than at 11:05 A.M. (scheduled flight arrival time). Thus Americans could continue to make promises and the Japanese would rarely find themselves promising something the company could not deliver. This solution recognized the values of both cultures without undermining either culture's management practices. As a synergistic solution, it was new and appropriate to both cultures (3:180–181).[6]

can we combine and leverage our various cultures' ways of working?"—focuses on synergy. The answer should be compatible with the assumptions of all represented cultures. Culturally synergistic solutions are novel and transcend the behavioral patterns of each individual culture (3:179). Selecting the best solution—evaluation—only becomes possible after the situation has been adequately described and interpreted from a cross-cultural perspective (see Chapter 3). The box "Creating Cultural Synergy: Uruguay and the Philippines" presents an example of the process of creating cultural synergy.

IMPLEMENTATION

Organizations must plan the implementation of culturally synergistic solutions carefully. Before organization members will understand the need for changes based on synergistic problem solving, they must develop cultural self-awareness (an understanding of their own cultural assumptions and patterns of behavior) as well as cross-cultural awareness (an understanding of the other cultures' assumptions and patterns of behavior). Without some understanding of the cultural dynamics involved, proposed changes often appear absurd; with cultural understanding, the organization can solve its problems and implement the changes needed to foster high-quality client service, employee effectiveness, and job satisfaction (3:180). The box "Creating Cultural Synergy: Japanese and American Scheduling" highlights a synergistic scheduling plan implemented by an American air freight company for its routes between Japan and the United States.

STRATEGIES THAT INCLUDE SYNERGY

Which strategies do the most effective managers use when working with global strategic alliance and joint venture partners? Which approaches work most effectively in negotiating across national borders and in working with global project teams? Do highly effective global managers always use synergy? No.

As shown in Figure 4-3, managers have five basic options to choose from in selecting their approach to multicultural situations. In all cross-cultural situations, managers must create a balance between continuing to work in their own way—that is, the way they manage at home—and adapting to the ways of other cultures. Exhibiting maximum flexibility and sensitivity, highly effective global managers use all five strategic options, selecting a specific option depending on the particular situation and people involved.

Cultural Dominance The first option is cultural dominance: continuing to use the approaches you use at home. Historically, companies having considerably more power than their counterparts—based on their

FIGURE 4-3   Global Strategic Options

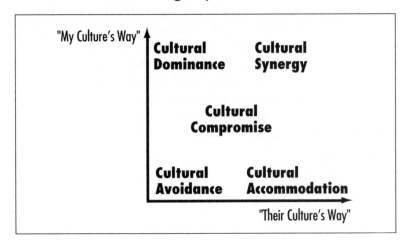

larger size, more advanced technology, or more significant financial resources—have often used a dominance approach. Individual managers often choose to use a cultural dominance approach when they strongly believe their way is the only right way, especially in situations involving ethical issues. One Swedish manager, for example, refused to lower the safety standards on his company's products, even though the lower standards were legally acceptable in the potential buyer's country. The Swede lost the contract because his bid, which included the higher safety standards, came in too high. Similarly, an American manager refused to accept a small, personal gift from a Korean client because his company, based on American practices, believed that gift giving represented a form of bribery. To the Korean, gift giving represented a form of relationship building. The American's behavior mystified the Korean— "How could a small personal gift be considered a bribe?" In both cases, home-culture-based personal ethics determined the manager's behavior; in both cases, it compromised the business relationship.

Cultural Accommodation The second approach, cultural accommodation, is the opposite of cultural dominance. Rather than attempting to maintain one's own home-country practices when working with colleagues from another culture, managers attempt to imitate the practices of their international colleagues. When working abroad, they attempt to blend into the local culture. They follow the maxim "When in Rome, do as the Romans do." Managers who consistently use cultural accommodation are often accused by their home-country colleagues of having "gone native," with executives from the home country often fearing that they will no longer fully represent either the home country's or the home organization's interests.

A German executive attempted to use cultural accommodation in Japan to get his first contract with a particularly important potential Japanese client. The German spent the first two weeks in Kobe and Osaka dining and playing golf with the Japanese, without scheduling any formal business meetings or product discussions. Although the German manager's boss in Munich became increasingly annoyed, thinking his colleague had confused a business trip with a vacation, the German executive was accommodating perfectly to the Japanese style of doing business: he was allowing the Japanese to get to know him (relationship building) before focusing on the details of the contract (task focus). The German got the contract.

Managers who learn the local language of countries in which they work are using a cultural accommodation strategy. Similarly, managers who denominate contracts in the local currency are using cultural accommodation. Their accommodation approach allows local managers to continue using their normal, comfortable ways of doing business. In 2005–06, Google used an accommodation strategy in China when the company agreed to implement Chinese-government-defined policies, including collecting web-based information for the Chinese government and launching a search engine that censors information on Tibet, Taiwan, human rights, and other topics considered sensitive to the Chinese government (17). China is recognized for operating "the most extensive, technologically sophisticated, and broad-reaching system of Internet filtering in the world" (17). Many people in Google's home country, the United States, found Google's accommodation strategy to be inappropriate, if not potentially unethical and illegal (29).

Cultural Compromise The third approach, cultural compromise, combines the first and second approaches. Cultural compromise implies that both sides concede something in order to work more successfully together. For example, French and Russian potential joint venture partners held initial meetings alternately in Moscow and Paris. Each had to travel to half the meetings, but neither experienced the inconvenience of always traveling and working away from their own headquarters every time.

In compromise solutions, the more powerful partner often gives up less than the less powerful partner. Both sides, however, make concessions for the business relationship to succeed. Home-country colleagues often label managers who give up too much as weak and sometimes even accuse them of "caving in."

Cultural Avoidance The fourth approach, cultural avoidance, is the choice to act as if no differences nor any potential conflicts exist. This approach, used more frequently by Asian managers than by their

Western counterparts, usually emphasizes "saving face" in lieu of openly and explicitly confronting the potentially conflictual details inherent in the business relationship. Managers use cultural avoidance most commonly when the unresolved issue is less important than maintaining the long-term business relationship or contract.

In negotiating the final details of a major construction contract in eastern Malaysia, for example, an American human resource manager thought he had resolved all potential disagreements regarding salaries and benefits. He therefore reacted with surprise when he saw that the Malaysian version of the benefits package included dental care for workers and their families, including the children of second, third, and fourth wives.[7] Even though the Americans had never considered including dental care, or any other benefits, for the families of workers' second, third, or fourth wives, and they knew that such benefits had never been discussed or promised, they chose not to confront the Malaysians. Perhaps the Malaysians, based on their cultural tradition, had assumed that "family" meant "all wives' families," whereas it had never occurred to the Americans that "family" might mean anything other than one wife's (or husband's) family. Rather than upsetting a project that would be good for both the Americans and Malaysians, the Americans chose "not to notice" the additional expense for benefits included in the contract.

Cultural Synergy As discussed in this chapter, the fifth approach, cultural synergy, develops new solutions to problems that leverage the cultural differences among all cultures involved while respecting each culture's uniqueness. Culturally synergistic solutions always go beyond what would be needed in a purely domestic situation. The use of foreign languages provides an excellent example. When businesspeople meet, they have to use language to communicate. If they speak different native languages, they must choose the language in which they will communicate. When a British company insists on working in English with its Swedish alliance partner, it is using cultural dominance. If the Swedes immediately agree, they are choosing to employ cultural accommodation. If each side chooses to speak in its own language and use interpreters, they are employing a compromise approach. However, when Norwegian and Austrian business partners choose to communicate in English, they are using synergy. Global businesspeople in both Norway and Austria often speak English, the international business language; however, neither speaks English as a native language. English allows multiple cultures to conduct business without one side capitulating and becoming disadvantaged by speaking the other's language. Similarly, denominating contracts in a basket of currencies—rather than in the currency of one of the countries involved—is a synergistic approach to managing the risk of future exchange-rate fluctuations.

SUMMARY

In a *Fortune* cover story on "What the Leaders of Tomorrow See," Corning's CEO asserted, "Future leaders will have to learn how to manage cultural diversity" (12:59). Cultural synergy is a powerful approach to managing the impact of cultural differences that encourages organizations to leverage their diversity, rather than to ignore or minimize it. Synergistic solutions create new forms of managing that recognize and transcend the array of unique ethnic cultures of employees and customers. Synergy, far from ignoring the presence of cultural diversity within the organization, recognizes both its potentially positive and negative impacts. Unlike the more commonly used cultural dominance and accommodation approaches, synergy emphasizes managing the impacts of diversity, rather than attempting to eliminate or ignore the diversity itself.

The synergy approach to problem solving involves three fundamental steps: cross-cultural situation description, cross-cultural interpretation, and cultural creativity. Global managers first define problems from the perspectives of all cultures involved. They then analyze the patterns that make each culture's behavior logical from within its own perspective. Only then can they create solutions that foster the organization's effectiveness and productivity without violating the norms of any culture involved.

The synergy approach creates organizational solutions to problems by using cultural diversity as a resource and an advantage to the organization. Synergy is most useful in resolving important issues in which cross-cultural interaction among employees and clients occurs daily. Organizations should not, however, consider synergy to be the only approach.

Introducing culturally synergistic problem solving to an organization for the first time involves managing change. The most fundamental change is one of perspective: executives must guide their organizations toward a more inclusive and more global world view. Many organizations find it helpful to begin the cultural synergy process by providing opportunities for managers to become more culturally self-aware (enhancing their recognition and understanding of their own culture's ways of doing business) and more cross-culturally aware (enhancing their recognition and understanding of the culturally based work styles of customers and colleagues from other cultures). With a heightened and more broadly based awareness of cultural dynamics, organizations can begin to address the culturally based conflict situations inherent in global management. Managers often initially address problems explicitly, formally, and slowly; yet later synergistic problem-solving sessions become more informal, implicit, and considerably less time-consuming. Knowledge acquired during initial sessions becomes part of the organization's increasingly global perspective and cross-cultural competence.

Cultural synergy is *an* approach, not *the* approach; it is one of five options that highly effective global managers use regularly. The synergistic problem-solving process is not a quick fix. It is a systematic process for increasing the options open to executives, managers, and employees working in increasingly global business environments. The synergy approach works equally effectively for competing successfully in multicultural domestic environments.

QUESTIONS FOR REFLECTION

1. **Choosing an Approach.** Select an organizational problem involving more than one culture that you are currently facing or have faced in the past. How would you develop a culturally synergistic solution to the problem?

2. **Reducing Cultural Blindness.** For many organizations, a major problem is cultural blindness. In the organizations you know, what factors cause managers to remain blind to the impact of cultural diversity? What would you recommend to decrease managers' work-related cultural blindness?

3. **Creating Cultural Synergy.** Select a cross-cultural conflict situation that is currently in the news or occurring in your organization. As a consultant, what would you recommend to help the parties involved create a culturally synergistic solution? Describe a potentially synergistic solution to the situation.

4. **Developing Skills for Synergy.** Reflecting on your own personality, experience, and work style, what do you see as your greatest skills in creating culturally synergistic solutions to global problems? How could you improve your skills at creating cultural synergy?

5. **Advantages of Cultural Diversity.** What advantages do global companies gain by using multicultural senior management teams? What are the advantages of using a homogeneous team of senior executives selected locally? Under what circumstances would you recommend each type of senior executive team?

NOTES

1. An increasing number of authors today include a statement about the potential lack of cultural generalizability in the "limitations" section of their research reports and articles.

2. The term *groupthink* was first coined by I. L. Janis (5). Reprinted by permission. See Chapter 5 for a more in-depth discussion of the topic.

3. From Adler (5); Copyright © 1983 NTL Institute.

4. From Adler (4); Copyright © 1983 Marcel Dekker, Inc., New York, NY.

5. From Adler (3); Copyright © 1980 Pfeiffer & Co. Reprinted with permission.

6. Clifford Clarke, president, Clarke Consulting Group, was instrumental in interpreting the cross-cultural air freight situation. His insight and creativity in creating cultural synergy with Japanese organizations continues to advance our global insight and practice.

7. According to Islamic tradition, a man may take up to four wives as long as he can support each of them and their children.

REFERENCES

1. Adler, N. J. "Cross-Cultural Management: Issues to Be Faced," *International Studies of Management and Organization,* vol. 13, no. 1–2 (1983), pp. 7–45.

2. Adler, N. J. "Cross-Cultural Management Research: The Ostrich and the Trend," *Academy of Management Review,* vol. 8, no. 2 (1983), pp. 226–232.

3. Adler, N. J. "Cultural Synergy: The Management of Cross-Cultural Organizations," in W. W. Burke and L. D. Goodstein, eds., *Trends and Issues in OD: Current Theory and Practice* (San Diego, Calif.: University Associates, 1980), pp. 163–184.

4. Adler, N. J. "Domestic Multiculturalism: Cross-Cultural Management in the Public Sector," in W. Eddy, ed., *Handbook on Public Organization Management* (New York: Marcel Dekker, 1983), pp. 481–499.

5. Adler, N. J. "Organizational Development in a Multicultural Environment," *Journal of Applied Behavioral Science,* vol. 19, no. 3 (1983), pp. 349–365.

6. Adler, N. J.; & Bartholomew, Susan. "Academic and Professional Communities of Discourse: Generating Knowledge on Transnational Human Resource Management," *Journal of International Business Studies,* vol. 23, no. 3 (1992), pp. 551–569.

7. Adler, N. J.; & Boyacigiller, Nakiye. "Global Organizational Behavior: Going Beyond Tradition," *Journal of International Management,* vol. 1, no. 1 (1995), pp. 73–86.

8. Adler, N. J.; & Laurent, André. Unpublished results from the Cultural Synergy Survey collected at INSEAD in 1980–1983 and in 1982 at major American and Canadian multinationals ($n = 145$).

9. Boyacigiller, Nakiye; & Adler, N. J. "Insiders and Outsiders: Bridging the Worlds of Organizational Behavior and International Management," in Brian Toyne & Doug Nigh, eds., *International Business Inquiry: An Emerging Vision* (Columbia, S.C.: University of South Carolina Press, 1997), pp. 396–416.

10. Boyacigiller, Nakiye; & Adler, N. J. "The Parochial Dinosaur: The Organizational Sciences in a Global Context," *Academy of Management Review,* vol. 16, no. 2 (1991), pp. 262–290.

11. Clark, T.; Gospel, H.; & Montgomery, John. "Running on the Spot? A Review of Twenty Years of Research on the Management of Human Resources in Comparative and International Perspective," *The International Journal of Human Resource Management,* vol. 10, no. 3 (1999), pp. 520–544.

12. Dumaine, B. "What the Leaders of Tomorrow See," *Fortune* (July 3, 1989), pp. 48–62.

13. Fuller, R. Buckminster. *Critical Path* (Washington, DC: St. Martin's Press/ World Future Society, 1981).

14. Godkin, L.; Braye, C. E.; & Cauch, C. L. "U.S.–Based Cross-Cultural Management Research in the Eighties," *Journal of Business and Economic Perspectives,* vol. 15, no. 2 (1989), pp. 37–45.

15. Hayles, Robert. "Costs and Benefits of Integrating Persons from Diverse Cultures in Organization," paper presented at the 20th International Congress of Applied Psychology, Edinburgh, Scotland, July 25–31, 1982.

16. Hofstede, Geert. *Culture's Consequences: International Differences in Work-Related Values* (Beverly Hills, Calif.: Sage, 1980).

17. "Internet Filtering in China in 2004–2005" (2006) as reported on the web at http://www.opennetinitiative.net/studies/china/ on February 22, 2006.

18. Janis, I. L. *Groupthink* (Boston, MA: Houghton Mifflin Company, 1982).

19. Laurent, André. "The Cultural Diversity of Western Conceptions of Management," *International Studies of Management and Organization,* vol. 13, no. 1–2 (1983), pp. 75–96.

20. Laurent, André; & Adler, N. J. "Managerial Skills for International Business," executive seminars held at INSEAD in Fontainebleau, France, August, 1981–1983.

21. McEvoy, G. M.; & Buller, P. F. "International Human Resource Management Publications: Even in the Eighties and Needs for the Nineties," Working Paper. Utah State University, 1992, pp. 1–21.

22. Moran, Robert T.; & Harris, Philip R. *Managing Cultural Synergy*, 3d ed. (Houston, Tex.: Gulf Publishing Company, 1983), Chapter 15, p. 303.

23. Ozbilgin, M. "'International' Human Resource Management: Academic Parochialism in Editorial Boards of the 'Top' 22 Journals on Human Resource Management," *Personnel Review*, vol. 33, no. 2 (2004), pp. 205–221.

24. Peng, T. K.; Peterson, Mark F.; & Shyi, Y. P. "Quantitative Methods in Cross-National Management Research: Trend and Equivalence Issues," *Journal of Organizational Behavior*, vol. 12, no. 1 (1990), pp. 87–107.

25. Prekel, Truda. "Multicultural Communication: A Challenge to Managers," paper delivered at the International Convention of the American Business Communication Association, New York, November 21, 1983, p. 11.

26. Ricks, David A. *Blunders in International Business*, 3d ed. (Cambridge, Mass.: Blackwell, 1998).

27. Stewart, Edward C. *American Cultural Patterns: A Cross-Cultural Perspective* (Chicago, Ill.: Intercultural Press, 1979).

28. Trompenaars, Fons; & Hampden-Turner, Charles. *Riding the Waves of Culture: Understanding Cultural Diversity in Business*, 2d ed. (New York: McGraw-Hill Book Company, 1998).

29. Zeller, Tom Jr. "Web Firms Are Grilled on Dealings in China," *New York Times* (February 16, 2006).

30. Ziller, R. C. "Homogeneity and Heterogeneity of Group Membership," in C. G. McClintock, ed., *Experimental Social Psychology* (New York: Holt, Rinehart, and Winston, 1972), pp. 385–411.

Chapter 5

Managing Multicultural Teams

It was once said that the sun never set on the British Empire. Today the sun does set on the British Empire, but not on the scores of global corporate empires including those of IBM, Unilever, Volkswagen, and Hitachi.

—Lester Brown, President of Worldwatch Institute (91:320)

Global business used to be a minor component of industrial activity; now it dominates. Global management used to involve simply sending one of "our" managers "over there" to sell products to foreign clients; now people from many countries work within the same companies, and in many cases, "we" have become the foreigners. Global management used to involve sending a few expatriates to direct operations abroad; now members of corporate boards, executives, managers, and workers represent every nationality. Today more than 100,000 firms headquartered in high-technology, free-market economies have operations outside their home countries (see 91:320).

By the beginning of the twenty-first century, global business had brought contact with foreign cultures home to almost every business. Today, with e-commerce, managers may work for foreign-owned firms without leaving their own communities, sell primarily to non-native clients, and negotiate with component suppliers worldwide, all while regularly attending global video conferences and web-based meetings with colleagues from around the world. Globally distributed design teams routinely develop innovative new products in e-meetings involving experts from five continents, none of whom ever have to leave home to participate in the telephone, video-conference, e-mail, and web-based discussions. Cross-cultural dialogue has thus become the foundation on which global business succeeds or fails.

MANAGING A MULTICULTURAL WORKFORCE

Both domestically and globally, the multicultural workforce has become a reality (61). The impact of multiculturalism, however, varies significantly based on the type of competitive environment and the

126

FIGURE 5-1   Importance of Cultural Diversity

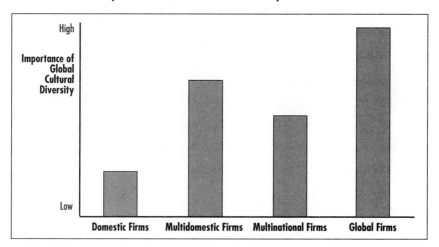

firm's overall strategy. As shown in Figure 5-1, prior to the 1980s, global cultural diversity had a minimal impact on domestic firms, even while domestic multiculturalism was strongly influencing the same firms' business outcomes. Sophisticated managers in U.S. firms, for example, coached their colleagues to appreciate and to effectively manage a workforce composed of African-American, Asian-American, Caucasian, Hispanic, and Aboriginal women and men. Assuming the domestic workforce to be homogeneous or defined by the norms of white men, while never appropriate, was no longer effective.

In multidomestic firms (those with fairly autonomous operations in multiple countries), the impact of culture is highly significant. Multidomestic firms must adapt their strategies, as well as their products and services, to the local culture in each country in which they operate. In multinational firms (those that are organized into global lines of business), by contrast, the impact of cultural differences is less than it is for multidomestic firms, because price and cost dominate all other considerations.

By the time firms adopt global strategies, the impact of cultural diversity becomes extremely important. Global firms must understand cultural dynamics to formulate their business strategies, to locate production facilities and manage worldwide supply chains, and to design and market culturally appropriate products and services, all while managing cross-cultural interaction throughout the organization, from the most senior executive committees to the shop floor. As more firms move from domestic, multidomestic, and multinational strategies to operating as truly global companies and alliances, the importance and

**FIGURE 5-2   Organizational Location of Global Cross-Cultural
Interaction: Internal and External**

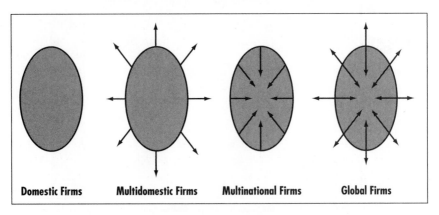

| Domestic Firms | Multidomestic Firms | Multinational Firms | Global Firms |

impact of cultural diversity increase markedly. In global firms, the effective management of cultural diversity, which was once a concept that was merely "nice to understand," becomes imperative for the firm's survival, let alone its success (3). (See Chapter 1 for a review of each strategy.)

Similar to the increasing importance of cultural diversity, the location of its impact varies with changes in the firm's competitive business environment and strategy. As shown in Figure 5-2, worldwide cultural diversity traditionally has not affected domestic firms' internal organizational culture nor their external relationships with clients. Domestic firms work domestically; only domestic multiculturalism—not global cultural diversity—directly impacts the internal dynamics of domestic firms and their relationships with the external environment. Today very few firms operate in a purely domestic environment; most no longer have the luxury of operating in a simple environment free from global influences.

In multidomestic firms, which focus primarily on exporting and producing abroad, cultural diversity strongly affects relationships external to the organization, given that it has both clients and employees in other countries. By contrast, multinational firms place less emphasis on managing cultural differences external to the firm, but must effectively manage the extensive multinational diversity within the firm. Whereas multidomestic firms primarily use expatriate managers to sell and work abroad, multinational firms hire people from around the world as employees and managers. In multidomestic firms, only expatriates have a high need to develop cultural sensitivity and cross-cultural management skills. By contrast, in multinational firms, because cultural diversity strongly affects internal organizational culture, many more employees and managers need cross-cultural management skills.

Global firms must continually manage cultural diversity both within the company and between the company and its external environment. To work effectively, everyone from the CEO to the lowest-level worker must use cross-cultural skills. This progression from culture's relative lack of importance to its critical importance, with respect to the firm's external environment as well as its internal organizational culture, underlies the general recognition that executives and managers must know how to work effectively in multinational and multicultural teams if they wish to succeed (3).

How do we manage people who differ from us? Research has shown that styles of leading, motivating, communicating, decision making, planning, organizing, and staffing vary among countries (see Chapters 6, 7 and 8). What happens when people from dissimilar cultures work together on a day-to-day basis within the same organization? How should organizations manage a multinational workforce?

This chapter investigates approaches to managing cultural diversity within organizations. It begins by reviewing domestic multiculturalism, an important source of multicultural dynamics in teams. It then focuses on cross-cultural interaction within teams: What types of problems does diversity most often cause within global teams? What are the potential advantages of well-managed, culturally diverse teams? How can leaders create world-class teams (61)? And, most importantly, how can management maximize the potential benefits and minimize the potential problems caused by diversity?

DOMESTIC MULTICULTURALISM

You do not have to go abroad to meet someone with a cultural background different from your own. With increasing immigration, a growing number of people working abroad, and the presence of indigenous and ethnic communities at home, managers who never leave home often face a multicultural workforce in domestic companies and organizations.

Multiple culturally distinct populations live in all countries of the world. Singapore, for example, has four cultural and linguistic groups: Chinese, Eurasian, Indian, and Malay. Belgium includes two linguistic groups, Flemish and French. India has 15 official languages: Hindi, Bengali, Telugu, Marathi, Tamil, Urdu, Gujarati, Malayalam, Kannada, Oriya, Punjabi, Assamese, Kashmiri, Sindhi, and Sanskrit. In addition, English, which is widely spoken in India, has associate status and frequently functions as a bridge among the linguistically diverse communities. Switzerland has four distinct ethnic communities: French, German, Italian, and Romansch. Canada, a multicultural country by national policy, uses two official languages, English and French. Many countries, including Australia, Canada, Israel, and the United States, have developed historically as havens for immigrants from around the world. Each immigrant community exhibits its own culturally unique lifestyle. Most of us are familiar with the typical foods of major ethnic groups: no one thinks spaghetti is Russian, tortillas are Chinese, or sushi is Senegalese. But many of us remain unaware of how extensively other cultures' lifestyles differ from our own. Even if we consider ourselves internationally sophisticated, many of us fail to recognize the culturally distinct attitudes and behaviors that our fellow citizens bring to the workplace (2).

The city of Los Angeles highlights the pervasiveness of domestic multiculturalism and its impact on the workplace. Since 1970 more than two million foreign immigrants have settled in Los Angeles (8:17). Of Los Angeles' 550,000 school children, 117,000 speak one of 104 languages more fluently than English, including 35 fluent only in Gujarati, a language of western India (8:18). Los Angeles no longer has a majority population but constantly "adjusts to the quirky, polyglot rhythms of 60,000 Samoans and 30,000 Thais, 200,000 Salvadorans and 175,000 Armenians" (8:18). Los Angeles is the second largest Mexican agglomeration after Mexico City (42:52); more Samoans live in Los Angeles than on the island of Samoa, 4,000 miles away (84:1); and more Israelis live there than in any other city outside of Israel (95). A former lieutenant governor of California recognized one central, inevitable fact more than two decades ago: "If the present trends continue, the emerging ethnic groups will constitute more than half the population of California by 1990, and . . . [California] will become the country's first Third World state" (51:35). His prediction became a reality, and the trends continue, with immigrants contributing hugely to the economy of the greater Los Angeles area. Since 1990, the Asian population of Los Angeles County has grown 37% to over 1.2 million. During the same period, the Hispanic population grew by 34% to over 4.5 million. Together, these two groups make up 58 percent of the county's total population (60).

Other cities and states in the United States reflect similar patterns, with the number of people born outside the country having reached 33 million (93). Of the 700,000 largely middle-class Cubans who left Cuba by 1978, more than 60 percent settled in Dade County, Florida (42:51). By 2002 Miami-Dade County led the U.S. in percentage of foreign-born residents, with over 60 percent of its population arriving from other countries (93). The borough of Queens in New York City has the second highest proportion of foreign-born residents (over 46%), and, with 140 distinct languages spoken, has arguably become the country's most ethnically diverse county (75;80;81). Such increases are not restricted to large urban settings: Iowa's foreign-born population increased by an estimated 26 percent, to nearly 98,000 in 2002 (93). These diverse communities have seen a resurgence of ethnic self-identity, both among new immigrants and among European populations that had previously appeared all but assimilated (76). Based on these and dozens of other similar statistics, multiculturalism has emerged as a dominant fact of domestic life. Citizens of most countries can neither ignore multiculturalism nor relegate it to the domain of global managers or diplomats.

Perhaps William Somerset Maugham best captured the essence of domestic multiculturalism in *The Trembling Leaf* in 1921, when he described Hawaii's domestic microcosm of Eastern and Western cultures—a state whose population of 1,227,000 is 25 percent Caucasian, 43 percent Asian, 9 percent Hawaiian and other Pacific Islander, 2 percent African American, and 21 percent mixed-race (94):

> *It is a meeting place of East and West, the very new rubs shoulders with the immeasurably old . . . you have come upon something singularly intriguing. All these strange people live close to each other, with different languages and different thoughts; they believe in different gods and they have different values; two passions alone they share, love and hunger. And somehow as you watch them, you have an impression of extraordinary vitality.*

TEAMS: THE ORGANIZATION IN MICROCOSM

Organizations consist of groups, and groups form the basic structure of organizations. Companies organize employees into many forms of temporary and permanent work groups, including departments, teams, task forces, subcommittees, committees, commissions, and boards. The quality of performance of such groups varies from poor to excellent, from totally unproductive to highly productive. Groups can espouse values and goals that society views as either desirable or destructive. Groups can accomplish much that is good, or they can cause great harm. From the organization's perspective, groups can be highly effective or totally ineffective. There is nothing implicitly good or bad, effective or ineffective, about a group (59).

The productivity of a work group—or team—depends on its task, its available resources, and its process. The team's goal defines its task. This task can involve a decision or recommendation, a project or report, or an action or series of actions. The team's resources include the people, information, materials, time, money, social capital, and energy available for accomplishing a particular task. A task force, for example, may have three or five people available; it may have one week or four months allocated to it; it may have a large budget or no budget at all; it may have very limited or completely unlimited access to IT resources and skills.

The team's process consists of the actual steps taken by individuals or the group when faced with a task. The team's process includes all intrapersonal and interpersonal actions taken by people to transform their resources into products and services, along with all nonproductive actions provoked by competing motivations, frustration, and inadequate understanding (90:8).

A team's actual productivity is therefore its potential productivity minus losses incurred due to faulty process (90:9).

**Actual productivity = Potential productivity −
Losses due to faulty process**

In other words, actual productivity depends on how well the team works together and uses its resources to accomplish the task.

TYPES OF DIVERSITY IN TEAMS

Team members can have very similar or quite different backgrounds, perspectives, and experience (9). Although diversity can occur on many characteristics, including gender, race, profession, nationality, age, and ethnicity, this chapter focuses on cultural differences (100). Homogeneous teams are those with all members coming from the same cultural group; multicultural teams are those with members coming from more than one culture (101). Multicultural teams can be divided into three types: token teams having a single member from another culture, bicultural teams having members from two cultures, and multicultural teams having members from three or more cultures.

HOMOGENEOUS TEAMS

In homogeneous teams, all members share a similar background. People on homogeneous teams generally perceive, interpret, and evaluate the world more similarly than do members of heterogeneous teams. An all-male team of Finnish bankers, for example, is homogeneous, based on gender, culture, and profession. A team of Mexican and Panamanian stockbrokers is professionally, but not culturally, homogeneous.

TOKEN TEAMS

In token teams all but one member comes from the same background. In a team of Australian lawyers and one British attorney, for example, the British attorney would be the token member. In such a token team, the British attorney would probably see and understand situations some-what differently from his Australian colleagues. In the last decade, pre-dominantly male management teams have begun to pay considerable attention to their few, often token, female members. Today many corpo-rations focus significantly more attention on leveraging the potential contributions of their token ethnic members.

BICULTURAL TEAMS
In bicultural teams, members represent two distinct cultures; for exam-ple, a fifty–fifty partnership between Peruvians and Bolivians, or a task force composed of Saudi Arabian and Jordanian managers, or a com-mittee of seven Spanish and three Portuguese executives. Bicultural teams must continually recognize and integrate the perspectives of both represented cultures. If the team has an unequal number of members from each culture, the culture of the group with more representatives is likely to dominate.

MULTICULTURAL TEAMS
In multicultural teams, members represent three or more ethnic back-grounds. United Nations agencies offer good examples of multicul-tural organizational structures, as do the committees of the European Union (EU) and the Association of Southeast Asian Nations (ASEAN). Today, an increasing number of corporate task forces are globally distanced teams—that is, teams composed of members from around the world who meet electronically.[1] The economic and politi-cal power structure of the represented members moderates a multi-cultural team's dynamics and, therefore, its effectiveness. To perform most effectively, multicultural teams need to recognize and integrate all represented cultures.

Although few studies describe cross-cultural interaction within management teams (13;66;67;69;85;89), considerable research exists on the conditions for effective team functioning within the United States (26;33;35;36;43;46;57;62;65;90;99). A growing literature describing team behavior in countries around the world, often with American comparisons, also exists (66;67;69;87). Researchers have studied such diverse peoples as black and white Americans (83), Arabs (14), the British (64), Canadians (88), Hispanics (19), Hong Kong and American Chinese (71), Indians (6;70), Japanese (18;73), Lebanese (21), New Zealanders (7), and South Africans, Nigerians, and Filipinos (34). By the beginning of the 21st century, more researchers began focusing specifically on multinational teams (24;25;31;50) and globally distanced teams (17;30;32;47;68). Research conclu-sively demonstrates that the behavior of people in work teams varies across cultures. Among other differences, researchers have found that team members from more collectivist cultures—such as those in China and the Middle East—frequently work more cooperatively with each other, enjoy working together more, and are less likely to "free ride," than their counterparts in more individualist cultures—such as those in Australia, Canada, and the United States (15;16;22;23).

CULTURAL DIVERSITY'S IMPACT ON TEAMS

Cultural diversity can have positive and negative impacts on a team's productivity (54;66;67;69;72;97;98). Diversity augments potential productivity, but at the same time greatly increases the complexity of processes members must manage for the team to realize its full potential (90:107). Multicultural teams thus have the potential to achieve higher productivity than homogeneous teams, but they also risk experiencing greater losses due to faulty process. As shown in the following model, actual productivity of multicultural teams can therefore be higher, lower, or the same as that of single-culture teams:

$$(\downarrow \text{ or} \uparrow) \ \begin{array}{c} \textbf{Actual} \\ \textbf{productivity} \end{array} = (\uparrow) \begin{array}{c} \textbf{Potential} \\ \textbf{productivity} \end{array} - (\uparrow) \begin{array}{c} \textbf{Losses due to} \\ \textbf{faulty process} \end{array}$$

Multicultural teams, for example, can have multiple perspectives on any given situation, thus potentially increasing their insight and, consequently, their productivity (63). Multicultural teams, however, also frequently experience greater difficulty than their homogeneous counterparts in evaluating and integrating these perspectives, thus causing losses in productivity due to faulty process.

LOSSES DUE TO FAULTY PROCESS
IN CULTURALLY DIVERSE TEAMS

Diversity makes team functioning more challenging because team members find it more difficult to see, understand, and act on situations in similar ways. Diversity makes reaching agreement more difficult. Team members from similar cultures find it easier to communicate clearly with one another and trust each other more readily. In culturally diverse teams, misperception, miscommunication, misinterpretation, and misevaluation abound (see Chapter 3). Because members of multicultural teams more frequently disagree on expectations, the appropriateness of relevant information, and the need for particular decisions, they generally experience higher levels of stress than do members of homogeneous teams. Diversity increases the ambiguity, complexity, and inherent confusion in team processes (see Chapter 4, Table 4-1). Process losses resulting from these issues diminish productivity (52;54).

Cohesiveness is the ability of team members to act as one. Team members' ability, when necessary, to perceive, interpret, and act on

**Table 5-1   Diversity in Multicultural Teams:
Advantages and Disadvantages**

Advantages	Disadvantages
Diversity permits increased creativity	**Diversity causes a lack of cohesion**
Wider range of perspectives	*Mistrust*
More and better ideas	Lower interpersonal attractiveness
Less groupthink	Inaccurate stereotyping
	More within-culture conversations
Diversity forces enhanced concentration to understand others'	*Miscommunication*
Ideas	Slower speech: Non-native speakers
Perspectives	and translation problems
Meanings	Less accuracy
Arguments	*Stress*
	More counterproductive behavior
Increased creativity can lead to generating	Less disagreement on content
	Tension
Better problem definitions	
More alternatives	**Lack of cohesion causes an inability to**
Better solutions	Validate ideas and people
Better decisions	Agree when agreement is needed
	Gain consensus on decisions
	Take concerted action
Teams can become	**Teams can become**
More effective	Less efficient
More productive	Less effective
	Less productive

situations in similar or mutually agreed upon ways determines the team's level of cohesiveness. Due to their lower level of similarity, members of multicultural teams initially exhibit less cohesion than most homogeneous teams.

As shown in Table 5-1, multicultural teams' higher levels of mistrust, miscommunication, and stress diminish their cohesion (45;47;78). More importantly, these attitudinal and perceptual communication problems also frequently diminish productivity. In addition to other challenges, globally distanced teams also lack physical proximity, and thus must rely on synchronous and asynchronous technology to communicate. The main process problems experienced by multicultural teams are discussed in the following section.

Attitudinal Problems: Dislike and Mistrust Members of culturally diverse teams express higher levels of mistrust than do their more homogeneous counterparts. Team members often find themselves more attracted to people from their own culture than to people from other cultures (92). Researchers in Belgium, for example, found that Walloon and Flemish individuals speak most frequently to colleagues from their own culture (82). Such mistrust usually results primarily from inadvertent cross-cultural misinterpretation rather than actual dislike. Many Indians, for example, look down when acknowledging authority, a behavior many European and North American managers misinterpret as signaling a lack of trustworthiness. As a result, European and North American team leaders often fail to develop sufficient trust in their Indian colleagues to delegate or share more than trivial responsibilities.

Perceptual Problems: Stereotyping Team members often inappropriately stereotype colleagues from other cultures rather than accurately seeing and assessing their skills and potential contributions to the accomplishment of a particular task (27). For instance, team members generally talk more to colleagues from higher-status cultures than to those from lower-status cultures. They assume, usually subconsciously, that national stereotypes apply to individual team members. Thus, in initial meetings, team members often inappropriately judge their colleagues from the most economically developed countries the most favorably (27). Members of one team of engineers, for example, assumed their American colleagues had more technological expertise than did their Moroccan colleagues simply because Morocco is less economically and technologically advanced than the United States. In a parallel situation, an Indian manager described the lack of respect granted him by many of his British colleagues who, he believed, "assume that I am underdeveloped simply because I come from an economically underdeveloped country." Both the initial stereotype and the Indian's resulting frustration interfered with the team's process and diminished the team's productivity.

Communication Problems: Inaccuracy, Misunderstanding, and Inefficiency Diversity can cause problems by disrupting communication (90). When all members do not fluently speak the team's working language, communication is slowed down (37). In linguistically diverse groups, some members must speak a foreign language or use an interpreter. Both diminish communication speed and increase the likelihood of errors (37).

Team members from diverse cultures often disagree over the meaning of important issues, such as the causes of particular events, how to determine admissible evidence, how to assess the relevance of specific information, and the possible conclusions that can be drawn (37). On many teams, disagreement remains implicit and, therefore, hidden; members assume they interpret things similarly when in fact the opposite is true. The following incident between an Indian and his Austrian task force leader highlights such an implicit misinterpretation:

> *When asked if his department could complete a project by a given date, the Indian department head said "yes" even though he knew he could not complete the project within the time frame, because he believed that the Austrian task force leader wanted "yes" for an answer. When the completion date arrived and the Indian had not finished the project, the Austrian showed dismay. The Indian's desire to act politely—to say what he thought the task force leader wanted to hear—seemed more important to him than accurately reporting his actual prediction of the completion date. Unfortunately, the Austrian valued accurate information more highly than politeness. Cross-cultural miscommunication disrupted the smooth functioning of work.[2]*

Stress Tension and stress levels in culturally diverse teams often exceed those in single-culture teams, due primarily to communication inaccuracies and a lack of trust (92). The deductive, analytical discussion style of the French, for example, often causes stress for the more inductive, pragmatic North Americans: the French continually want to discuss principles and historical precedent, whereas North Americans focus on specific details of the immediate situation.[3] Multicultural teams often exhibit symptoms of considerable social stress, including bickering, apathy, single-party (or single-culture) domination of discussions, stubbornness, and reprimanding (37). Alternatively, multicultural teams can show "a quiet climate of politeness and gradually increasing friendliness" (82); however, these rituals of politeness often merely reflect the team's superficial defense against weak cohesiveness (82). Ritual politeness leaves team members frustrated and usually becomes yet another hindrance blocking their realization of high productivity.

Decreased Effectiveness The previous examples demonstrate how cultural diversity can diminish effective team functioning in numerous serious ways. Studies have shown that members of multicultural teams use "more of their time and effort in creating cohesion and solidarity than [do] members of homogeneous groups" (48;79;82). If they remain unmanaged, cultural differences can paralyze a team's ability to act. For example, as described by one European manager,

> *In attempting to plan a new project, a three-person team composed of a British, French, and Swiss manager failed to reach agreement. To the French and Swiss managers, their British colleague seemed unable to embrace a systematic approach; he seemingly insisted on discussing every potential problem before even beginning to make a*

decision. *Whereas the French and Swiss managers agreed to examine everything before making a decision, they disagreed on the sequence and scheduling of operations. The Swiss, being the most pessimistic in his planning, allocated more time for each sub-operation than did his French colleague. The result of all these differences in planning style was that a project everyone had initially agreed upon was never initiated. If three French, three Swiss, or three British managers had discussed the project, the team would easily have made the needed decisions. The project would not have stalled for lack of agreement.*[4]

PRODUCTIVITY: POTENTIAL ADVANTAGES OF CULTURALLY DIVERSE TEAMS

Although they encounter more process problems than do homogeneous teams, culturally diverse teams also have the potential to achieve higher productivity, primarily because their greater diversity allows them to function more creatively. Effective teams need to perceive, interpret, and evaluate situations in numerous ways and then agree on the best options and directions. Multicultural teams generate alternatives easily because team diversity results in an array of diverging ideas. Leaders of all teams must constantly balance divergence with convergence; that is, generating new ideas (divergence) with gaining agreement on particular decisions and actions (convergence). Balancing creativity (divergence) and cohesion (convergence), however, is particularly challenging for leaders of multicultural teams.

As summarized in Table 5-1, multicultural teams have the potential to invent more options and create more solutions than do single-culture teams. Diversity makes it easier for teams to create more and better ideas (55). It allows them to avoid the trap of *groupthink* (44). It often forces members to pay closer attention to the contributions of their colleagues. Each of these advantages is discussed in the following sections (also see Table 4-1).

More and Better Ideas Due to the varied backgrounds of members of multicultural teams, they have the capacity to create more ideas, alternatives, and potential problem solutions than do homogeneous teams (40;56). Heterogeneous teams also frequently propose more inventive alternatives (39;79) and higher quality solutions to problems (40). Heterogeneous teams, however, are able to realize their potential only when they adequately manage the process problems associated with diversity. In the following example, a Swedish manager describes some of the advantages his pharmaceutical firm benefited from in moving from a single-culture to multicultural product design team:

We traditionally carried out product design at our Stockholm headquarters. Once, by accident or design, we brought in an international team to discuss the design of a new allergy product. Due to extreme differences in opinion on what constitutes good medical practice, the team designed the new product with maximum flexibility to suit the requirements of each country. We later discovered that the greater flexibility was a huge advantage in developing and marketing a wide range of internationally competitive products.[5]

Limited Groupthink *Groupthink* describes "a mode of thinking people engage in when they are deeply involved in a cohesive in-group, when [team] members' striving for unanimity overrides their motivation to realistically appraise alternative courses of action.... Groupthink refers to a deterioration of mental efficiency, reality testing, and moral judgment that results from in-group pressures" (44:9). Groupthink is a major source of ineffectiveness in teams.

The three major symptoms of groupthink are overestimating the team's power and morality, closed-mindedness, and pressures toward uniformity (44). Compared with their single-culture counterparts, multicultural teams are less likely to prematurely agree on a decision. They are also less likely to engage in the following counterproductive groupthink behaviors (44:175):

1. *Self-censoring* deviations from the apparent team consensus—caused by each member's inclination to minimize to themselves the importance of their doubts and counterarguments.

2. *Sharing an illusion of unanimity;* that is, assuming that judgements conform to the majority view—often a result of members' self-censorship of deviations, and augmented by the false assumption that silence implies consent.

3. *Directly pressuring* any member who expresses strong arguments against the team's stereotypes, illusions, or commitments, making it clear that this type of dissent is contrary to what the team expects from all loyal members.

4. The emergence of *self-appointed mindguards,* or members who protect the team from adverse information that might shatter the group's shared complacency about its effectiveness and the morality of its decisions.

The consequences of groupthink include incompletely surveying objectives and alternatives, failing to examine the risks inherent in preferred choices, failing to reappraise initially rejected alternatives, conducting poor information searches, introducing selective bias in processing available information, and failing to work out contingency plans (44:175). Multicultural teams are less susceptible to groupthink because they are less likely to subconsciously limit the range of perspectives, ideas, conclusions, and decisions they consider to those supported by the majority or by the team leaders.

CONDITIONS FOR HIGH-PERFORMING MULTICULTURAL TEAMS

Multicultural teams can potentially become the most effective and productive teams in an organization. Unfortunately, they frequently become the least productive.

Figure 5-3 shows the relative productivity of a series of four- to six-member problem-solving teams. Culturally diverse teams often perform either more or less effectively than their single-culture counterparts (53). What differentiates the most effective from the least effective teams? Why are culturally diverse teams usually either more or less effective than single-culture teams, but rarely equally effective?

The productivity of a team does not depend on the presence or absence of diversity, but rather on how well diversity is managed. When well managed, diversity becomes an asset and a productive resource for the team (6;28;40;54;66;67;74;96). When ignored, diversity causes process problems that diminish the team's productivity. Because diversity is more frequently ignored than well managed (see Chapter 4), culturally diverse teams often perform below expectations and below organizational norms.

As shown in Table 5-2, multicultural teams' productivity depends on their task, stage of development, and the ways in which they manage their diversity. Diversity becomes most valuable when the need for the team to

FIGURE 5-3   Team Effectiveness

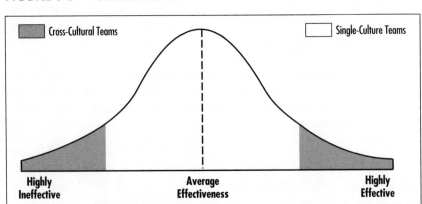

Source: Based on Kovach (53); adapted by Adler.

TABLE 5-2   Effectively Managing Team Diversity

	Effective	Ineffective
	Diversity can make teams most effective when:	Diversity renders teams least effective when:
Task	Innovative	Routine
Stage	Divergence (earlier)	Convergence (later)
Conditions	Differences recognized	Differences ignored
	Members selected for task-related abilities	Members selected based on ethnicity
	Mutual respect	Ethnocentrism
	Equal power	Cultural dominance
	Superordinate goal	Individual goals
	External feedback	No feedback (autonomy)

reach agreement (cohesion) remains low relative to the need to invent creative solutions. Diversity functions as an advantage only if the team recognizes when to leverage and when to minimize the impact of its diversity, and how creativity and agreement can be balanced. The team leader must accurately assess each situation and emphasize those aspects that best fit the team's overall goals and objectives, as well as its current task.

TASK: INNOVATIVE OR ROUTINE

Whether and how much diversity is desirable depends on the nature of the team's task. When a task requires team members to perform highly specialized roles, it is usually more advantageous to use a diverse team. When everyone must do the same thing, work generally progresses more smoothly if members think and behave similarly (90:106). Corporate consulting teams, for example, generally work most effectively when they include a range of specialists—finance, marketing, production, and strategy experts. Teams assembling radios, on the other hand, generally perform better when all members have similar levels of manual dexterity and coordination.

For some tasks, the ability of the most or the least competent member determines the team's potential productivity. For other tasks, the combination of abilities of all members determines the team's potential productivity. Reward schemes can alter members' performance. When managers reward employees with bonuses based on the best employee's performance, teams focus on helping their best member perform outstandingly. Olympic teams often work in this way: a country receives the gold medal for an individual event based on the performance of its top member. Alternatively, when managers reward an entire department based on the performance of the least productive employee (for example, based on the least productive member exceeding a certain minimal level), teams attempt to increase the productivity of their weakest member, often by coaching him or her. This approach reflects the philosophy behind the saying "A chain is only as strong as its weakest link." Using another approach, a manager might choose to give all employees a bonus based on the department's average productivity. Under this option, all department members individually and collectively strive to perform as well as possible. Firms often assess managers using this average scheme: managers' performance appraisals depend on their department's overall (or average) productivity. In some firms, managers allow employees to collectively select a reward system. In this case members of each department assess the task and range of abilities within the department and select a reward scheme accordingly.

Cultural diversity provides the biggest potential benefit to teams with challenging tasks that require creativity and innovation. Diversity becomes less helpful when team members work on simpler tasks involving repetitive or routine procedures. With the advent of robotics and computer-aided manufacturing processes for more routine tasks, organizational employees now face a much higher proportion of challenging and nonroutine tasks, almost all of which can benefit from well-managed diversity. The more senior the team members, the more likely they are to be involved in challenging, innovative projects and, therefore, the more likely they are to benefit from well-managed diversity. Well-managed diversity has therefore become extremely valuable for senior executive teams both within and across organizations.

STAGES: ENTRY, WORK, AND ACTION

Work teams progress through three basic stages: entry, work, and action. Early in its life, a team must develop cohesiveness. Members need to begin to know and to trust each other. After this initial entry stage, creativity becomes more important. Teams must create ways of defining their objectives, gathering and analyzing information, and developing alternative courses of action. Although diversity tends to hinder teams' initial development, it is highly valuable during the work stage. The team needs creativity (facilitated by divergence) to succeed. During the third and final stage, convergence again becomes important. Teams need to agree, or converge, on which decisions and actions to take. Cohesion, not creativity, fosters agreement. Whereas diversity is generally valuable during the work phase for planning and developing projects, it becomes much less helpful during this final implementation or "action" phase. Table 5-3 summarizes some of the advantages and disadvantages caused by diversity at each stage of a team's development.

Entry: Initial Team Formation In the initial stage, team members need to develop relationships and build trust. Team members from more

**TABLE 5-3   Managing Diversity Based on the Team's Stage
of Development**

Stage of Team Development	Process	Diversity Makes Process	Process Based On
Entry: Initial team formation	Trust building (developing cohesion)	More difficult	Using similarities and understanding differences
Work: Problem description and analysis	Ideation (creating ideas)	Easier	Using differences
Action: Decision making and implementation	Consensus building (agreeing and acting)	More difficult	Recognizing and creating similarities

task-oriented cultures, such as Germany, Switzerland, and the United States, spend relatively little time getting to know each other. Members from more relationship-oriented cultures, such as those in Latin America, the Middle East, and Southern Europe, generally spend considerably more time getting to know their teammates. When people from task- and relationship-oriented cultures join the same team, problems in this initial stage can result. While the task-oriented members become impatient to get down to business, their more relationship-oriented colleagues feel rushed and distrustful of their more hurried team members.

On first meeting, team members generally feel drawn to people who are most similar to themselves. They initially trust those people to whom they feel most attracted. Similarity therefore facilitates initial group formation, while visible differences hinder it. Not surprisingly, multicultural teams often find building initial relationships and trust more difficult and time-consuming than do their single-culture counterparts. To counteract this tendency, experienced leaders often focus initially on team members' complementary professional qualifications and equivalent status rather than on the dissimilarities in their cultural backgrounds. Once members have established professional similarity and respect, they can acknowledge their cultural diversity as a potential resource to the team rather than an imminent threat.

Work: Problem Description and Analysis After initial team formation, members define their work goals and objectives and assess the team's problem-solving potential. Although diversity often hinders the team's initial ability to build trust, well-managed diversity can enhance this second, work phase. During this work stage, teams can use their diversity to generate new perspectives and ideas and thus enhance their ability to create innovative problem definitions and solutions. As discussed previously, diverse teams generally are more able to see situations from multiple perspectives, interpret their perceptions within a wider variety of contexts, and create more numerous alternatives than are single-culture teams. Multicultural teams rarely succumb to groupthink; that is, to members blindly accepting a single definition of any situation.

Action: Decision Making and Implementation In the third stage, teams decide what to do and how to do it. Members agree on which alternatives appear best and which action plans appear most effective. Teams reach agreement by building consensus around a particular perspective. Similar to decision making, implementation also depends on consensus: teams must agree on the best way to proceed. These convergent processes—consensus building, agreement, concerted action, and implementation—usually prove easier for single-culture teams than for their multicultural counterparts. The very diversity that makes creating new ideas easier during the second stage renders building consensus and achieving agreement more difficult during the third stage.

MANAGING CULTURALLY DIVERSE TEAMS

Why are only some multicultural teams productive? And why are token teams (those with only one member from another culture) among the least productive (26)? The answer is that the most productive multicultural teams learn to use their diversity when it can enhance performance and to minimize the impact of diversity when it threatens to diminish performance. Multicultural teams that are able to create a synergistic culture outperform those teams that fail to integrate the cultures of individual members into a unified group culture. Token teams often fail to create a synergistic culture that integrates the perspective of the one, different token member into the whole. The leader must learn to help the team to integrate its diversity if the team is to function productively (1;41;66;67;99). "By integrating and building on the diverse perspectives of the various members of a team, solutions and strategies can be developed that produce greater results and are more innovative than the simple addition of each contribution alone" (66:5). Diversity leads to "higher performance only when members . . . [are] able to understand each other, [and to] combine and build on each others' ideas" (67:537); that is, when they communicate effectively with each other. Recent research suggests that all teams need the following communication skills to function effectively: They must be able to see situations from another person's perspective, create a shared social reality, explain problems appropriately, and establish agreed-upon norms for interacting. They must also be motivated to communicate, and have confidence that other team members are skilled enough to work effectively together (67 based on 10;11). Multicultural teams face substantially greater challenges than do single-culture teams in developing sufficient communication skills to achieve the prerequisite levels of integration needed for superior performance. Guidelines for increasing integration and minimizing diversity-related productivity losses due to faulty process follow.

MANAGING CULTURAL DIVERSITY

Task-Related Selection While acknowledging the team's diverse cultural background, leaders should select members based on their task-related abilities rather than basing their choices solely on ethnicity (77). "To maximize team effectiveness, members should be selected to be homogeneous in ability levels (thus facilitating accurate communication) and heterogeneous in attitudes (thus ensuring a wide range of solutions to problems)" (92).

Recognizing Differences Teams should not ignore or minimize cultural differences: "Many barriers to intercultural communication are due to ignorance of cultural differences rather than a rejection of those differences" (20). Teams, therefore, cannot begin to enhance communication without first recognizing and then understanding and respecting cross-cultural differences (12). Research indicates that "culturally trained leader[s], regardless of leadership style . . . achieve . . . high[er] levels of performance and rapport than do non-trained leaders" (29). To enhance the recognition of differences, team members should first describe each culture present without either interpreting or evaluating it. Before they can begin to increase understanding and respect, team members must become aware of their own stereotypes and the ways in which they might inadvertently limit their expectations of fellow team members from other cultures. Once members begin to recognize actual differences—that is, once they can differentiate their stereotypes from the actual personalities and behavior of team members (cultural description)—they can begin to understand why members from other cultures think, feel, and act the way they do (cultural interpretation). Subsequently, they can ask themselves what members from each culture can contribute and how their contributions complement those of other members (cultural creativity). In this way, creating effective multicultural teams follows the same process as creating cultural synergy (see Chapter 4). Team members' cultural intelligence—a combination of cognitive, motivational and behavioral attributes—may also contribute to cultural synergy (24).

Establishing a Vision or Superordinate Goal Members of diverse teams generally have more difficulty agreeing on their purpose and task than do members of homogeneous teams. Global alliances often become troubled because partners from different countries do not clearly understand each other's intent—their purpose, goals, and strategy—because they are initially unable to communicate with each other (38). This misunderstanding happens in part because teams set their overall purpose during the initial stage of team development, the stage during which individual differences tend to dominate and often interfere with team cohesion. To maximize effectiveness, leaders need to help teams agree on their vision or superordinate goal, a goal that transcends individual differences. Superordinate goals are often defined broadly, thus giving general direction and focus to the team's subsequent activities. Superordinate goals that require collaboration and cooperation usually decrease prejudice and increase mutual respect (86). This is particularly true when continued support of colleagues is required to achieve results that are important not only to the overall organization, but also to each member from the perspective of his or her own culture.

Equalizing Power   Teams generally produce more and better ideas if all members participate. Cultural dominance (disproportionate power vested in members of one culture relative to those from other cultures) is therefore counterproductive because it stifles nondominant team members' contributions. In multinational teams, leaders must guard against vesting disproportionate power in host-country members, members of the same nationality as the employing organization, members from the most technologically advanced or economically developed countries, or members with ideologies most consonant with their own. Team leaders should manage the distribution of power according to each member's ability to contribute to the task, not according to some preconceived gradient of relative cultural superiority.

Creating Mutual Respect   Ethnocentrism reflects a "view of things in which one's own group is the center of everything and all others are scaled and rated with reference to it" (58:8). Prejudice refers to judging other groups as inferior to one's own. Equal status, close contact, and cooperative efforts toward a common goal decrease prejudice (4;5). "The greater the opportunity for interethnic contacts, the less prejudiced and more frequent the development of cross-ethnic acceptance and friendship" (92:110). For most teams to work effectively, members must respect each other. Team leaders can enhance mutual respect by selecting members of equal ability, making prior accomplishments and task-related skills known to all team members, and minimizing premature judgments based on ethnic stereotypes.

Giving Feedback   Given the different perspectives present, culturally diverse teams have more trouble than do single-culture teams in agreeing collectively on what constitutes a good or bad idea or decision. Whereas single-culture teams rapidly develop judgment criteria based on members' similar values, multicultural teams usually experience difficulty and delay before eventually reaching agreement. To encourage effective functioning, managers should give team members positive feedback on their process and output—both as individuals and as a team—early in the team's life. Positive external feedback (given by the team leader or a senior manager who is not on the team) generally aids the team in viewing itself as a team, while additionally serving to teach team members to value the team's diversity, recognize contributions made by each member, and trust the team's collective judgment.

SUMMARY

The potential for superior productivity of culturally diverse teams is high; they possess a breadth of resources, insights, perspectives, and experiences that facilitates the creation of new and better ideas. Regrettably, culturally diverse teams rarely achieve their full potential. Process losses due to mistrust, misunderstanding, miscommunication, stress, and a lack of cohesion often negate the potential benefits of diversity to the team. Only if diversity is well managed can multicultural teams hope to achieve their full potential.

To function effectively, multicultural teams must therefore use their diversity to generate multiple perspectives, problem definitions, ideas, action alternatives, and solutions; learn to achieve consensus, including agreeing on specific decisions and directions, despite the diversity; and balance the simultaneous needs for creativity (divergence) and cohesion (convergence). If multicultural teams fail to generate many new ideas, they become no more effective than individuals working alone. If they fail to achieve consensus, their diversity paralyzes them. If multicultural teams fail to balance creativity and cohesion, they become awkwardly inefficient structures adding little value to the organization.

QUESTIONS FOR REFLECTION

1. **Managing Teams' Cultural Diversity.** As a team leader, what could you do to help a multinational team work more effectively than a domestic team? What major problems might occur and how might you best handle them?

2. **Multicultural Team Dynamics.** Think of the teams you have worked with or heard about. How have the group dynamics differed in multinational, bicultural, token, and single-culture teams?

3. **Types of Multicultural Teams.** As the leader of a task force made up of two Canadians, a German, three Japanese, and a Venezuelan, would you rather the team focus on a new research challenge or on current production problems? Why? How might you lead differently in each situation?

4. **Potential Productivity Losses.** Identify some potential productivity losses caused by faulty process that have occurred in multicultural teams you have worked with or observed. How might the team have minimized these problems?

5. **Creating Cultural Synergy.** Focus on a multinational political or economic team that is currently in the news. Using a culturally synergistic approach, how would you lead the team? What outcomes would you strive to achieve?

6. **Increasing Team Effectiveness.** Focus on a multicultural work team that you are currently involved with or aware of. Analyze the underlying cultural values affecting the team's functioning. How could you lead the team so that the probability of achieving synergy would increase?

7. **Globally Distanced Teams.** Imagine you have just been asked to lead a globally distanced multicultural marketing team. How would you convene and run your first three meetings? What strategies might you employ to maximize the team's chances for success given the unique challenges facing multicultural teams that in which members are not co-located? How would these strategies enable these groups to excel?

FILM NOTE

The two-part British Broadcasting Corporation video program, *It's a Jungle Out There* and *The Survival Guide,* presents the issues faced by multinational teams in learning how to function effectively. The first video, *It's a Jungle Out There,* presents the experiences of an eight-member, five-nationality multinational team of women and men, starting with the team's formation in England and continuing through its experiences on a three-country project in Africa. In the second video, *The Survival Guide,* Professor Adler assesses areas in which the team functions well and those in which it functions poorly. Her commentary is based on *International Dimensions of Organizational Behavior,* including material presented in Chapter 5. (The British Broadcasting Corporation, Open University Production Centre, Walton Hall, Milton Keynes, England MK7 68H; Tel: 44-1908-655-343; Fax: 44-1908-655-300). For additional video programs, see Notes 2 and 3 above.

NOTES

1. Globally distanced teams may be more or less "virtual." They face cultural challenges as well as those posed by time, distance and technology. Researchers studying Sabre, Inc., a leader in the travel industry, found five

challenges to virtual team success: building trust, maximizing process gains while minimizing process losses, overcoming feelings of isolation and detachment associated with virtual teamwork, balancing technical and inter-personal skills among team members, and assessment and recognition of team performance (49).

2. The film *Going International*, Part 2, by Copeland Griggs Productions, San Francisco, dramatizes a similar situation between an Indian and an American manager.

3. The film *The Heart of the Bull*, produced by V. P. Human Resources David Dotlich, documents the different working styles of French and American managers at the French computer company Groupe Bull.

4. Based on an incident described by a European manager attending the "Managerial Skills for International Business" executive seminar at INSEAD in Fontainebleau, France.

5. See Note 4.

REFERENCES

1. Abramson, F. "Factors Influencing the Entry of Canadian Software Manufacturers into the United States Market." Ph.D. dissertation, The University of Western Ontario, 1992.

2. Adler, N. J. "Domestic Multiculturalism: Cross-Cultural Management in the Public Sector," in W. Eddy, ed., *Handbook of Organization Management* (New York: Marcel Dekker, 1983), pp. 481–499.

3. Adler, N. J.; & Ghadar, F. "International Strategy from the Perspective of People and Culture: The North American Context," in A. M. Rugman, ed., *Research in Global Strategic Management: International Business Research for the Twenty-First Century; Canada's New Research Agenda*, vol. 1 (Greenwich, Conn.: JAI Press, 1990), pp. 179–205.

4. Allport, G. W. *The Nature of Prejudice* (Reading, Mass.: Addison-Wesley, 1954), p. 281.

5. Amir, Y. "Contact Hypothesis in Ethnic Relations," *Psychological Bulletin*, vol. 71 (1969), pp. 319–342; and Amir, Y. "The Role of Intergroup Contact in Change of Prejudice and Ethnic Relations," in P. A. Katz, ed., *Toward the Elimination of Racism* (New York: Pergamon, 1976).

6. Anderson, K. "The New Ellis Island," *Time* (June 13, 1983), pp. 16–23.

7. Anderson, L. R. "Leader Behavior, Member Attitudes and Task Performance of Intercultural Discussion Groups," *Journal of Social Psychology*, vol. 69 (1966), pp. 305–319.

8. Anderson, L. R. "Management of the Mixed-Cultural Work Group," *Organizational Behavior and Human Performance*, vol. 31, no. 3 (1983), pp. 303–330.

9. Bass, Bernard M. "A Plan to Use Programmed Group Exercises to Study Cross-Cultural Differences in Management Behavior," *International Journal of Psychology*, vol. 1, no. 4 (1966), pp. 315–322.

10. Blakar, R. M. *Communication: A Social Perspective on Clinical Issues* (Oslo: Universitetsforlaget, 1984).

11. Blakar, R. M. "Toward a Theory of Communication in Terms of Preconditions: A Conceptual Framework and Some Empirical Explorations," in H. Giles & R. N. St. Clair, eds., *Recent Advances in Language, Communication, and Social Psychology* (London: Lawrence Erlbaum Associates, 1985).

12. Brislin, Richard W. *Cross-Cultural Encounters* (New York: Pergamon, 1981).

13. Canney Davison, S. F. *Intercultural Processes in Multinational Teams.* Unpublished doctoral dissertation, London Business School (1995).

14. Chemers, M. M.; Fiedler, F. E.; Lekhyananda, D.; & Stolurow, L. M. "Some Effects of Cultural Training on Leadership in Heterocultural Task Groups," *International Journal of Psychology*, vol. 1, no. 4 (1966), pp. 301–314.

15. Chen, Chao C.; Chen, Xiao-Ping; & Meindl, James R. "How Can Cooperation Be Fostered? The Cultural Effects of Individualism-Collectivism," *Academy of Management Review*, vol. 23, no. 2 (1998), pp. 285–304.

16. Cox, T. H.; Lobel, S. A.; & McLeod, P. L. "Effects of Ethnic Group Cultural Differences on Cooperative and Competitive Behavior on a Group Task," *Academy of Management Journal*, vol. 34, no. 4 (1991), pp. 827–847.

17. Davison, S. C.; & Ekelund, B. Z. "Effective Team Processes for Global Teams," in H. W. Lane, M. L. Maznevski, M. E. Mendelhall, & J. McNett, eds., *The Blackwell Handbook of Global Management* (Malden, Mass.: Blackwell Publishing, 2004).

18. Davidson, W. H. "Small Group Activity at Musashi Semiconductor Works," *Sloan Management Review*, vol. 23, no. 3 (1982), pp. 3–14.

19. Delgado, M. "Hispanic Cultural Values: Implications for Groups," *Small Group Behavior*, vol. 12, no. 1 (1981), pp. 69–80.

20. Devonshire, C.; & Kremer, J. W. *Toward a Person-Centered Resolution of Intercultural Conflicts* (La Jolla, Calif.: Center for the Whole Person).

21. Diab, L. "A Study of Intragroup and Intergroup Competition Among Experimentally Produced Small Groups," *Genetic Psychology Monographs*, vol. 82 (1970), pp. 325–332.

22. Earley, P. Christopher. "East Meets West Meets Mideast: Further Explorations of Collectivistic and Individualistic Work Groups,"

Academy of Management Journal, vol. 36, no. 2 (1993), pp. 319–348.

23. Earley, P. Christopher. "Social Loafing and Collectivism: A Comparison of the United States and the People's Republic of China," *Administrative Science Quarterly*, vol. 34, no. 4 (1989), pp. 565–581.

24. Earley, P. Christopher; & Gardner, Heidi B. "Internal Dynamics and Cultural Intelligence in Multinational Teams," in J. L. C. Cheng, & M. A. Hitt (series eds.), *Advances in International Management*, vol. 18, and D. L. Shapiro, M. A. Von Glinow, & J. L. C. Cheng (vol. eds.), *Managing Multinational Teams: Global Perspectives* (Amsterdam/ New York: Elsevier/JAI, 2005), pp. 3–31.

25. Earley, P. Christopher; & Gibson, Cristina B. *Multinational Work Teams: A New Perspective* (Mahwah, N.J.: L. Erlbaum Associates, 2002).

26. Earley, P. Christopher; & Mosakowski, Elaine. "Creating Hybrid Team Cultures: An Empirical Test of Transnational Team Functioning," *Academy of Management Journal*, vol. 43, no. 1 (2000), pp. 26–49.

27. Ferrari, S. "Human Behavior in International Groups," *Management International Review*, vol. XII, no. 6 (1972), pp. 31–35.

28. Fiedler, F. E. "The Effect of Leadership and Cultural Heterogeneity on Group Performance: A Test of the Contingency Model," *Journal of Experimental Social Psychology*, vol. 2 (1966), pp. 237–264.

29. Fiedler, F. E.; Meuwese, W. A. T.; & Oonk, S. "Performance on Laboratory Tasks Requiring Group Creativity," *Acta Psychological*, vol. 18 (1961), pp. 110–119.

30. Gibson, C. B.; & Cohen, S. G. *Virtual Teams that Work: Creating Conditions for Virtual Team Effectiveness* (San Francisco: Jossey-Bass, 2003).

31. Gibson, C. B.; & Grubb, A.R. "Turning the Tide in Multinational Teams," in J. L. C. Cheng & M. A. Hitt (series eds.), *Advances in International Management*, vol. 18, and D. L. Shapiro, M. A. Von Glinow, & J. L. C. Cheng (vol. eds.), *Managing Multinational Teams: Global Perspectives* (Amsterdam/New York.: Elsevier/JAI, 2005), pp. 69–96.

32. Gluesing, J. C.; & Gibson, C. B. "Designing and Forming Global Teams," in H. W. Lane, M. L. Maznevski, M. E. Mendelhall, & J. McNett, eds., *The Blackwell Handbook of Global Management* (Malden, Mass.: Blackwell Publishing, 2004), pp. 199–226.

33. Hackman, J. R. "The Design of Work Teams," in J. W. Lorsch, ed., *Handbook of Organizational Behavior* (New York: Prentice Hall, 1987), pp. 315–341.

34. Hare, A. P. "Cultural Differences in Performances in Communication Networks in Africa, United States and the Philippines," *Sociology and Social Research*, vol. 54, no. 1 (1969), pp. 25–41.

35. Hare, A. P. *Handbook of Small Group Research* (New York: Free Press, 1976).

36. Harrison, D. A.; Price, K. H.; & Bell, M. P. "Beyond Relational Demography: Time and the Effects of Surface- and Deep-Level Diversity on Work Group Cohesion," *Academy of Management Journal*, vol. 41, no. 1 (1998), pp. 96–107.

37. Hayles, R. "Costs and Benefits of Integrating Persons from Diverse Cultures into Organizations." Paper presented at the 21st International Congress of Applied Psychology, Edinburgh, Scotland, July 1982.

38. Hitt, Michael A.; Tyler, Beverly B.; Hardee, Camilla; & Park, Daewoo. "Understanding Strategic Intent in the Global Marketplace," *Academy of Management Executive*, vol. 9, no. 2 (1995), pp. 12–19.

39. Hoffman, L. R. "Homogeneity of Member Personality and Its Effect on Group Problem-Solving," *Journal of Abnormal Psychology*, vol. 58 (1959), pp. 27–32.

40. Hoffman, L. R.; & Maier, N. R. F. "Quality and Acceptance of Problem Solutions by Members of Homogeneous and Heterogeneous Groups," *Journal of Abnormal Psychology*, vol. 62, no. 2 (1961), pp. 401–407.

41. Hurst, D. K.; Rush, J. C.; & White, R. E. "Top Management Teams and Organizational Renewal," *Strategic Management Journal* (1989), vol. 10 (Special Issue), pp. 87–105.

42. "It's Your Turn in the Sun: Now 19 Million and Growing Fast, Hispanics Are Becoming a Power," *Time*, vol. 112, no. 16 (1978), pp. 48–61.

43. Jackson, S. E.; May, K. E.; & Whitney, K. "Understanding the Dynamics of Diversity," in R. A. Guzzo, E. Salas, and Associates, eds., *Team Effectiveness and Decision Making in Organizations* (San Francisco: Jossey-Bass, 1995).

44. Janis, I. L. *Groupthink*, 2nd ed. (New York: Houghton Mifflin Company, 1982). Copyright © 1982 Houghton Mifflin Company. Reprinted by permission.

45. Jarvenpaa, S. L.; & Leidner, D. "Communication and Trust in Global Virtual Teams," *Organization Science*, vol. 10, no. 6 (1999), pp. 791–815.

46. Jewell, L. N.; & Reitz, H. J. *Group Effectiveness in Organizations* (Glenview, Ill.: Scott, Foresman, 1981).

47. Joshi, A.; Labianca, G.; & Caligiuri, P. M. "Getting Along Long Distance: Understanding Conflict in a Multinational Team through Network Analysis," *Journal of World Business*, vol. 37 (2002), pp. 277–284.

48. Katz, J.; Goldston, J.; & Benjamin, L. "Behavior and Productivity in Biracial Work Groups," *Human Relations*, vol. 11 (1958), pp. 123–151.

49. Kirkman, B. L.; Rosen, B.; Gibson, C. B.; Tesluk, P. E.; & McPherson, S. O. "Five Challenges to Virtual Team Success: Lessons from Sabre, Inc.," *Academy of Management Executive*, vol. 16, no. 3 (2003), pp. 67–79.

50. Kirkman, B. L.; & Shapiro, Debra L., "The Impact of Cultural Value Diversity on Multicultural Team Performance" in J. L. C. Cheng & M. A. Hitt (series eds.), *Advances in International Management*, vol. 18, and D. L. Shapiro, M. A. Von Glinow, & J. L. C. Cheng (vol eds.), *Managing Multinational Teams: Global Perspectives* (Amsterdam/ New York: Elsevier/JAI, 2005), pp. 33–67.

51. Kirsch, J. (citing former Lieutenant Governor M. Dymally of California) "Chicano Power," *New West*, vol. 3, no. 19 (1978), pp. 35–46.

52. Kirschmeyer, C.; & Cohen, A. "Multicultural Groups: Their Performance and Reactions with Constructive Conflict," *Group and Organization Management*, vol. 17, no. 2 (1992), pp. 153–170.

53. Kovach, Carol. Based on observations of 800 second-year MBAs in field study teams at UCLA, 1977–1980. Evaluation of teams was conducted by corporate clients and business faculty members in Los Angeles, California, 1980. Original model based on Kovach's paper, "Some Notes for Observing Group Process in Small Task-Oriented Groups," Graduate School of Management, University of California at Los Angeles, 1976.

54. Kumar, K.; Subramanian, R.; & Nonis, S. A. "Cultural Diversity's Impact on Group Process and Performance: Comparing Culturally Homogeneous and Culturally Diverse Work Groups Engaged in Problem-Solving Tasks," *Southern Management Association Proceedings* (1991).

55. Lattimer, Robert L. "The Case for Diversity in Global Business, and the Impact of Diversity on Team Performance," *Competitiveness Review*, vol. 8, no. 2 (1998), pp. 3–17.

56. Lattimer, Robert L. *Managing Diversity for Strategic and Competitive Advantage* (New York: Doubleday Books, 2000).

57. Lau, D. C.; & Murnighan, J. K. "Demographic Diversity and Faultlines: The Compositional Dynamics of Organizational Groups," *Academy of Management Review*, vol. 23, no. 2 (1998), pp. 325–340.

58. Levine, R. A.; & Campbell, D. T. *Ethnocentrism* (New York: Wiley, 1972).

59. Likert, R. "The Nature of Highly Effective Groups," in *New Patterns of Management* (New York: McGraw-Hill, 1961).

60. Los Angeles County Department of Regional Planning. *2000 Los Angeles County Demographic Profile* (October 4, 2000), http://planning.co.la.ca.us/ rsrch_LACountyProfile.pdf

61. McDermott, Lynda; Waite, Bill; & Brawley, Nolan. "Putting Together a World-Class Team," *Training and Development*, vol. 53, no. 1 (1999), pp. 46–51.

62. McGrath, J. E. *Groups: Interaction and Performance* (Upper Saddle River, N. J.: Prentice Hall, 1984).

63. McLeod, P. L.; & Lobe, S. A. "The Effects of Ethnic Diversity on Idea Generation in Small Groups," *Academy of Management Best Paper Proceedings* (1992), pp. 227–231.

64. Maier, N. R. F.; & Hoffman, L. R. "Group Decision in England and the United States," *Personnel Psychology*, vol. 15, no. 2 (1962), pp. 75–87.

65. Mann, L. "Cross-Cultural Studies of Small Groups," in H. Triandis, ed., *Handbook of Cross-Cultural Psychology*, vol. 5 (Boston: Allyn & Bacon, 1980).

66. Maznevski, M. L. "Process and Performance in Multicultural Teams." Working paper. London, Ontario, Canada: The University of Western Ontario, School of Business, 1995, p. 49.

67. Maznevski, M. L. "Understanding Our Differences: Performance in Decision-Making Groups with Diverse Members," *Human Relations*, vol. 47, no. 5 (1994), pp. 531–552.

68. Maznevski, M. L.; & Chuboda, K. M. "Bridging Space Over Time: Global Virtual Team Dynamics and Effectiveness," *Organization Science*, vol. 11, no. 5 (2000), pp. 473–492.

69. Maznevski, M. L.; & DiStefano, Joseph J. "Synergistic Performance in Multicultural Management Teams: A Communications Perspective," paper presented at the Academy of International Business Annual Meeting, Brussels, 1992.

70. Meade, R. "An Experimental Study of Leadership in India," *Journal of Social Psychology*, vol. 72 (1967), pp. 35–43.

71. Meade, R. "Leadership Studies of Chinese and Chinese-Americans," *Journal of Cross-Cultural Psychology*, vol. 1 (1970), pp. 325–332.

72. Milliken, F. J.; & Martins, L. L. "Searching for Common Threads: Understanding the Multiple Effects of Diversity in Organizational Groups," *Academy of Management Review*, vol. 21, no. 2 (1996), pp. 402–433.

73. Misumi, J. "Experimental Studies on Group Dynamics in Japan," *Psychologia*, vol. 2 (1959), pp. 229–235.

74. Mitchell, R. "Team Building by Disclosure of Internal Frames of Reference," *Journal of Applied Behavioral Science*, vol. 22, no. 1 (1986), pp. 15–28.

75. New York State Office of the State Comptroller. *Queens: An Economic Review* (January 2000), http://www.osc.state.ny.us/osdc/rpt1100/rpt1100.htm

76. Novack, M. *The Rise of the Unmeltable Ethnics* (New York: Macmillan, 1972).

77. "Over the Rainbow," *Economist* (November 22, 1997), p. 76.

78. Probst, Tahira M.; Carnevale, Peter J.; & Triandis, Harry C. "Cultural Values in Intergroup and Single-Group Social Dilemmas," *Organizational Behavior and Human Decision Processes*, vol. 77, no. 3 (1999), pp. 171–191.

79. Punnett, Betty Jane; & Clemens, Jason. "Cross-National Diversity: Implications for International Expansion Decisions," *Journal of World Business*, vol. 34, no. 2 (1999), pp. 128–138.

80. Queens Library, *Queens Borough Public Library Service Areas: A Language and Ethnic Profile Based on the 2000 US Census* (Spring 2003), http:// www.queenslibrary.org/pub/Census2000Ethic& LangProfile.pdf

81. Queens Library, *Quick Demographic Facts for Queens Library Service Areas* (2006), http://www.queenslibrary.org/pub/QuickFacts.asp

82. Rombauts, J. "Gedrag en Groepsbeleving in Etnisch-Homogene en Etnisch-Heterogene Groepen," *Tijdschrift Voor Opvoedkunde*, no. 1 (1962–1963).

83. Ruhe, J.; & Eastman, J. "Effects of Racial Composition on Small Work Groups," *Small Group Behavior*, vol. 8, no. 4 (1977), pp. 479–486.

84. "The Samoans Among Us," *The Los Angeles Times* (January 2, 1979), p. 1.

85. Schoonhoven, C. B.; & Woolley, J. L. "Top Management Teams in an International Context: An Assessment Review," in J. L. C. Cheng & M. A. Hitt (series eds.), *Advances in International Management*, vol. 18, and D. L. Shapiro, M. A. Von Glinow, & J. L. C. Cheng (vol eds.), *Managing Multinational Teams: Global Perspectives* (Amsterdam/New York: Elsevier/JAI, 2005), pp 249–280.

86. Sherif, M.; Harvey, O.; White, B.; Hood, W.; & Sherif, C. *Inter-Group Conflict and Cooperation: The Robbers Cave Experiment* (Norman, Okla.: Institute of Group Relations, 1961).

87. Shuter, R. "Cross-Cultural Small Group Research: A Review, an Analysis, and a Theory," *International Journal of Intercultural Relations*, vol. 1, no. 1 (1977), pp. 90–104.

88. Simard, L. M.; & Taylor, D. M. "The Potential for Bicultural Communication in a Dyadic Situation," *Canadian Journal of Behavioral Science*, vol. 5 (1973), pp. 211–225.

89. Snow, C. C.; Snell, S. A.; Canney Davidson, S.; & Hambrick, D. C. "Use Transnational Teams to Globalize Your Company," *Organizational Dynamics*, vol. 24, no. 4 (1996), pp. 50–67.

90. Steiner, I. D. *Group Process and Productivity* (New York: Academic Press, 1972).

91. Toffler, A. *The Third Wave* (New York: William Morrow, 1980).

92. Triandis, H. C.; Hall, E. R.; & Ewen, R. B. "Some Cognitive Factors Affecting Group Creativity," *Human Relations*, vol. 18, no. 1 (1965), pp. 33–35.

93. U.S. Census Bureau, *American Community Survey* (September 3, 2003), http://www.census.gov/Press-Release/www/releases/archives/american_ community_survey_acs/001311.html

94. U.S. Census Bureau, *Hawaii 2004 American Community Survey* (2004), http://factfinder.census.gov/servlet/ACSSAFFFacts?_event=Search&_ang=en&_sse=on&geo_id=04000US15&_state=04000US15

95. U. S. Office of Immigration. Personal conversation with immigration official (Los Angeles, November 1979).

96. Walsh, J. P.; Henderson, C. M.; & Deighton, J. "Negotiated Belief Structures and Decision Performance: An Empirical Investigation," *Organizational Behavior and Human Decision Processes*, vol. 42, no. 2 (1988), pp. 194–216.

97. Watson, W. E.; & Kumar, K. "Differences in Decision-Making Regarding Risk-Taking: A Comparison of Culturally Diverse and Culturally Homogeneous Task Groups," *International Journal of Intercultural Relations*, vol. 16, no. 1 (1992), pp. 53–66.

98. Watson, W. E.; Kumar, K.; & Michaelson, L. K. "Cultural Diversity's Impact on Interaction Process and Performance: Comparing Homogeneous and Diverse Task Groups," *Academy of Management Journal*, vol. 36, no. 3 (1993), pp. 590–602.

99. Watson, W. E., & Michaelson, L. K. "Group Interaction Behaviors That Affect Group Performance on an Intellective Task," *Group and Organization Studies*, vol. 13, no. 4 (1988), pp. 495–516.

100. Ziegler, S. "The Effectiveness of Cooperative Learning Teams for Increasing Cross-Ethnic Friendship: Additional Evidence," *Human Organization: The Journal of the Society for Applied Anthropology*, vol. 40, no. 3 (1981), pp. 264–268.

101. Ziller, R. C. "Homogeneity and Heterogeneity of Group Membership," in C. G. McClintock, ed., *Experimental Social Psychology* (New York: Holt, Rinehart and Winston, 1972), pp. 385–411.

Chapter 6

Leading Globally

---

*For all practical purposes, all business today is global. Those
individual businesses, firms, industries, and whole societies that
clearly understand the new rules of doing business in a world
economy will prosper; those that do not will perish.*

—Ian Mitroff (93:ix)

As global corporate citizens, companies worldwide strive to fulfill their
organizational and societal missions. They select leaders who articulate
a vision that can guide them toward achieving long-term economic viability and societal well-being. They expect their leaders to motivate and
inspire employees in consistent and effective ways. Leaders continually
create options and make decisions that influence the success of the
entire company.

This chapter reviews the ways in which corporate vision and leadership vary across cultures. Subsequent chapters will discuss how culture
influences motivation and how cross-cultural dynamics impact managerial decision making. Although some principles of leadership, motivation, and decision making apply almost everywhere, the ways in
which leaders adapt them to local conditions and work situations
determine their ultimate success or failure (67). Although approaches to
leadership, motivation, and decision making are interrelated, each
will be discussed separately.

Historically, most organization theories have been "Made in the
U.S.A." and therefore shaped by the political, economic, and cultural
context of the United States in the twentieth century (31). Although
some research has attempted to discover how American-based management theories can be altered to apply more broadly around the world,
and, perhaps more importantly, how management theories indigenous
to countries around the world operate, not enough is yet known to fully
understand the integrated nature of global organizational dynamics
(2;14;15;16;17;30).[1] Until such knowledge becomes more widely available,
it behooves us to resist the temptation to assume that any particular

157

theory applies everywhere. As cross-cultural psychologist Harry Triandis (114:139) astutely observed, culture's

> *influence for organizational behavior is that it operates at such a deep level that people are not aware of its influences. It results in unexamined patterns of thought that seem so natural that most theorists of social behavior fail to take them into account. As a result, many aspects of organizational theories produced in one culture may be inadequate in other cultures.*

Prudent leaders assume that current American-based theories apply to the United States; not, as it is so tempting to believe, to the world at large.

GLOBAL LEADERSHIP

To act comes from the Latin verb *agere* meaning "to set into motion" (78). The Anglo-Saxon origins of the verb *to lead* come from *laedere,* meaning "people on a journey" (29). Today's meaning of the word *leader,* therefore, denotes someone who sets ideas, people, organizations, and societies in motion; someone who takes the worlds of ideas, people, commerce, organizations, and societies on a journey. To lead such a journey requires vision, courage, and influence.

LEADERSHIP VISION

Leaders help to shape an organization's vision, the meaning within which organizational members work and live. Managers, by contrast, attempt to act competently within a vision (25;26). What is our vision of success? What do we want our society to look like? How do we ideally want our organizations to function? Who do we want to lead us? Leadership and vision fundamentally shape our understanding of a people and their institutions. Ask yourself what is most important to you about leading and leadership. See the Box "Global Leadership: Giving Oneself for Things Far Greater than Oneself."

The questions global leaders address are universal; the answers are often culturally specific. *The Way of Lao Tzu,* for example, captures a traditional Chinese vision of leadership from the sixth century B.C.E. (116:214):

> *I have three treasures. Guard and keep them.*
> *The first is deep love,*
> *The second is frugality,*
> *And the third is not to dare to be ahead of the world.*
> *Because of deep love, one is courageous.*
> *Because of frugality, one is generous.*
> *Because of not daring to be ahead of the world,*
> *one becomes the leader of the world.*

GLOBAL LEADERSHIP
Giving Oneself for Things Far
Greater Than Oneself

"To be human is to give yourself for things far greater than yourself" (35:194)
To lead is to give yourself for things far greater than yourself

When I was 11 years old, my Austrian mother explained to me that when she was my age she had wanted to have at least 6 children. Yet by the time she met my American father, just 8 years later, she no longer wanted any children. Losing most of her friends and family during World War II to Hitler's terror had convinced her that the world was not a fit place to raise children. Luckily, especially from my perspective, my father convinced my mother that within the family the two of them could create a bubble of love, and within that bubble their children could grow up in safety and happiness, protected from the inhumanity raging outside. Having grown up within the bubble of their love, and in sunny southern California rather than war-torn Europe, I never doubted that our role on earth, as human beings and as leaders, was to expand the bubble to encompass the world: or as the rabbis would exhort us, to return to our original task of *Tikun Olam*, the restoration of the world.

Of course, none of us can claim that the twenty-first century entered on a safe, secure, or loving note—a note imbued with peace, wisdom, compassion, and love. As we ask ourselves which of our twentieth-century legacies we wish to pass on to the children of the twenty-first century, we are humbled into shameful silence. Yes, we have advanced science, technology, and commerce, but at the price of a world torn asunder by a polluted environment, cities infested with social chaos and physical decay, an increasingly skewed income distribution that condemns large portions of the population to poverty (including people living in the world's most affluent societies), and rampant physical violence continuing to kill people in supposedly limited wars and seemingly random acts of violence. No, we did not exit the twentieth century with pride. Unless we collectively learn to treat each other and our planet in a more civilized way, it may soon become blasphemous to even consider ourselves a civilization (100).

And yet why not a more peaceful, sustainable, and compassionate society in the twenty-first century? Why not a global civilization that we could bequeath with pride to our children and our children's children? Naïvely idealistic? Perhaps; but only if we ignore the wisdom and approaches to learning of colleagues around the world who have dared to attempt to make a difference—only if we renege on our role as leaders and simply adapt to the future, rather than collectively attempting to improve it. As former U.S. Secretary of State Madeleine Albright admonishes us, "We have a responsibility in our time, as others have had in theirs, not to be prisoners of history, but to shape history. . . ." (20).

People want a change; they no longer want the narrow, circumscribed leadership of the twentieth century nor its outcomes. Perhaps it is not surprising that at this moment in history, countries around the world, most for the first time, are turning to women, rather than to the traditional cohort of

GLOBAL LEADERSHIP
Giving Oneself for Things Far
Greater Than Oneself (continued)

men, to lead them. They hope and imagine that women will bring a more inclusive and compassionate approach to leadership. A small but rapidly increasing number of women are now among the world's most prominent business and political leaders—women who serve as their country's president or prime minister or as CEO of a major global firm (3;4;5;12).

In Nicaragua, for example, former president Violetta Chamorro's ability to bring all the members of her family together every week for Sunday dinner achieved near legendary status. Symbolically, her dinners gave the nation hope that it could heal its civil-war-inflicted wounds and find a peace that would reunite all Nicaraguans (101:80). Why such elevated hopes from a Sunday night dinner? Because, of Chamorro's four adult children, two were prominent Sandanistas while the other two equally prominently opposed the Sandanistas, not an unusual split in war-torn Nicaragua (101:80). As Violetta Chamorro's children told their stories around her dining room table, others in the country began to believe that they too could "reach a deeper, more real consensus—including around such profoundly important issues as unity and peace—through the telling of their personal stories" (79). Implicitly, the Nicaraguans believed that by listening attentively to each other, with empathy, they could hear their core humanity and that of the nation (79). It is not coincidence that the symbol of hope, peace and unity was a dining room table and not a boardroom table (63;64). Such "holographic listening", as social-thinker Adam Kahane labels it—in which each story reflects the whole, rather than merely contributing a piece to the puzzle—opens up the possibility of communion and oneness, of transcending history to create a new future: "We have the greatest capacity to make a difference when we dare to open ourselves up, to expose our most honest nightmares and our most heartfelt dreams" (79).

Kahane points out that leaders who make a difference are extraordinarily committed, body and soul, to the changes they want to see in the world, to goals much larger than themselves (79). The lives of many of the world's first women leaders mirror commitments much larger than themselves. The personal commitment of Chandrika Kumaratunga, former president of war-torn Sri Lanka, for example, became a prism for the paradoxes of extraordinary leadership. When she was only eleven years old, her father, who was the country's founding father and its first prime minister, was assassinated, many believe due to his policies, which advantaged the Sinhalese and stripped the Tamil of many of their cultural rights. Her mother, who also served as prime minister, furthered the country's ethnically divisive policies. As an adult, Kumaratunga's husband, a politically involved citizen and noted actor, was murdered, in what many believe was Tamil-initiated violence. With the constant and very real threat of death to her and to her children, why did Kumaratunga

GLOBAL LEADERSHIP
Giving Oneself for Things Far
Greater Than Oneself (continued)

choose to stay in Sri Lanka and to run for office? And once she won, how did she find the courage to tell her mother—whom she later appointed to serve as prime minister—and the country that she was going to attempt to find a peaceful solution to Sri Lanka's seemingly interminable civil war by sitting down with the Tamil and listening to their stories? Kumaratunga, with both her father and husband murdered, chose to go outside the patterns of history and to say, "Enough! There has to be a better way." Her attempts to move Sri Lanka toward peace and unity have by no means met with unequivocal success. Yet for years, Kumaratunga persisted, even in the face of constant death threats and a bomb explosion that claimed one of her eyes. As Kumaratunga's life reminds us, leaders who influence history do so because they "live the paradox" (79). They have the courage to commit their lives to effecting the changes they want to see in the world. At the same time, they have the courage to engage with others—even their enemies. The challenge of leadership lies in complete commitment to change for the better; not in simplistic short-term evaluations of success and failure.

At the opening of the twenty-first century, my Jewish nephew Aaron married a deeply religious Catholic woman Karen. Although the couple told their families that their wedding ceremony and life together would be rooted in the two spiritual traditions, both families questioned the reality of the young couple's pronouncement when the invitations arrived announcing that the wedding would be celebrated at Holy Family Catholic Church with a Catholic priest, and no rabbi, presiding. Only as the priest opened the service in Hebrew with a traditional Jewish prayer did the tension subside. In one of the most moving and profoundly meaningful wedding ceremonies I have ever attended, the priest celebrated Aaron and Karen's unique individuality, including their two distinctly different spiritual traditions. He made no attempt to minimize or ignore the differences between Judaism and Christianity. After the bride and groom had exchanged vows, the priest reminded the gathering of friends and family of the hatred that has all too often separated Christian and Jewish communities. He then asked each of us to see Karen and Aaron as symbolic of the love that could unite the two traditions, the love that could replace the all too common hatred. What more powerful symbol of global leadership: love replacing hate, love bridging distinct individuality, love uniting bride and groom on their wedding day, love respecting and bridging differences among all peoples at all times.

Our capacity to see and to change the world co-evolves with our capacity to see and to change ourselves (79). As the marriage ceremony changed Aaron and Karen into husband and wife, so too did it change all of those present into people who more deeply understand what it means to unify diversity without extinguishing

GLOBAL LEADERSHIP
Giving Oneself for Things Far
Greater Than Oneself (continued)

individuality. As leaders, we can never close our eyes to the complexity of the world or to the profoundly influential interactions that define society. Goethe admonishes us that leaders know themselves only to the extent that they know the world; that they become aware of themselves only within the world, and aware of the world only within themselves (54).

"To be human is to find ourselves behind our names" (83).
To lead is to find ourselves behind our names.

Source: Adler (7).[2]

American Arthur Schlesinger expressed a very different leadership vision in *A Thousand Days,* the vision of U.S. President John F. Kennedy from the 1960s (103):

> *Above all . . . [President Kennedy] gave the world for an imperishable moment a vision of a leader who greatly understood the terror and the hope, the diversity and the possibility, of life on this planet and who made people look beyond nation and race to the future of humanity.*

Britain's Anita Roddick, founder and former CEO of the highly successful global firm, The Body Shop, describes her contemporary vision of corporate idealism:

> *Leaders in the business world should aspire to be true planetary citizens. They have global responsibilities since their decisions affect not just the world of business, but world problems of poverty, national security and the environment. Many, sad to say, duck these responsibilities, because their vision is material rather than moral* (101:226).

Integrating what Roddick has labeled "planetary citizenship" with shrewd business strategies, Indian-born C.K. Prahalad and American-born Stuart Hart coach executives to adopt bottom-of-the-pyramid strategies. According to these two global management professors, "Low-income markets present a prodigious opportunity for the world's wealthiest companies to seek their fortunes and bring prosperity to the aspiring poor" (99:2). They advise multinationals on how to reduce extreme poverty—and by extension global instability—while simultaneously earning significant profits. Prahalad and Hart coach companies to see a market that was previously invisible to them—and remains invisible to most of their competitors (61;62;97;98;99). That market is the four billion people who earn less than $1500 annually. It's an illusion that the world's poorest people do not constitute a market, do not possess buying power, and that companies cannot earn significant profits by serving the poor. Bottom-of-the-pyramid business strategies are by no means merely corporate philanthropy or some form of narrowly defined altruism. As Prahalad and Hart (99:4) explain,

> *Although complete income equality is an ideological pipe dream, the use of commercial development to bring people out of poverty and give them the chance for a better life is critical to the stability and health of the global economy and the continued success of Western MNCs.*

Such global strategies unambiguously work to the mutual benefit of business and society. See the Boxes on "Bottom-of-the-Pyramid Business Strategies" and "Micro-Lending" for examples on how multinationals are profiting by serving these no-longer-invisible markets.

As Prahalad and Hart (99:14) help individual companies embrace these new, highly profitable bottom-of-the-pyramid business strategies, they remind the entire private sector that:

> *It is tragic that . . . Western capitalists . . . have implicitly assumed that the rich will be served by the corporate sector, while governments and NGOs will protect the poor and the environment. This implicit divide is stronger than most realize. Managers in MNCs, public policymakers, and NGO activists all suffer from the historical division of roles. A huge opportunity lies in breaking this code—linking the poor and the rich across the world in a seamless market organized around the concept of sustainable growth and development.*
>
> *Collectively, we have only begun to scratch the surface of what is the biggest potential market opportunity in the history of commerce. Those in the private sector who commit their companies to a more inclusive capitalism have the opportunity to prosper and share their prosperity with those who are less fortunate. In a very real sense, the fortune at the bottom of the pyramid represents the loftiest of our global goals.*

Although each of these leaders' visions and strategies reflect different cultural perspectives, different centuries, and different target markets, each expresses the tension between immediate national and organizational concerns and the broader interests of humanity and the future. Research suggests that managers' perceptions of what they believe they should be doing varies more than their descriptions of

BOTTOM-OF-THE-PYRAMID BUSINESS STRATEGIES
Companies Reducing Poverty & Creating Fortunes

A number of companies are already using bottom-of-the-pyramid strategies to create wealth and reduce poverty.[3] Hindustan Lever (HLL), for example, created a new detergent that captured 38 percent of a market that neither Unilever, the parent company, nor its competitors realized existed (99:5). Using a new business model that emphasizes volume rather than high profit margins, Hindustan Lever formulated the detergent

> ". . . to substantially reduce the ratio of oil to water in the product, responding to the fact that the poor often wash their clothes in rivers and other public water systems. HLL decentralized the production, marketing, and distribution . . . to leverage the abundant labor pool in rural India, quickly creating sales channels through the thousands of small outlets where people at the bottom of the pyramid shop. HLL also changed the cost structure of its detergent business so it could [be introduced] . . . at a low price point."

During its first five years on the market, Hindustan Lever enjoyed an annual growth rate of 25 percent in profits and 20 percent in revenue (99:5). With bottom-of-the pyramid strategies, "the strategic challenge for managers is to visualize an active market where only abject poverty exists today. It takes tremendous imagination and creativity to engineer a market infrastructure out of a completely unorganized sector" (99:6).

Other examples of bottom-of-the-pyramid strategies include Honeywell's interest in offering micro-turbines as small-scale distributed energy solutions to extremely poor communities; The Body Shop's policy of trade-not-aid; and Starbucks' (together with Conservation International's) strategy to eliminate intermediaries from its business model and source coffee directly from farmers in Mexico's Chiapas region, thus enabling the company to provide coffee farmers with a reasonable standard of living and the company with a respectable profit.

Source: Based on Prahalad & Hart (99).

---

what they actually do (117). It is the tension between the reality of our world today and our aspirations for a better world tomorrow that gives rise to the need for societies to select leaders who can articulate a meaningful vision and guide them toward its realization. In *Beyond National Borders,* Kenichi Ohmae (96) captured a vision for Japan as it moved into the twenty-first century:

> *Of all the conceivable goals and achievements that Japan might seek to accomplish in the next century, only one, I believe, is worthy of Japan. It is to prove that without wielding military might, by human strength and resourcefulness alone, a major global power can alleviate the*

MICRO-LENDING
A Bottom-of-the-Pyramid Strategy

Micro-lending is one of the most important bottom-of-the-pyramid strategies. Micro-lending involves offering the poor very small loans at reasonable interest rates and within structures that are accessible to them.[3] Companies choosing to embrace micro-lending strategies make a profit by giving the poor access to reasonable borrowing power, and thus access to buying power.

> *"According to the International Labor Organization's World Employment Report 2001, nearly a billion people—roughly one-third of the world's work force—are either underemployed or have such low-paying jobs that they cannot support themselves or their families. Helping the world's poor elevate themselves above this desperation line is a business opportunity to do well and do good"* (99:6).

The business opportunity comes from the fact that, under the current system, money lenders in the poorest areas charge as much as 20 percent per day interest. Micro-lenders can charge much less and still make a substantial profit. Whereas the Grameen Bank, founded by Bangladeshi economist Muhammad Yunus, is the highly successful pioneer in this field—micro-lending is now a thriving business for the largest banks in a number of countries. "At the 1999 Microcredit Summit, the United Nations, in conjunction with several major MNCs, such as Citigroup Inc. and Monsanto Company, set a goal of making basic credit available to the 100 million poorest families in the world by the year 2005" (99:8). Whereas they have yet to achieve their goal, progress is being made.

Source: Based on Prahalad & Hart (99).

---

earth's disparities and injustices. . . . Now we must begin to think beyond national borders (96:11).

Historically, corporate visions have reflected the values and goals of the society in which they were conceived. Given the global nature of twenty-first century markets, corporate visions can no longer remain domestic, but must themselves be transnational. As witnessed with the economic integration of Europe into the European Union, the founding of the Association of South East Asian Nations (ASEAN) trading bloc, the increased trade generated by the North American Free Trade Agreement (NAFTA), and the omnipresence of the World Trade Organization (WTO), the world economy is erasing national borders. Whereas historic feuds remain nationally defined from a political perspective, economic pragmatism vanquishes them from a business perspective (49). Business leaders have chosen to transcend national boundaries in ways that remain beyond the realm of politicians and government diplomats. As business leaders know, if an idea or action is good for business, it is worth learning and doing no matter where in the world it originated. Global companies, more so than nations, already face the difficult questions involved in integrating visions based on divergent national and cultural values. The heated contemporary debates on outsourcing and offshoring highlight these challenges. Global companies' success in defining and implementing transnational visions will determine not only the future of the economy, but, more importantly, the future of society itself.

LEADERSHIP THEORIES

Leaders are individuals who significantly affect the thoughts and behaviors of others, not through coercion, but rather through persuasion (51). Global leadership therefore involves the ability to inspire and influence the thinking, attitudes, and behavior of people worldwide (23;24;25;26;52;84). The very word *leadership*

> *is a relatively new addition to the English language; it appeared approximately 200 years ago in writings about political influence in the British Parliament. However, from Egyptian hieroglyphics, we know that symbols for "leader" existed as early as 5,000 years ago. Simply put, leaders have existed in all cultures throughout history* (40:270).

In the past many people assumed that leaders were born, not made, and they attempted to identify the traits of great leaders. Although every society has had its great leaders, researchers found no consistent set of traits differentiating leaders from other people (113). North Americans, for example, value charisma in their leaders and identify such business and political leaders as Lee Iacocca, former CEO of Chrysler Corporation (75), and Bill Clinton, former president of the United States, as charismatic (36;37). By contrast, Germans do not value charisma in their contemporary leaders, because they associate charisma with the evil Hitler perpetrated during World War II. More generally, while the term *leader* evokes a positive image in the United States, for people in many parts of the world it evokes a quite negative image (40:271). For some Europeans, for example, ". . . everything seems to indicate that leadership is an unintended and undesirable consequence of democracy, or a 'perverse effect' as [is said] . . . in France" (59:241-242).

Going beyond the search for leaders' innate traits, researchers then tried to identify the types of behaviors outstanding leaders display. They found that the culture in which leaders grow up strongly influences their attitudes and behaviors (87:190-191):

Consider the implications for leadership of individual attitudes and expectations towards power. As a result of extended experiences with people who have wielded power over them when they were children, adults have expectations about how they should relate to others who have power and how they should behave in return. These attitudes are somewhat modified as a consequence of experiences with teachers, ministers, scout leaders, and other authority figures, but fundamental attitudes toward power are derived from the earliest and most intense experiences with authority figures. . . .

In spite of individual differences, however, these experiences reflect a strong common element in any given culture. As a result, there are generalized expectations about how authority is to be wielded, how the more powerful people should act toward the weaker, and what kinds of behavior the latter might expect from the former. It is expected that one will use social strength according to culturally established norms. Therefore, when acquiring control over others, one also incurs the effects of these expectations about power figures. In short, in a particular culture a person who becomes authoritative in direct relationships to others is expected to act in much the same way as a parent acts in the family. It means that as people develop their expectations of power and attitudes toward power, based on their earliest experiences with it, they will tend to work from these attitudes in every encounter. A superior who fails to conform to these expectations will be seen as an inadequate, unfair, or unjust leader.

Douglas McGregor's classic leadership theory describes two different sets of assumptions about the nature of human beings and what they want from their work environment (92; also see Chapter 2). According to McGregor, some leaders believe they must direct, control, and coerce people in order to motivate them to work. Such leaders assume that the more basic needs for safety, security, and certainty motivate people. By contrast, other leaders believe that they must provide people with freedom, autonomy, and responsibility in order to motivate them to work. These leaders assume that higher-order needs for achievement and self-actualization fundamentally motivate people. According to Anita Roddick (101:223, 225):

[People] . . . are looking for leadership that has vision. If you have a company with itsy-bitsy vision, you have an itsy-bitsy company. . . . If you employ people with small thinking and small ideas, you become a company of dwarves.

Leaders from different cultures vary in the assumptions they make about what motivates most people. In the United States, for example, many leaders assume that people's basic physiological needs for safety and security have been met and that therefore only opportunities to satisfy higher-order needs will motivate most people. They believe that denying these opportunities leads to alienation, lower productivity, and ultimately, high levels of turnover. Most leaders in the United States believe that the majority of the people who work for them want to develop interpersonal relationships characterized by trust and open communication. They therefore assume that people produce more when the workplace is most democratic.

Leaders in the People's Republic of China act similarly, but for very different reasons (106). According to historical explanations (95), the pre-1949 Chinese regarded satisfying lower-order needs as the main objective of the masses, with higher-order needs going unrecognized for all but the upper class. After the revolution two types of managers emerged: The first type, experts who possessed extensive technical expertise, tended to use a more controlling approach to get things done. The second type, leaders who possessed more political and ideological expertise and who were more skilled in managing people, tended to use a more inclusive approach. This second, more political, group of leaders believed that their leadership approach was closely tied to the philosophy of Chairman Mao. They strongly advocated a more egalitarian workplace in which all employees could improve their lot together, both economically and culturally. They strongly believed that leaders had to give workers' welfare prominence over production, and that material incentives that promoted self-interest and competition had to be discouraged. These leaders encouraged collaboration and broad participation in decision making by replacing individual rewards with collective rewards, and emphasizing democracy and decentralization. Today, more market-based motivations have re-emerged as a driving force among many Chinese businesspeople. Both American and Chinese leaders agree, but for very different reasons, that democratic organizations can perform efficiently and productively; that is, that global competitiveness without dehumanization is possible.

CULTURAL CONTINGENCY

Some researchers suggest that American approaches to leadership apply abroad (82;95). Most leaders, however, believe that they must adapt their style to the cultures of employees and clients; that is, they believe that leadership is culturally contingent (42). In their groundbreaking research, Haire, Ghiselli, and Porter (60) found that, although the 14 countries they studied showed more similarities than differences, the countries clustered along cultural rather than industrial lines. Hofstede (66;67) later concluded that participative leadership approaches, which were strongly encouraged by American theorists and managers, were not suitable for all cultures. Employees in high power-distance cultures, for example, expect managers to act as strong leaders; they become uncomfortable with leaders delegating discretionary decisions. Some cultures want their leaders to act as decisive, directive experts; others want leaders to act as participative problem solvers (see Figure 2-4). Laurent (86:75-76), for example, describes his difficulty explaining matrix management to French managers:

> *The idea of reporting to two bosses was so alien to [French] managers that mere consideration of such an organizing principle was an impossible, useless exercise. What was needed first was a thorough examination and probing of the holy principle of the single chain of command and the managers' recognition that this was a strong element of their own belief system rather than a constant element in nature.*

"Americans' extreme individualism, combined with their highly participative managerial climate, may render U.S. management practices unique; that is, differentiated from the approaches in most other areas of the world" (40:292;41;65). This conclusion is supported by recent research on leadership that found the United States unique in several respects among all of the Eastern and Western cultures studied (73).

Even in countries culturally well suited to more participative leadership (such as England, Sweden, and the United States), organizations must adapt the form of participation to the local culture (46). Although studies vary in the extent to which they see appropriate leadership styles as similar to those most acceptable in the United States (see, for example, descriptions of managers in Europe [94], Germany [85;115], India [80], and Israel [118]), the consensus today is that global managers must be flexible enough to alter their approach when crossing national borders and working with people from other cultures.[4]

GLOBAL LEADERSHIP COMPETENCIES

As organizations disperse globally, they have come to realize that leadership is a skill that most people need, not just a requirement of a few people at the top. In searching for the most important leadership competencies, companies have learned that emotional intelligence, not cognitive abilities, explains 90 percent of the difference between average and star performers (56:94). Asian, European, and U.S. companies headed by leaders with strong emotional intelligence outperform the yearly earnings goals of their competitors by up to 20 percent (56:95).

Globally, a company's success is clearly linked to the emotional intelligence of its leaders.

What is emotional intelligence? According to psychologist Daniel Goleman, it is a set of five individual and social competencies, including self-awareness, self-regulation, motivation, empathy, and social skills (32;55;56;57). Each competency is critical to effective leadership.

Self-awareness is "the ability to recognize and understand your moods, emotions, and drives, as well as their effects on" other people (56:95). Leaders with a high level of self-awareness exhibit self-confidence, realistic self-assessment, and a self-deprecating sense of humor.

Self-regulation, the second competency, is "the ability to control or redirect disruptive impulses and moods" along with "the propensity to suspend judgment—to think before acting" (56:95). Leaders with a high level of self-regulation exhibit trustworthiness, integrity, comfort with ambiguity, and openness to change.

Motivation, the third emotional-intelligence competency, is reflected in "a passion to work for reasons that go beyond money or status" and "a propensity to pursue goals with energy and persistence" (56:95). Leaders with a high level of motivation show a strong drive to achieve, optimism (even in the face of failure), and organizational commitment.

The fourth emotional-intelligence competency is *empathy,* "the ability to understand the emotional makeup of other people" and "skill in treating people according to their emotional reactions" (56:95). Leaders with a high level of empathy demonstrate an ability to build and retain talent in their organization, show cross-cultural sensitivity, and become known for offering great service to clients and customers.

The fifth emotional-intelligence competency is *social skill,* a "proficiency in managing relationships and building networks" along with an "ability to find common ground and to build rapport" (56:95). Leaders with a high level of social skill are effective at leading change, show a superior ability to build and lead teams, and become known for their persuasiveness.

Global Leadership: Going Beyond the Ordinary As former U.S. Secretary of State Madeleine Albright challenges us, "We have a responsibility in our time, as others have had in theirs, not to be prisoners of history, but to shape history" (20). Yet historically, leadership "that goes beyond the nation-state and seeks to address all human beings" has been "the most important, but rarest and most elusive, variety of leadership" (51:20). Today's global business environment demands that we strive to go beyond the ordinary leadership of prior centuries. Harvard professor Howard Gardner studied women and men whom society recognizes as extraordinary leaders. He discovered that extraordinary leaders become their organizations' and society's chiefs; that is, they "achieve their influence through the kinds of narratives or stories they tell about themselves, their society, and the people with whom they are dealing" (51). Without deeply understanding themselves, their organizations, and global society, they would be incapable of crafting and telling profoundly meaningful stories. Gardner discovered that extraordinary leaders worldwide possess three competencies that are similar to those Goleman recognized as emotional intelligence. According to Gardner, extraordinary leaders are better at reflecting, leveraging, and framing than are most people. First, extraordinary leaders spend a lot of time *reflecting;* they think about what they are trying to achieve, review how they are doing, and correct course when things are not going well (51). Second, extraordinary leaders are particularly good at *leveraging* (51). Because no leader is equally good at everything, extraordinary leaders find out what they are particularly good at and push this competitive advantage as hard as they can (51). Unlike ordinary leaders, they do not worry about activities that they are not good at (51). Perhaps the most surprising of the three competencies is *framing.* Extraordinary leaders take more risks than average leaders and are particularly good at learning from their failures. It is not that they fail less frequently than ordinary leaders; on the contrary, they fail more frequently. However, they learn more from their failures than do their more ordinary colleagues. Today's challenge is not just to be a leader, but rather to become a global leader who can meet the challenges of the twenty-first century—a leader who can rise to the challenge of shaping history.

Global Leadership: No Longer Men Alone As Carly Fiorina, former CEO of Hewlett Packard and the first woman to lead a *Fortune* top-20 firm, recognizes, "Anytime you have a fiercely competitive, change-oriented business where results count and merit matters, women will rise to the top" (45). A major shift is taking place in who is leading major companies and countries. Whereas the majority of senior leaders in the twentieth century were men, leadership is now shifting to include both women and men. As Harvard professor Rosabeth Moss Kanter (81:89) emphasizes, in a global economy, "Meritocracy—letting talent rise to the top regardless of where it is found and whether it is male or female—has become essential to business success."

Careful observation reveals a rapidly increasing number of countries and companies moving away, for the first time, from their historic men-only pattern of senior leadership. Of the 68 women who have served in their country's highest political leadership position—either as president or prime minister—more than half have come into office in just the last decade, all but ten of whom are the first woman their country has ever selected (3;5;10;11). Similarly, among the current women CEOs leading major global companies, almost all are the first woman whom their particular company has ever selected (4;5;6;9;13). The question is no longer, "Is the pattern changing?" but rather, "Which companies will take advantage of the trend and which will fall behind?" (8;18;19). Which companies and countries will lead in recognizing and understanding the talents women bring to leadership, and which will limit their potential by clinging to historic men-only patterns? Given the recency of women assuming very senior global leadership positions, it is important to recognize that almost all research conducted on senior leaders has been conducted on men. Only now, in the twenty-first century, are we beginning to understand women's unique patterns of leadership and accomplishment.

GLOBAL LEADERSHIP: CREATING A POSITIVE FUTURE

Klaus Schwab, president of the World Economic Forum, in a speech to the world's top business leaders gathered in Davos, Switzerland, described the twenty-first century's leadership challenge as business's relationship to the well-being of society:

> *In today's trust-starved climate, our market-driven system is under attack.... large parts of the population feel that business has become detached from society, that business interests are no longer aligned with societal interests ... The only way to respond to this new wave of anti-business sentiment is for business to take the lead and to reposition itself clearly and convincingly as part of society* (104).

How can business leaders simultaneously optimize financial, social, and environmental performance? How can they help to create a prosperous, sustainable society that benefits us all? Leadership at the intersection of business and society centers on a profound concern for the future of humanity and the earth. It recognizes that how we respond today to global ecological and economic change will reverberate across generations well into the future. It asks how we can leverage the strengths of business to address the most compelling challenges facing the world today. It is clear that a healthy world depends on the evolution of healthy organizations, and healthy organizations cannot exist without great leadership. Our common future depends on the extent to which managers and executives develop both a vision of a better world and an ability to lead others toward that vision.

To succeed as a global civilization in the twenty-first century, our ways of thinking about options and solutions need to expand to more prominently and explicitly include the private sector. This is not because the private sector has inherently better values than other sectors—it does not—but because of the private sector's global prominence and its worldwide structures and processes. For the first time in history, answers to questions of societal well-being—including questions of war and peace and of terrorism and security—may well be more in the hands of business people than in those of political, diplomatic, military, or humanitarian leaders.

Over the past 50 years, power has shifted dramatically from the public to the private sector. Today, 49 of the 100 largest economies in the world are multinational companies, not countries (90). Due to this shift in power, traditional perspectives that assumed government and intergovernmental agencies could or would take adequate care of society's welfare are no longer relevant either for society or for the economy; this applies to both the richest and the poorest nations and peoples.

Wal-Mart, for example, is now the nineteenth largest economy in the world, with sales exceeding $250 billion (90:128). If it were a country, Wal-Mart would be China's eighth largest trading partner (48;50). Wal-Mart's single-day revenue is larger than the annual gross domestic product of 36 independent countries (90:128). With over 1.3 million employees, Wal-Mart is now the world's largest employer. The company has more people in uniform than the entire United States Army (90:128). What Wal-Mart does in the world matters, not only to its own employees, customers, and suppliers, but to the global economy and society within which all companies operate and all people live. Global solutions cannot be conceived of or implemented without taking companies such as Wal-Mart into account.

United Nations' Secretary General Kofi Annan[5] has challenged business leaders to become co-creators of society's well-being:

> *Let us choose to unite the power of markets with the strengths of universal ideals . . . let us choose to reconcile the creative forces of private entrepreneurship with the needs of the disadvantaged and the requirements of future generations.*

Enlightened twenty-first century pleas for corporate global citizenship recognize that without the private sector, no attempt to create and maintain a peaceful, prosperous, equitable, and sustainable society can succeed. Many, however, rightfully question the role that business has taken. Whether they cite corporate greed and corruption—as brilliantly demonstrated in recent years by Arthur Andersen, Enron, Health South, Tyco, and WorldCom, among many others—or other forms of corporate malfeasance, the private sector is rarely perceived as a primary contributor to global society's security and well-being (see, among others, 38;39;91;105;112).

New York Times editorial writer Thomas Friedman suggests that the private sector's crime is not simply behavior that is ultimately exposed as criminal, but rather CEOs' lack of constructive engagement with the world's most serious problems; that is, CEOs' lack of global leadership. As Friedman labels it, many CEOs are simply "missing in action" (48). Equally seriously, many of these missing-in-action CEOs still view commitment to societal well-being not as a business strategy for superior performance—both fiscal and societal—but rather as a net drain on their companies' revenues and profits. Locked in an overly narrow definition of free enterprise, they continue to adhere to classical economist Milton Friedman's dictum that the only "social responsibility of business is to increase its profits" (47).

The challenge of twenty-first century global leadership is to contribute to the societal, ecological, and fiscal well-being of one's company and of the world. To contribute to the world, one must understand the world, including the rich interplay of cultures that define global society.

SUMMARY

Approaches to leadership vary across cultures. Global leaders today not only need to know how to inspire and lead people from a range of different cultures, they also need to create ways of leading people with very different backgrounds simultaneously. Moreover, the challenge of twenty-first century leadership is not simply business prosperity. Today's leadership challenge is to design innovative approaches that simultaneously create successful companies and successful societies.

QUESTIONS FOR REFLECTION

1. **World Leaders.** Publicly elected officials often display the leadership values and behaviors of their culture. Select two prominent world leaders and describe their behavior in cultural terms.

2. **Most Admired Global Leaders.** Select a global leader whom you strongly admire—known personally to you or not. List the qualities, characteristics, and behaviors that make you admire this particular leader. In what ways are the qualities, characteristics, and behaviors that you admire reflective of either your own cultural background or that of the particular leader you have chosen?

3. **Leadership Vision.** As you consider your current and future role in life, what is your vision of what you would like to contribute? In what ways does your choice reflect your culture? In what ways would you be considered unique, when seen from the perspective of your culture?

4. **Global Women Leaders.** Identify a woman leader from another culture whom you think is highly effective. How did she obtain her position of power? What was the reaction to her when she first

assumed power? Does her style of leadership differ significantly from that of her male contemporaries? What advantages does she have, as a leader, based on the fact that she is a woman?

NOTES

1. University of Pennsylvania Professor Robert House and his worldwide research team have conducted a major multi-domestic study of leadership to define leadership practices in countries around the world (68;69;70;71;72;77).

2. Adapted (2007) from Adler's "Global Leadership: Giving Oneself for Things Far Greater than Oneself" (7).

3. Adapted from Prahalad and Hart's "The Fortune at the Bottom of the Pyramid (99:5-6).

4. For an excellent review of current international cross-cultural leadership research see Dorfman (40). For other reviews and research on leadership, see references 21;22;33;34;43;44;53;58;74;95;107;108;109;110;111;119;120).

5. For further information on Kofi Annan's initiatives with the worldwide business community, see the United Nations Global Compact website at www.unglobalcompact.org.

REFERENCES

1. Adler, N. J. "Corporate Global Citizenship: Successfully Partnering with the World" in Gabriele Suder, ed., *Corporate Strategies under International Terrorism and Adversity* (Cheltenham, U.K: Edward Elgar Publishing, 2006), in press pp. 177–195.

2. Adler, N. J. "Cross-Cultural Management Research: The Ostrich and the Trend," *Academy of Management Review,* vol. 8, no. 2 (1983), pp. 226–232.

3. Adler, N. J. "Did You Hear? Global Leadership in Charity's World," *Journal of Management Inquiry,* vol. 7, no. 2 (1998), pp. 21–33.

4. Adler, N. J. "Global Entrepreneurs: Women, Myths, and History," *Global Focus,* vol. 1, no. 4 (1999), pp. 125–134.

5. Adler, N. J. "Global Leaders: A Dialogue with Future History," *International Management,* vol. 1, no. 2 (1997), pp. 21–33.

6. Adler, N. J. "Global Leaders: Women of Influence," in Gary Powell, ed., *Handbook of Gender in Organizations* (Thousand Oaks, Calif.: Sage, 1999), pp. 239–261.

7. Adler, N. J. "Global Leadership: Giving Oneself for Things Far Greater Than Oneself," *Insights, Journal of the Academy of International Business,* vol. 1, no. 2 (2001), pp. 13–15.

8. Adler, N. J. "Global Leadership: No Longer Men Alone," in Martin Gannon & Karen Newman (eds.), *Handbook of Cross-Cultural Management* (Oxford, England: Basil Blackwell, 2002), pp. 236–249.

9. Adler, N. J. "Global Leadership: Women Leaders," *Management International Review*, 37 (Special Issue 1, 1997), pp. 135–143.

10. Adler, N. J. "Global Women Political Leaders: An Invisible History, An Increasingly Important Future," *Leadership Quarterly*, vol. 7, no. 1 (1996), pp. 133–161.

11. Adler, N. J. "Societal Leadership: The Wisdom of Peace," in Suresh Srivastva, ed., *Executive Wisdom and Organizational Change* (San Francisco: Jossey-Bass, 1998), pp. 243–337.

12. Adler, N. J. "The Women's Global Leadership Forum: Enhancing One Company's Leadership Capacity," *Human Resource Management*, vol. 39, nos. 2 & 3 (2000), pp. 209–225.

13. Adler, N. J. "Twenty-First Century Leadership: Reality Beyond the Myths," in Richard Wright, volume ed., *Research in Global Strategic Management*, vol. 7, *International Entrepreneurship: Globalization of Emerging Business* (Greenwich, Conn.: JAI Press, 1999), pp. 173–190.

14. Adler, N. J.; & Bartholomew, Susan. "Academic and Professional Communities of Discourse: Generating Knowledge on Transnational Human Resource Management," *Journal of International Business Studies*, vol. 23, no. 3 (1992), pp. 551–569.

15. Adler, N. J.; & Boyacigiller, Nakiye. "Global Management and the 21st Century," in B. J. Punnett & O. Shenkar, eds. *Handbook of International Management Research* (Cambridge, Mass.: Blackwell, 1996), pp. 537–555.

16. Adler, N. J.; & Boyacigiller, Nakiye. "Global Organizational Behavior: Going Beyond Tradition," *Journal of International Management*, vol. 1, no. 3 (1995), pp. 73–86.

17. Adler, N. J.; & Boyacigiller, Nakiye. "Going Beyond Traditional HRM Scholarship," in R. N. Kanungo & D. M. Saunders, eds. *New Approaches to Employee Management.* vol. 3, *Employee Management Issues in Developing Countries* (Greenwich, Conn.: JAI Press, 1995), pp. 1–13.

18. Adler, N. J.; Brody, Laura W.; & Osland, Joyce S. "Advances in Global Leadership: The Women's Global Leadership Forum," in William H. Mobley, ed., *Advances in Global Leadership*, vol. 2 (Greenwich, Conn.: JAI Press, 2001), pp. 351–383.

19. Adler, N. J.; Brody, Laura W.; & Osland, Joyce S. "The Women's Global Leadership Forum: Enhancing One Company's Global Leadership Capability," *Human Resource Management*, vol. 39, nos. 2 and 3 (2000), pp. 209–225.

20. Albright, Madeleine K. *Harvard University Commencement Address* as reported in the *New York Times*, June 6, 1997, p. A8.

21. Al-Gratton, A. A. "Test of the Path-Goal Theory of Leadership in the Multinational Domain," *Group and Organization Studies*, vol. 10, no. 4 (1985), pp. 429–445.

22. Ayman, R. "Leadership Perception: The Role of Gender and Culture," *Leadership Theory and Research* (San Diego: Academic Press, 1993), pp. 137–166.

23. Bass, Bernard M. *Leadership and Performance Beyond Expectations* (New York: Free Press, 1985).

24. Bass, Bernard M.; & Stogdill, R. M. *The Handbook of Leadership,* 3rd ed. (New York: Free Press, 1989).

25. Bennis, Warren. *Why Leaders Can't Lead: The Unconscious Conspiracy Continues* (San Francisco: Jossey-Bass, 1989).

26. Bennis, Warren, & Nanus, Burt. *Leaders: Strategies for Taking Charge* (New York: Harper & Row, 1985).

27. Blake, R. R.; & Mouton, J. S. *The Managerial Grid* (Houston, Tex: Gulf Publishing, 1964).

28. Blake, R. R.; & Mouton, J. S. "Motivating Human Productivity in the People's Republic of China," *Group and Organization Studies,* vol. 4, no. 2 (1979), pp. 159–169.

29. Bolman, L.; & Deal, T. *Leading with Soul* (San Francisco: Jossey-Bass, 1995).

30. Boyacigiller, Nakiye; & Adler, N. J. "Insiders and Outsiders: Bridging the Worlds of Organizational Behavior and International Management," in Brian Toyne & Doug Nigh, eds., *International Business Inquiry: An Emerging Vision* (Columbia, S.C.: University of South Carolina Press, 1996), pp. 22–102.

31. Boyacigiller, Nakiye; & Adler, N. J. "The Parochial Dinosaur: The Organizational Sciences in a Global Context," *Academy of Management Review,* vol. 16, no. 2 (1991), pp. 262–290.

32. Boyatzis, R. E.; & McKee, A. *Resonant Leadership: Renewing Yourself and Connecting with Others through Mindfulness, Hope, and Compassion.* (Boston: Harvard Business School Press, 2005).

33. Chemers, M. M., "A Theoretical Framework for Examining the Effects of Cultural Differences on Leadership." Paper presented at the 23rd International Congress of Applied Psychology, Madrid, Spain, 1994.

34. Chemers, M. M.; & Ayman, R. "Directions for Leadership Research," *Leadership Theory and Research* (San Diego: Academic Press, 1993), pp. 321–332.

35. Chittister, J. Quote as cited in Frederick Franck; Janis Roze; & Richard Connolly, eds., *What Does It Mean To Be Human?* (Nyack, N.Y.: Circumstantial Productions, 1998).

36. Conger, J. A. *The Charismatic Leader: Behind the Mystique of Exceptional Leadership* (San Francisco: Jossey-Bass, 1989).

37. Conger, J. A.; & Kanungo, R. N., eds., *Charismatic Leadership* (San Francisco: Jossey-Bass, 1988).

38. Creswell, J. "Citigroup Agrees to Pay $2 Billion in Enron Scandal," *New York Times* (June 11, 2005a).

39. Creswell, J. "J. P. Morgan Chase Agrees to Pay Investors $2.2 Billion," *New York Times* (June 15, 2005b).

40. Dorfman, P. W. "International and Cross-Cultural Leadership," in B. J. Punnett & O. Shenkar, eds., *Handbook for International Management Research* (Cambridge, Mass.: Blackwell, 1996), pp. 267–349.

41. Dorfman, P. W.; & Howell, J. P. "Dimensions of National Culture and Effective Leadership Patterns: Hofstede Revisited," *Advances in International Comparative Management,* vol. 3 (Greenwich, Conn.: JAI Press, 1988), pp. 127–150.

42. Dorfman, P. W.; Howell, J. P.; Hibino, S.; Lee, J. K.; Tate, U.; & Bautista, A. "Leadership in Western and Asian Countries: Commonalties and Differences in Effective Leadership Processes Across Cultures," *Leadership Quarterly,* vol. 8 (1997), pp. 233–274.

43. Dorfman, P. W.; & Ronen, S. "The Universality of Leadership Theories: Challenges and Paradoxes." Paper presented at the National Academy of Management annual meeting, Miami, Florida, 1991.

44. Erez, M.; & Earley, P. Christopher. *Culture, Self-Identity and Work* (New York: Oxford University Press, 1993).

45. Fiorina, Carly. "Anytime You Have a Fiercely Competitive Business," *Nortel World* (November 1999), p. 8.

46. Foy, N.; & Gadon, H. "Worker Participation Contrasts in Three Countries," *Harvard Business Review* (May–June 1976), pp. 71–84.

47. Friedman, Milton L. "The Social Responsibility of Business is to Increase its Profits," *New York Times Magazine* (September 13, 1970), pp. 32–33, 122–126.

48. Friedman, Thomas L. "It's a Flat World After All," *New York Times* op-ed (April 3, 2005).

49. Friedman, Thomas L. *The Lexus and the Olive Tree* (New York: Farrar, Straus, Giroux, 1999).

50. Friedman, Thomas L. *The World is Flat: A Brief History of the Twenty-First Century* (New York: Farrar, Straus & Giroux, 2005).

51. Gardner, Howard. *Leading Minds: An Anatomy of Leadership* (New York: Basic Books, 1995).

52. Gardner, John W. *Gardner on Leadership* (New York: The Free Press, 1989).

53. Gerstner, C. R.; & Day, D. D. "Cross-Cultural Comparison of Leadership Prototypes," *Leadership Quarterly,* vol. 5, no. 1 (1994), pp. 121–134.

54. Goethe, J. W. Von *Goethe's Scientific Studies.* Translated by D. Miller, Edited by A. P. Cottrell & D. Miller (Boston, Mass.:

Suhkamp Insel, 1985); statement is paraphrased from Goethe as cited in Kahane (79).

55. Goleman, Daniel. *Emotional Intelligence* (New York: Bantam, 1995).

56. Goleman, Daniel. "What Makes a Leader," *Harvard Business Review* (November–December 1998), pp. 92–102. Also see Goleman, Daniel. "Leadership That Gets Results," *Harvard Business Review* (March–April 2000), pp. 78–90; and Goleman, Daniel. *Emotional Intelligence at Work* (New York: Bantam, 1998).

57. Goleman, Daniel; Boyatzis, R. E.; & McKee, A. *Primal Leadership: Realizing the Power of Emotional Intelligence.* (Boston: Harvard Business School Press, 2002).

58. Graen, G. B.; & Wakabayashi, M. "Cross-Cultural Leadership Makings: Bridging American and Japanese Diversity for Team Advantage," *Handbook of Industrial and Organizational Psychology,* vol. 4, 2rd ed. (Palo Alto, Calif.: Consulting Psychologists Press, 1994), pp. 415–446.

59. Grauman, C. F.; & Moscovici, S. *Changing Conceptions of Leadership* (New York: Springer-Verlag, 1986).

60. Haire, M.; Ghiselli, E. E.; & Porter, L. W. "Cultural Patterns in the Role of the Manager," *Industrial Relations,* vol. 2, no. 2 (1963), pp. 95–117.

61. Hart, S. L. *Capitalism at the Crossroads* (Upper Saddle River, N.J.: Wharton School Publishing, Pearson Education, 2005).

62. Hart, S. L.; & Christiansen, C. M. "The Great Leap: Driving Innovation from the Base of the Pyramid," *Sloan Management Review,* vol. 44, no. 1, pp. 51–56 (2002).

63. Hassink, Jacqueline. *Queen Bees: Female Power Stations* (Amsterdam: Menno van de Koppel, 1999).

64. Hassink, Jacqueline. *The Table of Power* (Amsterdam: Menno van de Koppel, 1996). Artist Hassink created a photo essay on tables of power (board room tables) and relationship (dining room tables) of both male and female CEOs worldwide.

65. Hofstede, Geert. *Cultures and Organizations: Software of the Mind* (London: McGraw-Hill, 1991).

66. Hofstede, Geert. *Culture's Consequences: International Differences in Work-Related Values* (Beverly Hills, Calif.: Sage, 1980).

67. Hofstede, Geert. "Motivation, Leadership and Organization: Do American Theories Apply Abroad?" *Organizational Dynamics,* vol. 9, no. 1 (1980), pp. 42–63.

68. House, Robert J. "GLOBE: The Global Leadership and Organizational Behavior Effectiveness Research Program," *Polish Psychological Bulletin,* vol. 28, no. 3 (1997), pp. 215–254.

69. House, Robert J.; & Aditya, R. N. "The Social Scientific Study of Leadership: Quo Vadis?" *Journal of Management,* vol. 23, no. 3 (1997), pp. 409–473.

70. House, Robert J.; Hanges, Paul J.; Javidan, Mansour; Dorfman, Peter W.; & Gupta, Vipin, eds., *Culture, Leadership, and Organizations: The GLOBE Study of 62 Societies.* (Thousand Oaks, Calif.: Sage Publications, 2004).

71. House, Robert J.; Hanges, Paul J.; Ruiz-Quintanilla, S. Antonio; Dorfman, Peter W.; Javidan, Mansour; Dickson, Marcus; Gupta, Vipin; & GLOBE Country Co-Investigators. "Cultural Influences on Leadership and Organizations: Project Globe," in William H. Mobley, M. Jocelyne Gessner, & Val Arnold, eds., *Advances in Global Leadership,* vol. 1 (1999), pp. 171–233.

72. House, Robert J.; Wright, N. S.; & Aditya, R. N. "Cross-Cultural Research on Organizational Leadership: A Critical Analysis and a Proposed Theory," in P. C. Earley & M. Erez, eds., *New Perspectives in International Industrial/Organizational Psychology* (San Francisco: New Lexington, 1997), pp. 535–625.

73. Howell, J. P.; Dorfman, P. W.; Hibino, S.; Lee, J. K.; & Tate, U. "Leadership in Western and Asian Countries: Commonalities and Differences in Effective Leadership Processes and Substitutes Across Cultures." Center for Business Research, New Mexico State University (1994).

74. Hunt, J. W. *Leadership: A New Synthesis* (Newbury Park, Calif.: Sage, 1991).

75. Iacocca, L.; & Novak, W. *Iacocca* (New York: Bantam, 1984).

76. Jain, C. H.; & Kanungo, R. *Behavioral Issues in Management: The Canadian Context* (Toronto: McGraw-Hill Ryerson, 1977), pp. 85–99.

77. Javidan, M.; Dorfman, P. W.; de Luque, M. S.; & House, R. J., "In the Eye of the Beholder: Cross Cultural Lessons in Leadership from Project GLOBE," *Academy of Management Perspectives,* vol. 20, no.1 (2006), pp. 67–90.

78. Jennings, E. *The Anatomy of Leadership* (New York: Harper and Row, 1960).

79. Kahane, Adam. Keynote Address delivered to *Fast Company's* Real Time Conference in Orlando, Florida, May 2000 and published as "How to Change the World: Lessons for Entrepreneurs from Activists," *Reflections,* vol. 2, no. 3 (2001), pp. 16 –26.

80. Kakar, S. "Authority Patterns and Subordinate Behavior in Indian Organizations," *Administrative Science Quarterly,* vol. 16, no. 3 (1971), pp. 298–308.

81. Kanter, Rosabeth Moss. Comments on Nancy A. Nichols' *Reach for the Top: Women and the Changing Facts of Work Life* (Boston: Harvard Business School Press), as cited in the book review by John R. Hook in *The Academy of Management Executive,* vol. 8, no. 2 (1994), pp. 87–89.

82. Kaufman, F. "Decision Making—Eastern and Western Style," *Business Horizons*, vol. 13, no. 6 (1970), pp. 81–86.

83. Krieger, David. Quote as cited in F. Frank; J. Roze; & R. Connolly, eds., *What Does It Mean To Be Human?* (Nyack, N.Y.: Circumstantial Productions, 1998).

84. Kotter, J. *The Leadership Factor* (New York: Free Press, 1988).

85. Kuchinke, K. Peter. "Leadership and Culture: Work-Related Values and Leadership Styles Among One Company's U.S. and German Telecommunication Employees," *Human Resource Development Quarterly*, vol. 10, no. 2 (1999), pp. 135–154.

86. Laurent, André. "The Cultural Diversity of Western Conceptions of Management," *International Studies of Management and Organization*, vol. 13, nos. 1–2 (1983), pp. 75–96.

87. Levinson, Harry. *Executive* (Cambridge, Mass.: Harvard University Press, 1968, 1981) as cited in R. H. Mason and R. S. Spich, *Management: An International Perspective* (Homewood, Ill.: Irwin, 1987), pp. 190–191. Reprinted by permission of the publisher. Copyright © 1968, 1971, 1981 by the President and Fellows of Harvard College.

88. Likert, R. *The Human Organization* (New York: McGraw-Hill, 1967).

89. Likert, R. *New Patterns of Management* (New York: McGraw-Hill, 1961).

90. Mau, Bruce & The Institute Without Boundaries. *Massive Change* (London: Phaidon Press, 2004).

91. McClean, B.; & Elkind P. *The Smartest Guys in the Room: The Amazing Rise and Scandalous Fall of Enron* (New York: Portfolio, Penguin Group, 2003).

92. McGregor, D. *The Human Side of Enterprise* (New York: McGraw-Hill, 1960).

93. Mitroff, I. I. *Business Not as Usual* (San Francisco: Jossey-Bass, 1987).

94. Nath, R.; & Narayanan, V. K. "A Comparative Study of Managerial Support, Trust, Openness, Decision-Making, and Job Enrichment," *Academy of Management Proceedings*, vol. 40 (1980), pp. 48–52.

95. Oh, T. K. "Theory Y in the People's Republic of China," *California Management Review*, vol. 19, no. 2 (1976), pp. 77–84.

96. Ohmae, K. *Beyond National Borders* (Homewood, Ill.: Dow Jones-Irwin, 1987).

97. Prahalad, C. K. The *Fortune at the Bottom of the Pyramid: Eradicating Poverty through Profits* (Upper Saddle River, N.J.: Wharton School Publishing, Pearson Education, 2005).

98. Prahalad, C. K.; & Hammond, A. "Serving the World's Poor, Profitably," *Harvard Business Review*, vol. 80, no. 9, pp.48–57.

99. Prahalad, C. K.; & Hart, S. L. "The Fortune at the Bottom of the Pyramid," *Strategy and Business*, vol. 26, no. 1 (2002), pp. 2–14.

100. Rechtschaffen, Stephan. *Timeshifting* (New York: Bantam Doubleday Dell Audio Publishing, 1996).

101. Roddick, Anita. *Body and Soul* (New York: Crown, 1991).

102. Saint-Germain, Michelle A. "Women in Power in Nicaragua: Myth and Reality" in Michael A. Genovese, ed., *Women as National Leaders.* (Newbury Park, Calif.: Sage, 1993).

103. Schlesinger, A. M., Jr. *A Thousand Days* (Boston: Houghton Mifflin, 1965).

104. Schwab, Klaus. Remarks as reported in *Newsweek,* February 24, 2003, p. 10.

105. Scott, A. O. "Those You Love to Hate: A Look at the Mighty Laid Low," *New York Times*, April 22, 2005.

106. Shenkar, Oded; Ronen, Simcha; Shefy, Erella; & Chow, Irene Hau Siu. "The Role Structure of Chinese Managers," *Human Relations,* vol. 51, no.1 (1998), pp. 51–72.

107. Smith, P. B.; Misumi, S.; Tayeb, M.; Peterson, M.; & Bond, M. "On the Generality of Leadership Style Measures across Cultures," *Journal of Occupational Psychology,* vol. 62, no. 2 (1989), pp. 97–109.

108. Smith, P. B.; & Peterson, M. F. "Leadership as Event Management: A Cross-Cultural Survey Based upon Middle Managers from 25 Nations." Paper presented in the symposium on Cross-Cultural Studies of Event Management at the 23rd International Congress of Applied Psychology, Madrid, Spain, 1994.

109. Smith, P. B.; & Peterson, M. F. *Leadership, Organizations and Culture* (London: Sage, 1988).

110. Smith, P. B.; Peterson, M. F.; Misumi, J.; & Bond, M. "A Cross-Cultural Test of Japanese PM Leadership Theory," *Applied Psychology: An International Review,* vol. 41, no. 1 (1992), pp. 5–19.

111. Smith, P. B.; Peterson, M. F.; Misumi, J.; & Tayeb, M. "Testing Leadership Theory Cross-Culturally," *Recent Advances in Social Psychology: An International Perspective* (Amsterdam: North-Holland, 1989), pp. 383–391.

112. Sorkin, Ross. "Ex-Chief and Aide Guilty of Looting Millions at Tyco," *New York Times* (June 18, 2005).

113. Stogdill, R. M. "Personal Factors Associated with Leadership: A Survey of the Literature," *Journal of Psychology,* vol. 25 (1948), pp. 37–71.

114. Triandis, H. C. "Dimensions of Cultural Variations as Parameters of Organizational Theories," *International Studies of Management and Organization,* vol. 12, no. 4 (1983), pp. 139–169.

115. Tscheulin, D. "Leader Behavior Measurement in German Industry," *Journal of Applied Psychology,* vol. 57 (1973), pp. 28–31.

116. Tzu, Lao. *The Way of Lao Tzu (Tao-Te Ching): Translated with Introductory Essays, Comments and Notes by Wing-Tsit Chan* (Indianapolis, Ind.: Bobbs-Merrill, 1963). As cited in "Lao Leader Behaviors," *Management International Review,* vol. 19 (1979), p. 214. (Lao Tzu wrote in the sixth century B.C.E.)

117. Van Fleet, D.; & Al-Tuhaih, S. "A Cross-Cultural Analysis of Perceived Leader Behaviors," *Management International Review,* vol. 19 (April 1979), pp. 81–88.

118. Vardi, Y.; Shrom, A.; & Jacobson, D. "A Study of Leadership Beliefs of Israeli Managers," *Academy of Management Journal,* vol. 23, no. 2 (1980), pp. 367–374.

119. Xu, L. C. "A Cross-Cultural Study of the Leadership Behavior of Chinese and Japanese Executives," *Asia Pacific Journal of Management,* vol. 4, no. 3 (1987), pp. 203–209.

120. Yukl, Gary A. *Leadership in Organizations,* 3d ed. (Upper Saddle River, N.J.: Prentice Hall, 1994).

Chapter 7

Motivating People From Around the World: Inspiring People to Contribute

---

You and I belong to the same family. All people on earth belong to the same family, the human family.

—Thor Heyerdahl, Norway[1]

What inspires people to give their best to an organization? What can a company do to consistently attain high productivity and job satisfaction? What energizes members of an organization to produce high-quality work? What directs and channels their behavior to accomplish organizational goals? How do global organizations maintain desired behavior? What influences from within employees and from their environment encourage them to outperform the competition (73;74)?

One global high-technology firm based in Silicon Valley in California thought it had the answer. The firm created the "Dragon Slayer Campaign" with posters encouraging employees to "Slay the Dragon." Unfortunately, the American management had not realized that dragons symbolize good luck to the Chinese and that their campaign was not encouraging Chinese employees to beat the competition but rather to destroy their good luck. Understandably, Chinese employees took down the posters and forced the firm to end the campaign.

Numerous motivation theories address these questions and, like the majority of leadership theories discussed in Chapter 6, most have been developed in the United States (23;47). Each attempts to explain why human beings behave in the ways they do and what managers can do to encourage certain types of behavior while discouraging others. Let's look at a few of the historically well-recognized motivation theories and determine whether they are universal or culture bound.

HIERARCHIES OF NEEDS

Psychologist Abraham Maslow (51;52;53) suggested that human beings' five basic needs form a hierarchy: from physiological, to safety, to social, to esteem, to self-actualization needs. According to this theory, higher-order needs (i.e., esteem and self-actualization) only become activated, and thus motivate behavior, after lower-order needs have been satisfied.

Does Maslow's theory, which he based on Americans, hold for employees outside the United States?[2] Hofstede (33;34) and Trompenaars (78) have shown that it does not always hold (see Chapter 2). For instance, in countries higher on uncertainty avoidance (such as Greece and Japan) as compared with those lower on uncertainty avoidance (such as the United States), security motivates employees more strongly than does self-actualization. As a result, employees in high-uncertainty-avoidance countries often consider job security and long-term employment more important than holding a more interesting or challenging job. Also contrasting with the American pattern, social needs often dominate the motivation of workers in countries such as Denmark, Norway, and Sweden that stress the quality of life (Hofstede's quality-of-life dimension) over materialism and productivity (Hofstede's career success dimension).[3] People in more collectivist countries, such as Pakistan, tend to stress social needs over the more individualistic ego and self-actualization needs stressed in countries such as the United States. Researchers Ronen and Shenkar helped expand our understanding of collectivism with a parallel concept, "collectualization," which they define as the "realization of self through behavior aimed at enhancing the in-group's welfare" (65). Given the conflicting patterns of motivation of people in individual versus group-oriented cultures, managers using Americans' highly individualist motivation theories must ask:

> *In what cultural and historical context does the greatest good involve being able to break apart from one's collective base to stand alone, self-sufficient and self-contained? In the context of an individualistic society in which individualism and self-containment is the ideal, the person who most separates . . . [himself or herself] from the group is thereby seen as embodying that ideal most strongly; the person who remains wedded to a group is not . . . [the] esteemed ideal* (67:776).

Economically developing countries, in contrast to the United States and most advanced economies, often exhibit relatively high uncertainty avoidance, low individualism, high power distance, and a relatively low emphasis on career success (3;31;32;34;38). Community dominates individualism, for example, in most East African nations. The community

> *dominates all aspects of African thought. Dances are communal and worship is communal. Property was held communally before the colonial era and there are attempts today to reinstate that practice. This inbuilt bias toward the community means that individualism is always seen as a deviance* (56:35).

The African norm most clearly valued ". . . is traditional communal responsibility, revealed partly in the condemnation of self-seeking individualism" (68:358). Clearly the motivation of employees from more collective-oriented cultures differs from that of their more individualistic American counterparts.

Numerous research studies testing the hierarchies of needs in different cultures demonstrate similar, but not identical, rank ordering in such diverse cultures as Argentina (35), Anglophone and Francophone Canada (40), Chile (35), India (35;39), Japan (63), Korea (13;42), Liberia (35), Libya (12) Mexico (63;64), the Middle East (3;6;7), Peru (75;81), Russia (18), South Africa (35), Thailand (63), Turkey (63), and Venezuela (63). Although the conflicting patterns of research findings fail to offer definitive conclusions, they strongly indicate that we should not assume that the rank ordering of motivational needs holds universally (34;10). In summary,

> *Studies have found that an individual's frame of reference will determine the order of importance of his needs. It has also been found that his frame of reference is in part determined by his culture. Therefore, it can be said that an individual's needs are partially bound by culture* (60).

Human needs may well include fundamental or universal aspects, but their importance and the ways in which they express themselves vary across cultures.

THREE MOTIVES: ACHIEVEMENT, POWER, AND AFFILIATION

David McClelland, another American theorist, suggested that three important motives drive people: the needs for achievement, power, and affiliation (49). Although McClelland later focused on executives' needs for power (50), he initially emphasized the need for achievement as fundamental in explaining why some societies produce more than others (48). In his famous studies in India, for example, he found that entrepreneurs trained in the need for achievement performed better than did untrained entrepreneurs (also see 36).

Comparative research has shown achievement motivation to be relatively robust across cultures (66). Managers in New Zealand, for example, follow the same pattern observed in the United States (28).

WHAT MOTIVATES A PERSON?
A New Hotel on Tahiti

A major hotel chain chose to develop a new hotel on the island of Tahiti. The developer contracted with a Tahitian skilled in carving large wooden *ti'i* (totems). The hotel desired a number of these *ti'i* to provide the site with local island atmosphere. The Tahitian quoted a price for carving the first *ti'i* and then higher and higher prices for each succeeding totem. This, of course, astonished the hotel developer, who asserted that this was no way to do business. Didn't the Tahitian understand the concept of quantity discounts? The Tahitian artisan, equally mystified, also tried to explain: "No, it is you who doesn't understand. Carving the first *ti'i* is fun. Carving each additional *ti'i* becomes less fun" (55:134).

Hofstede, however, questions how universal the needs for achievement, power, and affiliation really are (34). Hofstede begins by pointing out that the word *achievement* itself is hardly translatable into any language other than English (34:55). Based on his analysis, Hofstede found that countries with a high need for achievement also have a high need to produce (Hofstede's career success dimension) and a strong willingness to accept risk (Hofstede's weak uncertainty avoidance). As shown in Figure 2-5 (p. 58), Anglo countries such as Canada, Great Britain, and the United States (characterized by weak uncertainty avoidance combined with a strong commitment to career success) follow the high achievement motivation pattern, and countries such as Chile and Portugal (strong uncertainty avoidance combined with an equally strong commitment to quality of life) follow the low achievement motivation pattern. Although helpful in explaining human behavior, the needs for achievement, power, and affiliation have not been shown to be universal (see the box "What Motivates a Person? A New Hotel on Tahiti").

THE TWO-FACTOR MOTIVATION THEORY

Frederick Herzberg (26;27) suggested that certain extrinsic factors (those associated with the environment surrounding a job) have only the power to demotivate employees, whereas intrinsic factors (those associated with the job itself) have the power to energize, or motivate, people. The extrinsic and potentially demotivating factors largely correspond to the lower-order physiological and safety needs in Maslow's need hierarchy. They include factors associated with job dissatisfaction, such as poor working conditions, supervision, relations with co-workers, salary, company policy, and administration. Intrinsic factors, or motivators, which correspond to the higher-order needs on the need hierarchy, include the work itself, responsibility, recognition for work well done, achievement, and advancement.

More recent research has questioned Herzberg's two categories. Studies have shown, for example, that people sometimes continue a particular course of action because they have made a prior public commitment to it and not because it continues to be rewarding (72). Similarly, some people, who gain intrinsic satisfaction from a particular activity, switch to explaining their motivation in extrinsic terms after having received an extrinsic reward (often labeled as retrospective sense-making [see 72, among others] or the "overjustification hypothesis" [46]; also see cognitive evaluation theory [15]). Others indicate that some behavior is random and neither as goal oriented nor as rational as many American motivation theories would suggest (62).

Hofstede (33:385-388;34) again points out that culture influences factors that motivate and demotivate behavior. According to his dimensions, it is not surprising that the highly individualistic, productivity-oriented American culture has focused on job enrichment (the restructuring of individual jobs to increase productivity); whereas the more quality-of-life oriented and slightly more collectivist societies of Sweden and Norway have developed sociotechnical systems and new approaches to the quality of working life (such as the restructuring of employees into work groups to achieve the same ends).

When researchers tested Herzberg's two-factor theory outside the United States, they failed to confirm his initial findings (29). Results in New Zealand, for example, failed to replicate those in the United States. In New Zealand, supervision and interpersonal relationships appear to contribute significantly to satisfaction and not merely to reducing dissatisfaction (28). Similarly, in the former Panama Canal Zone, researchers found that citizens of Asia, Canada, Europe, Latin America, the Republic of Panama, and the West Indies cited certain extrinsic factors as satisfiers with greater frequency than did their American counterparts (14).

Similar to other motivation theories, the universality of Herzberg's two-factor theory cannot be assumed. In every culture, certain factors act as motivators and others act as demotivators. Specific motivators and their relative importance are unique to each culture and, all too frequently, to each situation. Managers entering a new culture should observe which factors appear important and not assume that their prior experience in other cultures is transferable.

EXPECTANCY THEORIES

Expectancy theories (44;79;80) claim that people are driven by the expectation that their acts will produce certain results. Workers assess both their ability to perform a task and the probable type of reward for successful performance (continued employment, a paycheck, or the ability to support one's family, for example). According to expectancy theories, the likelihood that an action will lead to certain outcomes or goals (E), multiplied by the attractiveness of the outcome $(V$, its valence) equals motivation $(M = E \times V)$ (45). Expectancy theories depend on the extent to which people believe they have control over the outcomes of their efforts, as well as on managers' abilities to identify desired rewards, both of which vary across cultures. Although expectancy theories have clearly advanced our understanding of motivation, they equally clearly vary cross-culturally.[4]

A review of our understanding of motivation (71:650-651) underscores the prevalent assumption that "whether the driving force is thought to be prior reinforcement, need fulfillment, or expectancies of future gain, the individual is assumed to be a rational maximizer of personal utility." Unfortunately, this individual, calculative view of motivation has questionable applicability in many regions outside the United States and therefore indicates "a fundamental omission in our motivation theories" (71:651; also see 11;19;43).

In countries where individualism dominates, for example, employees see their relationship with the organization from a calculative perspective; whereas in collectivist societies, the ties between the individual and the organization rely on a moral component (4;11;57). Clearly people become committed to organizations for very different reasons in individualistic and collectivist societies (72). Employees with collectivist values make organizational commitments because of their personal ties to managers, owners, and co-workers (collectivism) and much less because of the nature of the job or the particular compensation scheme (individualistic incentives [11]). In Brazil, for example, where people's personal and work lives are highly integrated, it is common for major firms

> to help employees with personal financial problems. For example, because of a lack of public social services, employees may have an illness in the family which puts them in a precarious financial position. The personnel departments of larger Brazilian firms regularly provide assistance to employees in such a situation, thus mitigating the impact of the employees' problems on the functioning of the firm (38:292).

Given its individualistic orientation, it is not surprising that the United States exhibits a pattern different from that of Brazil. While Brazilians expect their firms to take care of employees' personal needs, Americans have no such expectations and therefore much less loyalty to their employers. It is not a coincidence that the United States (and not Brazil) has the most executive search firms and the highest level of executive and managerial mobility in the world (11).

As discussed in Chapter 1 (see discussion of the dominance-harmony cultural dimension), people in different cultures vary in the amount of control they believe they have over their environment. Most Americans strongly believe that they control the relevant aspects of their environment. American managers believe that they directly influence the world in which they work (that is, they have a high level of internal attribution). Most American managers, for example, believe that "where there is a will, there is a way." By contrast, many managers in other parts of the world believe that they only partially control their work environment and the outcomes of their own behavior (that is, they attribute the causes of some events to external circumstances). Many Muslim managers, for example, believe that things will happen only if God wills them to happen (external attribution). Many Latin American managers believe that it is important to be from the right family and social class (external attribution). Many Hong Kong Chinese executives believe that there is an element of *joss*, or luck, involved in all transactions (external attribution). In contrast, most American managers believe that effective problem solving and hard work will get the job done (internal attribution). Expectancy theories work best in explaining the motivation of people in cultures that emphasize internal attribution.

The rewards people want from work also vary greatly across cultures. As discussed in reference to the needs hierarchy, security is very important to some people, congenial relationships are paramount for others, and individual status and respect (career success) dominate for others. A classic study investigated the work goals of 19,000 employees in a large multinational electrical equipment manufacturer operating in 46 countries and reported the results for such countries as Argentina, Australia, Austria, Belgium, Brazil, Canada, Chile, Colombia, Denmark, Finland, France, Germany, India, Israel, Japan, Mexico, New Zealand, Norway, Peru, South Africa, Sweden, Switzerland, the United Kingdom, the United States, and Venezuela (69). In every country, the five most important goals included achievement, especially individual achievement. Next in importance were the immediate environment, general features of the organization, and employment conditions such as pay and work hours. Some of the major differences among the cultural groups included the following (69):

- English-speaking countries ranked higher on individual achievement and lower on the desire for security.

- French-speaking countries, although similar to the English-speaking countries, gave greater importance to security and somewhat less to challenging work.

- Northern European countries expressed less interest in "getting ahead" and work recognition goals and put more emphasis on job accomplishment; in addition, they showed more concern for people and less for the organization as a whole (it was important for them that the job not interfere with their personal lives).

- Latin American and Southern European countries found individual achievement somewhat less important; Southern Europeans placed the highest emphasis on job security, while both groups of countries emphasized fringe benefits.

- Germany ranked high on security and fringe benefits and among the highest on "getting ahead."

- Japan, although low on advancement, also ranked second highest on challenge and lowest on autonomy, with a strong emphasis on good working conditions and a friendly working environment.

Expectancy theories are universal to the extent that they do not specify the types of rewards that motivate a given group of employees (54). Managers themselves must determine the level and types of reward most sought after by a particular group. Although this study's conclusions support the idea that basic human needs are similar, they highlight the fact that culture and environment determine how human needs can best be met.

Global human resource systems are replete with examples of overgeneralization resulting from overreliance on U.S.-based reward structures. For example (as described in Chapter 1), raising the salaries of a particular group of Mexican workers motivated them to work fewer, not more, hours. As the Mexicans explained, "We can now make enough money to live and enjoy life [one of their primary values] in less time than before. Now we do not have to work so many hours." In another example, an expatriate Canadian manager in Japan decided to promote one of his Japanese sales representatives to manager (a status reward). To the surprise of the Canadian, the promotion diminished the new Japanese manager's performance. Why? Japanese have a high need for harmony—to fit in with their work colleagues. The promotion, an individualistic reward, separated the new manager from his colleagues, embarrassed him, and therefore diminished his motivation to work.

CULTURAL INTELLIGENCE

New theories are beginning to address the cultural void in motivation theories. Cultural intelligence, for example, refers to "a person's capability to adapt effectively to new cultural contexts" (16:59). The three aspects of cultural intelligence—cognitive, motivational, and behavioral—help to explain motivation as well as other managerial behaviors.

Cognitive aspects of cultural intelligence include thinking, learning and strategizing (17:105). They explain how we learn to think. Cultural intelligence helps us to understand how our perceptions can aid or hinder our cross-cultural understanding when faced with new situations.

Motivational aspects of cultural intelligence include effectiveness, confidence, persistence, value congruence, and the level of affinity or attraction toward a new culture (17:105). Motivational aspects of cultural intelligence explain how strongly we hold our particular cultural values and norms toward a new culture when encountering it for the first time.

Behavioral aspects of cultural intelligence include a person's range of possible actions and responses that can be used in intercultural encounters, as well as the ability to acquire new behaviors when needed (17:108). "Knowing" what to do and exerting the effort to learn new behaviors is not enough; it is also important to be able to draw on a repertoire of previously learned behaviors that are appropriate for the particular situation (17:108).

Although definitions of "intelligence" are culture bound (77:25), developing the cognitive, motivational, and behavioral aspects of cultural intelligence can powerfully increase international managers' efficacy when interacting across cultures. Culturally intelligent managers suspend judgment and understand the nuances of diverse situations, while striving to contain their instinctive ethnocentrism (77).

BEYOND MOTIVATION: INSPIRATION

People commit to work long into the night and contribute everything they have to give, not when they are merely motivated, but when they are inspired. People become inspired when they are working for some higher purpose that they believe in. As described in the Box "Universal Inspiration: Beyond Motivation," Norske Skog inspired its employees worldwide by committing to improve the world for their children's sake. As you read Norske Skog's story, think about other companies you know of that have taken similar strategies. Consider what approaches you might use that would inspire the people you work with.

BEYOND MOTIVATION
Universal Inspiration

September 2001 was not a good month for the world. The month opened with the United Nations–sponsored World Conference Against Racism in Durban, South Africa.[5] As the world watched with high expectations, the conference drowned in a cacophony of intolerance, expressed by official delegates from more than 160 countries as well as by thousands of representatives of non-governmental organizations. "The meeting, which was intended to celebrate tolerance and diversity, became an international symbol of divisiveness. . . ." (76). According to the world press, the results "reflect less a new international unity than a collective exhaustion" (70:A1). As one delegate summarized, "Far too much of the time at this conference has been consumed by bitter, divisive exchanges on issues which have done nothing to advance the cause of combating racism . . . [The final documents] contain language which will do nothing to achieve greater peace . . ." (70:A1/A12).

One week later, on September 11th, terrorists destroyed the World Trade Center and parts of the Pentagon, killing more than 3,000 people. In the immediate aftermath, public rhetoric and behavior, especially in the United States, became increasingly susceptible to simplistic definitions of good and evil and to the call for large-scale military retaliation—(rhetoric that inevitably increases the possibility of further loss of innocent lives). The escalation of ignorance-based hatred attempting to pit the Western world against Islamic communities and nations became palpable. Perhaps the danger, absurdity, and pain can best be symbolized by the fate of a woman living far from both Durban and the World Trade Center. As the woman, a Montreal doctor, made her usual hospital rounds the week after the terrorist attacks, she was strangled. Why? Strictly because she was Muslim wearing the traditional headscarf. Her status as a physician and good citizen, working daily to save the lives of her fellow human beings, was obliterated in the eyes of her attacker solely because she practiced a religion he failed to understand. During the same week, miles away in the Middle East, Israeli children admitted to reporters that they no longer "imagine ever having a Palestinian friend" nor did their Palestinian counterparts imagine having an Israeli friend. None could foresee living in peace. As one 13 year old murmured, while staring at his hands, "It'll end by war. Either we'll die or they'll die" (30:6).

The New York-based director of the Center for the Advancement of Human Rights, after spending a week in Durban, concluded, "Sadly, hate . . . was all too evident at this global conference in the new South Africa in which so many placed their hopes" (21). Hate and intolerance, optimism reduced to hopelessness, compassion eclipsed by anger, ignorance motivating senseless action: Is this the scenario that will define the twenty-first century; that will define our children's future? Possibly, but hopefully not.

Although from the perspective of September 2001 it may seem otherwise, the twenty-first century is not just a time of terrorism, intolerance, and fear. It also heralds an era of unprecedented global communication, global contact, and global commerce (20). However, the ability of global companies to work successfully across cultures, while better than the track record of participants at

BEYOND MOTIVATION
Universal Inspiration (continued)

U.N. racism conferences, remains humbling. Historically, over 50 percent of all international joint ventures fail.[6] As everyone who watched the much-touted Daimler/Chrysler debacle knows, in this case, unfortunately, the statistics don't lie. The seeds of failure become particularly evident when one overhears the chorus of Daimler/Chrysler's American managers blaming the company's 50 percent drop in value on the "bull-headed, dominant, and just plain dishonest" German managers, while Daimler/Chrysler's German managers, with equal vehemence, blame the company's problems on the Americans being "unworldly and too focused on the bottom line" (41).[7] One wonders, at times, why societies choose to continue to become more globally interconnected and companies choose to continue to expand beyond their borders, when the track record of global cross-cultural relations remains so dismal. Weaving the peoples of the world together into a global "human family" is clearly not easy. Our historical approaches beg for new perspectives.

Norske Skog, a Norwegian-based global company, may give us a glimpse at just such a new perspective; one with positive implications both for companies and for society. Until almost the end of the twentieth century, Norske Skog was a domestic paper company with operations almost exclusively in Norway. Then, over a period of five years, the company expanded throughout Europe. Then, following the pattern taken by so many other companies, Norske Skog went global. Among its other acquisitions, it bought a New Zealand-based company with operations throughout Asia and the Americas. In a mere five years, Norske Skog more than doubled its size and went from being a local Norwegian company to the most global firm in its industry. The immediate challenges facing Norske Skog were the same as those that face all newly global companies: How to create a global organizational culture in which people from throughout the world are inspired to work effectively together? How to benefit from the company's newly acquired global scale, scope, and diversity? How to reap the benefits of employees' cultural diversity, rather than allowing such diversity to undermine the company's future success?

Norske Skog's initial response to creating an organizational culture that would be appropriately globally integrated, locally responsive, and skilled at worldwide learning in many ways replicated that of other global companies (9). In one fundamental respect, however, the company's strategy did not at all follow traditional approaches. Rather than relying solely on Norske Skog's and other companies' experience, or the plethora of global strategies offered by management consultants, Norske Skog went beyond traditional approaches and chose a process that inspired everyone to give their very best to the company. They chose to include the perspectives of children in their deliberations. By reaching out to their children, they forced themselves to consider the impacts of their decisions on the company and on society for generations to come.

BEYOND MOTIVATION
Universal Inspiration (continued)

Immediately following the New Zealand acquisition, Norske Skog invited the children of its employees on four continents to help them understand what global cooperation means, and could mean, for society, companies, and individuals. The children did not shy away from the task. In paintings, essays, and sculptural models, they told their parents and the company what it would mean to them to know and to work with people from around the world, people very different from themselves. They expressed their hopes and their fears.[8] Trude Jorid Mosling, an 11-year-old from Norway, for example, told the company:

> We have to be good to the world we live in. Even if we don't have the same culture, and even if some of us are white and some are brown, it doesn't make any difference. . . . Actually it's good that there are differences . . . because . . . we can teach each other things. . . .

From half way around the world, another 11-year-old, Julia McKean of Sydney, Australia, explained that by effectively communicating across cultures, differences among the peoples of the world can become a potential benefit—what managers, but not 11-year-olds, often refer to as cultural synergy. Julia wrote:

> I think that people communicating together, freely and happily, is what people need to do to live together in peace. Without communication the world would become one big war. In our world there are many people who believe in different religions and gods, there are people with different coloured skin, people who speak different languages and people who look different. If all these people stayed in groups where everyone was the same, our world would not be as good a place to live. . . . Without communication the different groups of people would become enemies and fight against each other.

Catherine Goodfellow, a 13-year-old Australian with wisdom well beyond her years—wisdom that appears to have been scarce among the adults deliberating in Durban—added her perspective:

> We will never have a human race that is the same. People will always have different eye, skin and hair colour, [different] races, religions and values. Instead of letting our vast differences draw us apart, we should let them bring us together.

The children, while inherently optimistic, did not shirk from the pain in the world, even when it affected children living very differently from themselves. For example, 12-year-old Nicole Cordova, a Brazilian, reported:

> I am sad when I see thin . . . children on TV, dying of hunger and diseases. . . . The mothers have no tears left to cry. It is sad and humiliating to see such scenes.

BEYOND MOTIVATION
Universal Inspiration (continued)

Nor did the children ignore that different perspectives can lead to conflict. An Australian, Catherine Goodfellow, reflected,

> *It is inevitable that people will have ideas that come into conflict. . . . [Yet,] only through the cooperation of people with different cultural roots can greater equality and knowledge be achieved.*

Perhaps 8-year-old Canadian Jesse Swanson, in his painting and words, found the essence of global cooperation that has eluded so many companies and countries (see Jesse's painting on the next page).

The children spoke in words that everyone can understand. And the children's words and images brought the best of the adults—their parents—into the company's discussions. No longer limited to their professional roles—and thus to their sophisticated knowledge of what is not possible—the adults began discussing what their newly formed global company could, and should, accomplish from the broader, more optimistic, and more idealistic perspectives of professionals who are also (or perhaps, foremost) parents and human beings. As the company presented the children's stories, pictures, and sculptural models, they implicitly invited those fuller human beings, with their differences, into the room. Everyone immediately understood that in forming a global organizational culture, they were playing for much greater stakes than merely the success of the company. They were publicly and collectively taking responsibility for the type of world they would pass on to their children. The definition of winning suddenly far surpassed simply achieving a healthy bottom line. Winning became nothing less than the legacy they would be creating for their children and the world's children.

Are the employees and executives at Norske Skog inspired to work with each other? Yes. Are they inspired to cooperate on a global basis? Yes. Will the company beat the odds against succeeding as a global joint venture? Well, if the initial post-merger results are any indication, the answer will also be yes.

From 1999 to 2001, turnover doubled from approximately USD $2 billion to approximately USD $4 billion. Over the same period, earnings more than doubled, with margins being among the highest in the industry. In 2005, Norske Skog delivered the best total shareholder return in the paper industry, even though the newsprint industry had entered a slump in 2002. Norske Skog has grown from being a modest player to becoming the second largest supplier of newsprint in the world. Beginning in 1999, production of publication paper increased 40 percent over one year and 87 percent over two years.

Norske Skog's success story, moreover, is not limited to the financial and productivity indicators of a very healthy bottom line. The company also leads its industry in environmentally sound practices, including having become the world's largest user of recycled fibres for publication paper and, in the Southern Hemisphere, the largest user of plantation (rather than virgin) forests. Similarly, in the area of industrial relations, the company, drawing on its roots in the managerial cultures of

Jesse Swanson's Picture and Ideas

The lamp represents the guiding light in the quest for world peace and cooperation.

The lamp is for everyone to hold.

Scandinavia, has been able to maintain an organizational culture that continues to strongly encourage employee involvement. Employees continue to hold positions on the Board of Directors, and the company continues to consult and inform union representatives prior to each major expansion or divestment, even during periods of rapid change.

In their 2004 annual report, Norske Skog included CEO Jan Oksum's public commitment to a business strategy focused simultaneously on world benefit and outstanding financial performance. Norske Skog clearly rejects the "great trade-off illusion"—that doing good can only be accomplished at the expense of doing well. As the CEO states (59):

BEYOND MOTIVATION
Universal Inspiration (continued)

We have committed ourselves to contribute to sustainable development. Customers, suppliers and the world at large can rely on us. We take work on environmental issues seriously. Our values build on the UN universal declaration of human rights. These are not just fine words to us, but commitments which are demonstrated in specific actions. We were accordingly the first international pulp and paper company to sign a global agreement on employee rights with the International Federation of Chemical, Energy, Mine and General Workers' Unions (ICEM). On that basis, we have also developed a close and good collaboration with our unions through several channels, most recently the creation of a Global Employee Forum. The latter provides a common meeting place for employees and management, where we can give and receive information and discuss relevant issues relating to Norske Skog.

We also accept our social responsibility to the local communities in which our operations are pursued. Mills and employees involve themselves in a number of areas in these communities. We support many activities which help to improve the quality of life, health and knowledge.

Together with our customers, we are making a contribution internationally to improve reading skills among children and young people. We cooperate with the World Association of Newspapers on introducing the Newspapers in Education programme, particularly in new democracies where working conditions for a free press have improved. This commitment has both social and commercial objectives. International surveys show that the level of reading skills is not acceptable, even in Western countries. We are doing our bit to reverse this trend. Newspaper and magazine publishers must attract new generations of regular readers to survive in the future. It is clearly in our own interest that they succeed in this effort. Using newspapers in education is one instrument in that respect.

Will Norske Skog do well in the future? No one knows for sure. But most observers are not willing to bet against the company, not when their children's future is at stake.

The same week that Norske Skog held its first-year, global executive meeting in Oslo, the U.N. Conference on Racism in Durban, South Africa was collapsing into racist name calling, with countries and delegates quitting the meeting in disgust. The contrast with the dynamics at Norske Skog' meeting was immense. A for-profit, private-sector company found a way to commit itself to constructive, worldwide communication and action while many diplomats were failing at the same task?

One week after Norske Skog's global executive meeting, terrorists destroyed the World Trade Center in New York City. No one doubts that too many adults on this planet have failed to live together peacefully while respecting cultural, racial, and national differences. As we listen to the voices of children—recognizing that many of us have become too jaded and corroded by experience-based cynicism to

BEYOND MOTIVATION
Universal Inspiration (continued)

actually hear the relevance of their perspectives—maybe we should try again not just to listen, but to hear what they are saying.

"The moral universe rests upon the breath of school children."[9]

Source: Adapted in 2007 from Adler's "Global Companies, Global Society: There is a Better Way" (1).[10]

SUMMARY

Motivation is culture bound. Most motivation theories in use today were developed in the United States by Americans and focus on Americans. Of those that were not, many have been strongly influenced by American theories. Americans' strong emphasis on individualism has led to expectancy and equity theories of motivation: theories that emphasize rational, individual thought as the primary basis of human behavior. The emphasis placed on achievement is not surprising given Americans' willingness to accept risk and their high concern for performance. These theories therefore do not offer universal explanations of motivation; rather, they reflect Americans' values (19;34;43).

Unfortunately, many Americans as well as managers from other countries have treated American theories as the best or only way to understand motivation. They are neither. American motivation theories—too often assumed to reflect universal values—have failed to provide consistently useful explanations for behavior outside the United States. Managers must therefore guard against imposing domestic American management theories on their global business practices (19;37).

QUESTIONS FOR REFLECTION

1. **Cultural Roots of Motivation.** What are your own assumptions about motivation? Why do you think people work? List your own motivation assumptions and then analyze them from a cross-cultural perspective. In what ways are your assumptions similar to those of most of the people from your country? In what ways do they differ?

2. **Multinational Motivation.** Choose a country you have never lived or worked in. Then imagine that you have just been selected to become the new managing director in the country you selected—a country in which your company has decided to open a new industrial

complex. Neither you nor your company has ever worked in this country before. What would you do to motivate the employees from the foreign country to join your company and to work hard once employed?

3. **Inspiration Beyond Motivation.** What are some of the reasons that people would be extremely committed to work for a company? Imagine that they would be willing to work late and on the weekends because they are so committed. Which of the reasons you have identified are universal; that is, which do you think would be true worldwide? Which are culture specific? Why do you believe some of the reasons would strongly motivate people in some cultures but not in others?

4. **Designing Your Own Firm.** Imagine that you are starting your own company. Describe the company. Why, beyond receiving a paycheck, would people want to work for your company? How would you attract the best and the brightest people worldwide to work for your firm?

NOTES

1. Thor Heyerdahl is most known for his many explorations on his raft, the Kon-Tiki, each with crews of different creeds and cultural backgrounds. His voyages show that people can live and work together in peace.

2. Although Maslow's hierarchy has been questioned within the United States, it has become one of the accepted bases for explaining and understanding behavior within organizations. The validity of generalizing from this U.S.–based acceptance to worldwide applicability is questioned in this chapter.

3. Hofstede (32) originally labeled this dimension "masculinity/femininity." To better reflect its underlying meaning, it has been relabeled in this book as "career success/quality of life." For a more in-depth discussion of this dimension, see Chapter 2.

4. "After reviewing the literature, Ambrose & Kulik (1999) concluded that little or no advances have been made in expectancy theory research in the past decade" (43).

5. The official title of the U.N. Conference was the United Nations' World Conference Against Racism, Racial Discrimination, Xenophobia and Related Intolerance.

6. For research on the instability of international joint ventures, see Yan and Zeng's summary (82). Although the definitions (complete termination versus significant change of ownership) and overall results vary, numerous studies have reported substantial international joint venture instability, including 55% termination reported by Harrigan (24); 49% termination reported by Barkema and Vermeulen (8); and 68% instability through termination or acquisition reported by Park and Russo (61). Also see

Hammel's classic article "Competition for Competence and Inter-Partner Learning within International Strategic Alliances" (22).

7. Among many other reports on Daimler/Chrysler, see Jamison's "Far from a merger of equals" (41).

8. All children's quotes are published in the Norske Skog company booklet, "Only through the Cooperation of People with Different Cultural Roots Can Greater Equality and Knowledge Be Achieved" (58).

9. Based on Psalm VIII, 3 and Deuteronomy XXXI, 12, as traditionally interpreted by the rabbis and cited in *The Pentateuch and Haftorahs* (25:888).

10. An earlier version of this article was published by Adler (2) in the *Journal of Management Inquiry*. Reprinted by permission of Sage Publications, Inc.

REFERENCES

1. Adler, N. J. "Global Companies, Global Society: There is a Better Way" in Larraine Segil, Marshall Goldsmith, & James Belasco, eds., *Partnering: The New Face of Leadership* (New York: AMACOM, 2003), pp. 223–230.

2. Adler, N. J. "Global Companies, Global Society: There is a Better Way" *Journal of Management Inquiry*, vol. 11 (No. 3), 2002, pp. 255–260.

3. Adler, N. J.; & Boyacigiller, Nakiye. "Global Organizational Behavior: Going Beyond Tradition," *Journal of International Management*, vol. 1, no. 3 (1995), pp. 73–86.

4. Allen, Douglas B.; Miller, E. L.; & Nath, R. "North America," in R. Nath, ed., *Comparative Management* (Cambridge, Mass.: Ballinger, 1988), pp. 23–54.

5. Ambrose, Maureen L.; & Kulik, Carol T. "Old Friends, New Faces: Motivation Research in the 1990s," *Journal of Management*, vol. 25, no. 3 (1999), pp. 231–292.

6. Badawy, M. K. "Managerial Attitudes and Need Orientations of Mideastern Executives: An Empirical Cross-Cultural Analysis," *Academy of Management Proceedings*, vol. 39 (1979), pp. 293–297.

7. Badawy, M. K. "Styles of Mideastern Managers," *California Management Review*, vol. 22, no. 3 (1980), pp. 51–59.

8. Barkema, Harry; & Vermeulen, Freek. "What Differences in the Cultural Backgrounds of Partners are Detrimental for International Joint Ventures?" *Journal of International Business Studies*, vol. 28, no. 4 (1997), pp. 845–64.

9. Bartlett, Christopher; & Ghoshal, Sumantra. *Managing Across Borders: The Transnational Solution*, 2nd ed. (Boston: Harvard Business School Press, 1998).

10. Bluntt, P.; & Jones, M. L. *Managing African Organizations* (Berlin: Walter de Gruyter, 1992).

11. Boyacigiller, Nakiye; & Adler, N. J. "The Parochial Dinosaur: The Organizational Sciences in a Global Context," *Academy of Management Review,* vol. 16, no. 2 (1991), pp. 262–290.

12. Buera, A.; & Glueck, W. "Need Satisfaction of Libyan Managers," *Management International Review,* vol. 19, no. 1 (1979), pp. 113–123.

13. Chung, K. H.; Lee, H. C.; & Jung, K. H. *Korean Management: Global Strategy and Cultural Transformation* (Berlin: Walter de Gruyter, 1997).

14. Crabbs, R. A. "Work Motivation in the Culturally Complex Panama Canal Company," *Academy of Management Proceedings* (1973), pp. 119–126.

15. Deci, E.; & Ryan, R. "The Empirical Exploration of Intrinsic Motivational Processes," in L. Berkowitz, ed., *Advances in Experimental Social Psychology* (New York: Academic Press, 1980).

16. Earley, P. Christopher; & Ang, Soon. *Cultural Intelligence: Individual Interactions Across Cultures* (Stanford, Calif.: Stanford University Press, 2003).

17. Earley, P. Christopher; & Peterson, Randall S. "The Elusive Cultural Chameleon: Cultural Intelligence as a New Approach to Intercultural Training for the Global Manager," *Academy of Management Learning and Education,* vol. 3, no.1 (2004), pp. 100–115.

18. Elenkov, D. S. "Can American Management Concepts Work in Russia? A Cross-Cultural Comparative Study," *California Management Review,* vol. 40, no. 4 (1998), pp. 133–157.

19. Erez, Miriam; Kleinbeck, Uwe; & Thierry, Henk, eds., *Work Motivation in the Context of a Globalizing Economy.* (Mahwah, N.J.: Lawrence Erlbaum Associates, 2001).

20. Friedman, Thomas L. *The Lexus and the Olive Tree* (New York: Farrar, Straus, Giroux, 1999).

21. Gaer, Felice D., Director of the Jacob Blaustein Center for the Advancement of Human Rights, as reported in Rachel L. Swarns' "Race Talks Finally Reach Accord On Slavery and Palestinian Plight," *The New York Times* (September 9, 2001), p. 14.

22. Hammel, Gary. "Competition for Competence and Inter-Partner Learning within International Strategic Alliances," *Strategic Management Journal,* vol. 12, no. 1 (1991), pp. 83–103.

23. Hammer, W. C. "Motivation Theories and Work Applications," in S. Kerr, ed., *Organizational Behavior* (Columbus, Ohio: Grid Publishing, 1979), pp. 41–58.

24. Harrigan, Kathryn R. "Strategic Alliances and Partner Asymmetries" in F. Contractor & P. Lorange, eds., *Cooperative Strategies in International Business* (Lexington, Mass.: Lexington Books, 1988), pp. 205–226.

25. Hertz, J. H., ed. *The Pentateuch and Haftorahs,* 2nd ed. (London: Socino Press, 1971), p. 888.

26. Herzberg, F. "One More Time: How Do You Motivate Employees?" *Harvard Business Review* (January–February 1968), pp. 54–62.

27. Herzberg, F.; Mausner, B.; & Snyderman, B. *The Motivation to Work,* 2nd ed. (New York: Wiley, 1959).

28. Hines, G. H. "Achievement, Motivation, Occupations and Labor Turnover in New Zealand," *Journal of Applied Psychology,* vol. 58, no. 3 (1973), pp. 313–317.

29. Hines, G. H. "Cross-Cultural Differences in Two-Factor Theory," *Journal of Applied Psychology,* vol. 58, no. 5 (1973), pp. 375–377.

30. Hockstader, Lee. "Eighth Grade in the Mideast: A Curriculum of Hatred," *International Herald Tribune* (September 6, 2001).

31. Hofstede, Geert. *Cultures and Organizations: Software of the Mind* (London: McGraw-Hill, 1991).

32. Hofstede, Geert. *Culture's Consequences: International Differences in Work-Related Values* (Beverly Hills, Calif.: Sage, 1980).

33. Hofstede, Geert. *Culture's Consequences: Comparing Values, Behaviors, Institutions, and Organizations Across Nations,* 2nd ed. (Thousand Oaks, Calif.: Sage, 2001).

34. Hofstede, Geert. "Motivation, Leadership and Organization: Do American Theories Apply Abroad?" *Organizational Dynamics,* vol. 9, no. 1 (1980), pp. 42–63.

35. Howell, P.; Strauss, J.; & Sorensen, P. F. "Research Note: Cultural and Situational Determinants of Job Satisfaction among Management in Liberia," *Journal of Management Studies* (May 1975), pp. 225–227.

36. Hundal, P. S. "A Study of Entrepreneurial Motivation: Comparison of Fast- and Slow-Progressing Small Scale Industrial Entrepreneurs in Punjab, India," *Journal of Applied Psychology,* vol. 55, no. 4 (1971), pp. 317–323.

37. Illman, P. E. "Motivating the Overseas Work Force," in *Developing Overseas Managers and Managers Overseas* (New York: AMACOM, 1980), pp. 83–106.

38. Jaeger, A. M.; & Kanungo, R. N., eds., *Management in Developing Countries* (London: Routledge, 1990).

39. Jaggi, B. "Need Importance of Indian Managers," *Management International Review,* vol. 19, no. 1 (1979), pp. 107–113.

40. Jain, C. H.; & Kanungo, R. *Behavioral Issues in Management: The Canadian Context* (Toronto: McGraw-Hill Ryerson, 1977), pp. 85–99.

41. Jamison, B. "Far From a Merger of Equals," *ABCnews.com* (January 25, 2001).

42. Koch, M.; Nam, S. H.; & Steers, R. M. "Human Resource Management in South Korea," in L. Moore & D. Jennings, eds., *Human Resource Management on the Pacific Rim* (Berlin: Walter de Gruyter, 1995), pp. 217–242.

43. Latham, G. P.; & Pinder, C. C. "Work Motivation Theory and Research at the Dawn of the Twenty-First Century," *Annual Review of Psychology*, vol. 56 (2005), pp. 485–516.

44. Lawler, E. E., III. "Job Design and Employee Motivation," *Personnel Psychology*, vol. 22 (1969), pp. 426–435.

45. Lawler, E. E., III. *Pay and Organizational Effectiveness: A Psychological View* (New York: McGraw-Hill, 1971).

46. Lepper, M.; Greene, D.; & Nisbett, R. (1973). "Undermining Children's Intrinsic Interest With Extrinsic Rewards: A Test of the 'Overjustification' Hypothesis," *Journal of Personality and Social Psychology*, 28, 129–137.

47. Leung, Kwok. "Different Carrots for Different Rabbits: Effects of Individualism–Collectivism and Power Distance on Work Motivation" in Miriam Erez, Uwe Kleinbeck, & Henk Thierry, eds., *Work Motivation in the Context of a Globalizing Economy* (Mahwah, N.J.: Lawrence Erlbaum Associates, 2001), pp. 329–339.

48. McClelland, D. C. *The Achieving Society* (Princeton, N.J.: Van Nostrand, 1961).

49. McClelland, D. C.; Atkinson, J. W.; Clark, R. A.; & Lowell, E. L. *The Achievement Motive* (New York: Appleton-Century-Crofts, 1953).

50. McClelland, D. C.; & Burnham, D. H. "Power Is the Great Motivator," *Harvard Business Review*, vol. 54, no. 1 (1976), pp. 100–110.

51. Maslow, A. H. *Motivation and Personality* (New York: Harper & Row, 1954).

52. Maslow, A. H. "A Theory of Human Motivation," *Psychology Review* (July 1943), pp. 370–396.

53. Maslow, A. H. *Toward a Psychology of Being* (Princeton, N.J.: Van Nostrand, 1962).

54. Matsui, T.; & Terai, I. "A Cross-Cultural Study of the Validity of the Expectancy Theory of Work Motivation," *Journal of Applied Psychology*, vol. 60, no. 2 (1979), pp. 263–265.

55. Miller, J. J.; & Kilpatrick, J. A. *Issues for Managers: An International Perspective* (Homewood, Ill.: Irwin, 1987).

56. Mutiso, G. C. M. *Socio-Political Thought in African Literature: Weusi* (New York: Barnes and Noble, 1974).

57. Nath, R.; & Narayanan, V. K. "A Comparative Study of Managerial Support, Trust, Openness, Decision-Making, and Job Enrichment," *Academy of Management Proceedings*, vol. 40 (1980), pp. 48–52.

58. Norske Skog. "Only Through the Cooperation of People With Different Cultural Roots Can Greater Equality and Knowledge Be Achieved," *Norske Skog Company Booklet* (Oslo, Norway: Norske Skog, 2001).

59. Oksum, Jan. "CEO's Statement" *Norske Skog Annual Report* (Oslo, Norway, 2004), pp. 4–5.

60. O'Reilly, C. A.; & Roberts, K. H. "Job Satisfaction among Whites and Nonwhites," *Journal of Applied Psychology,* vol. 57, no. 3 (1973), pp. 295–299.

61. Park, Seung H.; & Russo, Michael V. "When Competition Eclipses Cooperation: An Event History Analysis of Joint Venture Failure," *Management Science,* vol. 42, no. 6 (1996), pp. 875–890.

62. Pfeffer, J. *Organizations and Organization Theory* (Boston: Pitman, 1982).

63. Reitz, H. J. "The Relative Importance of Five Categories of Needs among Industrial Workers in Eight Countries," *Academy of Management Proceedings* (1975), pp. 270–273.

64. Reitz, J.; & Grof, G. *Similarities and Differences Among Mexican Workers, in Attitudes to Worker Motivation* (Bloomington, Ind.: Indiana University, 1973).

65. Ronen, Simcha. "Self Actualization vs. Collectualization," in Miriam Erez, Uwe Kleinbeck, & Henk Thierry, eds., *Work Motivation in the Context of a Globalizing Economy* (Mahwah, N.J.: Lawrence Erlbaum Associates, 2001), pp. 341–368.

66. Sagie, A.; Elizur, D.; & Yamauchi, H. "The Structure and Strength of Achievement Motivation: A Cross-Cultural Comparison," *Journal of Organizational Behavior,* vol. 17, no. 5 (1996), pp. 431–444.

67. Sampson, E. D. "Psychology and the American Ideal," *Journal of Personality and Social Psychology,* vol. 35, no. 11 (November 1977), pp. 767–782.

68. Shelton, A. J. "Behavior and Cultural Value in West African Stories," *Literary Sources for the Study of Culture Contact, Africa,* vol. 34 (1964), pp. 353–359.

69. Sirota, D.; & Greenwood, M. J. "Understanding Your Overseas Workforce," *Harvard Business Review,* vol. 14 (January–February 1971), pp. 53–60.

70. Slackman, Michael. "Divisive U.N. Race Talks End in Accord," *Los Angeles Times* (September 9, 2001).

71. Staw, B. M. "Organizational Behavior: A Review and Reformulation of the Field's Outcome Variables," *Annual Review of Psychology,* vol. 35 (1984), pp. 627–666.

72. Staw, B. M. "Rationality and Justification in Organizational Life," in B. M. Staw & L. L. Cummings, eds., *Research in Organizational Behavior*, vol. 2 (Greenwich, Conn.: JAI Press, 1980), pp. 45–80.

73. Steers, R. M.; & Porter, L. W., eds., *Motivation and Work Behavior* (New York: McGraw-Hill, 1975).

74. Steers, Richard M.; & Sanchez-Runde, Carlos. "Culture, Motivation, and Work Behavior," in Martin J. Gannon & Karen L. Newman, eds., *Handbook of Cross-Cultural Management* (London: Basil Blackwell, 2001), pp. 190–216.

75. Stephens, D.; Kedia, B.; & Ezell, D. "Managerial Need Structures in U.S. and Peruvian Industries," *Management International Review*, vol. 19 (1979), pp. 27–39.

76. Swarns, Rachel L. "Race Talks Finally Reach Accord on Slavery and Palestinian Plight," *New York Times* (September 9, 2001), p. A1.

77. Triandis, Harry C. "Cultural Intelligence in Organizations," *Group and Organization Management*, vol. 31, no. 1 (2006), pp. 20-26.

78. Trompenaars, Fons; & Hampden-Turner, Charles. *Riding the Waves of Culture* (London: The Economist Books, 1998).

79. Vroom, V. H. *Work and Motivation* (New York: Wiley, 1964).

80. Vroom, V. H.; & Yetton, P. W. *Leadership and Decision Making* (Pittsburgh, Penn.: University of Pittsburgh Press, 1973).

81. Williams, L. K.; Whyte, W. F.; & Green, C. S. "Do Cultural Differences Affect Workers' Attitudes?" *Industrial Relations,* vol. 5 (1966), pp. 105–117.

82. Yan, Aimin; & Zeng, Ming. "International Joint Venture Instability: A Critique of Previous Research, A Reconceptualization, and Directions for Future Research," *Journal of International Business Studies*, vol. 30, no. 2 (1999), pp. 397–414.

Chapter 8

Multinational Decision Making

It could be argued that the essence of living is free choice—the process of making decisions. To be deprived of choices is to lose all meaning (4:59).

Decision making plays a central role in management; for some people, management *is* decision making (24). The higher the level of management, the greater the number, the higher the complexity, and the more significant the impact of the decisions made. Leadership involves making decisions that affect whole organizations, divisions within organizations, and increasingly today, society itself. Motivational efforts, when viewed from the perspective of decision making, are simply the choices leaders make in attempting to positively influence the behavior of their colleagues, clients, and employees. Similarly, planning can be viewed as making sets of related decisions among available options. The ultimate dilemma faced by all decision makers is that no amount of sophistication can allay the fact that all knowledge is about the past and all decisions are about the future. Decision makers always act on the basis of inadequate and incomplete knowledge. With the 21st century's rapid and discontinuous changes in society, the economy, and technology, this is even more true today than it has ever been in the past. Good decision makers in every culture are those who learn not only to cope with the ambiguity and uncertainty of reality, but to thrive on it. In the past, managers could successfully base their decisions primarily on their own experience and their own culture; today such a circumscribed domestic perspective no longer works.

Organization theorists have argued for years about how people make decisions. Some believe that managerial decision making reflects a conscious, rational process in which managers select criteria and use them to evaluate alternative solutions to particular problems. In choosing profit maximization as a prime decision-making criterion, for example, private-sector managers might assess a range of business opportunities relative to their potential to generate profit. Alternatively,

207

an equally rational decision rule might be *satisficing;* that is, meeting acceptable standards on several criteria rather than maximizing performance on a single criterion. When satisficing, managers might assess alternatives until they identify at least one option that would generate an acceptable profit margin while at the same time integrating new, ecologically sound industrial processes. Without further search they would select that alternative. However, no decision-making process, no matter how sophisticated, will produce effective outcomes if it is not based on superior options.

Contact with other cultures creates new challenges when we attempt to use strictly objective, rational processes. As futurist Robert Theobold (28:42) observed,

> *"We are all having increasing problems as we come to understand that different people have profoundly different visions of reality, and that there is no objective way of sorting out which of these visions is correct."*

Increasingly today, given the complexity and rapidly changing nature of social, cultural, and business environments, experts recognize that managers do not make all of their decisions using time-consuming logical and rational decision-making processes, but rather make many of their most important decisions instantly and intuitively (6). Intuitive decision making works best when managers allow themselves to instantly recognize cues as patterns, which in turn allow them to act based on their past experience and the sense they have made of their experience (14:28). In short, action is based on intuition and intuition is based on instantly recognizing and evaluating prior experience.

Noted psychoanalyst Sigmund Freud believed that human decision making was almost completely irrational—that forces outside of our conscious control drive decision making. Herbert Simon (23;24), in his administrative theory of individual decision making, describes the process managers use to make decisions as "bounded rationality." According to Simon, managers make choices based on simplified rather than real situations. This "subjective rationality" narrows and alters the objective facts. Because managers from different cultures perceive the world differently, their subjective rationalities differ, as do their ways of simplifying complex realities into perceived environments in which they become capable of making choices.

Along this rational/irrational spectrum, some theorists believe that one best way exists to make decisions; others believe that the best way depends on the particular situation one faces. In certain situations, for example, companies should maximize profit; in others they should attempt to maximize societal well-being and the firm's financial performance simultaneously; in yet other situations they should satisfice; and in still others they should base their decisions on intuition rather than on traditional, rational economic analysis. In this chapter we will look at some of the ways in which decision making is culturally contingent; that is, the ways in which the best approach depends on the values, beliefs, attitudes, and behavioral patterns of the people involved (2). Cultural contingency is, in fact, just one more contingency in the "fit" models of decision making; the decision-making style must fit the culture.

Traditional decision-making processes involve five basic steps (3, based on 4;24):

1.   Problem recognition
2.   Information search
3.   Construction of alternatives
4.   Choice
5.   Implementation

These steps suggest the following cross-cultural questions: Do managers from different cultures perceive problems in similar ways? Do they gather similar types and amounts of information while investigating a problem? Do they construct similar types of solutions? Do they use similar strategies for choosing between alternatives? Do they implement their decisions in similar ways? The answer to each question is no. As illustrated in Table 8-1, at each step culture influences the ways in which managers make decisions and solve problems.

TABLE 8-1 Cultural Contingencies of Decision Making

Five Steps in Decision Making	Cultural Variations	
1. Problem Recognition	*Problem Solving* We should change the situation.	*Situation Acceptance* Some situations should be accepted as they are.
2. Information Search	*Gathering "facts"*	*Gathering ideas and possibilities*
3. Construction of Alternatives	*New, future-oriented alternatives* Adults can learn and change.	*Past-, present-, and future-oriented alternatives* Adults cannot change.
4. Choice	*Individual decision making* Decision-making responsibility is delegated. Decisions are made quickly. Decision rule: Is it true or false?	*Team decision making* Senior managers often make decisions. Decisions are made slowly. Decision rule: Is it good or bad?
5. Implementation	*Slow* Managed from the top Responsibility of one person	*Fast* Involves participation of all levels Responsibility of team

PROBLEM RECOGNITION

When is a problem a problem? When do people from different cultures recognize that a problem exists? Based on differences in a society's orientation to activity—to "getting things done" (see Chapter 1)—some cultures emphasize solving problems while others accept situations as they are. In certain cultures, such as the United States, managers perceive most situations as problems to be solved, as opportunities for improvement through change. Other cultures, such as those of the Indonesians, Malays, Thais, and most aboriginal peoples in North America, tend to see no need to change most situations, but rather frequently accept life as it is.

If a problem-solving manager receives a notice that a prime supplier will be three months late in delivering needed construction materials, she will immediately attempt to speed up delivery or find an alternate supplier. If, by contrast, a situation-accepting manager receives a similar notice of delay, he might simply accept that the project will be delayed. Situation-accepting managers believe that they neither can nor should alter every situation that confronts them. Problem-solving managers believe that they both can and should change situations to their own benefit. Situation-accepting managers generally believe that fate or God's will intervenes in the production process (external attribution), whereas problem-solving managers are more likely to believe that they are the prime or only influence on the same process (internal attribution). Consequently, when considering exactly the same situation, American managers might identify a problem long before their Indonesian, Malay, or Thai counterparts would choose to define the situation as a problem. Comparative research has demonstrated that managers' perceptions of situations and their definitions of problems indeed vary across cultures.

INFORMATION SEARCH

After recognizing that a problem exists, where does the manager gather information to solve it? The noted psychoanalyst Carl Jung suggested two primary modes of gathering information (i.e., of perceiving): sensing and intuition. Sensors primarily use their five senses to gather information and facts about a situation; intuitive people more frequently gather ideas from the past and future in their attempt to understand the situation. Sensors rely on facts and often employ a more inductive information-gathering style; intuitive people rely more heavily on images and often employ a more deductive style. Cervantes' *Don Quixote*, the archetypal intuitive, symbolically captures the thinking pattern of intuitive people:

> *When life itself seems lunatic, who knows where madness lies?*
> *Perhaps to be too practical is madness. To surrender dreams—this*
> *too may be madness. To seek treasure where there is only trash. Too*

much sanity may be madness. And the maddest of all, to see life as it is and not as it should be.[1]

Today, Canadian designer Bruce Mau, in his work on "massive change," challenges us in a way similar to the mythic Don Quixote, by asking "Now that we can do anything, what do we want to do?" (15). Similarly, Benjamin Zander, Boston Philharmonic conductor and winner of one of the Davos World Economic Forum's top leadership awards, works with executives in engaging the "art of possibility" (29).

Cultures vary in the extent to which one or the other style of data gathering–of perceiving the world–dominates. During the 1973 Yom Kippur war in the Middle East, for example, the Americans, in a manner typical of sensors, assessed the situation pessimistically for the Israelis because one hundred million Arabs were at war with fewer than eight million Israelis. The Americans based their perception of the situation on fact-oriented, empirical evidence. The Israelis, who are typically more intuitive, based their predictions on their image of the future— the continued existence of a free and democratic Jewish state—and therefore remained more optimistic. Moreover, the Israelis felt that the relative number of Arabs and Israelis was relevant in determining how they would fight the war but was irrelevant in influencing their beliefs about who would win the war. In a similar contrast of perceptual styles, many English Canadians—typically sensors—questioned the economic viability of Quebec if the province separated from the rest of Canada. They consequently predicted that people of Quebec would vote to remain a part of Canada in the referendum on separation. Many French Canadians, more typically using intuitive perceptions, continued to reiterate their vision of a culturally and linguistically distinct Francophone nation. These French Canadians, while recognizing the economic consequences of separation, considered them less relevant to the validity of their over-all goal (see 19). While the province eventually opted to remain in Canada, the vote was almost evenly split between those wishing to separate from Canada and those choosing to keep the country intact.

CONSTRUCTING ALTERNATIVES

What types of alternatives do we construct? Are they predominantly new ideas or ideas rooted in the past? Are they ideas that demand large or moderate amounts of change? Based on a culture's underlying values, the types of alternatives they most seriously consider vary. People from more future-oriented cultures, such as California, tend to generate more new alternatives. Think, for example, of the number of ideas generated by Silicon Valley firms. People from more conservative, past-oriented cultures, such as England, tend to search for historical patterns on which to base alternatives. Californians, when attempting to minimize urban congestion, would be more likely to consider "flying cars" and networks of home offices connected through the Internet; the British would be more likely to consider improved traffic control (such as their implementation in 2006 of a toll to access the London city center by car) and rapid transit mechanisms. Both societies consider both types of alternatives; but, in each, one type is preferred (16:35). For some past-oriented Africans, acquiring a modern education is equivalent to rejecting the ways of their ancestors. Such an attitude contrasts sharply with the support of more future-oriented Californians for the world-renowned University of California system (16:35) (see time dimension in Chapter 1).

Similarly, some cultures believe that adults can change, whereas other cultures believe that adults basically remain unchangeable (see discussion of how people see themselves in Chapter 2). Cultures that believe in change stress alternatives such as adult education and on-the-job training; those that believe in permanence stress initial selection. Today, a company's orientation toward change is often reflected in its approach to technology: "Can we train our present employees to learn to use each new generation of technology (thus believing change is possible), or must we hire new, generally younger employees who are already comfortable with the range of e-commerce options (thus believing change is not possible)?" Given Americans' strong belief in employees' and managers' ability to learn and to change, it is not surprising that the American Society for Training and Development has over 70,000 members.

CHOICE

Who makes the decisions for a company? Are decisions made quickly or slowly? Are information and alternatives discussed sequentially or holistically? Based on a culture's view of the relationships among people (see Chapters 1 and 2), either individuals or groups will hold primary decision-making responsibility. In North American business, individuals usually make decisions. The popular expression "the buck stops here" reflects the belief that ultimately a single person holds responsibility for a particular decision. In Japan, groups make decisions; most Japanese would find it inconceivable for an individual to make a decision prior to consulting his or her immediate colleagues and gaining their agreement (5;12;13;17;28). Whether made individually or collectively, "the trick in decision making is to avoid becoming mindlessly global or hopelessly local" (22:56).

At what level are decisions made? In more hierarchical cultures (see 9); power distance dimension, Chapter 2), only senior executives make important decisions. Lower-level personnel hold responsibility for implementing decisions. Most lower-level Indian employees, for example, would wonder about the competence of a superior who consulted them on routine decisions. The majority of Indian managers prefer a

more directive style, and up to 85 percent of their surveyed subordinates believe they work better under supervision (11). By contrast, most
lower-level Swedish employees expect to make most of their own decisions about day-to-day operations. Thus, it is not surprising that
Swedes, not Indians, experimented with some of the first autonomous
work groups. At Volvo's Kalmar plant, Swedish management gave
groups of employees total responsibility for producing cars (7). The
group, not senior management, took responsibility for allocating and
scheduling tasks as well as for allocating rewards among employees.
Senior management could only delegate this amount of discretion to
the shop floor in a low-power-distance country.

Are decisions made slowly or quickly? American businesspeople pride
themselves on being quick decision makers. In the United States, being
called "decisive" is a compliment: "A good decision executed quickly beats
a brilliant decision implemented slowly" (22:54). By contrast, many other
cultures downplay time urgency—some cultures even increase a decision's value based on the length of time spent on making it. When managers from quick-paced cultures, such as the United States, attempt to
conduct business with people from more slow-paced cultures, such as
Egypt and Pakistan, the mismatched timing causes problems. Americans,
for example, typically become frustrated at Egyptians' slow, deliberate
pace and begin to believe that their Middle Eastern counterparts lack
interest in getting the job done. Egyptians, on the other hand, in observing the Americans' "overly hasty race" to make decisions, typically conclude that Americans' unwillingness to take more time reflects the lack of
importance they place on the business relationship and the particular
work at hand. Time (as discussed in Chapter 1) is a crucial dimension in
understanding business behavior cross-culturally.

How much risk is too much? As described by Hofstede in Chapter 2,
cultures vary in their uncertainty avoidance (9;10). Managers in some
cultures take more risks than those from other cultures. The extent to
which managers enjoy experimenting, trying previously untried alternatives, depends on their aversion to risk.

In what order do businesspeople discuss alternatives? When do they
eliminate alternatives? When do they select one particular alternative?
As will be discussed in Chapter 9, some holistic cultures, such as China
and Japan (27), discuss all alternatives before making any decisions;
other more sequence-oriented cultures, such as Canada, Germany, and
the United States, usually discuss alternatives in a preplanned sequence
and make incremental decisions as each alternative is discussed.

The overall process of decision making can be described in Jungian
terms, with some people acting primarily as "thinkers" and others primarily as "feelers." Thinkers generally process data and make decisions

by questioning whether an alternative is correct or incorrect, true or false. Feelers, while equally logical, question whether an alternative is good or bad. Thinkers orient themselves around a belief in absolute truth, whereas feelers orient themselves around a model of "fit": Is there a good or bad fit between this alternative and what we are trying to accomplish? In selecting a new manager, the thinker might stress the individual's expertise and track record. The feeler might stress the candidate's ability to use good judgment and fit in with other members of the organization. Both are equally logical and valid systems for decision making, but each can lead to very different choices.

IMPLEMENTATION

If decisions are to have any value, they must be implemented. Again, depending on the culture, implementation can be quick or slow, innovative or disruptive, managed from the top or involve participation from all levels within the organization, and managed by an individual or a group. Some of the most difficult global business decisions involve ethical considerations. In a survey of *Harvard Business Review* readers (1), almost half agreed that American business executives tend not to apply ethical laws immediately to work, but rather are preoccupied chiefly with gain. Only 5 percent listed social responsibility as a factor influencing ethical business standards. Half of the respondents attributed unethical practices to superiors who were interested in results no matter how they were attained. Within this context, the ethical failings of almost everyone involved with Enron's meteoric rise and precipitous collapse become more understandable, although no more excusable. Global business decisions are often even more difficult to make than domestic decisions because the basis of what is believed to be "right" and "wrong" is culturally determined (25;26).

ETHICAL DECISION MAKING

British former CEO Anita Roddick defines corporate leadership as moral leadership:

> *Authority to lead should be founded on a moral vision rather than a desire to create the biggest or the richest company in the world. I don't understand how anybody can be a leader without a clearly defined moral vision. If your ambitions and interests do not extend beyond the role of making money or expanding your business, as far as I am concerned you are morally bankrupt* (21:226).

As global leaders, each of us must define our own moral imperatives. Our moral vision guides our personal and organizational behavior, it frames the goals we set, the trade-offs we are willing to consider, and the decisions we make.

Managing across cultures confronts leaders with profound ethical questions as they attempt to adhere to the highest standards of integrity while making and implementing culturally appropriate decisions. Consider the following real situation of "Local Justice and Integrity" (see box) that took place just as Western multinationals were beginning

LOCAL JUSTICE AND INTEGRITY

A major North American company operating in Asia discovered one of the local employees stealing company property of minimal value. The senior managers at the location, all of whom were expatriate Americans, had little doubt about the employee's guilt.

Following the company's standard worldwide procedure, the North American managing director reported the case to the local police. Similar to many other North American companies, this company believed that it was best to let officials from the local culture deal with theft and similar violations in whatever way they found most appropriate, rather than imposing the system of justice from their home culture. The local police arrived at the company, arrested the employee, took him to the police station, and interrogated him according to local procedures. The employee confessed. The police then took the employee outside and shot him dead.

The North American managing director was devastated. For months, he was haunted by the fact that his action, taken because he thought it was culturally appropriate and fair, had led to the murder of an employee.

Questions for Reflection

1. How should employees be treated when they compromise integrity? Does a company's belief in maintaining the highest level of integrity limit its ability to consider culturally based values differences—and more important, their consequences—between the company's culture and local national cultures?
2. Should companies review their policies on the prevention of theft and the promotion of personal honesty in the light of cultural differences? In which situations, if at all, can companies use worldwide standards and procedures? Must companies define integrity issues differently in each country or region of the world?

Senior Management Committee Decisions

3. Given the company's belief in maintaining the highest respect for people while maintaining the highest personal integrity, how should it handle future situations such as this one?
4. If you were the North American managing director, what would you personally have done in this situation? Why? Knowing how the situation turned out, what would you recommend that future managing directors do in similar situations?

to increase their presence in China. Review the situation both from the perspective of the North American expatriate managing director who made the decision and from the perspective of the local Chinese authorities who responded to the information provided to them by the expatriate managing director. Imagine that you are on the senior management committee of the Western multinational and decide what you would do in this situation. Use the *Questions for Reflection* following the description of the situation to guide your analysis.

The box on "Ethical Decision Making" that follows presents four additional cross-cultural business decisions demanding ethical considerations. As you read each, observe the criteria you would use at each stage of the decision-making process: problem recognition, information search, construction of alternatives, choice, and implementation. To what extent are your criteria culturally determined (20;26)? Under what conditions would you be willing to modify your perspective and decision (8)?

ETHICAL DECISION MAKING
A Global Perspective

In each of the four following situations, first decide what you personally would do and why. Note what information you would use to investigate the question, what alternatives you would consider, and what criteria you would use to make the decision. After making your initial decision on your own, meet with a group of your colleagues—preferably including people from other cultures—and make a group decision as to what should be done. Again, assess the type of information you would consider, the range of alternatives you generate, the criteria you use to decide, and your implementation plan. Next, develop a contrasting-culture decision; that is, make the opposite decision based on assumptions of a culture that is very different from your own. Finally, following the suggestions in Chapter 4 for creating synergistic solutions, develop a decision and implementation plan that both you and members of the contrasting culture could accept and support. The situations are not easy. Each is based on a true situation in which at least one manager believed colleagues, clients, or competitors from other parts of the world were acting unethically.

Situation 1: *Facilitating Decisions in the Middle East*

You are the marketing director for a global construction company. Your company has bid on a substantial project in the Middle East that it wants very much to get. Yesterday the cousin of the minister who will award the contract suggested that he might be of help. You know that with his help the chances of your company winning the contract would increase substantially. For his assistance, the minister expects $200,000. You would have to pay this amount in addition to the standard

ETHICAL DECISION MAKING
A Global Perspective (continued)

fees to your agent. If you refuse to make the requested payment, you are certain that the minister will go to your competitor (who won the last three contracts), and that they will make the payment (and probably get this contract, too).

Your company has not established a worldwide code of conduct yet, although it formed a committee some time ago to consider one. The government of your country recently passed an ethical business practices act. The pertinent paragraph is somewhat vague but implies that this kind of payment would probably be a violation of the act. The person to whom you report, and those above him, do not want to become involved. The decision is yours to make.

Situation 2: *Hazardous Materials in West Africa*

For one year you have been the international vice-president of a global company that produces and markets chemicals. The minister of agriculture in a small, economically developing country in West Africa has requested a series of large shipments over the next five years of a special insecticide that only your company produces. The minister believes that this insecticide is the only chemical that will rid one of his country's most important crops of a new infestation that threatens to destroy it. You know, however, that one other insecticide would probably be equally effective. The alternative product is produced in another country by a competitor and has never been allowed in your own country.

Your insecticide, MIM, is highly toxic. After years of debate, your government has just passed a law forbidding its use in your country. Evidence shows that dangerous amounts are easily ingested by humans through the residue it leaves on vegetables, through animals that eat the crops, and through the water supply. After careful consideration, you tell the minister about this evidence. He still insists on using your company's product, arguing that it is necessary and that will be used intelligently. You are quite sure that, 10 years from now, insecticide-caused damage to the health of some of his people will begin to become evident.

Both the president and executive vice president of your firm feel strongly that your company should fill the order. In addition to questioning their own government's position, they are very concerned about the large inventory of MIM the company has on hand and the serious financial setback its prohibition will cause the company. They have made it clear, however, that the decision is up to you.

Although the company has a code of conduct and your government has an ethical business practices act, neither adequately covers hazardous materials.

Situation 3: *The Southeast Asian Advertising Campaign*

You are the new marketing manager for a very large, profitable global company that manufactures automobile tires. Your advertising agency has just presented elaborate plans for introducing a new tire into the Southeast Asian market for your approval. The promotional material clearly implies that your company's new tire

ETHICAL DECISION MAKING
A Global Perspective (continued)

is better than all local products. In fact, it is better than some, but not as good as others. The proposed advertising material tries to attract potential buyers by explaining that for six months your product will be sold at a reduced price. Actually, the price is reduced from a hypothetical high price that the firm established only so they could reduce it. The proposed advertisement further claims that your company has tested the tire under the most adverse conditions. In reality the new tire has not been tested in the prolonged heat and humidity of the tropics. Finally, the proposed advertisement assures buyers that they will be safer in their cars riding on your company's tires than ever before. The truth is, however, that they would be equally safe using a competitor's tire that has been available for two years.

You know your product is good. You also know the proposed advertising is deceptive. Your superior has never been concerned about such deceptive practices, believing that advertisements must present products as distinctive in order to achieve and maintain a competitive edge. Senior management of your company is counting on a very favorable reception for this tire in Southeast Asia and to its introduction making a significant contribution to the bottom line. They are counting on you to see that the tire gets this reception and succeeds.

Whether you go with the proposed advertisement or not is up to you. Your company has a code of conduct and your government has an ethical business practices act, but neither covers advertising practices.

Situation 4: *Cultural Conflict in the Middle East*

You became quite upset last week when you read a strong editorial in the *New York Times*, written by a prominent journalist, that strongly criticized your company, especially its major project in a conservative Muslim country.

As the international vice president, you hold responsibility for this project, which is to build and run a large steel plant. Based on the figures, this plant makes a lot of sense, both for your company and for the government of the country that approved the project. But as the journalist pointed out, the company plans to build the steel plant in a rural area, which will have a very disruptive effect upon the values and customs of the people in the whole region. The project will have many negative consequences. Young people from other towns will move to work at the plant, thereby breaking up families and eliminating the families' primary source of financial and personal security. Working the second or third shift will further interfere with family responsibilities as well as religious observances. Working year-round will certainly mean that many people will find themselves unable to return home to help with the harvest. As the company pays the young people more and more, they will gain greater influence, thereby overturning centuries-old patterns of authority. And, of course, the Westerners whom the company brings in will probably not live up to local moral standards nor show due respect to local women.

ETHICAL DECISION MAKING
A Global Perspective (continued)

The journalist ended by charging your company with cultural imperialism and claiming that your plant, if actually built and put into operation, would disrupt the traditional values and relationships that have provided stability for the country through many generations.

You had known that the new steel plant would cause some social changes, but you had not realized how profound they could be. You have now examined other evidence and discovered that a factory built several years ago by another foreign firm in a similar location is causing exactly the types of problems described by the New York Times journalist—and more. Widespread concern in the country over these problems has become one reason for the increasing influence of traditionalists and nationalists in the country, who argue for getting rid of all foreign firms, and particularly those from your country, because of their disruptive priorities and practices.

Your company has a code of conduct and your government has an ethical business practices act, but neither deals with the destruction of traditional values and relationships. You are on your own here. A lot is at stake for the company and for the people of the region into which you had planned to move. The decision is yours.[2]

SUMMARY

Effective styles of management vary among cultures. Whereas managers in all countries must analyze situations, design viable options, and make decisions, the ways in which they approach these core managerial behaviors remain, in part, determined by their own cultural backgrounds and those of their work environments. Far from learning only one way to assess situations and options, managers working across cultures must become flexible enough to adapt to each particular situation and country. In moving from domestic to global management, leaders must develop a wider range of thinking patterns and behaviors, along with the ability to select the pattern best suited to each particular situation. Effective global managers must become chameleons capable of acting in many ways, not experts rigidly adhering to any one approach.

Most management theories have been developed in the United States by Americans. The questions they raise—How can I lead most effectively? How should I motivate the workforce? How can I make the best decisions?—are universal, but the solutions remain culturally specific. Rather than being applicable worldwide, many traditional models effectively guide thinking and action only within the American context within which they were developed. Based on the cultural context of their operations, global managers must constantly decide to use more directive or democratic styles of leadership, more individual- or group-oriented motivation schemes, more long-term or short-term criteria for decision making. Their decisions, to be most effective and most appropriate, must depend on the particular culture, industry, organization, and individuals involved. Far from being useless, traditional models guide the questions we ask. Only observation and analysis of each culture and situation can guide our answers.

QUESTIONS FOR REFLECTION

1. **Global Decision Making.** Your company has just formed a strategic alliance with a company from another part of the world. Your company has appointed you to lead the transition team, which includes executives from Canada, Mexico, Singapore, and Switzerland. The team must make many decisions about the alliance right away. What would you do as a team leader to ensure that the decision-making process in the transition team quickly becomes as effective as possible?

2. **Multiple Decision-Making Criteria.** Your company, which is known around the world as a "good corporate citizen" has decided to expand its manufacturing facilities in China. You are the vice president responsible for Asian operations and are concerned that China's air, water, and soil have deteriorated at an alarming rate as a consequence of the approaches both industry and the Chinese government have taken to foster the country's rapid economic development. What do you recommend that your company do to take into consideration the nature of the current environmental crises, China's new and proposed environmental legislation, and your company's decision to benefit from the cost advantages of expanded operations in this rapidly developing economy?

3. **Deciding to Operate in Russia.** Your company, which is headquartered in Latin America, is very seriously considering expanding operations to Russia. Some of your colleagues are quite concerned about what has been described as the "wild west" business environment in Russia, and the level of corruption—both real and perceived. What process would you recommend that your company use for deciding if this is the right time to invest in operations in Russia?

4. **Intuitive Decision Making.** Think of a time when you made an "instant" decision based on your intuition that involved people from other cultures. In what ways was it a good decision? In what ways could the decision have been better? Reflecting on the decision now, after the fact, what prior experience do you think your

subconscious drew on when you made the decision (even if you were not aware of it at the time you made the decision)?

NOTE

1. The quotation is from the play *Man of La Mancha* (as found in Otis L. Guernsey, Jr., New York: Dodd, Mead, 1966, p. 214), which is based on the book *Don Quixote* by Miguel Cervantes.

2. Adapted by Adler, 2007; from George W. Renwick and Robert T. Moran, *Basic Responsibility and International Business Ethics* (19).

REFERENCES

1. Brenner, S. N.; & Molander, E. A. "Is the Ethics of Business Changing?" *Harvard Business Review* (January–February 1977), pp. 70–71.

2. Chu, P. C.; Spires, Eric E.; & Sueyoshi, Toshiyuki. "Cross-Cultural Differences in Choice Behavior and Use of Decision Aids: A Comparison of Japan and the United States," *Organizational Behavior & Human Decision Processes*, vol. 77, no. 2 (1999), pp. 147–170.

3. Dewey, J. *How We Think* (Boston: D.C. Heath, 1933).

4. Driver, M. J. "Individual Decision Making and Creativity," in S. Kerr, ed., *Organizational Behavior* (Columbus, Ohio: Grid Publishing, 1979), pp. 59–91.

5. Drucker, P. F. "What We Can Learn from Japanese Management," *Harvard Business Review* (March–April 1971), pp. 110–122.

6. Gladwell, Malcolm. *Blink* (New York: Little, Brown and Company, 2005).

7. Gyllenhammer, P. G. "How Volvo Adapts Work to People," *Harvard Business Review*, vol. 55, no. 4 (1977), pp. 102–113.

8. Hendry, John. "Universalizability and Reciprocity in International Business Ethics," *Business Ethics Quarterly*, vol. 9, no. 3 (1999), pp. 405–420.

9. Hofstede, Geert. *Culture's Consequences: Comparing Values, Behaviors, Institutions, and Organizations Across Nations*, 2nd ed. (Thousand Oaks, Calif.: Sage, 2001).

10. Hofstede, Geert. "Motivation, Leadership and Organization: Do American Theories Apply Abroad?" *Organizational Dynamics*, vol. 9, no. 1 (1980), pp. 42–63.

11. Kakar, S. "Authority Patterns and Subordinate Behavior in Indian Organizations," *Administrative Science Quarterly*, vol. 16, no. 3 (1971), pp. 298–308.

12. Kavcic, B.; Rus, V.; & Tannenbaum, A. S. "Control, Participation, and Effectiveness in Four Yugoslavian Industrial Organizations," *Administrative Science Quarterly*, vol. 16, no. 1 (1971), pp. 74–86.

13. Keizan, W. "Decision Making by Socialist Managers in Complex Organizations," *International Studies of Management and Organization*, vol. 9, no. 4 (1979), pp. 63–77.

14. Klein, Gary. *The Power of Intuition* (New York: Doubleday, 2003).

15. Mau, Bruce & The Institute Without Boundaries. *Massive Change.* (London: Phaidon Press Ltd., 2004)

16. Mutiso, G. C. M. *Socio-Political Thought in African Literature: Weusi* (New York: Barnes and Noble, 1974).

17. Pascale, R. T. "Communication and Decision Making Across Cultures: Japanese and American Comparisons," *Administrative Science Quarterly*, vol. 23 (March 1978), pp. 91–110.

18. Punnett, B. J. "Language, Cultural Values and Preferred Leadership Styles: A Comparison of Anglophones and Francophones in Ottawa," *Canadian Journal of Behavioral Sciences*, vol. 23, no. 2 (1991), pp. 241–244.

19. Renwick, George W.; & Moran, Robert T. *Basic Responsibility and International Business Ethics (BRIBE).* (Glendale, Ariz.: American Graduate School of International Management, January 1982).

20. Robertson, Chris; & Fadil, Paul A. "Ethical Decision Making in Multinational Organizations: A Culture-Based Model," *Journal of Business Ethics*, vol. 19, no. 4, Part 1 (1999), pp. 385–392.

21. Roddick, Anita. *Body and Soul* (New York: Crown, 1991).

22. Rogers, Paul; & Blenko, Maria. "Who has the D? How Clear Decision Roles Enhance Organizational Performance," *Harvard Business Review*, January 2006, pp. 53–61.

23. Simon, Herbert A. *Administrative Behavior* (New York: The Free Press, 1957).

24. Simon, Herbert A. *The New Science of Management Decision* (New York: Harper & Row, 1960).

25. Su, Shu-Hui. "Cultural Differences in Determining the Ethical Perception and Decision-making of Future Accounting Professionals: A Comparison between Accounting Students from Taiwan and the United States," *Journal of American Academy of Business*, vol. 9, no. 1 (2006), pp. 147–158.

26. Tadepalli, Raghu; Moreno, Abel; & Trevino, Salvador. "Do American and Mexican Purchasing Managers Perceive Ethical Situations Differently?" *Industrial Marketing Management*, vol. 28, no. 4 (1999), pp. 369–380.

27. Takamiya, S. "Group Decision Making in Japanese Management," *International Studies of Management and Organization*, vol. 2, no. 2 (1972), pp. 183–196.

28. Theobald, Robert. "Management of Complex Systems: A Growing Societal Challenge," in F. Feather, ed., *Through the 80s: Thinking Globally, Acting Locally* (Washington, DC: World Future Society, 1980), pp. 42–51.

29. Zander, Rosamund Stone; & Zander, Benjamin. *The Art of Possibility: Transforming Professional and Personal Life* (Boston: Harvard Business School Press, 2000).

Chapter 9

Negotiating Globally

---

*Let us not be blind to our differences—but let us also direct
attention to our common interests and the means by
which those differences can be resolved.*

—John F. Kennedy, Former President of the United States (42)

A crucial aspect of all interorganizational relationships, including strategic alliances, joint ventures, mergers and acquisitions, licensing and distribution agreements, and sales of products and services, involves negotiating. As global business becomes the dominant form of business, business negotiations among people from different countries and cultures become more prevalent. To succeed in such negotiations, businesspeople need to know how to communicate with and influence members of cultures other than their own (4).

A growing body of research documents the range of different cultures' negotiating styles (48;64;65;73;74). Research can be found, for example, describing the negotiating behavior of Brazilians (25;28), Canadians (3), Chinese (5;35;38;43;44;47;54;61;68), French (16;53), Japanese (1;9;12;24;27;32;46;66;67;72), Mexicans (20;75), Middle Eastern Arabs (7;51;81), and Russians (8;11;58), among many others (6;13;31;33;78). Do Russians bargain with the same expectations and approaches as Arabs? No. Are Arab negotiating styles similar to those of Americans? Again, no. Russians, Arabs, and Americans—to choose three distinctly different cultures—negotiate in notably different ways.

As shown in Table 9-1 (15;23), Russians typically use an axiomatic approach to negotiating—they base their arguments on asserted ideals.

Russians generally do not expect to develop a continuing relationship with their bargaining partners and therefore see little need for relationship building. As a negotiation progresses, Russians make few, if any, concessions and view their counterparts' concessions as signs of weakness. Russians often start with extreme positions, ignore deadlines, and, due to their very limited authority, frequently check back with headquarters.

TABLE 9-1   Styles of Persuasion Vary Across Cultures

	North Americans	Arabs	Russians
Primary nego-tiating style and process	Factual appeals made to logic	Affective appeals made to emotions	Axiomatic appeals made to ideals
Conflict: Counterparts' arguments countered with...	Objective facts	Subjective feelings	Asserted ideals
Making concessions	Small concessions made early to establish a relationship	Concessions made throughout as a part of the bargaining process	Few, if any, concessions made
Response to counterparts' concessions	Usually reciprocate counterparts' concessions	Almost always reciprocate counterparts' concessions	View counterparts' concessions as weakness and almost never reciprocate
Relationship	Short term	Long term	No continuing relationship
Authority	Broad	Broad	Limited
Initial position	Moderate	Extreme	Extreme
Deadlines	Very important	Casual	Ignored

Source: Glenn, Witmeyer, & Stevenson (23); adapted by Adler, 2007.[1]

By contrast, Arabs typically use an affective approach to negotiating (23)—they counter the other side's arguments with emotional appeals based on subjective feelings. Arabs generally want to build long-term relationships with their bargaining partners. Therefore, they are often willing to make concessions throughout the bargaining process and almost always reciprocate their opponents' concessions. Most Arabs do not feel limited by time or authority; they frequently approach deadlines very casually and rarely lack the broad authority necessary to discuss and to agree on all issues pertinent to the negotiation.

Americans differ from both Russians and Arabs. Americans typically use a factual approach to negotiating (23); they attempt to counter the other side's arguments with logical appeals based on objective facts. Americans make small concessions early in the negotiation in an attempt to establish a relationship, and they generally expect their bargaining partners to do likewise. Americans, far from casual about time and authority, generally take deadlines very seriously and have broad authority.

What happens when Russians begin negotiating with Arabs or Americans? Who persuades whom when styles of negotiating differ? Who wins when bargainers from each culture define the process of negotiating, the rules of the game, differently? How can I get what my company and I want from our negotiation partner while maintaining a good relationship? To succeed in global business, negotiators must continually face and solve these dilemmas.

NEGOTIATING GLOBALLY

Negotiation is a process in which at least one individual tries to persuade another individual to change his or her ideas or behavior (14:152). Business negotiations often involve one party attempting to influence another to make a particular decision or sign a contract. Negotiating is the process in which at least two partners with different needs and viewpoints try to reach agreement on matters of mutual interest (14:152). A negotiation becomes cross-cultural when the parties involved belong to different cultures and therefore do not share the same ways of thinking, feeling, and behaving (14:152). All global negotiations are cross-cultural. Some domestic negotiations, in spanning two or more ethnic groups, are also cross-cultural. Therefore, a Singaporean businessperson negotiating a new e-commerce agreement with a Brazilian, a U.N. official negotiating with ambassadors from several countries concerning the agenda for an upcoming world trade summit, Mexican executives considering a potential strategic alliance with Swedes, and French- and Flemish-speaking Belgians determining national language legislation are all negotiating cross-culturally.

Effective cross-cultural negotiation is one of the most important global business skills a manager can possess (17;18;40;80). Global negotiations contain all of the complexity of domestic negotiations, with the added dimension of cultural diversity. Global managers spend more than 50 percent of their time in formal and informal negotiations (52). As highlighted in Tables 9-1 and 9-2, negotiating styles vary markedly across cultures. Countries vary on such key aspects as the amount and type of preparation for a negotiation, the relative emphasis on task versus interpersonal relationships, the use of general principles versus specific details, the number of people present, and the extent of the negotiators' authority.

According to global negotiations experts, negotiating is not always the best approach to doing business (56). Sometimes the best strategy is "take it or leave it," at other times it is bargaining, and, on some occasions, focusing on problem solving is most appropriate and effective (56:6.24). Negotiating, compared with bargaining and the take-it-or-leave-it approach, demands more time. Managers should negotiate when the value of the exchange and of the relationship is important—as

TABLE 9-2 Styles of Negotiation Vary Across Cultures

Japanese	North American	Latin American
Emotional sensitivity highly valued	Emotional sensitivity not highly valued	Emotional sensitivity valued
Hide emotions	Deal straightforwardly or impersonally	Emotionally expressive and passionate
Subtle power plays; conciliation	Litigation used more than conciliation	Explicit power plays; use others' weaknesses
Loyal to employer; employer takes care of employees	Little commitment to employer; either side can break ties if necessary	Loyal to employer (who is often family)
Team decision making by consensus	Team provides input to decision maker	Decisions come down from one individual
Face-saving crucial; decisions often made to save someone from embarrassment	Decisions based on cost-benefit analysis; face-saving not generally important	Face-saving crucial in decision making to preserve honor and dignity
Decision makers openly influenced by special interests	Decision makers influenced by special interests, but often not considered ethical	Inclusion of special interests of decision maker expected and condoned
Not argumentative; quiet when right	Argumentative, but impersonal, when right or wrong	Argumentative and passionate when right or wrong
Written statements must be accurate and valid	Great importance given to documentation as evidential proof	Impatient with documentation, seen as an obstacle to understanding general principles
Step-by-step approach to decision making	Methodically organized decision making	Impulsive, spontaneous decision making
Good of the team is the ultimate aim	Profit motive or individual benefit is the ultimate aim	What is good for the team is good for the individual
Cultivate a good emotional climate for decision making; get to know decision makers	Decision making impersonal; personal involvements seen as conflict of interest and avoided	Good personal relationships necessary for good decision making

Source: Casse (14); adapted by Adler, 2007.[2]

FIGURE 9-1   When to Negotiate

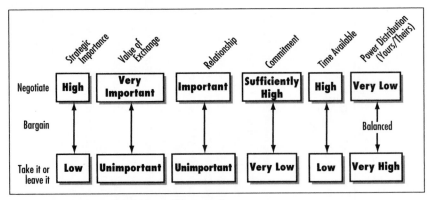

Source: Raider (56); adapted by Adler, 2007.[3]

it is, for example, within the growing number of global strategic alliances. As summarized in Figure 9-1, negotiating is generally the preferred strategy for creating win-win solutions in global business. Businesspeople should consider negotiating when any of the following conditions exist:

- Their power position is low relative to that of their counterpart.
- The trust level is high.
- Sufficient time is available to explore each party's multiple needs, resources, and options.
- Commitment, not mere compliance, is important to ensure that all parties carry out the agreement.

In discussing negotiation, this chapter uses the terms negotiator, bargaining partner, counterpart, and opponent interchangeably.

Cultural diversity makes communicating effectively more difficult (see Chapter 3). Because people from different cultures perceive, interpret, and evaluate the world differently, accurately communicating needs and interests in ways that people from other cultures will understand becomes more challenging, as does fully understanding their words and meanings. Although communication becomes more difficult across cultures, creating mutually beneficial options often becomes easier. When negotiators overcome communication barriers, identifying win-win solutions—mutually beneficial solutions in which both parties gain—becomes easier. For instance, based on their different perspectives, a seller from one culture may no longer want to keep a particular business, whereas a buyer from another culture may find the same business an especially attractive prospect.

In negotiations between Americans and Japanese, American owners traditionally concern themselves more with the viability of the enterprise, and in particular with its predicted long- and short-term future revenues and profits. Japanese buyers, on the other hand, generally show more interest in market share and in the property and physical plant. A Japanese buyer may find an enterprise particularly valuable for one set of reasons, whereas the American owner may place it on the market for an entirely different set of reasons. Similarly, Vietnamese, with their higher unemployment and lower wage rates, find producing labor-intensive products a more attractive prospect than do Swiss manufacturers who face high wage rates and negligible unemployment. Differences, rather than similarities, form the basis of mutually beneficial solutions. The probability that experienced international negotiators will identify substantial areas of difference, and therefore substantial areas for mutual gain, is greater in multicultural than in single-culture situations.

In some situations, negotiators are able to go beyond mutually beneficial agreements to create synergistic opportunities (see Chapter 4). Whereas mutually beneficial agreements focus on comparative advantage—the exchange of benefits more highly valued by one party than the other—synergy uses differently valued benefits as a resource in creating new options that would never have become possible without the initial differences. Differences, the source of cross-cultural communication complexities and problems, ultimately become the primary resource in creating mutually beneficial, synergistic solutions.

NEGOTIATING SUCCESSFULLY: THE PEOPLE, THE SITUATION, AND THE PROCESS

Each of the three areas on which the success of a negotiation depends—individual characteristics, situational contingencies, and strategic and tactical processes—vary considerably across cultures (19;23;24;29). Although all three affect outcomes, negotiators have the most influence on the process: the strategy and tactics employed in negotiations. Negotiators can determine the success or failure of a negotiation most directly by managing the negotiation process. The following section discusses each of the three areas, highlights cultural variations, and recommends the most effective approaches. Effective negotiators base their strategy and tactics on the characteristics of the specific situation and the particular people involved. Although managers would find it easier if just one best way to negotiate existed, no such consistency or any guaranteed formula for success exists.

QUALITIES OF A GOOD NEGOTIATOR

What qualities does a good negotiator possess? According to negotiation expert John Graham's extensive research (24), the answer depends on the cultures involved. As shown in Table 9-3, American managers believe that effective negotiators act highly rationally. Brazilian managers, to the surprise of many Americans, hold an almost identical view, differing only in replacing integrity with competitiveness as one of the seven most important qualities of effective negotiators. By contrast, the opinions of Japanese negotiators differ quite markedly from those of both Americans and Brazilians. Japanese see an interpersonal, rather than a rational, negotiating style as leading to success. Japanese differ from Americans in stressing both verbal expressiveness and listening ability, whereas Americans only emphasize verbal ability. In contrast to American negotiators, Brazilians, Chinese, managers in Taiwan and Japanese emphasize negotiators' rational skills and, to a lesser extent, their interpersonal skills. To the Chinese, a successful negotiator must be an interesting person and should show persistence and determination, the ability to win respect and confidence, preparation and planning skills, product knowledge, good judgment, and intelligence.

The role that individual qualities play varies across cultures. Favorable outcomes are most strongly influenced by negotiators' own characteristics in Brazil, opponents' characteristics in the United States, the negotiator's role in Japan (the buyer always does better), and a mixture of the

TABLE 9-3   Individual Characteristics Negotiators See as Most Important for Success Vary by Culture

American Negotiators	Japanese Negotiators	Chinese (Taiwan) Negotiators	Brazilian Negotiators
1. Preparation and planning skill	Dedication to job	Persistence and determination	Preparation and planning skill
2. Thinking under pressure	Perceive and exploit power	Win respect and confidence	Thinking under pressure
3. Judgment and intelligence	Win respect and confidence	Preparation and planning skill	Judgment and intelligence
4. Verbal expressiveness	Integrity	Product knowledge	Verbal expressiveness
5. Product knowledge	Demonstrate listening skill	Interesting	Product knowledge
6. Perceive and exploit power	Broad perspective	Judgment and intelligence	Perceive and exploit power
7. Integrity	Verbal expressiveness		Competitiveness

Source: John L. Graham, The Paul Merage School of Business, University of California, Irvine.

negotiators' and their counterparts' characteristics in Taiwan (24). Specifically, Brazilian negotiators achieve higher profits when they act more deceptively and in their own self-interest, when they express higher self-esteem, and when their bargaining partners act with more honesty. American negotiators achieve greater success when their counterparts are honest, not self-interested, introverted, not particularly interesting as people, and made to feel uncomfortable by the negotiators' actions. By contrast, as described previously, Japanese buyers always do better than sellers. Both Japanese buyers and sellers can improve their positions by making their bargaining partners feel more comfortable. In Taiwan, negotiators do better when they act deceptively and when their counterparts are neither self-interested nor have particularly attractive personalities.

BUYER/SELLER RELATIONSHIP

The hierarchical relationship between buyers and sellers is crucial in understanding how negotiating styles differ across cultures (24). As shown in Figure 9-2, Japanese buyers and sellers, for example, maintain a vertical, hierarchical relationship: buyers generally get most of what they ask for. Sellers, however, expect buyers to take care of them. When the Japanese explain this system to Americans, the Americans frequently ask, "But won't the seller get taken?" The answer is no, because in Japan the group that is higher in the hierarchy takes care of the lower group: management takes care of workers, government takes care of industry, and buyers take care of sellers. *Amae*—indulgent dependence—explains the buyer-seller relationship in Japan.

FIGURE 9-2   The Relationship of Buyers to Sellers

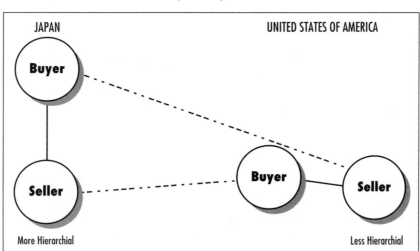

JAPAN   UNITED STATES OF AMERICA

Buyer

Seller   Buyer   Seller

More Hierarchial   Less Hierarchial

Buyers and sellers in the United States, by contrast, maintain a less hierarchical, more equal, relationship. The American norm is not *amae*, but rather independent competition: "May the best person win." Buyers do not expect to take care of sellers; they expect to take care of themselves by getting the best deal possible for their company.

Predictably, problems can arise when Japanese and American buyers and sellers negotiate with each other (32:28-29). From the American perspective, being a buyer in Japan is extremely advantageous. According to some Japanese, "Americans ask for the moon!" Many Japanese, in describing their initial negotiations with Americans, say, "When we first came to the United States, we took a beating. As sellers, we gave the American buyers everything they wanted." But because they were working under a different set of expectations, the Americans did not then "take care of" the Japanese sellers. The Japanese thought the Americans took advantage of them, while the Americans believed they had merely driven a hard bargain.

In the reverse situation, American sellers, not trusting Japanese buyers to take care of them, act as equals. They thus fail to behave with appropriate deference to the buyer; the Japanese, not surprisingly, perceive the Americans as arrogant. All too frequently, negotiations collapse as a result. Unfortunately, both sides frequently attribute the collapse to unacceptable product or service quality and price, rather than to the actual cause—cross-cultural differences.

When negotiators bargain with people from diverse cultures, the most important individual characteristics they can possess are good listening skills, an orientation toward people, a willingness to use team assistance, high self-esteem, high aspirations, and an attractive personality, along with credibility and influence within the home organization (30). These individual characteristics, although significant, are not necessarily the most important factors determining negotiated outcomes. It is therefore unfortunate that many companies emphasize individual characteristics in selecting members of their negotiating teams rather than training those selected to understand and more skillfully manage the negotiation process.

NEGOTIATION CONTINGENCIES: CHARACTERISTICS OF THE SITUATION LEADING TO SUCCESS OR FAILURE

Situations in which negotiators find themselves vary widely. Effective negotiators recognize and manage the impact of each situational aspect of the bargaining process from both their own and their opponents' cultural perspectives. In preparing for global negotiations, they imagine what the situation might look like through the eyes of the other countries' teams: What do they need? What do they want? What is important to them? Who has power? What is at stake? What is their time frame? Where do they draw their personal and organizational bottom lines? What is their best alternative to a negotiated solution? Situational contingencies influence success just as individual characteristics do, but they are rarely as critical to success as the strategy and tactics used.

Location Should you meet at their office, your office, or at a neutral location? Negotiation wisdom generally advises teams to meet at their own or a neutral location. Meeting in another country disadvantages negotiators because it increases travel-related stress and cost, reduces familiarity, and reduces the traveling negotiators' ease of access to expertise. Meeting at home allows a team to control the situation more easily. A division of Caterpillar of California, for example, increased its control over a particularly important negotiation by taking international clients out on their yacht. They gained the advantage of removing their clients from interruptions and distractions while— given the planned absence of wireless connectivity—limiting their ease of access to expertise.

Many negotiators select neutral locations. Business entertainment remains a common type of neutral location, used primarily to get to know and improve relations with members of the opposing team. Heavy users of business entertainment, the Japanese traditionally spent almost two percent of their GNP on *settai* (entertaining clients)—even more than they historically spent on national defense after World War II (1.5%). Whereas defense spending has been increasing and business entertainment decreasing somewhat in recent years, the amount spent by Japanese entertaining their clients remains significant. Americans generally consider such high business entertainment costs absurd, but perhaps Americans' extraordinarily high legal expenses reflect the cost of insufficient relationship building.

In choosing neutral locations, business negotiators often select resorts geographically located somewhere between each company's headquarters. Asian and North American negotiators, for example, have frequently selected Hawaii for business meetings; both sides travel, both sides have reduced access to expertise, and as a consequence, the incentive increases for both sides to conclude the negotiation as quickly as possible. The opportunity cost of executives' time, along with the cost of travel and hotels, usually, but not always, increases pressure to conclude negotiations expeditiously. In one negotiation between an American and a Russian company, negotiators conducted the sessions at a resort in the south of France. The Russian negotiators made it clear that they did not want to end their "vacation" early by concluding the bargaining prematurely.

Physical Arrangements In traditional American negotiations, the two teams face each other, often sitting on opposite sides of a boardroom table. Unfortunately, this arrangement maximizes competition. By contrast, sitting at right angles facilitates cooperation. If negotiators view the process as a collaborative search for mutually beneficial outcomes (win-win solutions), the physical arrangements should support cooperation, not competition. As an alternative to the boardroom table, negotiators from both teams may choose to sit on the same side of the table, "facing the problem" (18). In this way they compete with the problem, not with the people. The Japanese, in posting all information related to a negotiation on the walls, structure the environment so that all parties involved "face the problem" holistically.

Participants Who should attend the formal negotiating sessions? Americans tend to want to "go it alone"—they consider extra team members an unnecessary expense. This strategy is usually ineffective in global negotiations, in which the involvement of more team members tends to be better. Why? First, the physical presence of more people communicates greater power and importance—an essential nonverbal message. Second, as discussed earlier, communicating cross-culturally is complex and difficult. Giving some team members primary responsibility for listening to the discussion and observing nonverbal cues while other members focus primarily on conducting substantive negotiations has repeatedly proven to be an extremely effective strategy.

Who should be present at a negotiation? Should the press be present? Will public opinion make it easier or more difficult to develop mutually beneficial solutions? Should the union have direct representation? Should bargainers keep government agencies informed during the negotiation or only present them with the final agreement? The power that government, unions, and public opinion have over business negotiators varies considerably across cultures. Negotiating with government officials from such open democracies as Australia, Canada, and New Zealand, for example, requires broader public debate than is generally necessary in the more tightly controlled governments of Albania, Cuba, Iran, Kenya, and North Korea. Effective global negotiators carefully manage access to the proceedings.

Time Limits The duration of a negotiation can vary markedly across cultures. Americans, being particularly impatient, often expect negotiations to take a minimum amount of time. During the Paris Peace Talks, designed to negotiate an end to the Vietnam War, the U.S. team arrived in Paris and made hotel reservations for a week. Their Vietnamese counterparts leased a château for a year. As the negotiations proceeded, timing forced the frustrated Americans to continually renew their weekly reservations to accommodate the more measured pace of the Vietnamese.

Negotiators generally make more concessions as their deadline approaches. Americans' sense of urgency puts them at a disadvantage with respect to their less hurried bargaining partners. Negotiators from outside the United States often recognize Americans' time consciousness, achievement orientation, and impatience. They know that Americans will make more concessions close to their deadline (time consciousness) in order to get a signed contract (achievement orientation). One Brazilian company, for example, invited a group of Americans to Brazil to negotiate a contract the week before Christmas. The Brazilians, aware that the Americans would want to return to the United States by Christmas with a signed contract, knew that they could push hard for concessions and an early agreement. The final agreement definitely favored the Brazilians.

Some negotiators attempt to discover their opponents' deadline and refuse to make major concessions until after that deadline has passed. The local team may determine their opponents' deadlines by checking hotel reservations or politely offering to reconfirm return airline tickets. Effective global negotiators determine the best alternative to not meeting their deadline. If they find the best alternative acceptable, they may choose a less hurried pace than they had originally planned or than they typically use at home.

Status Differences The United States prides itself on its egalitarian, informal approach to life, in which titles do not seem particularly important and ceremonies are often considered a waste of time. Americans often attempt to minimize status differences during negotiations: for example, they use first names to promote equality and informality. Unfortunately this approach, which succeeds at putting Americans at ease, often makes people from other cultures uncomfortable. Most countries respect hierarchy and formality more than the United States does; and most negotiators from these countries feel more comfortable in formal situations with explicit status differences. The Japanese, for example, must know the other person's company and position before being able to select the grammatically correct form of address. For this reason, the Japanese always exchange business cards— *meishi*—before a business conversation begins. For similar reasons, German negotiators would almost never address colleagues on their own team, let alone those from another team, by first name. Such informality would severely insult their sense of propriety, hierarchy, and respect.

Age, like title, connotes seniority and demands respect in most countries of the world. Sending a young, albeit brilliant, North American expert to Indonesia to lead a negotiating team is more likely to insult senior Indonesian officials than it is to facilitate a successful exchange of technical information. In almost all cases, North Americans need to increase formality in dress, vocabulary, behavior, and style when working outside of the United States.

NEGOTIATION PROCESS

Process is the single most important factor influencing the success or failure of a negotiation. An effective process includes managing the negotiation's overall strategy or approach, its stages, and the specific tactics used. As with other aspects of negotiating, process varies markedly across cultures (2;10;33;41;60;69;80). An effective process reflects the situational characteristics and personal backgrounds of the negotiators involved. It balances the position, procedure, timing, and roles of negotiators.

NEGOTIATION STRATEGY:
A CULTURALLY SYNERGISTIC APPROACH

In *Getting to Yes*, based on the work of the Harvard International Negotiation Project, Fisher and Ury (20) propose a principled approach to negotiating. As shown in Table 9-4, this approach includes four steps:

- Separating the people from the problem
- Focusing on interests, not on positions
- Insisting on objective criteria (and never yielding to pressure)
- Inventing options for mutual gain

Does this principled approach become easier or harder when negotiating globally? Let's analyze the principled approach from a cross-cultural perspective. Cultural differences make communicating more difficult. Steps 1, 2, and 3 therefore become more difficult: understanding opponents, their interests, and their assessment criteria becomes more complex and fraught with cross-cultural communication pitfalls. By contrast, step 4 can become easier. Inventing options for mutual gain requires recognizing and using differences. The fewer identical options sought by both negotiating teams, the greater the chances of simultaneously satisfying each teams' needs. If teams recognize, clearly communicate, and understand cross-cultural differences (steps 1, 2, and 3), they can become the basis for constructing win-win solutions. Western European countries that import Indonesian batiks, for example, exchange an economically developed market for a labor-intensive good. The Europeans could not afford to hand make batiks in Europe, and the Indonesians could not command as high a price in

TABLE 9-4   Traditional, Principled, & Synergistic Approaches to Negotiating Globally

Traditional Approach *Competitive*	Principled Approach *Collaborative/Individual*	Synergistic Approach *Collaborative/Cultural*
Preparation	**Preparation**	**Preparation**
• Clarify economic issues	• Clarify interests	• Clarify interests
		• Cross-cultural training
Relationship Building	**Relationship Building**	**Relationship Building**
• Assess counterparts	• Separate the people from the problem	• Separate the people from the problem
		• Create style and pace appropriate to all parties
Information Exchange	**Information Exchange**	**Information Exchange**
• Exchange task-related information	• Exchange task- and participant-related information	• Exchange task- and participant-related information
• Clarify positions	• Clarify interests	• Clarify interests, customary approaches, and potentially acceptable approaches
Persuasion	**Designing Options for Mutual Gain**	**Designing Options for Mutual Gain Appropriate to All Cultures Involved**
Concessions	**Choose Best Option**	**Choose Best Option**
	• Insist on using objective criteria	• Insist on using criteria appropriate to all cultures involved
	• Never yield to pressure	• Never yield to pressure
Agreement	**Agreement**	**Agreement**
		• Translate and back-translate agreement
		• Renegotiate if necessary

Source: Table 9-4 is based on the work of George Renwick (unpublished); adapted by Adler, 2007.[4]

stable currencies within their own country. This culturally synergistic approach, which uses cultural differences as a resource rather than a hindrance to organizational functioning, allows global negotiators to maximize benefits to all parties. Each step of the principled approach will be discussed as it relates to the four stages of the formal negotiation process.

Dutch cross-cultural scholar Geert Hofstede (34) cautions managers that the principled approach includes hidden cultural assumptions that fit best with the American culture of the approach's co-creators, Fisher and Ury. He asks global managers to recognize, first, that the principled approach assumes an individualistic values set. In collectivist cultures, relationship prevails, so people are central to negotiating issues and resolving problems (34). See the box entitled "Malays Negotiating with Americans" in this chapter for an example of the Malays' more people-centered negotiating style clashing with the Americans' more issue-oriented style. In collectivist cultures, both the issue and the people must be addressed. Second, the principled approach assumes a "not-too-large power distance" context (that is, a low acceptance of hierarchy) in which negotiating positions are less likely to be linked to issues of power (34). Third, the principled approach assumes a "not-too-large uncertainty avoidance," rather than the "what is different is dangerous" mentality that is more likely to prevail in cultures that strongly avoid uncertainty (34). And fourth, according to Hofstede, the principled approach "assumes a shared objectivity among the parties" (34).

STAGES OF A NEGOTIATION

To prepare for an initial meeting, effective negotiators analyze the situation in terms of their own and their counterparts' needs, goals, and underlying cultural values, determine the limits to their authority, assess power positions and relationships, identify facts to be confirmed, set an agenda, establish overall and alternative concession strategies, and make team assignments. They also determine their *best alternative to a negotiated solution* (20); that is, the most favorable outcome in the event that they fail to reach agreement. This best alternative to a negotiated solution, unlike a conventional *bottom line,* protects negotiators "from accepting terms that are too unfavorable and from rejecting terms it would be in . . . [their] interest to accept" (20:104).

Planning The Huthwaite Research Group conducted a study in the United Kingdom on the behavior of successful negotiators (56). The researchers interviewed and observed 48 successful negotiators in more than 100 negotiations. Negotiators were only considered successful if they were rated as effective by both sides, had a track record of significant success, and had a low incidence of implementation failure. As highlighted in Table 9-5, successful negotiators' planning behavior differed in the following ways from that of their less-skilled colleagues (56):

- *Planning time.* Both skilled and average negotiators use about the same amount of time for planning. "It is not the amount of planning time that makes the difference, but how the time is used" (56).
- *Exploring options.* Skilled negotiators consider twice as wide a range of action options and outcomes as do their less-skilled colleagues. The greater the number of options, the greater the chances for success.

TABLE 9-5   Skilled Negotiators Prepare Differently than Average Negotiators

Preparing for a Negotiation	Skilled Negotiators	Average Negotiators
Planning Time *Overall time spent planning*	No significant difference	No significant difference
Exploration of Options *Number of options and outcomes considered per issue*	5.1	2.6
Common Ground *Percentage of comments about areas of anticipated common ground*	38%	11%
Long Term *Percentage of comments about long-term considerations of issues*	8.5%	4%
Planned Order: Issues versus Sequences *Average use of sequences during planning per session*	Issues 2.1	Sequences 4.9
Setting Limits	Range	Fixed-point

Source: Rackham (55); adapted by Adler, 2007.[5]

- ***Establishing common ground.*** Although all negotiators focus more on areas of conflict than agreement, skilled negotiators spend over three times as much time focusing on common ground.

- ***Focusing on the long term.*** All negotiators spend the vast majority of their time on short-term issues. Skilled negotiators, however, spend more than twice as much time focusing on long-term issues.

- ***Using issue versus sequence planning.*** Average negotiators use sequence planning. They plan to discuss point A, then point B, then point C, and so on. Skilled negotiators, by contrast, use issue planning. They discuss each issue independently, without any pre-determined sequence or order.

- ***Setting limits.*** Average negotiators set single point objectives, such as requesting $70 per unit. Skilled negotiators set range objectives, such as requesting $50 to $100 per unit. Setting ranges gives skilled negotiators more bargaining flexibility.

Following the preparation, formal negotiations usually proceed through four fairly distinct stages (26;30):

1. Interpersonal relationship building (learning about the people)
2. Exchanging task-related information (learning about the economic, legal, technical, political and logistical issues)
3. Persuading
4. Making concessions and agreements

Countries vary in the emphasis placed on each phase and the style used to approach it. As shown in Table 9-4, effective bargainers can approach each stage of the negotiation through "principled" strategies:

- to build interpersonal relationships, principled negotiators separate the people from the problem;
- to exchange task-related information, principled negotiators focus on interests, not on positions;
- to effectively persuade the other team, principled negotiators invent options for mutual gain, rather than relying on preconceived positions and high pressure "dirty tricks"; and
- to make appropriate concessions and reach agreement, principled negotiators insist on using objective decision criteria.

Interpersonal Relationship Building The first phase of a face-to-face negotiation involves getting to know the other people and helping them to feel comfortable. Every negotiation involves the relationship (you and them) and the substance (what you and they want). During relationship building, parties develop respect and trust for members of the other team. *Non-task sounding* begins the relationship-building process of discovering general areas of similarity and difference in both the relationship and the substance. Similarities become the basis for personal relationships and trust; differences, the basis for mutual exchange. The strategy of separating the people from the problem implies that negotiators can reject their partners' suggestions without rejecting the people themselves, that they can disagree with their counterparts' analysis without labeling them negatively, and that they can enjoy and trust their counterparts as individuals while rejecting their proposals.

Being particularly task- and efficiency-oriented, Americans usually see little need to "waste time" on getting to know people in non-task-related conversations. Americans want to "get down to business" almost immediately—to discussing and agreeing on task-related issues, often after only five to ten minutes. The U.S. legal system also supports a task-oriented approach. Americans base their transactions on written contracts. Businesspeople in the United States trust the legal system to enforce written agreements (contracts) once all parties involved have signed them. Americans consequently focus on signing contracts rather than developing meaningful relationships with members of their partner teams. The American approach and legal system, however, is not replicated in most countries. Many areas of the world have neither strong nor consistently dependable legal systems to enforce contracts. Enforcement mechanisms are personal. People keep commitments to people, not to contracts. People honor contracts if they like and respect the people with whom they are conducting business. They emphasize the personal relationship, not the written agreement.

Americans need to emphasize building relationships with their global partners. They need to discuss broader topics than just business, including the arts, history, culture, and current economic conditions of the countries involved. Effective negotiators view lunch, dinner, reception, ceremony, and tour invitations as times for interpersonal relationship building and therefore as key to the negotiating process. When American negotiators, often frustrated by seemingly endless formalities, ceremonies, and "small talk," ask how long they must wait before beginning to "do business," the answer is simple: wait until your counterparts bring up business (and they will). Realize that the work of conducting a successful negotiation has already begun, even if business has yet to be mentioned.

Exchanging Task-Related Information The substance of a negotiation is interests: yours and theirs. Negotiators should therefore focus on presenting their situation and needs, and on understanding their counterparts' situation and needs. Presenting interests—a situation and needs—is not the same as stating a position. A position articulates only one solution for a particular situation from one party's perspective (usually the solution prepared prior to the negotiation). Stating positions limits the ways in which your interests (and by implication, your counterparts' interests) can be met. If, for example, based on an analysis of my personal and family needs (housing, clothing, food, transportation, children's education, health care, and entertainment), I tell my employer that I must have a minimum foreign service salary of $250,000 (a position) to transfer to Hong Kong and she refuses to go above $200,000, we quickly arrive at an impasse. My employer finds $250,000, my one solution to my needs, unacceptable. If, on the other hand, I present my situation and needs, my employer may offer me $200,000 plus company-paid medical insurance, company-owned housing, and use of a company car. Would this offer meet my needs? Perhaps. Would it meet my initial position? No. Focusing on interests rather than positions allows both sides to draw on the widest possible range of mutually agreeable solutions.

In negotiating, cross-cultural miscommunication causes numerous problems. For example, the Iranians' misinterpretation of a bargaining offer presented in English by the United Nations made the Iranian hostage crisis more difficult to resolve:

> *In early 1980, United Nations Secretary-General Waldheim flew to Iran to deal with the hostage . . . [crisis]. His efforts were seriously set*

> *back when Iranian national radio and television broadcast in Persian a remark he reportedly made on his arrival in Tehran: "I have come as a mediator to work out a compromise." Within an hour of the broadcast, his car was being stoned by angry Iranians* (20:34). *Why?*
>
> *In Persian, the word compromise . . . lacks the positive meaning it has in English (a "midway solution both sides can live with") and has only a negative meaning ("her virtue was compromised" or "our integrity was compromised"). Similarly, the word "mediator" in Persian suggests "meddler," someone who is barging in uninvited.*

A clear understanding of the interests of negotiators from other cultures is difficult. Verbal and nonverbal barriers significantly influence understanding and outcomes. Misperception, misinterpretation, and misevaluation pervade cross-cultural situations. To begin to understand, effective negotiators try to see the situation from both their own and the other parties' perspectives. Many negotiators use role reversal: they prepare for the negotiation as if they were the other party. Reversing roles forces them to appreciate the situation and issues from the other negotiating team's point of view.

Persuading In principled, synergistic negotiations, bargainers emphasize creating mutually beneficial options, whereas more traditional negotiators often emphasize persuading the other party to accept a particular option. Creating mutually beneficial options is particularly important for global negotiators. (This chapter reviews the most common methods of persuasion used both domestically and globally in the section on negotiating tactics.)

In successful negotiations, all parties' interests and needs are recognized and satisfied, and therefore all parties win. Effective synergistic negotiators view their counterparts' interests and needs as a part of their own problem. Mutually beneficial options derive from (a) understanding each party's real interests, values, and needs, (b) identifying areas of similarity and difference, and (c) creating new options based primarily on the differences between the parties. Identifying interests more highly valued by one party than the other and using such differences as a resource underlies the creation of mutually beneficial options.

In cross-cultural negotiations, the possibilities for inventing mutually beneficial options exceed those in single-culture situations due to the inherent differences among the parties. If, for example, a company tells its employees that they cannot all take their vacations at the same time, management will probably have a problem in selecting who will receive time off during the holiday season. If all employees are Christian, most will want their vacation during Christmas week. If some employees are Christian and others Jewish, some will be happiest with a Christmas vacation while others will prefer time off during Hanukkah (which rarely coincides with Christmas), Pesah, or the high holidays. Cross-cultural differences, when recognized, facilitate mutually beneficial solutions that are often impossible when all employees share similar cultural and religious backgrounds.

Making Concessions and Reaching Agreement In this fourth stage of negotiation, principled negotiators insist on using objective criteria in deciding how to make concessions and to reach agreement, rather than resorting to a series of dirty tricks. Although numerous high-pressure tactics exist, such tactics diminish both the relationships between the negotiating partners and the possibility of developing synergistic solutions. (Specific tactics to avoid will be discussed later.)

Concessions, large or small, can be made at any time during a negotiation. Although the research is not definitive, it appears that negotiators who make numerous early concessions disadvantage themselves in comparison with those making fewer concessions primarily at the end of the bargaining sessions (59). Americans generally negotiate sequentially: they discuss and attempt to agree on one issue at a time. Throughout the bargaining process, Americans make many small concessions, which they expect their counterparts to reciprocate; then they finalize the list of concessions into an overall agreement. In some ways, making small concessions reflects Americans' task-oriented form of relationship building. Negotiators from many other cultures, unlike most Americans, discuss all issues prior to making any concessions. These negotiators view concessions as relative and make them only as they reach a final agreement. This holistic approach to negotiating is particularly evident in Asia.

Similar to many Asians, most Russian negotiators make very few, if any, concessions during a negotiation and rarely reciprocate the other party's concessions. Unlike many of their colleagues, Russian negotiators generally view concessions as signs of weakness, not as gestures of goodwill, flexibility, or trust. In the seven rounds of postwar negotiations between the former Soviet and U.S. governments, for example, the United States made 82 percent of its concessions in the first round, considerably more than did the Russians (39). Mikhail Gorbachev's and Boris Yeltsin's styles in implementing political change in the former Soviet Union highlight the Russian approach to negotiation.

No single approach to concessions has proven to succeed more consistently than any other in negotiating globally. Effective global negotiators respect their own and their counterparts' domestic styles, and when appropriate, adjust accordingly. The following story highlights differences in whom Malaysians and Americans select to negotiate and how negotiators from these two contrasting cultures perform.

CONTRASTING STYLES
Malays Negotiating With Americans

Americans' patterns of negotiating differ depending on the context. Government officials working out a treaty, for example, negotiate somewhat differently from business executives "hammering out" a contract. The pattern portrayed here reflects that of business executives.

American businesspeople usually begin a series of negotiating sessions in a cordial manner, but they express their intent to "get things under way." They are very clear as to what they and their company want, when they want it, and how they will go about getting it; they have planned their strategy carefully. And they have done what they could to "psych out" their negotiation counterparts.

From the outset, American negotiators urge everyone to dispense with the formalities and get down to the business at hand. As soon as possible they express their determination, saying something like, "O.K., let's get down to brass tacks."

Americans usually state their position (at least their first position) early and definitively. They plan before long to "really get down to the nitty-gritty." They want to "zero in" on the knotty problems and get to the point where "the rubber meets the road" (the point, that is, where "the action" begins). Once the negotiations are "really rolling," Americans usually deal directly with obstacles as they come up, trying to clear them away in quick order, and becoming impatient and frustrated if they cannot.

Most of what Americans want to convey, of course, they put into words: spoken words—often many of them. Their approach, therefore, is highly verbal, quite visible, and thoroughly planned. They outline their alternatives and prepare their counterproposals, contingencies, back-up positions, bluffs, guarantees, and tests of compliance ahead of time; all carefully calculated, and, of course, including lots of numbers. Toward the end of the negotiation, they see that the agreement includes some bail-out provisions, but they usually don't worry too much about them. Making and meeting business commitments "on schedule" is what American business people's lives are all about—they are not too concerned about getting out of a contract. If they have to get out, then they have to, and they will find a way when the time comes.

Americans experience real satisfaction when all the problems have been "worked out," especially if they have been able to get provisions very favorable to their company—and to their own reputation as "tough negotiators." They rest securely when everything is "down in black and white" and the contract is initialed or signed.

Afterwards, Americans enjoy themselves; they relax "over some drinks" and carry on some "small talk" and "joke around" with their own team and their counterparts.

Malay patterns of negotiation, as might be expected, differ markedly from those of Americans. When they are buying something, Malays bargain with the merchant; and when they are working, they socialize with their boss and co-workers. Their purpose is to develop a sense of relationship with the other person.

CONTRASTING STYLES
Malays Negotiating With Americans (continued)

The relationship then provides the basis, or context, for the exchange. Malays take the same patterns and preferences into their business-negotiating sessions. When all is said and done, it is not the piece of paper they trust, it is the people and their relationships with the people.

Malay negotiators begin to develop the context for negotiating through the interaction routines appropriate to this and similar occasions. These routines are as complicated and subtle as customary American routines; they are cordial but quite formal. Like Americans using their own routines, Malays understand the Malay routines but are seldom consciously aware of them. Neither Malays nor Americans understand very clearly the routines of the other.

To form the preliminary context, it is important to Malays that the proper forms of address be known beforehand and used, and that a variety of topics be talked about that are unrelated to the business to be transacted. This preliminary interaction may continue for quite a while. Malay negotiators want their counterparts to participate comfortably, patiently, and with interest. As in other interactions, it is not the particular words spoken that are of most importance to Malays; rather they listen primarily to the attitudes the words convey, attitudes toward the Malays themselves and toward the matters being negotiated. Attitudes are important to the relationship. At this point and throughout the negotiations, Malays remain concerned as much about the quality of the relationship as the quantity of work accomplished. Motivation is more important to Malays than momentum.

Malay negotiators, as in other situations, are also aware of feelings—their own and those of their counterparts, and the effects of the exchanges upon both. They are also aware of, and concerned about, how they look in the eyes of their own team, how their counterparts look in the eyes of the other team, and how both they and their counterparts will look in the eyes of their respective superiors after the negotiations.

Malays are alert to style, both their own and that of their counterparts. They consider displaying manners as more important than scoring points. Malays value the way one negotiates as well as what one negotiates. Grace and finesse show respect for the other and for the matters under consideration. Negotiating, like other interaction, is something of an art form. Balance and restraint are therefore essential.

The agenda Malays work through in the course of the negotiation usually remains quite flexible. Their strategy is usually rather simple. Malays express their positions in more general terms than do Americans, but hold them no less strongly. They offer their proposals to the other party rather than argue them. Malays do not enjoy sparring. They deeply dislike combat.

In response to a strong assertion, Malay negotiators usually express their respect by replying indirectly. The stronger the assertion and the more direct the demands, the more indirect the reply—at least the verbal reply.

CONTRASTING STYLES
Malays Negotiating With Americans (continued)

Malay teams usually formulate their position gradually and carefully. By the time they present their position, they usually have quite a lot of themselves invested in it. Directly rejecting the position, therefore, is sometimes felt to be a rejection of the people holding the position. Negotiating for Malays is not quite the game that it is for some Americans.

If Malays and their team have arrived at a position from which they and those whom they represent cannot move, they will not move. If it requires a concession from their counterparts, Malays will not try to force the concession. If the counterparts see that a concession is necessary, and make it, Malays, as polite and considerate people, recognize the move and respect the people who made it. The Malay team usually does not consider a concession as a sign that they can press harder and extract further concessions. Instead, Malays consider a concession by either side as evidence of strength and a basis for subsequent reconciliation and cooperation.

What about getting out of a contract? Making and meeting business commitments is not central to Malays' lives. They have other, often prior, commitments. They therefore enter into contracts cautiously and prefer to have an exit provided.

In addition, Malays are less certain of their control over the future (even their control over their own country) than are Americans. Malays, therefore, often find promising specific kinds of performance by specific dates, especially in a long-term contract where the stakes are high, difficult. They find promising even more difficult, of course, if they are not certain whether they can trust the people to whom they are making commitments and from whom they are accepting commitments. Malays therefore give a great deal of thought to a contract and to the contracting parties before signing it. And Malays become uneasy if provisions have not been made for a respectable withdrawal should future circumstances make their compliance impossible.

Source: Renwick (57); adapted by Adler, 2007.[6]

NEGOTIATION TACTICS

Negotiating includes both verbal and nonverbal tactics. Whereas most Americans consider verbal tactics most important, many people from other countries do not agree. According to one study, words communicate only 7 percent of meaning, with tone of voice communicating 38 percent and facial expression 55 percent (50). Both verbal and nonverbal behavior often cause problems cross-culturally. According to global negotiations experts, "It's hard to read the writing on the wall if you don't know the language, much less where to find the wall" (56:3.18). In the following section, we review some of the most common verbal and nonverbal negotiating tactics. Several "dirty tricks" are described, which, although common, do not particularly help in arriving at mutually beneficial agreements.

VERBAL TACTICS

Negotiators use many verbal tactics. Research (26) has shown that negotiators do better—their profits increase—as (a) the number of questions asked increases; (b) the number of commitments made prior to the final agreement stage decreases; and (c) the amount of the initial request increases (that is, sellers ask for more and buyers offer less). Consequently, in most cultures, effective negotiators start by having high expectations and making high initial offers (or requests), proceed by asking a lot of questions, and refrain from making many commitments until the final stage of the negotiation.

Initial Offers The Chinese (47;54) and Russians (36) habitually use extreme initial offers and requests as their opening bargaining strategy. By contrast, Swedes initially request a price close to the one they expect to get. Americans negotiating domestically consistently reach higher and more satisfactory outcomes using extreme rather than moderate opening offers (59). Other research also suggests that negotiators starting with extreme positions have a higher probability of reaching an agreement (44).

Why do extreme initial positions help? Although not yet thoroughly researched in cross-cultural contexts, some scholars believe that extreme positions (a) demonstrate to counterparts that the negotiator will not be exploited (59), (b) allow negotiators to gain more than expected, (c) prolong the negotiating process, thus allowing negotiators to gain more information about their counterparts, (d) modify counterparts' beliefs about the negotiator's preferences, (e) create more room to make subsequent concessions and thus to exhibit cooperation, and (f) communicate negotiators' willingness to play the game according to "usual" norms (79:727). Exceptions to the advantages of high initial offers also exist. Japanese diplomats who make extreme opening offers in global negotiations, for example, often have them treated as phony by the other team (1). More importantly, extreme offers appear to discourage synergistic agreements. The following news report (in the box "Negotiating for Olympic Coverage") highlights the contrasting expectations of American and Japanese negotiators.

Range of Tactics Some of the more common tactics used in negotiating include promises, threats, recommendations, warnings, rewards, punishments, normative appeals, commitments, self-disclosure, questions, and commands. Table 9-6 describes each briefly. The use and

NEGOTIATING FOR OLYMPIC COVERAGE

The Olympic Committee for the Los Angeles Olympics negotiated television broadcasting rights with various countries. From the American Broadcasting Company (ABC), the Olympic Committee received $225 million. From the Japanese, the Committee received $18.5 million. Why did the Japanese pay so much less?

The Japanese originally offered $6 million for the rights and the Olympic Committee countered with $90 million. The Committee's goal was $10 million. The Japanese argued that theirs was a smaller market than that of the United States. Moreover, the Japanese had only one Japanese television station bidding, whereas the Americans had all three major networks bidding up the price (ABC, CBS, and NBC). High expectations (for a low price), convincing arguments (smaller market), and little competition resulted in a final cost to the Japanese network that was one-twelfth that of its American counterparts.

Source: John L. Graham, The Paul Merage School of Business, University of California, Irvine.

meaning of many of these tactics vary across cultures. As shown in Table 9-7, negotiators from Asia (Japanese), North America (Americans), and South America (Brazilians) use very different verbal tactics in negotiating (28). Brazilians, for example, say "no" nine times more frequently than do Americans, and almost fifteen times more frequently than do the Japanese. Similarly, Brazilians make more initial concessions than do Americans, who in turn make more than the Japanese (28).

The British Huthwaite study, documenting successful negotiators' behavior, analyzed the verbal behavior of skilled and average negotiators (56:6.6–6.13). As shown in Table 9-8, the most skillful British negotiators use fewer irritators, counterproposals, and defend/attack spirals, less argument dilution, and more behavioral labels, active listening, questions, and feeling commentaries. Each of these negotiating tactics will now be briefly described (56).

- *Irritators* refer to words that, although having negligible value in persuading counterparts, cause annoyance. Irritators include such phrases as "generous offer," "fair price," and "reasonable arrangement." Average negotiators use over four times as many irritators as do skilled negotiators.

- *Counterproposals* involve negotiators responding to their counterparts' proposals by simply offering their own proposal. Average negotiators use counterproposals twice as often as skilled negotiators. Skilled negotiators clarify their understanding of counterparts' suggestions before responding with their own proposals.

TABLE 9-6   Verbal Negotiating Tactics

Tactic	Description	Example
Promise *(conditional, positive)*	I will do something you want me to do, if you do something I want you to do.	I will lower the price by $50 if you increase the order by 100 units.
Threat *(conditional, negative)*	I will do something you don't want me to do, if you do something I don't want you to do.	I'll walk out of the negotiation if you leak this story to the press.
Recommendation *(third party positive)*	If you do something I want you to do, a third party will do something you want.	If you lower your price, more teenagers will be able to buy your product.
Warning *(third party negative)*	If you do something I don't want you to do, a third party will do something you don't want.	If you don't settle, the journalists will spill this whole sordid story on the evening news nationwide.
Reward *(unconditional, positive)*	I will give you something positive (something you want) now, on the spot.	Let's make it easier on you next time and meet closer to your office. I have really appreciated your willingness to meet in my city.
Punishment *(unconditional, negative)*	I will give you something negative (something you don't want) now, on the spot.	I refuse to listen to your screaming. I am leaving.
Normative Appeal	I appeal to a societal norm.	Everybody else buys our product for $50 per unit.
Commitment *(unconditional, positive)*	I will do something you want.	I will deliver 100 units by June 15.
Self-Disclosure	I will tell you something about myself.	We have had to lay off 100 employees this month. We really need to sign a major contract by the end of the year.
Question	I ask you something about yourself.	Can you tell me more about your Brazilian operation?
Command	I order you to do something.	Lower your price.

- *Defend/attack spiral.* Negotiating, by definition, involves conflict. That conflict often leads to heated, value-laden accusations and defensive statements. Average negotiators frequently respond defensively and often attack the other team, first gently and then harder and harder. Skilled negotiators, by contrast, rarely respond defensively. Although they also rarely attack, when they do so, they hit hard and without warning. Average negotiators attack more than three times as frequently as do skilled negotiators.

- *Behavioral labeling* refers to describing what you plan to say before you say it. For example, "Can I ask a question?" and "Can I make a suggestion?" are behavioral labels for asking a question and making a suggestion. Behavioral labels forewarn counterparts. For all behavior

TABLE 9-7   Verbal Negotiating Behaviors Vary Across Cultures

Verbal Negotiating Behaviors (Tactics)	Average Number of Times Tactic Was Used in Half-Hour Negotiating Sessions		
	Japan	United States of America	Brazil
Promise	7	8	3
Threat	4	4	2
Recommendation	7	4	5
Warning	2	1	1
Reward	1	2	2
Punishment	1	3	3
Normative appeal	4	2	1
Commitment	15	13	8
Self-disclosure	34	36	39
Question	20	20	22
Command	8	6	14
Saying "No" (per 30 minutes)	5.7	9.0	83.4
Profit level of first offers (80 maximum)	61.5	57.3	75.2
Initial concessions	6.5	7.1	9.4

Source: Graham (28); adapted by Adler, 2007.[7]

TABLE 9-8   How Successful Negotiators Negotiate

Negotiating Behavior	Skilled Negotiators	Average Negotiators
Use of *irritators* per hour of face-to-face negotiating time	2.3	10.8
Frequency of *counterproposals* per hour of face-to-face negotiating time	1.7	3.1
Percent of negotiator's time classified as a *defense/attack spiral*	1.9%	6.3%
Percent of all negotiator's behavior immediately preceded by a *behavioral label:*		
Disagreeing	0.4%	1.5%
All behavior except disagreeing	6.4%	1.2%
Percent of negotiator's time spent *actively listening:*		
Testing for understanding	9.7%	4.1%
Summarizing	7.5%	4.2%
Questions, as a percent of all negotiating behavior	21.3%	9.6%
Feelings commentary, giving internal information as a percent of all negotiating behavior	12.1%	7.8%
Argument dilution, average number of reasons given by negotiators to back each argument or case they advance	1.8	3.0

Source: Rackham (55); adapted by Adler, 2007.[8]

except disagreement, skilled negotiators use labeling over five times as often as their average colleagues. Average negotiators label disagreement three times as often as do skilled negotiators.

- *Active listening* involves demonstrating to oneself and one's counterpart that the previous statement has been understood. Active listening does not convey agreement or approval, it strictly reflects understanding. Skilled negotiators use two powerful active listening techniques—testing for understanding and summarizing—more than twice as often as their average colleagues.

- *Questions* are a primary method of gathering information. Skilled negotiators ask more than twice as many questions as do average negotiators.

- *Feelings commentary* involves describing what a person feels about a situation. A negotiator might say, "I'm uncertain how to react to what you've just said. If the information you've given me is true, then I would like to accept it; yet I feel some doubts inside me about its accuracy. So part of me feels happy and part feels suspicious. Can you help me resolve this?" Skilled negotiators give almost twice as much feelings commentary as do average negotiators.

- *Argument dilution.* Weak arguments generally dilute strong arguments. Skilled negotiators know that the fewer arguments, the better. Average negotiators use almost twice as many reasons to back each of their positions as do skilled negotiators.

In summary, the Huthwaite group found that skilled British negotiators avoid irritators, counterproposals, defend/attack spirals, and argument dilution. They use behavioral labeling (except for disagreement), active listening, questions, and feelings commentaries. Unfortunately, this important study has not yet been replicated worldwide.

NONVERBAL TACTICS

Nonverbal behavior refers to what negotiators do rather than what they say. It involves how they say their words, rather than the words themselves. Nonverbal behavior includes tone of voice, facial expressions, body distance, dress, gestures, timing, silences, and symbols. Nonverbal behavior is complex and multifaceted; it sends multiple messages, many of which are responded to subconsciously. Negotiators frequently respond more emotionally and powerfully to the nonverbal than to the verbal message, often leading to positive or negative spirals that directly affect the outcome of the negotiation (22).

As with verbal behavior (language), nonverbal behavior varies markedly across cultures. As shown in Table 9-9, the extent to which Americans, Brazilians, and Japanese use silence, conversational overlaps, facial gazing, and touching during a negotiation varies considerably (28).

TABLE 9-9   Nonverbal Negotiating Behaviors Vary Across Cultures

Behaviors (Tactics)	Americans	Brazilians	Japanese
Silent Periods Number of silent periods greater than 10 seconds, per 30 minute negotiation	3.5	0	5.5
Conversational Overlaps Number of overlaps per 10 minutes	10.3	28.6	12.6
Facial Gazing Minutes of gazing per 10 minutes	3.3	5.2	1.3
Touching Not including handshaking, per 30 minutes	0	4.7	0

Source: Graham (28); adapted by Adler, 2007.[9]

Silence Japanese use the most silence, Americans a moderate amount, and Brazilians almost none at all. Americans often respond to silence by assuming that the other team disagrees or has not accepted their offer. Moreover, they tend to argue and make concessions in response to silence. This response does not cause problems in negotiating with Brazilians, but it severely disadvantages Americans when they negotiate with Japanese. While the Japanese silently consider the Americans' offer, the Americans interpret the silence as rejection and respond by making concessions (e.g., by lowering the price). Similar dynamics occur when non-native English speakers negotiate in English. As the non-native English speakers hesitate, to make certain that they fully understand the meaning of the English words, Americans frequently assume that they are rejecting the Americans' position. Again, they tend to misinterpret the silence as rejection and respond by making unnecessary concessions.

Conversational Overlaps Conversational overlaps are the opposite of silent periods; they occur when more than one person speaks at the same time. As shown in Table 9-9 and Figure 9-3, Brazilian negotiators interrupt each other more than twice as often as do either American or Japanese negotiators (28). Multiple members of the Brazilian team frequently talk simultaneously. By contrast, when Japanese or American negotiators are interrupted, one or the other speaker generally stops talking—thus minimizing the conversational overlap. Cultures such as the American and, even more so, the Japanese, in which people do not talk while another person is talking, generally interpret conversational overlaps as rude and disrespectful behavior.[10]

Facial Gazing Facial gazing involves looking directly in the face of one's counterpart. Eye contact is one of the most intense forms of facial gazing.

FIGURE 9-3   Conversational Overlaps: Who Interrupts Whom?

COUNTRY	PATTERN	DESCRIPTION
Brazil		Overlapping
Japan		Silent Periods
United States of America		Alternating

Negotiators in some cultures interrupt each other; in other cultures, they do not. A two-person negotiation is diagrammed above for three countries. A line indicates that either negotiator one or two is speaking, but not both. Blanks indicate that both negotiators are silent. Overlaps indicate that both negotiators are speaking at the same time.

Source: Graham (28); adapted by Adler, 2007.[11]

The amount of eye contact and facial gazing often communicates the level of intimacy in a relationship—the more eye contact, the more intimacy. Confusion occurs when the appropriate amount of gazing for one culture communicates too much or too little intimacy for people from another culture. In both cases bargaining partners from the other culture feel uncomfortable. Brazilians use four times as much facial gazing as Japanese, and one and one-half times more than Americans (28).

Touching Whether negotiators touch each other during bargaining sessions depends on the cultures involved. Without including hand-shaking, Brazilian negotiators touch each other almost five times every half hour, whereas there is no physical contact between American or Japanese negotiators (28). Similar to facial gazing, touching communicates intimacy. A hug—a *double abrazo*—in Mexico communicates the development of a trusting relationship, whereas the same gesture offends Germans, for whom it communicates an inappropriately high level of intimacy.

DIRTY TRICKS

Some domestic and global negotiators do not search for mutually benefi-cial agreements. In attempting to gain the most for themselves, some nego-tiators resort to "dirty tricks," tactics designed to pressure opponents into undesirable concessions and agreements. For example, your counterpart might attempt to exploit your jet lag by scheduling a meeting immediately after you arrive and then insisting that he take you out for dinner and enter-tainment; thus guaranteeing that you will feel exhausted by the time the negotiations open on the following day (49). If you suspect that your clients might use such a tactic, simply arrive a day earlier than they expect, go to your hotel, and get some rest. In general, negotiators can reduce the use of dirty tricks by (20):

- Not using them themselves
- Recognizing them when their counterparts use them, explicitly pointing them out, and negotiating about their use (i.e., establish-ing the "rules of the game")
- Knowing what the cost of walking out is if the other party refuses to use principled negotiation (i.e., knowing ahead of time what the best alternative is to a negotiated solution)
- Realizing that tactics that appear "dirty" to people from another culture may be acceptable to your team

Avoiding dirty tricks is more complex in an international context than it is in a domestic context. Effective negotiators systematically question their own interpretations of their counterparts' tactics rather than naïvely assuming that others' tactics have the same intended mean-ings as they would within the negotiator's home culture. Table 9-10 out-lines a series of commonly used dirty tricks, including various types of deliberate deception, psychological warfare, and positional pressure tactics (20).

Reviewing the range of dirty tricks from a cross-cultural perspective reveals some of the possible misinterpretations global negotiators face. Brazilians, for example, expect more deception among negotiators who do not know each other than do Americans. Brazilians are therefore more likely to use "phony facts" during the initial stages of a global negotiation than are some of their counterparts (28;70). The recommen-dation therefore is: "Unless you have good reason to trust someone, don't!" (20).

A negotiating team's discretion (the extent of its authority) varies across cultures. Under communist regimes, Russians and Eastern Europeans traditionally had very limited authority; they had to check with their superiors if they wanted to deviate at all from the planned agenda. Americans, by contrast, generally have extensive authority; they expect to make the most important decisions at the negotiating table. When the other team has limited authority, experts recommend making all commitments tentative and conditional on the ability of the other party to accept and commit to their side of the deal (23). In cross-cultural business situations, negotiators must remember that the other parties may not be using limited authority as a form of deliberate

TABLE 9-10   What If They Use Dirty Tricks?
Principled Responses to Unprincipled Tactics

Unprincipled Tactics	Examples of Unprincipled Tactics (Ex) and Principled Responses (PR)
Deliberate Deception	**Tactics designed to make you believe something that is not true.**
Phony Facts	PR: *Unless you have good reason to trust someone, don't.*
Ambiguous Authority	PR: *"Alright. We'll treat it as a joint draft to which neither side is committed," or, "Good, you take it to your boss and I'll sleep on it. Then tomorrow either of us can suggest changes."*
Dubious Intentions	PR: *Call their cards and build in a compliance system. Note that less than full disclosure is not the same as deception.*
Psychological Warfare	**Tactics designed to make you feel uncomfortable, so that you will have a subconscious desire to end the negotiation as soon as possible.**
Stressful Situation	Ex: *Room too hot or too cold, no private place to talk, their turf, too much touching, etc.*
	PR: *Bring it up and change it.*
Personal Attacks	Ex: *Opponent comments on your clothes, your appearance ("Were you up all night?"), your status (by interrupting with other business, making you wait), your intelligence (making you repeat things, not listening), refusing to make eye contact.*
	PR: *Recognizing it usually nullifies it. Bringing it up usually ends it.*
Good Guy/ Bad Guy Routine	Ex: *"The price is $4,000" (bad guy). "But, we can offer you $3,800" (good guy).*
	PR: *"Why do you think $4,000 is reasonable; what is your principle?" Followed by a warning: "If the price is $4,000, X will happen."*
Positional Pressure Tactics	**Bargaining tactics designed to structure a situation so that only one side can effectively make concessions.**
Refuse to Negotiate	PR: *Ask why they refuse to negotiate. Will they be seen as weak? Suggest alternatives: negotiate through third parties, negotiate in private, send letters, etc.*
Extreme Demands	Ex: *Asking for $100,000 when it is only worth $25,000.*
	PR: *Ask why it is a reasonable demand (price). Bring tactic to their attention.*
Escalating Demands	Ex: *Making one concession and then adding new demands or reopening old demands.*
	PR: *Call the tactic to their attention and then take a break while you consider which issues you are willing to continue to negotiate on.*
Lock-in Tactics	Ex: *Committing to a course of action, usually publicly. Paradoxically, you strengthen your bargaining position as you weaken your control over the situation.*
	PR: *Don't take lock-in seriously. Resist lock-in on principle: "I understand you are publicly committed to X, but my practice is never to yield to pressure."*

(continued)

TABLE 9-10   (continued)

Unprincipled Tactics	Examples of Unprincipled Tactics (Ex) and Principled Responses (PR)
Hard-hearted Partner	Ex: *"I would agree, but my partner (i.e., boss) won't."*
	PR: *Get it in writing and/or negotiate directly with hard-hearted partner.*
Calculated Delay	Ex: *Waiting for the 11ᵗʰ hour. (Danger: If the 11ᵗʰ hour arrives, the other side may continue waiting.)*
	PR: *Make delaying tactic explicit and negotiate about it. Also create objective deadlines (such as starting to negotiate with another firm).*
Take It or Leave It	PR: *Ignore it. Or, explicitly recognize it, let them know what they have to lose if no agreement is reached, and look for a face-saving way for them to back off.*

Source: Fisher & Ury (20); adapted by Adler, 2007.

deception; they may simply come from cultures where the authorities delegate very little discretion to individual team members.

Psychological warfare (tactics designed to make the other person feel uncomfortable) has different meanings in different cultures. A common psychological trick, for example, involves too much touching or too little eye contact. As discussed earlier, both extremes make people uncomfortable; both make them want to get out of the situation quickly (and therefore conclude the negotiation as soon as possible). Problems arise in defining appropriate versus extreme amounts of touching and eye contact across cultures. Latins touch much more than Canadians, who in turn touch more than Swedes. Arabs maintain much greater eye contact than do Americans, who in turn use more than the Japanese. What appears to be a dirty trick from a domestic perspective may, in fact, simply express another culture's typical behavior. As with other potentially inappropriate tactics, negotiators must differentiate intended psychological warfare from both intended and unintended expressions of a culture's normal behavior patterns. Review the two global international management situations—"Off the Books Payments" and "Extremely High Freight Forwarding Fees"—described at the end of this chapter and decide whether the parties involved are using dirty tricks or culturally appropriate behavior.

WHOSE STYLE TO USE?

When should global negotiators continue to use their own cultural style of negotiating and when should they adopt the style of their counterparts? Global negotiations expert Stephen Weiss suggests that

FIGURE 9-4   **Whose Style to Use? Yours or Theirs?
Culturally Responsive Negotiating Strategies**

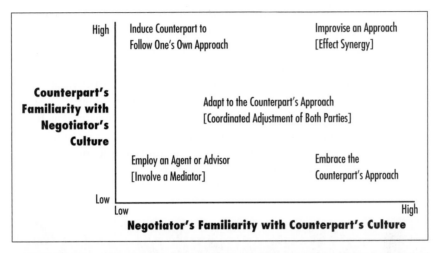

Brackets indicate a joint strategy requiring deliberate consultation with one's counterpart. At each level of cultural familiarity, negotiators can consider as feasible the strategies at that level or any lower level.

Source: Weiss (75); adapted by Adler, 2007.[12]

negotiators have five options, depending on the nature of the negotiation and the level of cross-cultural knowledge each negotiating team has (71;74;76;77). As outlined in Figure 9-4, if neither team is familiar with the other's culture, it would be best to consider employing agents to represent the teams. If your team has a high knowledge of their culture, but their team has a limited knowledge of your team's culture, you have the option of embracing their cultural approach to negotiating. If the opposite is true, and they have a high knowledge of your culture while you only have a limited knowledge of their culture, you can attempt to induce your counterparts to follow your culture's approach to negotiating. If both teams have a moderate knowledge of their counterparts' culture, both teams can adapt somewhat to each other's style. In the ideal situation, in which both teams have an in-depth knowledge of the other's culture, the two teams can improvise an approach that works for them both; that is, they can create a culturally synergistic approach to the negotiation (see Chapter 4). Although no option guarantees a positive outcome, the higher the cross-cultural knowledge on the part of both negotiating teams, the more options open to them and the greater their chances of reaching a satisfactory agreement.

NEGOTIATING ACROSS CULTURES: ETHICAL CHALLENGES

Global firms constantly confront cross-cultural business negotiations that challenge their notions of effective and ethical behavior. Review the following two situations, "Off the Books Payments" and "Extremely High Freight-Forwarding Fees." In each case the senior management team of a major North American–based transnational firm must ethically and effectively manage the immediate situation as well as set a policy to guide their company's behavior in the future. Analyze each situation from both cultures' perspectives before choosing how to manage the immediate situation and prior to recommending a more general corporate policy governing all such situations.

OFF THE BOOKS PAYMENTS

Prestige, a North American-based global firm, sent American Frank Quick to the Middle East to scout out possibilities for increasing the market for a particular Prestige product. Two other global firms compete directly with Prestige for this market, Companies Y and Z.

Frank has spent a year in one Middle Eastern country and has made considerable progress. He has made it quite clear to prospective buyers that Prestige offers a much better product than does the competition. Frank has been working especially hard to obtain a large order from the top officials of a large local company, Ajax, rather than having Ajax place their order with either Company Y or Z.

Ajax presently buys some products from Prestige and some from Companies Y and Z. While admitting that it regards Prestige's products as uniformly superior, Ajax claims it chooses to spread its business among the three suppliers as a hedge against possible failure of supply. Nonetheless, Frank is persisting in his dogged efforts to make Prestige Ajax's sole supplier.

Recently, Ajax's vice president of purchasing invited Frank to his office and informed him that Ajax would be willing to gradually taper off business with Companies Y and Z, primarily because Prestige offers a better product. He adds, however, that under-the-table payments are rather common in his country, and proceeds to hint broadly that he accepts substantial payments from both of the other two companies. Subtly, he indicates that if Prestige pays him an amount equal to the combined payments of Companies Y and Z, Prestige will become his exclusive supplier. However, if Prestige refuses, he will keep Prestige's present contract at its existing level, while expanding Ajax's business with Companies Y and Z, who, he claims, are prepared to make even greater payments than in the past.

OFF THE BOOKS PAYMENTS (continued)

Questions for Reflection

1. Under these circumstances, can Prestige continue to conduct any business with Ajax?
2. Does Prestige have an obligation to make public the described under-the-table payments of Companies Y and Z? How much loyalty does Prestige owe to other global firms operating in the host country's business community?
3. Will making this information public force Companies Y and Z to lose their contracts with Ajax? Will such behavior work to Prestige's advantage or disadvantage?

Senior Management Committee Decisions

1. What should Prestige advise Frank to do? What should Prestige's overall policy on such payments be? Should Prestige walk away from companies or individuals who accept under-the-table payments?
2. Should Prestige expose the other companies? Why? Why not? What moral grounds does a company have to try to change the behavior of other companies?
3. What moral grounds does a company have to try to change the country?
4. What would you do if you were in Frank's position?

EXTREMELY HIGH FREIGHT-FORWARDING FEES

In a certain Asian country the only way companies can get raw materials, parts, and finished products through local customs is to use a local freight-forwarding agent at the airport, seaport, or other point of entry. These agents charge forwarding fees that seem extremely high to many outsiders. The explanation, though hard to pin down, appears to be that the freight-forwarding agents use some of the money that companies pay them to make under-the-table payments to local customs officials. When agents make such payments, shipments appear to clear customs more quickly, thus helping to reduce the companies' cycle time.

Business has long been conducted in this way in this country, ostensibly because the government underpays local customs officials and offers them annual raises that do not keep pace with inflation. According to common knowledge, the government assumes that officials will receive part of their income from direct payments from companies and individuals needing customs assistance.

EXTREMELY HIGH FREIGHT-FORWARDING FEES (continued)

When Prestige, a North American–based global company, originally entered this country some years ago, it did not believe that the government allowed this practice, or that it even took place. However, in the intervening years, the political milieu changed, along with a certain loosening of discipline among civil servants, due in part to surging inflation. Recently, expatriates working for Prestige in this country have become increasingly convinced that the situation has become unacceptable, that such payments do not reflect good ethical practice, and that therefore they do not reflect good business practice.

Questions for Reflection

1. Given Prestige's corporate beliefs in the highest level of integrity and the utmost respect for people, what type of respect should Prestige's global managers show to customs and freight-forwarding agents who expect and accept unofficial payments from companies or individuals? How would your behavior change if you knew that typical customs officials in this particular country believe that, far from doing anything unethical, they would be acting unethically, given the inflationary situation, if they failed to accept some additional unofficial payments needed to feed their families and to educate their children? Would knowing the customs agents' appreciation of the situation change your judgment or behavior?
2. Who is to blame? Should Prestige blame the government rather than the individual customs and freight-forwarding agents? Does Prestige have any right to interfere with the procedures of customs and freight-forwarding agents in this, or any other, country?
3. Knowing that such practices exist, what responsibility does Prestige's management have in the host country? Should Prestige make it clear in a quiet but firm way that the company will not participate in such practices? To whom? Are there circumstances under which Prestige should publicly state its position on this issue? What other alternatives does Prestige have?
4. Should an individual Prestige manager who learns about such unofficial payments and reports them to his or her immediate supervisor without apparent effect, report the situation directly to senior management?

Senior Management Committee Decisions

1. What constitutes ethical behavior in this case?
2. What should Prestige's policy be toward such payments in this country? In all countries?
3. How should Prestige implement this policy?
4. As an individual, what would you be willing to do if you were working in this country? What would you be unwilling to do? Why?

SUMMARY

"When in Rome, do as the Romans do?" No, when in Rome, or Beijing, or Prague, act like an effective foreigner. Lucian Pye, in his excellent book, *Chinese Commercial Negotiating Style*, recommends that foreigners conducting business in the People's Republic of China (54:xii):

> *(a) practice patience; (b) accept prolonged periods of no movement; (c) control against exaggerated expectations, and discount Chinese rhetoric about future prospects; (d) expect that the Chinese will try to influence by shaming; (e) resist the temptation to believe that difficulties may have been caused by one's own mistakes; and (f) try to understand Chinese cultural traits, but never believe that a foreigner can practice them better than the Chinese.*

Pye recommends recognizing and understanding the cultural differences, not trying to become a member of the other culture.

Negotiating styles clearly vary across cultures (4;10;21;34:435-437;37;63;66; 67;68). Words and behavior that effectively persuade people at home may fail to influence businesspeople from other countries. The cultural context of a negotiation significantly influences who should become a member of the negotiating team, where the parties should conduct the negotiation, and which approach—including strategy and tactics—negotiators should use. Negotiating globally requires acute observation skills and a more tentative approach to understanding meaning than its domestic counterpart. Not only does negotiating globally require that negotiators not jump to conclusions, it also rarely allows negotiators to conclude a negotiation definitively.

In preparing to negotiate globally, team members should learn as much as possible about the cultures of their negotiation partners—including their negotiating patterns and especially their style of negotiating with outsiders (4)—and then approach the actual meetings with the widest possible range of options and alternatives in behavior and substance. In initial meetings, negotiators should emphasize developing a relationship with their counterparts (remembering to let *them* bring up business). During the discussions, negotiators should assume differences exist in negotiating styles until similarity is proven. Negotiators can more easily move from an expectation of difference to an acceptance of similarity than recoup their losses from mistakes incurred in acting as if negotiation partners from other cultures bargain just like members of the home culture do when in fact they do not. Effective negotiators generally have high expectations and make high initial offers (or requests), proceed by asking a lot of questions, and refrain from making many commitments until the final stage of the negotiation. When bargaining, effective negotiators generally use fewer irritators, counterproposals, and defend/attack spirals; less argument dilution; and more behavioral labels, active listening, and feeling commentaries than do less skilled negotiators.

The most effective negotiators approach bargaining sessions searching for synergistic solutions—solutions in which both sides win. The art of negotiating lies in developing creative options and alternatives, not in using persuasive tactics that more often result in giving offense than in gaining acceptance.

QUESTIONS FOR REFLECTION

1. **Stages of a Negotiation.** Review the four stages of negotiation. Analyze your own negotiating style. Which stages do you emphasize more and which less? In what ways could your natural style of negotiating—the style that you use at home with businesspeople from your own culture—cause problems when negotiating abroad?

2. **Culturally Synergistic Negotiating.** Why does the synergistic negotiating style succeed most frequently in negotiations involving businesspeople from more than one culture?

3. **Preparing for a Negotiation.** How would you prepare for and negotiate with businesspeople from Mumbai, India? From Paris, France? From Stockholm, Sweden? From Rio de Janeiro, Brazil? From Gaborone, Botswana? In each culture, what would you make certain you did at the first session? What would you avoid doing at the first session?

4. **Cultural Self-Awareness.** When negotiators from another culture hear that someone is coming to negotiate with them from your country, what do they expect? What is the stereotype—the most commonly expected behavior—of negotiators from your country? How could you use that stereotype to your advantage? In what ways could the stereotype of negotiators from your culture disadvantage you? In what ways could you overcome the disadvantages associated with the stereotype of negotiators from your culture?

5. **Learning from Success.** Think about the most successful cross-cultural negotiation you have ever seen or been involved with. Describe it. What allowed it to be so successful? What can you learn from this successful negotiation to make your future negotiations more successful?

NOTES

1. Reprinted with permission from Pergamon Press, Ltd.

2. Reprinted with permission of Intercultural Press, Inc., Yarmouth, Maine. Copyright, 1982. Out of print. Adapted by Adler from Pierre Casse,

Training for the Multicultural Manager (Yarmouth, ME: Intercultural Press, 1982).

3. Adapted by Adler from Ellen Raider, "Strategy Assessment," in *International Negotiations* (Plymouth Mass.: Situation Management Systems, 1982). Reprinted with permission of Coleman Raider International.

4. The traditional approach is based on Graham and Herberger (30), the principled approach is based on Fisher and Ury (20), and the synergistic approach is based on Adler (see Chapter 4).

5. Copyright © 1976. Reprinted by permission of Huthwaite, Inc.

6. Copyright © 1985. Reprinted by permission of the author (57).

7. Reprinted with permission of *The Journal International Business Studies*, Newark, N.J.

8. Copyright © 1976. Reprinted by permission of Huthwaite, Inc.

9. Reprinted with permission of *The Journal International Business Studies*, Newark, N.J.

10. Deborah Tannen, Professor of Linguistics at Georgetown University, studied conversational overlaps and interruptions in conversation. She found distinct differences among regional ethnic groups in the United States, as well as between the United States and other national groups. A New Yorker may considered rude by a polite Californian, and that same polite Californian may be considered rude by New Englanders (62:188-215).

11. Reprinted with permission of *The Journal International Business Studies*, Newark, N.J.

12. Copyright © Sloan Management Review, Reprinted with permission.

REFERENCES

1. Adair, Wendy L. "Exploring the Norm of Reciprocity in the Global Market: U.S. and Japanese Intra- and Inter-Cultural Negotiations," in S. J. Havlovic, ed., *59th Annual Meeting of The Academy of Management: Proceedings*, 1999.

2. Adair, Wendi L.; & Brett, Jeanne M. "Culture and Negotiation Processes," in Michele J. Gelfand and Jeanne M. Brett, eds. *The Handbook of Negotiation and Culture* (Stanford, Calif.: Stanford University Press, 2004), pp. 158–176.

3. Adler, N. J.; & Graham, John L. "Business Negotiations: Canadians Are Not Just Like Americans," *Canadian Journal of Administrative Sciences*, vol. 4, no. 3 (1987), pp. 211–238.

4. Adler, N. J.; & Graham, John L. "Cross-Cultural Interaction: The International Comparison Fallacy," *Journal of International Business Studies*, vol. 20, no. 3 (1989), pp. 515–537.

5. Adler, N. J.; Graham John L.; & Brahm, R. "Strategy Implementation: A Comparison of Face-to-Face Negotiations in The People's

Republic of China," *Strategic Management Journal,* vol. 13, no. 7 (1992), pp. 449–466.

6. Adler, N. J.; Schwartz, T.; & Graham, John L. "Business Negotiations in Canada (French and English Speakers), Mexico, and the United States," *Journal of Business Research,* vol. 15, no. 4 (1987), pp. 411–429.

7. Al-Ghamdi, Salem M. "Success and Failure in Saudi-American Negotiations: American Views," *International Negotiation,* vol. 4, no. 1 (1999), pp. 23–36.

8. Beliaev, E.; Mullen, T.; & Punnett, B. J. "Understanding the Cultural Environment: U.S.A.-U.S.S.R. Trade Negotiation," *California Management Review,* vol. 27, no. 2 (1985), pp. 100–112.

9. Blaker, M. *Japanese International Negotiating Style* (New York: Columbia University Press, 1977).

10. Brett, Jeanne M. *Negotiating Globally: How to Negotiate Deals, Resolve Disputes, and Make Decisions Across Cultural Boundaries* (San Francisco: Jossey Bass, 2001).

11. Brett, Jeanne M.; Adair, Wendy L.; Lempereur, A.; Okumura, T.; Tinsley, Catherine; & Lytle, A. "Culture and Joint Gains in Negotiation," *Negotiation Journal,* vol. 14, no. 1 (1998), pp. 61–86.

12. Brett, Jeanne M.; & Okumura, Tetsushi. "Inter- and Intracultural Negotiation: U.S. and Japanese Negotiators," *Academy of Management Journal,* vol. 41, no. 5 (1998), pp. 495–510.

13. Campbell, N.; Graham, J. L.; Jolibert, A.; & Meissner, H. "Marketing Negotiations in France, Germany, the United Kingdom, and the United States," *Journal of Marketing,* vol. 52, no. 2 (1988), pp. 49–62.

14. Casse, Pierre. *Training for the Cross-Cultural Mind,* 2nd ed. (Washington, DC: Society for Intercultural Education, Training, and Research, 1981).

15. Cohen, H. *You Can Negotiate Anything* (Secaucus, N. J.: Lyle Stuart, 1980).

16. Dupont, C. *La négociation: Conduite, théorie, applications* (Paris: Dalloz, 1982).

17. Fayweather, John; & Kapoor, A. "Simulated International Business Negotiations," *Journal of International Business Studies,* vol. 3 (Spring 1972), pp. 19–31.

18. Fayweather, John; & Kapoor, A. *Strategy and Negotiation for the International Corporation* (Cambridge, Mass.: Ballinger, 1976), pp. 29–50.

19. Fisher, Glenn. *International Negotiations: A Cross-Cultural Perspective* (Chicago: Intercultural Press, 1980).

20. Fisher, R.; & Ury, W. *Getting to Yes* (New York: Houghton Mifflin, 1981).

21. Gelfand, Michele J.; & Brett, Jeanne M., eds. *The Handbook of Negotiation and Culture* (Stanford, Calif.: Stanford University Press, 2004).

22. George, Jennifer M.; Jones Gareth R.; & Gonzalez, Jorge A. "The Role of Affect in Cross-Cultural Negotiations," *Journal of International Business Studies,* vol. 29, no. 4 (1998), pp. 749–772.

23. Glenn, E. S.; Witmeyer, D. & Stevenson, K. A. "Cultural Styles of Persuasion," *International Journal of Intercultural Relations,* vol. 1, no. 3 (1977), pp. 52–66.

24. Graham, John L. "Brazilian, Japanese, and American Business Negotiations," *Journal of International Business Studies,* vol. 14, no. 1 (1983), pp. 47–61.

25. Graham, John L. "Deference Given the Buyer: Variations Across Twelve Cultures," in P. Lorange & F. Contractor, eds., *Cooperative Strategies in International Business* (Lexington, Mass.: Lexington Books, 1987).

26. Graham, John L. "An Exploratory Study of the Process of Marketing Negotiations Using a Cross-Cultural Perspective," in R. Scarcella, E. Andersen, & S. Krashen, eds., *Developing Communicative Competence in a Second Language* (Rowley, Mass.: Newbury House Publishers, 1989).

27. Graham, John L. "A Hidden Cause of America's Trade Deficit with Japan," *Columbia Journal of World Business* (Fall 1981), pp. 5–15.

28. Graham, John L. "The Influence of Culture on the Process of Business Negotiations," *Journal of International Business Studies,* vol. 16, no. 1 (1985), pp. 81–96.

29. Graham, John L. "The Problem-Solving Approach to Interorganizational Negotiations: A Laboratory Test," *Journal of Business Research,* vol. 14 (1986), pp. 271–286.

30. Graham, John L.; & Herberger, R. A., Jr. "Negotiators Abroad—Don't Shoot from the Hip," *Harvard Business Review* (July–August 1983), pp. 160–168.

31. Graham, John L.; Kim, D. K.; Lin, C. Y.; & Robinson, M. "Buyer-Seller Negotiations Around the Pacific Rim: Differences in Fundamental Exchange Process," *Journal of Consumer Research,* vol. 15 (June 1988), pp. 48–54.

32. Graham, John L.; & Sano, Y. *Smart Bargaining: Doing Business with the Japanese* (Cambridge, Mass.: Ballinger, 1984).

33. Harnett, O. L.; & Cummings, L. L. *Bargaining Behavior: An International Study* (Houston, Tex.: Dane Publications, 1980).

34. Hofstede, Geert. *Culture's Consequences: Comparing Values, Behaviors, Institutions and Organizations Across Cultures,* 2nd ed. (Thousand Oaks, Calif.: Sage Publications, 2001), pp. 435–437.

35. Hofstede, Geert; & Bond, Michael H. "Confucius and Economic Growth: New Trends into Culture's Consequences," *Organizational Dynamics,* vol. 16, no. 4 (1988), pp. 4–21.

36. Ikle, F. C. *How Nations Negotiate* (New York: Harper & Row, 1964), pp. 225–255.

37. Jastram, R. W. "The Nakado Negotiators," *California Management Review,* vol. 17, no. 2 (1974), pp. 88–90.

38. Jehn, Karen; & Weigelt, Keith. "Chinese Thought, Game Theory, and Strategic International Negotiations," *International Negotiation,* vol. 4, no. 1 (1999), pp. 79–93.

39. Jensen, L. "Soviet-American Behavior in Disarmament Negotiations," in I. W. Zartman, ed., *The 50 Percent Solution* (New York: Anchor, 1976).

40. Kapoor, A. "MNC Negotiations: Characteristics and Planning Implications," *Columbia Journal of World Business* (Winter 1974), pp. 121–130.

41. Kapoor, A. "Negotiation Strategies in International Business-Government Relations: A Study in India," *Journal of International Business Studies,* vol. 1–2 (Summer 1970), pp. 21–42.

42. Kennedy, John F. Address given at American University, Washington, D.C., June 10, 1963.

43. Kirkbride, P. S.; Tang, Sara F. Y.; & Westwood, R. I. "Chinese Conflict Preferences and Negotiating Behaviour: Cultural and Psychological Influences," *Organizational Studies,* vol. 12, no. 3 (1991), pp. 365–386.

44. Komorita, S. S.; & Brenner, A. R. "Bargaining and Concession-Making Under Bilateral Monopoly," *Journal of Personality and Social Psychology,* vol. 9 (1968), pp. 15–20.

45. Krauthammer, C. "Deep Down, We're All Alike, Right? Wrong," *Time* (August 15, 1983), p. 30.

46. Kumar, Rajesh. "Communicative Conflict in Intercultural Negotiations: The Case of American and Japanese Business Negotiations," *International Negotiation,* vol. 4, no. 1 (1999), pp. 63–78.

47. Lall, A. *How Communist China Negotiates* (New York: Columbia University Press, 1966).

48. Lewicki, Roy J.; Weiss, Stephen E.; & Lewin, D. "Models of Conflict, Negotiation and Third Party Intervention: A Review and Synthesis," *Journal of Organizational Behavior,* vol. 13 (1992), pp. 209–252.

49. Lunz, Steve. "Identify and counter these 'dirty dozen' buyer tricks," in *Selling,* September 2005, pp. 6–7.

50. Mehrabian, A.; & Ferris, S. R. "Inference of Attitudes from Nonverbal Communication in Two Channels," *Journal of*

Consulting Psychology, vol. 31, no. 3 (1967), pp. 248–252. Also see Mehrabian, A. "Communicating Without Words," *Psychology Today* (September 1968), p. 53.

51. Muna, F. A. *The Arab Mind* (New York: Scribners, 1973).

52. Perlmutter, Howard. "More Than 50 Percent of International Managers' Time Is Spent in Negotiating—in Interpersonal Transaction Time Influencing Other Managers," statement made at Academy of Management Meetings, Dallas, Texas, August 1983, and at The Wharton School, University of Pennsylvania, 1984.

53. Plantey, A. *La Négociation Internationale: Principes et Méthodes* (Paris: Editions du Centre National de la Recherche Scientifique, 1980).

54. Pye, Lucian. *Chinese Commercial Negotiating Style* (Cambridge, Mass.: Oelgeschlager, Gunn and Hain, Publishers, 1982).

55. Rackham, N. *The Behavior of Successful Negotiators* (Reston, Va.: Huthwaite Research Group, 1976).

56. Raider, Ellen. *International Negotiations: A Training Program for Corporate Executives and Diplomats* (Brooklyn, N.Y.: Ellen Raider International, Inc.; and Plymouth, Mass.: Situation Management Systems, Inc., 1982); Berlew, D.; Moore, A.; & Harrison, R. *Positive Negotiation Programs* (Plymouth, Mass.: Situation Management Systems, Inc., 1978, 1980, and 1983).

57. Renwick, George. *Malays and Americans: Definite Differences, Unique Opportunities* (Yarmouth, Maine: Intercultural Press, 1985). Copyright © 1985. Reprinted by permission of the author.

58. Roemer, Christina; Garb, Paula; Neu, Joyce; & Graham, John L. "A Comparison of American and Russian Patterns of Behavior in Buyer-Seller Negotiations Using Observational Measures," *International Negotiation,* vol. 4, no. 1 (1999), pp. 37–61.

59. Rubin, J. Z., & Brown, B. R. *The Social Psychology of Bargaining and Negotiation* (New York: Academic Press, 1976).

60. Sawyer, J., & Guetzkow, H. "Bargaining and Negotiation in International Relations," in H. C. Kelman, ed., *International Behavior: A Social Psychological Analysis* (New York: Holt, Rinehart and Winston, 1965), pp. 464–520.

61. Tang, Sara F. Y., & Kirkbride, Paul S. "Developing Conflict Management Skills in Hong Kong: An Analysis of Some Cross-Cultural Implications," *Management Education and Development,* vol. 17, part 3 (1986), pp. 287–301.

62. Tannen, Deborah. *You Just Don't Understand: Women and Men in Conversation* (New York: Ballantine Books, 1990), pp. 188–215.

63. Terasawa, Y. "The Japanese Perspective in International Business Negotiations." Paper presented at the Academy of Management Meetings, Dallas, Texas, August 16, 1983.

64. Tinsley, Catherine H. "Models of Conflict Resolution in Japanese, German and American Cultures," *Journal of Applied Psychology*, vol. 83 (1998), pp. 316–323.

65. Tinsley, Catherine H.; & Weiss, Stephen E. "Examining International Business Negotiations and Directions for the Future," *International Negotiation*, vol. 4, no. 1 (1999), pp. 95–97.

66. Tung, Rosalie L. *Business Negotiations with the Japanese* (Lexington, Mass.: Lexington Books, 1984).

67. Tung, Rosalie L. "How to Negotiate with the Japanese," *California Management Review*, vol. 26, no. 4 (1984), pp. 62–77.

68. Tung, Rosalie L. "U.S.-China Trade Negotiations: Practices, Procedures and Outcomes," *Journal of International Business Studies*, vol. 13 (1982), pp. 25–38.

69. Van Zandt, H. F. "How to Negotiate in Japan," *Harvard Business Review* (November–December 1977), pp. 72–80.

70. Volkema, Roger J. "Ethnicality in Negotiations: An Analysis of Perceptual Similarities and Differences Between Brazil and the United States," *Journal of Business Research*, vol. 45, no. 1 (1999), pp. 59–67.

71. Weiss, Stephen E. "Analysis of Complex Negotiations in International Business: The RBC Perspective," *Organization Science*, vol. 4, no. 2 (1993), pp. 269–300.

72. Weiss, Stephen E. "Creating the GM-Toyota Joint Venture: A Case in Complex Negotiation," *Columbia Journal of World Business*, vol. 22, no. 2 (1987), pp. 23–37.

73. Weiss, Stephen E. "International Business Negotiation in a Globalizing World: Reflections on the Contributions and Future of a (Sub) Field," *International Negotiation*, vol. 11, no. 2 (2006), pp. 287–316.

74. Weiss, Stephen E. "International Negotiations: Bricks, Mortar, and Prospects," in B. J. Punnett & O. Shenkar, eds., *Handbook for International Management Research* (Cambridge, Mass.: Blackwell, 1996), pp. 209–265.

75. Weiss, Stephen E. "The Long Path to the IBM-Mexico Agreement: An Analysis of the Microcomputer Investment Negotiations, 1983–1985," *Journal of International Business Studies*, vol. 21, no. 4 (1990), pp. 565–596.

76. Weiss, Stephen E. "Negotiating with 'Romans'—Part 1," *Sloan Management Review* (Winter 1994), pp. 51–62.

77. Weiss, Stephen E. "Negotiating with 'Romans'—Part 2," *Sloan Management Review* (Spring 1994), pp. 85–100.

78. Weiss, Stephen E.; & Strip, W. G. "Negotiating with Foreign Business Persons." Working paper # 85–86, New York University, New York, 1985.

79. Weiss-Wik, S., "Enhancing Negotiators' Successfulness," *Journal of Conflict Resolution*, vol. 27, no. 4 (1983), pp. 706–739.

80. Wells, L. T. "Negotiating with Third World Governments," *Harvard Business Review* (January–February 1977), pp. 72–80.

81. Wright, P. "Doing Business in Islamic Markets," *Harvard Business Review*, vol. 59, no. 1 (1981), pp. 34ff.

PART 3

Managing
Global
Managers

Chapter 10

Managing Cross-Cultural Transitions: Moving Abroad and Coming Back Home

---

If a man does not keep pace with his companions,
perhaps it is because he hears a different drummer.
Let him step to the music which he hears,
however measured or far away.

—Henry David Thoreau, Walden

Global assignments have become an increasingly important, if not essential, part of managers' careers and a source of competitive advantage for global firms (14;18;60;95). However, this has not always been the case. Historically, companies have sent managers to live and work abroad for many reasons, depending primarily on the extent of globalization of their industry and the firm's specific business strategy (1;11;23;28;41;62;63;79). As shown in Table 10-1, domestic firms, of course, have no business need to send anyone abroad. Multi-domestic firms, by contrast, send people abroad primarily to transfer technology and, more importantly from the perspective of the firm, to maintain control over highly autonomous operations in countries around the world. Multi-domestic firms generally select home-country nationals—people who are known and trusted at headquarters—and send them abroad as *expatriates* to get a particular job done. Because the headquarters of multi-domestic firms often (although generally erroneously) view their international operations as simply replicating what has already been achieved at home, they rarely choose high-potential or top performers for expatriate assignments; rather, they frequently settle for average performers. When expatriates who have been sent abroad by multi-domestic firms return home, they often find no jobs waiting for them, little value given by their firms to the international experience they have gained, and gain little benefit to their overall careers.

TABLE 10-1   A Company's Business Strategy Determines the Nature of Its Global Assignments

Business Strategy	Domestic	Multidomestic	Multinational	Global
Global Assignments	None	Expatriates	Expatriates and inpatriates	Expatriates, inpatriates, and transpatriates
Who Sent	No one	Home-country nationals sent abroad	Home-country nationals sent abroad and local nationals brought to headquarters	People sent from any country to any country
	—	Average performers	Good performers	High-potential managers and top executives
Purpose	—	Project (to get job done abroad)	Project and career development	Project, career, and organizational development
Career Impact	—	Negative for domestic career	Good for global career	Essential for executive suite
Professional Re-entry	—	Extremely difficult	Somewhat difficult	Easy
Global Organizational Learning	None	None	Limited	Extensive

Luckily for expatriates, the implications of global assignments become more positive as firms increase their commitment to global business. In contrast to both domestic and multi-domestic firms, multinational firms operate highly integrated global lines of business. Multinational firms also send expatriates abroad; but rather than selecting average performers, they choose their best performers—both senior managers who can take responsibility for worldwide lines of business and more junior high-potential managers who can benefit from worldwide experience in their career development. Because multinationals are highly integrated, they stay in close contact with their expatriates while they are abroad and carefully fit them back into the organization when they return home. Professional re-entry is therefore considerably easier for expatriates returning from global assignments in multinational firms than for those returning to multi-domestic firms.

In addition to sending home-country managers abroad as expatriates, multinationals also bring managers from local cultures around the world—*inpatriates*—into the home country on assignments designed to help them learn about the headquarter's organizational culture and

A PORTRAIT OF TODAY'S EXPATRIATES

Most expatriates are married men, representing 55 to 66 percent of those sent abroad. Since 1996, however, the proportion of married men among all expatriates has been decreasing. Single men comprise the second largest group of employees sent abroad, between 16 and 29 percent of the total. Over the last decade, the proportion of single men has increased. Seven to 10 percent of the expatriates companies send abroad are single women; an additional 5 to 10 percent are married women. Men and women accompanied by significant others remain the least common expatriates, averaging only 1 to 3 percent for each group.

In 2003, the most recent year for which accurate data exists, 86 percent of married expatriates were accompanied by their spouses, which is consistent with historical averages. Fifty-one percent of expatriates were accompanied by children, a decrease compared with the historical average of 59 percent.

Sixty percent of companies offer some type of cross-cultural pre-departure training; however, such training is mandatory at only a quarter of the companies. Twenty-eight percent of the companies offering training offer it to the entire family, 27 percent offer it to the expatriate and spouse (but not the children), and 5 percent offer it only to the expatriate.[1]

---

approach to doing business. The headquarters then returns the inpatriates back to their local cultures to manage local operations. Unfortunately, multinationals' corporate learning at this stage is generally only one-way: while teaching the inpatriates about the headquarter's culture, multinationals rarely spend much time learning from the inpatriates about their countries' local cultures and business environments.

Expatriate assignments in global firms differ markedly from those in domestic, multi-domestic, and multinational firms. Because global firms operate in highly competitive, complexly networked global business environments, they need executives who understand the world and have had experience working in numerous countries across several continents. Global firms therefore select the best people from anywhere in the world to send on assignments to anywhere else in the world. Rather than limiting themselves to transfers into and out of headquarters— that is, rather than limiting themselves either to expatriates (home-country nationals sent out to the rest of the world) or inpatriates (people from throughout the world brought into headquarters)—global firms select *transpatriates*. The prime role of transpatriates is organizational development; they act as the "glue" that holds the globally distributed firm together. For transpatriates to fulfill this role effectively, the company must stay in close contact with them and actively learn as much as possible from them, both while they work abroad and after they have either returned home or moved on to a new global assignment. Unlike their counterparts in domestic, multi-domestic, and multinational firms, managers working abroad for global firms find that their experience abroad helps, rather than hinders, their career progress.

Although multi-domestic, multinational, and global firms send people abroad for different reasons, in each case the person experiences a predictable series of stages in transferring from a domestic to a global assignment and back home again. As shown in Figure 10-1, companies recruit potential global managers either from within the organization or from other companies. The company then chooses whether to select the candidate for a global assignment, and the recruit chooses whether to accept the assignment. Next, many companies provide orientation sessions describing the global project and local foreign culture as well as the logistical arrangements for moving to the new country (17;19;24;36;48;49).

FIGURE 10-1   The Expatriate's Global Career Cycle

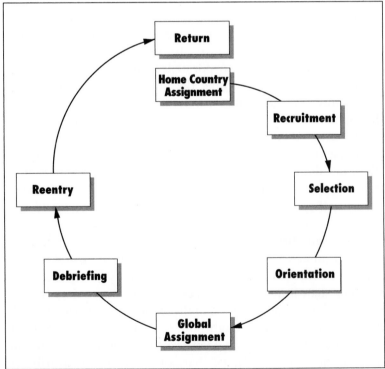

Oriented managers, usually accompanied by their families, then proceed abroad to accomplish the assignment. When managers come back to their home country, they either return to a position within the same organization or leave the organization to find a position elsewhere. Few companies conduct re-entry or debriefing sessions. The complete expatriate global career cycle thus includes two major international transitions: cross-cultural entry and home-country re-entry. Successful global companies understand and carefully manage each phase of the expatriate global career cycle (22;23;37;38;40;42;43;45;57;72;73;83; 91;99;101;102;103;105).[*]

ENTERING A NEW CULTURE

Cross-cultural adjustment includes adjusting to the job, to interactions with host nationals, and to the general nonwork environment of the host country (21; also see 20;88). As shown in Figure 10-2, cross-cultural adjustment to a country can be depicted as a U-shaped curve (53). In the initial phase, at the top of the curve, expatriates often feel very positive and excited as they discover the new culture. Business travelers, as compared with expatriates, often have the luxury of remaining at this stage. This initial phase is often followed by a period of disillusionment, during which it is no longer romantic to try to take a cab without knowing where to find the taxi stand; or to wait anxiously on Saturday for the arrival of an important letter, only to discover that weekend mail delivery does not exist; or to try to converse intelligently using a severely limited vocabulary. The bottom of the U-shaped curve is marked by *culture shock*—the frustration and confusion that result from being bombarded by too many new and uninterpretable cues. Following the culture shock phase, expatriates begin adapting to the new culture: they generally begin feeling more positive, working more effectively, and living a more satisfying life. Neither the highs of the initial phase nor the lows of the culture shock phase usually characterize this subsequent adjustment phase.

EXPERIENCING CULTURE SHOCK

Does everyone suffer from culture shock, or does it only afflict globally inexperienced managers and businesspeople moving to significantly different countries? Surprisingly, the most effective global managers often suffer the most severe culture shock (81). By contrast, global managers who are not particularly effective describe themselves as suffering little or no culture shock. Culture shock is not a disease, but

---

[*] *Note that in the following sections, the word expatriate is used to refer to expatriates, inpatriates, and transpatriates.*

rather a natural response to the stress of immersing oneself in a new environment. Economically and linguistically similar countries can cause as much culture shock as more dissimilar countries. Quebec-based executives initially experience culture shock when working in France, as do Australians transferring to Canada. Severe culture shock is often a positive sign indicating that the expatriate is becoming deeply involved in the new culture instead of remaining isolated in an expatriate ghetto. Experienced expatriates therefore should view culture shock as a sign that they are doing something right, not wrong. For them, the most important question is how best to manage the stress caused by culture shock, not how to avoid the culture shock itself.

What exactly is culture shock? Culture shock is the expatriate's reaction to a new, unpredictable, and therefore uncertain environment (13). As discussed in Chapter 3, culture shock results from a breakdown in an expatriate's selective perception and effective interpretation systems. Global managers who have recently arrived in a foreign country constantly need to ask such questions as "To what should I pay attention?" and "What does it mean?" Millions of sights, sounds, smells, tastes, and feelings bombard global managers, and they find it difficult to know which ones to treat as meaningful and which ones are unimportant and can therefore be screened out. Upon entering a new culture, global managers lack an interpretation system based on the local culture and are therefore forced to inappropriately and ineffectively use their home cultures' interpretive systems.

During the initial period in a new culture, global managers often find that other people's behavior does not seem to make sense,

FIGURE 10-2   Culture Shock Cycle

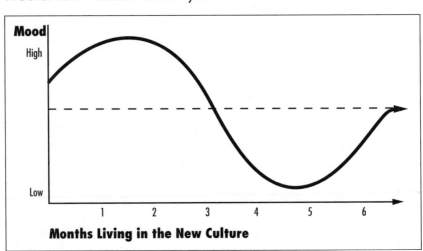

and—even more disconcerting—that their own behavior does not produce expected results. They find that the environment makes new demands for which they have neither ready-made answers nor the ability to develop new, culturally appropriate responses. A North American newly arrived in the Middle East, for example, described her experience:

> My third day in Israel, accompanied by a queasy stomach, I ventured forth into the corner market to buy something light and easy to digest. As yet unable to read Hebrew, I decided to pick up what looked like a small yogurt container that was sitting near the cheese. Not being 100 percent sure it contained yogurt, I peered inside; to my delight, it held a thick, white, yogurt-looking substance. I purchased my "yogurt" and went home to eat—soap, liquid soap! How was I to know that soap came in packages resembling yogurt containers, or that market items in this Israeli market were not neatly divided into edible and inedible sections, as I remembered them in the United States? My now "clean" stomach became a bit more fragile and my confidence waned.

Stress Change causes stress; expatriates face many changes in leaving their home country and organization and transferring to a new country and a new job. Separation from friends, family, children (perhaps for the first time), and parents (perhaps elderly or ill) increases stress. When expatriates arrive in a new country, different perceptions and conflicting values exacerbate the stress. Global managers see situations that they neither understand nor believe to be ethically correct. Some North American expatriates, for example, feel appalled by the poverty in many economically developing countries, especially in contrast to their own relatively luxurious international hotels and expatriate homes.

Stress-related culture shock may take many forms: anger, anxiety, disappointment, embarrassment, frustration, identity confusion, impatience, and physiological responses such as sleeplessness, stomachaches, headaches, and trembling hands. As one executive recalled, "There's some kind of traumatic reaction to it. It evidenced itself in my insomnia. There was something there . . . waking up at 4 A.M. every morning." Because culture shock is a sign that expatriates are beginning to let go of their home culture and engage with the new culture, the appropriate response is not to try to eliminate the culture shock but rather to manage the stress it causes.

Successful expatriates use many highly effective and creative stress management mechanisms for coping with culture shock. The most appropriate method depends on the particular individual and situation involved. Some people participate in regular physical exercise, some practice meditation and relaxation techniques, while others keep a journal ("Yell at the paper, not at the people!"). Many of the most effective global managers create *stability zones* (81). They spend most of their time totally immersed in the new culture, then briefly retreat into an environment—a stability zone—that closely resembles home. Examples of successful stability zones used by executives include checking into a home-country hotel for the weekend, going to an international club and talking only with other compatriots, playing a musical instrument, listening to familiar music, or watching movies in one's native language.

On the job, managers can reduce the stress caused by culture shock by recognizing it and modifying their expectations and behavior accordingly. They can establish priorities and focus their limited energy on only the most important tasks; they can clearly define their responsibilities and educate the home office concerning the cultural and business differences between the new country, headquarters, and other parts of the world; and they can realize that in their new position they will work neither as efficiently nor as effectively, especially initially, as they did previously. The exact nature of the stability zone and stress management techniques is less important than global managers' recognition of the highly stressful nature of moving into a new culture and their development of at least one stress-reduction technique that works for them.

Adjusting to Living and Working Abroad After three to six months abroad, most expatriates escape the most severe level of culture shock and the "low" it causes and begin living a more normal life. Little by little, they learn what the new culture considers important and what it considers meaningful. They learn when "yes" means "yes," when it means "maybe," and when it means "no." They learn what to focus on and what to ignore. They learn to differentiate individual behavior from behavior reflecting a cultural pattern. One expatriate, for example, showed his confusion—his inability to differentiate idiosyncratic from culturally patterned behavior—by asking, "Is it that Budi is lazy while most Indonesians work very hard to fulfill their work commitments [idiosyncratic behavior], or is it that most Indonesians work slowly and rarely finish their work [behavior reflecting a cultural pattern]?" The most successful expatriates rapidly learn the local language well enough to make themselves understood in day-to-day conversations.

In addition to time (usually at least three to six months), the key to escaping the culture shock "low" is cross-cultural appreciation and problem solving. Successful expatriates recognize that the foreign environment makes many demands for which they must find or create solutions. In so doing, they realize that blaming others—host nationals, the company, or one's spouse—for their frustrations, no matter how tempting, is not useful. Commonly used ineffective approaches include:

- **Blaming the host nationals.** "These *foreigners* [who, in fact, are the natives] are stupid; anyone with any intelligence would never have laid out a city this way! Addresses seem to be scattered randomly down the streets."

- **Blaming the company.** "Why didn't the company tell me that street numbers in Tokyo are not sequential? How do they expect me to find our clients, let alone make sales? The least the company could have done is give me a map and a guide."

- **Blaming one's spouse.** "Here I've been traveling for the last two weeks, eating strange food, trying to get these foreigners to sign the biggest contract that the firm has ever negotiated, and I come home to hear you complaining that the kids can't take a bath because the plumber doesn't speak English. Some help you are!"

Although it is tempting to blame others, it is almost always an unproductive stress management technique and never a good problem-solving approach.

The most successful global managers recognize that they do not fully understand the situation and must find ways to get reliable information and expertise. Their need to make immediate decisions versus their lack of sufficient knowledge on which to base those decisions causes both the tension experienced by successful global managers and the often inappropriate decisions made by their less effective colleagues. Company-sponsored cross-cultural communication and management programs give expatriates (as well as global business travelers) the skills they need to manage culture shock and work more effectively worldwide.

Experienced expatriates and host nationals who have previously faced and dealt effectively with the same or similar situations can often best empathize with the newcomer's dilemmas.

> *An Italian colleague of mine described the horror of his first day in Philadelphia. He handed his secretary a stack of letters and manuscripts and told her to type them. Each day he expected her to present him with the finished work and each day he received nothing. Only at the end of a disappointing, frustrating, and unproductive week did an Italian friend of his explain that "In the United States, secretaries have more status than in Italy. You must ask them if they can do your typing, not tell them to do your typing. U.S. organizations*

*are more egalitarian and less hierarchical than Italian firms."
Sheepishly, my Italian colleague began to ask; slowly, he began to
receive typed pages.*

Host nationals, although often invaluable as cultural informants, can
be somewhat inarticulate in describing their own culture. People do
not consciously learn the do's and don'ts of their native culture.
Rather, as children, they mimic the behavior of their parents and
other adults. Eventually, with maturity, they can perform the behaviors, but they cannot explain them. A Hungarian businessperson
meeting with an Arab, for example, will not maintain sufficient eye
contact. To the Arab, the Hungarian seems shifty-eyed and not to be
trusted. If asked, the Arab will not be able to describe how often and
how long appropriate eye contact should last. He can do it, but he
can't explain it. The frustrated Hungarian knows that he is doing
something wrong but cannot find out how to behave correctly.

Whatever the source of information, patience and creativity
remain essential. Effective global managers "know that they do not
know." They recognize that they are in a difficult situation and that
they will not act as effectively abroad as they did at home, especially
in the initial stages. They recognize the need for good stress management techniques, including stability zones, that will not harm their
relationship with colleagues, clients, or family. They also recognize
that all members of the family experience culture shock in adjusting
to a new country and that the transition often affects the spouse more
profoundly than the employee (see Chapter 11). Successful expatriates, and their companies, therefore view cross-cultural adjustment as
a systemic issue, not as an individual problem (74).

MANAGING EXPATRIATES EFFECTIVELY, EQUITABLY, AND ETHICALLY

Managing cross-cultural transitions effectively, equitably, and ethically
presents challenges for even the most sophisticated global firms.
Described in the following boxes are two real situations in which a company must develop an effective, equitable, and ethical policy both for
the immediate situation and for all such future situations in their
worldwide operations. For both cases, "Adjusting to America" and "The
Morality of Having Fun," analyze the situation from both cultural perspectives before recommending a response to the specific situation and
a more general corporate policy. As you consider T. S.'s situation in the
first case, "Adjusting to America," keep in mind that the United States is
now considered the third most difficult country in the world to adjust
to (after China and Japan) (48).

ADJUSTING TO AMERICA

T.S. comes from a country that is culturally quite different from the United States and received his education entirely outside the United States. He is a devout member of a profoundly different religious tradition that has only recently gained some prominence among Americans.

Prestige, a North American–based global company, regards T.S. as one of its finest young executives. A year ago, Prestige offered T.S. a promotion from his current upper middle-management position in his native country to a higher position in the United States. T.S. very much looked forward to the new assignment, both for the additional challenge as well as for the opportunity to advance the good of the company. A number of American managers at Prestige who had also wanted the position resisted T.S.'s appointment. However, top management's careful assessment convinced them that T.S. was indeed the most qualified person for the job.

T.S.'s wife and two young children felt happy about his success and were eager to be loyal to him. They expressed uneasiness, however, about moving to the United States, fearing that it would require considerable cultural and family adjustment.

As feared, the adjustment to America proved extremely difficult, even though T.S. did everything he could to make his family feel at home. A major problem was the lack of servants. In their home country, T.S. and his wife lived at a high socioeconomic level, with T.S.'s salary allowing them to employ two servants to do the household chores. Indeed, even as children, both T.S. and his wife had grown up in families sufficiently affluent to afford servants to attend to their needs. (In T.S.'s home country, middle-class citizens can easily afford servants who are paid a quite low wage.)

T.S. and his family now feel a deep need for similar services in the United States. Based on his cultural background, T.S., who ordinarily shuns making waves, is now requesting that Prestige provide him with an extra allowance to hire two servants, explaining to the company that this would "only be fair."

Questions for Reflection

1. Prestige regularly gives American expatriates assigned to T.S.'s home country allowances for servants, along with numerous other benefits such as liberal educational allowances for spouses. Does not a policy of the highest respect for people dictate that the company should offer T.S. and his family a lifestyle similar to that which they have grown accustomed since childhood? Is not T.S.'s request reasonable?

2. Should Prestige offer all expatriates transferred to a given country, who hold similar level positions, the same allowances? Should Singaporeans, for example, transferred by Prestige to a country such as China receive the same allowances as those given to American expatriates of the same grade and position?

ADJUSTING TO AMERICA (continued)

Senior Management Committee Decisions

1. Should Prestige pay for two servants for T.S.'s family? Why? Why not?
2. When a company transfers managers and executives across borders, does the highest respect for people mean treating everyone the same? Does it mean treating people as they were treated back home? Does it mean treating people as the host country treats its own citizens? On what principle(s) should Prestige base its corporate expatriate policy?
3. Which parts of the expatriate package should be universal? Which parts should be based on accepted practices in the home country? Which parts should be based on the typical practices of the host country?

COMING HOME: RE-ENTERING ONE'S OWN CULTURE

Cross-cultural re-entry is the transition from the foreign country back into one's home country (10;26;56;57;61;98;108).[2] Similar to cross-cultural entry, re-entry involves readjusting to the home-country work and nonwork environments, as well as to interacting again with home-country friends and colleagues (17). It involves facing previously familiar surroundings after living and working abroad for a significant period of time. Until the 1980s, companies assumed that re-entry was a relatively easy transition, but since then many have considered it a significant problem (75;77). According to Business International Corporation,

> *Repatriating executives from . . . [global] assignments is a top management challenge that goes far beyond the superficial problems and costs of physical relocation. . . . The assumption is that since these individuals are returning home . . . they should have no trouble adapting. . . . However, experience has shown that repatriation is anything but simple* (27:74).

Historically, 20 percent of the employees who complete global assignments want to leave their company when they come home. According to a *Wall Street Journal* report on a survey of thirty-four global companies, "Bosses might quickly become sensitive if they added up the cost to the company of unhappy . . . [returning employees]" (110).

Re-entry experiences frequently surprise returnees (26). When transferring abroad, people generally expect new and unfamiliar situations, whereas they do not expect any surprises when returning home (92).

THE MORALITY OF HAVING FUN

I.M. Urgin, a native of a non-Western country, is a devoted family man with three young children. He recently left his senior management position with a local telecommunications company and joined Prestige, a North American–based global company, receiving a raise commensurate with his new, more senior position. I.M. felt thrilled to work for a truly global company.

The new position required I.M. to leave his native country in order to live and work in another country in the region that has a religion, values system, and overall culture quite different from his own. I.M.'s home culture, for example, does not consider it bad to frequent prostitutes. Some wives even encourage their husbands to go to prostitutes on occasion, as is the case with I.M.'s wife. By contrast, the new host country holds quite different cultural values concerning prostitution. Prostitution is illegal, although the host country officials often overlook the law.

After arriving in the host country, I.M. continues his previous habits, although on a more limited basis than previously. One of I.M.'s associates at Prestige, a native of the host country, becomes deeply concerned about the legality and morality of I.M.'s actions, and suggests that he stop. I.M. becomes irate. He rigorously defends himself by stating that North American expatriate managers from Prestige living in I.M.'s home country actually form romantic liaisons with local women, including with local Prestige women. I.M. angrily contends that these romantic liaisons create a much more serious problem than going to prostitutes, because the North American men might eventually leave their wives as a result of such relationships. I.M.'s colleague further argues that in addition to North American culture frowning upon such behavior, it might also upset the local people, with consequent bad effects on the morale of local Prestige workers. I.M. heatedly concludes that "having fun with prostitutes" is much better, and certainly less undesirable, than the North Americans' behavior.

Questions for Reflection

1. Who is to judge the morality here? Must I.M. adhere to the host country's ethics?
2. Does the fact that I.M.'s colleague has pointed out the situation force I.M. into a new moral context in which formerly innocent acts may now be considered unethical and illegal? What if I.M. comes to think of himself as guilty but remains unable to change his behavior?
3. Even if I.M. thinks his behavior is blameless, does his behavior endanger the integrity of the company? Do the North Americans' "romantic liaisons" in I.M.'s home country endanger the integrity of the company? Does sexual promiscuity signal a readiness to engage in unethical business practices? How much does an individual's private life impinge on his or her work?

THE MORALITY OF HAVING FUN
(continued)

4.   Does I.M.'s colleague have any right to report I.M.'s activities to senior management? Does he have a duty to do so?

Senior Management Committee Decision

1.   When is the private life behavior of a manager a concern of the company? When it is illegal? When it is immoral? When it reflects badly on the company from any culture's perspective? Never?

2.   Should Prestige ask I.M. to stop going to prostitutes? Should the company require that he stop? Similarly, should the company ask the North Americans in I.M.'s home country to stop forming "romantic liaisons" with locals? Should the company require employees to refrain from such behavior?

3.   For you personally, what areas of your private life do you believe are of no concern to the company? The way you raise your children? The way you treat your spouse? The way you treat your parents? The way you treat members of the community?

Most returnees expect neither re-entry shock nor trauma; they expect to slip easily back into their previous organization, job, and lifestyle. As reported by three expatriate managers:

> *"I don't expect changes. . . . Because it was only a short stay overseas, I expect to just slip right back into my old mold."*

> *"I expect to have the same friends, the same activities, and the same family connections."*

> *"I do not anticipate culture shock at re-entry. . . . I don't expect much trauma."*

Returnees come back neither to the world they left nor to the world they are anticipating. While abroad, the expatriate changes, the organization changes, and the country changes. Moreover, during the culture shock phase of adjusting to another country, expatriates often idealize their home country, remembering only the good aspects of home—in essence, creating something to hold on to and to dream about.

> *As I shivered in Quebec's minus thirty-five degree winter, I remembered Los Angeles' blue sky and sunshine, driving to the beach on a warm January morning. . . . I didn't remember skies opaque with smog, freeways so clogged with cars that driving anywhere was*

impossible, nor did I remember my car being broken into while parked at the beach.

When returning home, expatriates face real changes; the gap between the way it was and the way it is, and the gap between their idealized memories and reality. Most feel surprised both at their feelings and by reality. Returnees often describe re-entry as a more difficult transition than their initial entry into the new country at the beginning of their expatriate assignment.

> *Going home is a harder move. The foreign move has the excitement of being new . . . more confusing, but exciting. Re-entry is frightening . . . I'll be happy to be home . . . but I really wonder if I can adjust back.*

Returnees describe stages similar to those of culture shock—first being in a high mood, quickly plummeting to a very low mood, and then slowly returning to their normal mood. The initial high mood, as expressed in the following comments, often lasts only a short time:

> "*I was pleasantly surprised by our neighbors. They really went overboard to welcome us back.*"

> "*It's cleaner . . . and just a reasonable number of people . . . fantastic! . . . freedom of mobility . . . quality of life is higher here and I notice it more.*"

For most returnees the initial high mood lasts less than a month, and many report it lasting only a few hours. The low period therefore begins earlier in re-entry than it does in the entry transition. Returnees' lowest times usually occur during the second and third months after their return. As American managers returning from assignments in South America describe:

> "*Some of my friends couldn't even imagine the foreign country. . . . They asked me how it was, but they just wanted to hear 'fine.'*"

> "*In Venezuela, getting things done was a hassle . . . and we said, 'In the United States it would be so easy.' When we came home, everything was delayed and frustrating. Here in the United States! The U.S. was a continual Venezuela story . . . and we had always said, 'This will never happen at home . . . HA!'*"

> "*Calling friends, my sister, my mom. . . . Everyone was so busy with their lives that they didn't have time to just talk. They cut me off . . . I understand, but . . .*"

> "*I came back with so many stories to share, but my friends and family couldn't understand them. It was as if my years overseas were unshareable.*"

By the sixth month back home, returnees generally accept their situation and report feeling "average"—neither much better nor much worse than usual.

PROFESSIONAL RE-ENTRY

Just as the new environment and lifestyle can cause problems when entering another culture, so too can the professional transition back into the home organization (15;16;17;35). Professional re-entry is often more difficult than personal re-entry, especially for returnees to multi-domestic companies in which global experience is not considered critical to overall corporate success (15;16;17;89). Most managers expect a global assignment to help their career; yet historically they have returned to discover that, at best, it has had a neutral effect. Multi-domestic companies promote fewer than half of their returning expatriate managers (58:1;110). For many, especially in the short run, the impact on their career is negative. Historically, more than two thirds of returnees to multi-domestic companies have suffered from the *out-of-sight, out-of-mind syndrome* (58:1;59). Managers returning to North American companies described their experience as follows:

> *"My colleagues react indifferently to my global assignment. . . . They view me as doing a job I did in the past; they don't see me as having gained anything while overseas."*
>
> *"The organization has changed . . . work habits, norms, and procedures have changed, and I have lost touch with all that. . . . I'm a beginner again!"*
>
> *"I had no specific re-entry job to return to. I wanted to leave international and return to domestic. Working abroad magnifies problems while isolating effects. You deal with more problems, but the home office doesn't know the details of the good or bad effects. Managerially, I'm out of touch."*
>
> *"I lost time. My career stopped when I left and started again when I returned."*

Similarly, many managers complain that their re-entry jobs bore them. Almost half of surveyed repatriated executives found their re-entry position less satisfying than their global assignment (11;58). They describe their positions abroad as offering more challenge and excitement. They miss the greater responsibility, authority, status, decision-making autonomy, and variety that their global assignments offered them. Returnees frequently feel disappointed, discouraged, and angry when they realize that their re-entry positions do not live up to their expectations:

> *"I'm bored at work. . . . I run upstairs to see what [another returning colleague] is doing. He says, 'Nothing.' Me, too."*

> *"In a lot of ways, the red tape and nonsense that we're experiencing now since we re-entered are a lot worse. Maybe I didn't recognize these things before [going abroad] or maybe I'd learned to live with them."*

> *"While overseas, I realized that the home office doesn't do anything right . . . bosses call bosses to get anything done. I had to talk to seven people to get one answer. It's a real bureaucracy."*

The transition from one organizational culture to another and from one set of organizational assumptions and behaviors to another can be difficult and stressful. Returnees experience organizational culture shock at the same time that they are experiencing societal culture shock.

Luckily for returnees, the evolution of business from less globally integrated multi-domestic strategies and structures to today's highly networked and integrated multinational and global strategies and structures is making professional re-entry easier. Due to increasing global competitiveness and worldwide integration, expatriates are no longer as isolated when abroad, nor do companies view their global experience as irrelevant when they return.

EFFECTIVENESS

Are returnees effective during their initial period back in the home organization? Yes and no. As shown in Figures 10-3 and 10-4, returnees and their bosses do not agree: home-country bosses often see returnees as more effective than the returnees see themselves. Historically, returnees described themselves as initially ineffective followed by increasing effectiveness. By contrast, home-country bosses and colleagues describe the same returnees as initially effective followed by increasingly higher effectiveness. Home-country bosses, especially in companies with multi-domestic strategies, tend to compare expatriates' re-entry performance with their prior predeparture performance without realizing that the expatriates have developed professionally while abroad and can now handle higher levels of complexity and responsibility than they could previously. By contrast, returnees generally see themselves as accomplishing relatively little during their first few months back in comparison with the greater breadth and challenge of their work abroad. This pattern of companies consistently underutilizing returnees is dysfunctional for the organization and leads to dissatisfaction among returnees, which in turn causes many of them to leave the firm (12;16).

XENOPHOBIC RESPONSE

In addition to disagreeing about their overall effectiveness, returnees and their bosses also disagree about which returnees are most effective. Returnees who see themselves as highly effective are rarely seen as such by their bosses; similarly, returnees who see themselves as ineffective are infrequently rated as such by their bosses. Home-country bosses and

FIGURE 10-3   Returnees Assess Their Re-Entry Effectiveness

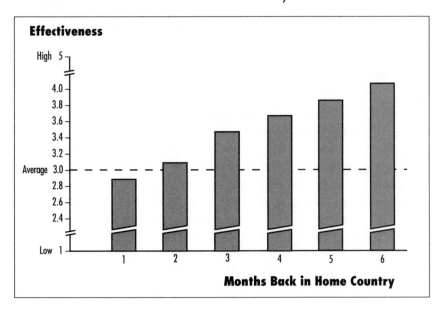

FIGURE 10-4   Home-Country Bosses and Colleagues
              Assess Returnees' Effectiveness

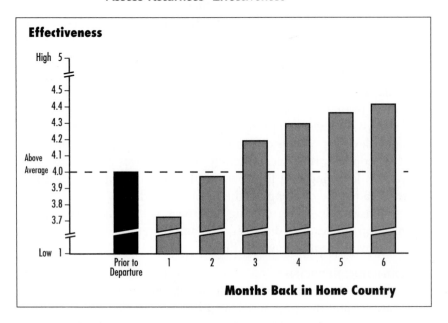

colleagues generally assess those returnees who appear "least foreign" as most effective—that is, those returnees who do not know or use foreign languages, do not have foreign friends, and were not born in a foreign country. Moreover, companies have historically ranked as most effective those returnees who did not explicitly use the skills and knowledge gained while abroad on their job back home. This *xenophobic response*—bosses' and colleagues' fear and rejection of things foreign—severely handicaps organizations that want to learn from the experience of their employees around the world. Although multi-domestic firms competing primarily in individual domestic markets around the world may have tolerated this response, it is no longer acceptable in today's highly competitive global markets. As many experts have observed, business today is a learning race and only those companies that learn from their clients, managers, and employees worldwide will survive and prosper in the twenty-first century.

In contrast to the xenophobic assessments of their home-country bosses, returnees who recognize and use their global learning and skills to the greatest extent and who are least limited by their home culture rank themselves as most effective. Returnees who speak foreign languages, have friends from around the world, and know about other cultures rate themselves more highly than do their less globally knowledgeable and involved colleagues.

WHAT DO MANAGERS LEARN ABROAD?

Today, most returning expatriates regard their global experience as essential for a successful career, primarily because it allows them to acquire experiences and skills that are rarely available at home (100). In reviewing their experiences abroad, returnees report that they improve their managerial skills more than their technical skills. As highlighted in the "Skills Expatriates Learn Abroad" box, returnees report having enhanced many important professional skills, including many of those seen as critical for success in today's rapidly changing, highly competitive global business environment. In addition to enhanced professional skills, returnees often report significant personal growth—most commonly, an improved self-image and increased self-confidence.

When recognized and used, skills acquired abroad can increase the returnee's contribution to the home organization. However, if the returnee's xenophobic boss associates these same skills with the foreign country, the boss's rating of the returnee's effectiveness generally decreases. While both unfortunate and counterproductive, the boss's response is not surprising, given that until recently most firms operated as domestic or multi-domestic organizations and transferred employees abroad primarily to get a job done, rather than to develop either the worldwide organization or the expatriate's career—as is often the primary goal in today's more

SKILLS EXPATRIATES LEARN ABROAD

Expatriates Primarily Learn Managerial Skills, Not Technical Skills

"Working abroad makes you more knowledgeable about the questions to ask than about the answers."

"I learned how to work in two cultures . . . to compromise, not to be a dictator. It's similar to working with two professional cultures at home . . . like marketing and engineering."

"I am more open-minded . . . more able to deal with a wider range of people . . . because, while abroad, I ran into many other points of view."

Tolerance for Ambiguity

"Because I only understood a fraction of what was really going on abroad, maybe 50 percent, I had to make decisions on a fraction of the necessary information. Now I can tolerate nonclosure and ambiguity much better."

"Things you never thought you would put up with, you learn to put up with . . ."

Multiple Perspectives

"I learned what it feels like to be a foreigner . . . I could see things from their perspective."
"I learned to anticipate . . . it's the role of a diplomat."
"I always thought I was right, until I went abroad."

Ability to Work with and Manage Others

"I increased my tolerance for other people. For the first time, I was the underdog, the minority. I became a soft-headed screamer. I am definitely better now at working with others."

"I used to be more ruthless than I am now . . . I was the All-American manager. Now, I stop and realize the human impact. I see others as resources. I do more communicating with others in the organization."[3]

globally networked multinational and transnational organizations. The multi-domestic's narrow definition of the expatriate's role, combined with its inherently parochial belief that "our home-country's way of working is the best way"—often labeled as the *not-invented-here syndrome*—severely diminished the perceived value of returnees to most home organizations.

TRANSITION STRATEGIES

The strategies returnees use to fit back into their formerly familiar home country and home organization vary markedly (82). As shown in Table 10-2, some returnees become resocialized, some become alienated, and others become proactive.

Resocialized Returnees Resocialized returnees are most common among corporate expatriates who work for multi-domestic firms that lack a global orientation. Resocialized returnees neither recognize nor use their globally acquired skills and knowledge. They simply try to fit back into the domestic corporate structure; that is, to act like managers who have never been away. In treating their experience abroad as non-transferable, they negate the possibility that it could enhance their home-country effectiveness, either at work or at home. Historically, because few home-organization bosses (especially in multi-domestic companies) appreciated returnees' increased potential contribution, they often felt satisfied with this "fit-back-in" strategy. Resocialization precludes both the individual and the organization gaining very much from the expatriate experience. This lack of individual and organizational learning is particularly unfortunate today, when it has become necessary for global firms to engage in continual worldwide learning just to compete, let alone succeed.

Alienated Returnees These returnees are more common among employees who have had a series of global assignments than those who have had a single such assignment, more common among spouses than employees, and more common among volunteers (e.g., Peace Corps and Canadian University Students Overseas) than among corporate returnees. While working abroad, future alienated returnees often "go native"—they assimilate the values and lifestyle of the foreign culture. When they return, they continue to see the foreign culture as better than their own culture, believing that it offers a richer way of life. They reject their home culture, and in so doing frequently become personally isolated. Alienated returnees, in believing that they cannot fit back in or use their globally acquired skills and knowledge in their home environment, often feel professionally unproductive and personally unsatisfied. Similar to resocialized returnees, they contribute little to the home organization as a result of their global experience. The home organization generally recognizes the alienated returnees' diminished productivity and evaluates them as ineffective.

Proactive Returnees These returnees reject neither their own nor the foreign culture. Rather, they combine aspects of both in creating new approaches to working and to living. Proactive returnees usually feel optimistic and creative; they recognize and use their globally acquired skills and knowledge to contribute within the work environment and to modify their personal lifestyle. They see themselves as more effective and more satisfied with their jobs than do users of the other re-entry strategies. Proactive returnees develop highly sophisticated skills at perceiving their environment—whether abroad or at home—and at describing situations, rather than simply comparing and evaluating them. They easily identify similarities and differences without needing to classify one as good and the other as bad. Proactive returnees therefore contribute by creating new, synergistic ways of perceiving and

TABLE 10-2   Coping Strategies: Approaches to Returning Home

Returnee Oriented Toward Home Country ←

Resocialized Returnees attempt to fit back in when they return to their home country. They do not recognize that they have learned skills that they could use at home. In general they are neither aware of changes in themselves nor in their environment. They are rated as highly effective by their bosses and themselves and feel quite satisfied with their re-entry positions and performance. Most resocialized returnees distance themselves from their global experience. Similarly, while living abroad, most resocialized returnees *rejected the foreign country.* Many lived in expatriate ghettos separate from the host nationals and were labeled as "Ugly Foreigners."

Proactive Returnees attempt to integrate their global and their home-country experiences. They recognize changes in themselves and their environment, and try to use the skills and learning they acquired abroad. Whereas proactive returnees rate themselves as effective and satisfied with their job, their bosses only rate them as moderately so. Proactive expatriates aim to effectively *integrate the home and foreign cultures'* ways of life; their approach was to attempt to adapt to living abroad without "going native."

Alienated Returnees often disassociate themselves from the home culture and home organization. Although they recognize that they have acquired skills and knowledge while abroad, they see no way to use them at home. Alienated returnees do not see themselves as particularly effective, nor, in general, do their bosses. They receive the least recognition of the three types of returnees. As expatriates, they *rejected the home culture.* Their approach to living abroad was to try to *go native*—to assimilate into the foreign culture.

Returnee Oriented Toward Foreign Country →

working within the home organization based on their experience both at home and abroad. This synergistic approach—the combining of multiple cultures' ways of working—allows returnees to work more effectively with their multicultural colleagues and clients, to make decisions based on a wider range of alternatives, and to act as leaders in the realm of both ideas and action. Proactive returnees' potential for contributing to the organization thus exceeds that of both domestic employees and other returnees; in order to benefit, however, the home organization must be open to using the returnees' potential contributions and not simply attempt to fit them back in.

MANAGING RE-ENTRY

What makes some returnees more proactive than others? What allows some returnees to contribute more than others (see 15;16;17;50;51;52)? Support provided by the company during re-entry can dramatically decrease the number of returnees who choose to quit the organization (8;16;46;57;90). Companies can use two primary processes—communication and validation—to increase the probability of returnees engaging in a more effective re-entry coping mode.

Communicating with Expatriates While Abroad How can companies close the gap between what returnees expect and the actual reality of the country and company to which they are returning (92)? The level of communication with expatriates refers to the extent to which expatriates receive information and recognize changes while abroad. Expatriates who maintain close contact with the home organization while abroad become more proactive, more effective, and more satisfied in their re-entry jobs. Returnees who perform the best recognize both positive and negative changes in themselves, their organization, their industry, and their country. Given the higher levels of integration and interdependence in today's global companies—especially in comparison to the multi-domestic companies of the last few decades—and the ease of e-mail, cell phone, video conferencing, and other forms of instant, worldwide communication, today's returnees are much more likely than their predecessors to have maintained close contact with their home organization while abroad.

Validating the Experience of Expatriates at Re-entry Validation involves the amount of recognition, including promotions, expatriates receive upon returning home. Returnees who receive more recognition from bosses and colleagues for their work abroad as well as for their potential future contributions do better than less recognized returnees. Returnees whom the company promotes better than those not promoted (51). Organizations that treat expatriates and returnees as if they were "out of sight and out of mind," on vacation, or so far behind that they could not possibly contribute usefully, diminish returnees' proactivity.

Most organizations do not consciously choose to ignore or to fail to accommodate returnees. Many expatriates, however, return home when they complete their global assignment, which rarely coincides with when the company has another appropriate position available. Historically, few companies have used sophisticated global career-path systems. One returnee, an engineer, explained that his *Fortune 50* company simply gave him a desk and a phone when he returned and told him to find himself a job within the company. Another engineer, even though he had no human resource management experience, was put in charge of designing re-entry procedures for future expatriates, because "Clearly we don't know what to do with you or with the others who will be coming back." External validation through recognizing and valuing global and re-entry experiences is one of the most powerful management techniques for increasing returnees' satisfaction and effectiveness. Equally important, it is one of the most effective ways for global companies to acquire an up-to-date understanding of the worldwide business environment.

Returnees can facilitate their own re-entry by using skills similar to those they used in adjusting abroad. Perhaps most important, they must recognize the highly stressful nature of the re-entry transition and manage it accordingly. Unfortunately, the natural assumption that the home country is familiar often blinds returnees to the reality of the re-entry transition and strips them of the very skills that they need and so successfully developed while working abroad. Clearly, managers returning to global organizations using an integrated, worldwide perspective find the re-entry transition much easier than do those who work for domestic or multi-domestic companies.

UNDERUTILIZED GLOBAL MANAGERS

The global business environment is highly competitive. Success depends on corporate excellence. To compete, today's global companies must select the best people and manage them appropriately. Unfortunately, many organizations frequently fail to profit from their employees' global experience. To benefit fully from their investment, organizations and returnees need to better understand the re-entry transition. Both must identify job skills acquired or enhanced while abroad and systematically find ways to productively use them. The home organization needs to understand the importance of staying in contact with expatriates, planning for their return, and recognizing the value of their worldwide experience. The attitudes of managers who stay at home must change, as must evaluation and reward schemes. Increasing effectiveness at each stage in the expatriate global career cycle is neither easily nor superficially accomplished, but rather takes a major commitment on the part of the company.

Just as predeparture training can assist expatriates in adjusting to living and working abroad (65), re-entry debriefings facilitate the transition back into the home organization as well as significantly increase home organization learning (73). In debriefing sessions, management asks returnees to describe what they learned abroad. Together returnees and home organization personnel integrate the new appreciations and create synergistic approaches to the ongoing management of worldwide operations. Re-entry sessions, in addition to identifying what was learned abroad, facilitate the transition back into the home organization and home community. As a part of a re-entry session, experts describe both the personal and professional re-entry transition and suggest proactive approaches to managing each. By including home-country managers in debriefing and re-entry sessions, the organization increases the global sophistication of all its managers and significantly decreases organizational parochialism and xenophobia. Both home-based and expatriate managers learn to transcend their own experience and integrate their perceptions and understandings of the organization on a global basis.

As home organization personnel become more multicultural and their clientele becomes more global, the need for globally skilled managers also increases. Both companies and expatriates need to cultivate their understanding of the entry and re-entry transitions and develop organizational strategies that benefit both parties (79). Companies can no longer afford to send any but their best people abroad. Neither the companies nor the individuals can afford to let the best fail.

COACHING WOMEN FOR GLOBAL MANAGERIAL SUCCESS

Companies often hesitate to send women abroad on global assignments (29;30). According to *Business Week*, "American women seeking to climb the corporate ladder via overseas positions face steep odds" (64). Women account for approximately 30 percent of MBA students, and yet they average only 14 percent of those chosen for international assignments by U.S. corporations (64). Historic highs in the percentage of managerial women sent abroad were reached in 2001 (16%) and in 2003 (18%) (48;49;78;87;109). One reason the percentages are so low is that the women's male counterparts overestimate the problems awaiting women working outside their home country. Executive coaches often help managers who are considering sending their most senior and highest potential women abroad as well as coaching the current and future women expatriates themselves. As you read "Coaching Executives: Women Succeeding in Global Careers,"

COACHING EXECUTIVES:
Women Succeeding in Global Careers

Executive coaches bring perspective. They offer a context of meaning beyond a manager's or executive's individual position, organization, and industry. By quietly asking questions that are beyond the bottom line, coaches offer executives opportunities to more consciously consider the types of contributions they make to their company and to choose the kinds of contributions they would like to make more broadly in the world. Such questions as:

- What does success mean to you?

- In what ways is your work helping society?

- Why would your daughter be proud to tell her daughter about your accomplishments?

often appear illegitimate when taken out of the privacy of executive coaching dialogues. In the public glare of business-as-usual, such questions frequently fail to appear sufficiently pragmatic to warrant executive time. And yet the conversations, reflection, and learning that such questions generate often bring soul, along with deep motivation, back into the pragmatism of professionalism. Context, deep meaning, and soul are without counterparts in the pragmatism of successful careers, successful lives, and successful societies.

How does coaching women executives differ from coaching men?

While few people question whether the world of business has gone global, most assumptions about building a global career and succeeding as a global executive remain based on the experience of men. Many of the most fundamental assumptions about executive success remain parochial, limited not only to the experience of men, but often to the experience of men working within their own home country. If companies continue to believe current parochial assumptions about business success, few, if any, women will venture into the world beyond their national borders, and even fewer will succeed once there. To succeed in a global economy, both companies and women managers need to go beyond the myths and erroneous assumptions of history.

Because so few women worked as international managers in the twentieth century, let alone as global executives, ignorance and misleading myths abound. Not surprisingly, many women, especially in such Anglo cultures as the United States, believe that they must emulate men to succeed. Fearing to differentiate themselves in any way from their successful male predecessors and contemporaries, many women become reticent to openly challenge the abundant myths about the barriers women supposedly face when attempting to conduct business abroad. Executive coaching allows women managers and executives to ask societally unacceptable, and therefore publicly unaskable, questions, such as:

- "Is it true that as a woman I cannot succeed in the Middle East?"

- "Will I insult their culture if I lead the negotiating team in Saudi Arabia?"

COACHING EXECUTIVES:
Women Succeeding in Global Careers (continued)

- "Is it true that our company's expansion into South Asia will be jeopardized if I head up the project?"

- "Even if I succeed in getting the CEO to send me to Korea, will I fail once I am there? I have heard that Korean businessmen just ignore women; that they would never take a businesswoman seriously."

- "Will our German joint venture partners be annoyed when they see that my company has sent me as the lead engineer?"

- "Will men in Latin America really think that my company has sent me as some kind of sexual plaything? What do I need to do to get Latin men to respect me?"

As I listen to women telling their stories and asking their unaskable questions, my most frequent response is "Why?" Why do you think that that might happen to you? What reality do you want to be true for you? How can you go beyond all the negative scenarios that you and others in your company imagine will occur? Why do you think foreigners will be more prejudiced against you than are some of the executives you have already successfully dealt with here at home? How can you go beyond history's erroneous assumptions to create your own reality? In the privacy of executive coaching dialogues, we laugh, question, and explore a world that has literally remained foreign to all too many women and companies. In the process, we lay to rest the misleading belief that women cannot succeed abroad, or, if they do succeed, that they must act like men.

Myth #1: Global experience is not that important

Lisette, an executive in a major consumer products company with two teenagers in high school, recently turned down an assignment in Brussels. Annoyed with her, Lisette's boss tells her that he will not consider her for a senior vice presidency because she is not mobile. He emphasizes that her promising career will plateau if she does not willingly move abroad to take an expatriate assignment. Lisette challenges the importance of global experience. She knows that neither her boss, nor his boss—the CEO—have had much experience abroad beyond regularly boarding airplanes. Given that she is currently the highest ranking woman in the company, the requirement that she gain global experience looks suspiciously like the latest hurdle her boss is putting in the way of her career progress, the latest hurdle defining the glass ceiling.

My response to Lisette's angry phone call is a resounding "No!" Business has gone global. Requiring global experience reflects neither sexism nor a new variant of the glass ceiling. "Your boss is right. If you choose not to get global experience, it is *you* who are choosing to remain well below the glass ceiling. No man or woman should be promoted into the executive ranks of a twenty-first-century company without having a deep understanding and appreciation of global business dynamics.

COACHING EXECUTIVES:
Women Succeeding in Global Careers (continued)

Your boss and the CEO grew their careers in another era, an era of domestic or, at most, multi-domestic business. Unless your aim is to progress backward through history and to attempt to have a parochial nineteenth- or twentieth-century career, you would not dare consider limiting your experience to domestic stay-at-home assignments."

Lisette doesn't like hearing what I am saying, but she believes me. She knows that as an executive coach, I am an outsider and that therefore I am on her side and I will tell her the truth, even if it is an inconvenient truth that she would rather not hear. Recognizing the truth, however, does not imply resignation to a career stopped by a seemingly impenetrable global glass ceiling. The outwardly para-doxical question I raise with Lisette is "How can you gain significant internation-al experience *and* keep your commitment to not moving during your children's formative high school years?" Asking paradoxical questions—such as "How can you both move abroad and not move abroad?"—and then helping executives resolve them is a very important part of executive coaching.

Myth #2: Given my family commitments, I cannot take a global assignment

In reflecting on her situation, Lisette realized that expatriation, while a pow-erful way to gain global experience, was not the only option open to her. As we brainstormed options, Lisette discovered that she could significantly increase her global experience in a number of innovative ways. She suggested participating on more global task forces and increasing her international business travel. Her most creative idea was to take short two-month assignments in Europe and Asia while her two teenagers were away each summer at camp. For Lisette, as well as for many other executive women, the problem is the form in which global experience has traditionally been offered (multiyear expatriate assignments), not the require-ment for global experience itself. The trap for Lisette would have been to reject global experience because it was "packaged" in its traditional, and to her, unac-ceptable, form, such as a three- to five-year expatriate assignment. The trap for me as a coach would have been to accept her boss's definitions of reality rather than to help Lisette to think beyond the mythology surrounding the corporation's increasingly anachronistic requirements. As Lisette's subsequent discussions with the CEO revealed, expatriation, as a developmental strategy, was a better fit for the company's needs in the past when business strategy required key executives to only have an in-depth knowledge of a single foreign culture. By contrast, today's globally integrated business strategies require key executives to understand mul-tiple cultures and their interaction. The option that Lisette was suggesting for her-self—shorter term exposure to multiple countries—is actually preferable in many cases to the company's traditional emphasis on a single, longer-term expatriate assignment.

COACHING EXECUTIVES:
Women Succeeding in Global Careers (continued)

Myth #3: For global managers, being a woman is a disadvantage

This pervasive and erroneous myth seems to find its way into the thinking of the vast majority of today's executives, both male and female. Valana, a senior financial analyst for a major pharmaceutical company, was offered a regional vice-presidency in Japan. Given the company's new start-up operations in Pakistan, the position in Japan would involve considerable travel to this Islamic country. Valana felt simultaneously excited and cautious. Would she, as a woman, be able to succeed in Japan and Pakistan, both countries reputed to be hostile to women managers and executives? She worried that if she openly raised her fears with her boss, he would change his mind; that, once again, the company would assume that it could not send women abroad. To make sure that she did not ruin the opportunity to work abroad for herself, or for other women, she chose not to raise her concerns inside the company but rather relied on the confidentiality inherent in the executive coaching relationship.

Myth #4: Certain cultures make it impossible for woman executives to succeed

Valana's initial fear was that no woman could succeed in Japan or Pakistan. Her real fear was that if she accepted the position, she would be setting herself up for failure. When I asked her why she believed she would fail in either of these two Asian countries, she immediately cited the cultural limitations placed on most women in Japan as well as in most Islamic countries: "The scarcity of Japanese and Pakistani women executives says it all. Even with all your travelling, how many Japanese or Pakistani women executives do you know? Not many!" Unconsciously, yet understandably, Valana had fallen into the *Gaijin Trap*. She had assumed that, as a woman, she would be treated similarly to the local Japanese and Pakistani women, few of whom are given the cultural latitude to succeed in major multinational businesses. Her mistake was not in her statistics: both countries have extremely few women executives. Rather, her mistake was in overemphasizing the salience of being a woman. Based on the actual experience of women executives who have worked abroad, we know that women from outside a particular region are treated as foreigners who happen to be women. They are not treated in the same way as local women. While both the Japanese and Pakistanis limit the roles that local women can take in business, neither culture confuses foreign women with local women. Valana's freedom to succeed lies in the fact that she is visibly foreign. The trap for Valana would be to assume that the Japanese could not tell that she is not Japanese (or that the Pakistanis could not tell that she not Pakistani); they can. To get accurate tips on how to succeed in such cultures, I suggested that Valana restrict her advice-gathering to conversations with other North American and European women who had worked for major multinationals in Japan or Pakistan. From them she could learn the nuances of showing respect for each culture

COACHING EXECUTIVES:
Women Succeeding in Global Careers (continued)

without limiting her potential success. I strongly advised that she disregard suggestions made by both men and women who had not had direct experience with women working in the particular countries in which she would be working. Without direct experience, even the best-intentioned colleagues unconsciously pass on myths disguised as advice. The only thing that eradicates the myth that women cannot succeed abroad—and, simultaneously, the fear that such myths engender in both women executives and the companies that consider sending women on global assignments—is learning about the actual experience of foreign women executives who have worked abroad, the majority of whom unquestionably succeed.[4]

Over the next couple of weeks, Valana talked with many expatriate women executives, coming back to me frequently to question whether their suggestions would really be advisable for her. Among her many questions, Valana asked if it was true that women executives did not have to stay up drinking until late into the night in order to do business with Japanese firms. My answer, "Absolutely true." Whereas behavior among men in Japan is fairly codified and almost always includes a lot of business entertainment and drinking, the newness of women conducting significant business in Japan means that male/female business behavior has yet to become codified. Given the ambiguity, women at this point in history have more latitude than do men to conduct business in ways that feel most comfortable to them. As one highly successful American woman executive, who had been based in Tokyo for years, laughingly related to me, "Among all of my male colleagues, I am the only one who has consistently maintained relationships with Japanese clients without needing to put my liver in jeopardy! I can get away with conducting business over lunch and a Perrier; the men can't."

Myth #5: Public is public, and private is private: To be taken seriously, a woman executive must hide her role as a wife and mother

The myth, albeit false, is that foreigners will not take a businesswoman seriously unless she focuses 100 percent on work. American women, who come from one of the most task-oriented cultures in the world, often fall into the trap of emulating American businessmen. They try to focus almost exclusively on business, to the detriment of both their worldwide business success and their private life. Perhaps one particularly successful businesswoman's experience says it all. On a business trip to Hong Kong, Katia, a marketing vice president for a global telecommunications firm, was negotiating her first major contract with a consortium of Chinese, Malaysian, and Thai companies. The negotiations were not going well and seemed in jeopardy of failure. At a very tense moment in the deliberations, Katia glanced at her watch, stood up, and apologized for needing to take a ten-minute break. While receiving quizzical looks from the group of businessmen, he explained that it was bedtime for her seven-year-old daughter back home in Chicago, and that she always called to say goodnight to her daughter no matter where she was in the world.

COACHING EXECUTIVES:
Women Succeeding in Global Careers (continued)

Returning ten minutes later, Katia was surprised to discover that the tension around the negotiating table had melted. As she entered the room, the Thai executive asked how her daughter was doing. Then the lead Chinese negotiator asked Katia if she had a picture of her daughter. Other negotiators expressed how difficult they imagined it must be for a mother to be so far away from her daughter. After this brief exchange of warm interest and concern, the negotiations continued, now clearly with a focus on efficiently finding a mutually beneficial agreement. At noon the following day, the negotiation that had appeared irreversibly stuck came to a successful conclusion.

Most women from Anglo-Saxon cultures, especially those from the United States, have been coached by their colleagues to separate their private life from their professional life. To succeed abroad, however, these same women need to unlearn the advice that their Anglo-Saxon colleagues have given them. Unlike the task-oriented Anglo-Saxon countries, most other cultures emphasize relationship building. In countries such as China, Malaysia, and Thailand, people will only conduct business with people whom they know, like, and trust. Revealing who you are as a whole person, including unmasking some aspects of your private life, allows colleagues from relationship-building cultures to get to know you and, therefore, to want to do business with you. It is not that people from relationship-oriented cultures are not concerned about getting the task accomplished; they are. It is just that relationship must precede task. Katia's relationship with her daughter added the dimension of wholeness that she needed to succeed.

Today Katia laughs at the number of her women friends who are also global executives who carry pictures of their children very visibly in their business card cases. Why? Because from the first moment of contact, clients know that they are a whole person—a wife, mother, and businesswoman. As Katia's story spread, rumors began circulating that even single women were borrowing pictures of Katia's children to ensure their success abroad.

Executive Coaching: Reaching Beyond the Myths of History

For both women and men, coaching dialogues foster a depth of questioning that allows executives to escape the bounded thinking of their own professional, organizational, and national cultures. For women, coaching sessions encourage exploring alternatives that reach beyond the accepted "wisdom" gained by successful men working worldwide with other men. At their best, coaching sessions provide the time, space, and learning opportunities that allow executives to offer profound and wise counsel to themselves.

Source: Adapted from Adler's "Coaching Global Executives: Women Succeeding in a World Beyond Here," in Marshall Goldsmith, Lawrence Lyons, & Alyssa Freas, eds., *Coaching for Leadership* (San Francisco: Jossey-Bass, 2000), pp. 347–356. Reprinted by permission John Wiley & Sons.

ask yourself from whom you get your best coaching advice. The box describes one executive coach's approach to helping companies and women executives separate the facts from the myths surrounding successful, and not so successful, global careers.

SUMMARY

Transitions are a part of a global manager's career path. Expatriate, inpatriate, and transpatriate managers are sent to other countries, and return home again after they have completed one or a series of global assignments. Transitions, whether entry or re-entry, involve managing the stress that accompanies moving into an unfamiliar environment. In moving abroad, culture shock causes stress. In moving back home, unmet expectations and a lack of validation cause stress. Returning expatriates need to identify what they have learned abroad and how it can benefit the organization. They need to integrate their global perspective with the home-country perspective in proactive ways that enhance successful global careers. Organizations need to focus on what they can learn from expatriates as well as from returnees. Finally, for the benefit of all, both companies and managers need to be open to the innovative ways in which women succeed—ways that are not necessarily identical to those of men.

QUESTIONS FOR REFLECTION

1. **Global Strategy.** Given today's globally competitive business environment, what are the main reasons why companies send managers abroad?

2. **Global Skills.** Of the skills learned on a global assignment, which are the most valuable to returning managers? How can the organization best use returnees' skills?

3. **Managing Re-entry.** How might companies best help expatriates manage the re-entry transition? What can home-country managers do to make a returnee's transition as easy as possible for the returnee and as beneficial as possible for the company?

4. **Global Career Planning.** If your company offered you an expatriate assignment today to work for three years in an area of the world that is completely new to you, why would you want to go? Why would you reject going?

5. **Managing Culture Shock.** What is culture shock? If you have experienced culture shock, describe what it felt like. What would you recommend to minimize the impact of culture shock on global managers?

6. **Global Women Managers.** Imagine that your company is considering sending a team of women engineers to India and Dubai on an important assignment. What would you recommend that the company, and the women, do to increase their chances of success?

NOTES

1. Data is based on 1993 to 2004 surveys sponsored by GMAC Global Relocation Services, The National Foreign Trade Council and the Society of Human Resource Management's Global Forum (48;49).

2. The original research and quotations on re-entry, unless otherwise cited, are drawn from Adler's initial major re-entry study (4) as summarized in Adler's "Re-entry: Managing Cross-Cultural Transitions" (5).

3. From Adler's "Re-entry: Managing Cross-Cultural Transitions" (5). Copyright © 1981 by Sage Publications. Reprinted by permissions of Sage Publications, Inc.

4. For research documenting expatriate women managers success abroad, see Adler's "Competitive Frontiers: Women Managing Across Borders" (2) along with Adler's "One World: Women Leading & Managing Worldwide" (6) for a summary of research on women in international management. For additional research on women expatriates, see Caligiuri and other researchers (9;29;30;33;34;36;39;44;47;54;55;66;67;68;69;70;71;76;80;84;85;86;87;93;94;96; 97;104;106;107). For a more in-depth discussion of women's global leadership and international management careers, see Adler and Izraeli's *Competitive Frontiers: Women Managers in a Global Economy* (7) and Adler's "Global Leaders: A Dialogue with Future History" (3).

REFERENCES

1. Adler, N. J. "Coaching Global Executives: Women Succeeding in a World Beyond Here," in Marshall Goldsmith, Lawrence Lyons, & Alyssa Freas, eds., *Coaching for Leadership* (San Francisco: Jossey-Bass, 2000), pp. 347–356.

2. Adler, N. J. "Competitive Frontiers: Women Managing Across Borders," in N. J. Adler, & Dafna N. Izraeli, eds., *Competitive Frontiers: Women Managers in a Global Economy* (Cambridge, Mass.: Blackwell Publishing, 1994), pp. 22–40.

3. Adler, N. J. "Global Leaders: A Dialogue with Future History," *International Management*, vol.1 no. 2, 1997, pp. 21–33.

4. Adler, N. J. *Re-entry: A Study of the Dynamic Coping Processes Used by Repatriated Employees to Enhance Effectiveness in the Organization and Personal Learning During the Transition Back into the Home Country* (Los Angeles, Calif.: UCLA dissertation, 1980).

5. Adler, N. J. "Re-entry: Managing Cross-Culture Transitions," *Group and Organization Studies,* vol. 6, no. 3 (1981), pp. 341–356.

6. Adler, N. J. "One World: Women Leading & Managing Worldwide" in Diana Bilimoria & Sandy Kristin Piderit, eds., *Handbook on Women in Business and Management* (Cheltenham, U.K.: Edward Elgar Publishing, 2007), pp. 330–355.

7. Adler, N. J.; & Izraeli, Dafna N., eds., *Competitive Frontiers: Women Managers in a Global Economy* (Cambridge, Mass.: Blackwell Publishing, 1994).

8. Allen, Douglas; & Alvarez, Sharon. "Empowering Expatriates and Organizations to Improve Repatriation Effectiveness," *Human Resource Planning*, vol. 21, no. 4 (1998), pp. 29–39.

9. Altman, Y.; & Shortland, S. "Women, Aliens and International Assignments," *Women in Management Review*, vol. 16 no. 3 (2001), pp. 141–145.

10. Austin, C. N. *Cross-Cultural Re-entry: An Annotated Bibliography* (Abilene, Tex.: Abilene Christian University Press, 1983).

11. Barham, K.; & Antal, A. B. "Competences for the Pan-European Manager," in P. Kirkbride, ed., *Human Resource Management in Europe* (London: Routledge, 1994), pp. 222–241.

12. Baughn, C. "Personal and Organizational Factors Associated with Effective Repatriation," in Jan Selmer, ed., *Expatriate Management: New Ideas for International Business* (Westport, Conn.: Quorum Books, 1995), pp. 215–230.

13. Black, J. Stuart. "Locus of Control, Social Support, Stress, and Adjustment in International Assignments," *Asia-Pacific Journal of Management*, vol. 7 (1990), pp. 1–29.

14. Black, J. Stuart; & Gregersen, Hal B. "The Right Way to Manage Expatriates," *Harvard Business Review* (March–April 1999), pp. 52–62.

15. Black, J. Stuart; & Gregersen, Hal B. "When Yankee Comes Home: Factors Related to Expatriate and Spouse Repatriation Adjustment," *Journal of International Business Studies*, vol. 22, no. 4 (1991), pp. 671–695.

16. Black, J. Stuart; Gregersen, Hal B.; & Mendenhall, Mark E. *Global Assignments: Successfully Expatriating and Repatriating International Managers* (San Francisco: Jossey-Bass, 1992).

17. Black, J. Stuart; Gregersen, Hal B.; & Mendenhall, Mark E. "Toward a Theoretical Framework of Repatriation Adjustment," *Journal of International Business Studies*, vol. 23, no. 4 (1992), pp. 737–760.

18. Black, J. Stuart; Gregersen, Hal B.; Mendenhall, Mark E.; & Stroh, L. K. *Global Assignments* (New York: Addison-Wesley, 1999).

19. Black, J. Stuart; & Mendenhall, Mark E. "Cross-Cultural Training Effectiveness: A Review and Theoretical Framework for Future Research," *Academy of Management Review*, vol. 15 (1990), pp. 113–136.

20. Black, J. Stuart; Mendenhall, Mark E.; & Oddou, G. "Toward a Comprehensive Model of International Adjustment: An Integration of Multiple Theoretical Perspectives," *Academy of Management Review,* vol. 16 (1991), pp. 291–317.

21. Black, J. Stuart; & Stephens, G. K. "The Influence of the Spouses on American Expatriate Adjustment in Overseas Assignments," *Journal of Management,* vol. 15 (1989), pp. 529–544.

22. Borg, M. *International Transfers of Managers in Multinational Corporations,* (Uppsala, Sweden: Acta Universitatis Upsaliensis, Studia Oeconomiae Negotiorum, no. 27, 1988).

23. Boyacigiller, Nakiye. "The Role of Expatriates in the Management of Interdependence, Complexity and Risk in Multinational Corporations," *Journal of International Business Studies,* vol. 21, no. 3 (1990), pp. 357–381.

24. Brewster, C. "Current Issues in Expatriation," *International Studies of Management and Organization,* vol. 24, no. 3 (1994).

25. Brewster, C. *The Management of Expatriates* (London: Kogan Page, 1991).

26. Brislin, R. W.; & Van Buren, H. "Can They Go Home Again?" *International Educational and Cultural Exchange,* vol. 1, no. 4 (1974), pp. 19–24.

27. Business International Corporation. "Successful Repatriation Demands Attention, Care, and a Dash of Ingenuity," *Business International,* vol. 25, no. 9 (1978), pp. 57–65.

28. Caligiuri, P. M. "Performance Measurement in a Cross-National Context: Evaluating the Success of Global Assignments," in W. Bennett, D. Woehr, & C. Lance, eds., *Performance Measurement: Current Perspectives and Future Challenges* (Mahwah, N.J.: Lawrence Erlbaum, 2005).

29. Caligiuri, P. M.; & Cascio, W. "Can We Send Her There? Maximizing the Success of Western Women on Global Assignments," *Journal of World Business,* vol. 33, no. 4 (1998), pp. 394–416.

30. Caligiuri, P. M.; & Cascio, W. "Sending Women on Global Assignments: Challenges, Myths and Solutions," *World at Work Journal,* vol. 9, no. 2 (2000), pp. 34–41.

31. Caligiuri, P. M.; Hyland, M.; & Joshi, A. "Families on Global Assignments: Applying Work/Family Theories Abroad," in A. Rahim, ed., *Current Topics in Management* (Greenwich, Conn.: JAI Press, vol. 3, 1998), pp. 313–328.

32. Caligiuri, P. M.; Hyland, M.; Joshi, A.; & Bross, A. "A Theoretical Framework for Examining the Relationship Between Family Adjustment and Expatriate Adjustment to Working in the Host Country," *Journal of Applied Psychology,* vol. 83, no. 4 (1998), pp. 598–614.

33. Caligiuri, P. M.; Joshi, A.; & Lazarova, M. "Factors Influencing the Adjustment of Women on Global Assignments," *International Journal of Human Resource Management,* vol. 10, no. 2 (1999), pp. 163–179.

34. Caligiuri, P. M.; & Lazarova, M. "A Model for the Influence of Social Interaction and Social Support on Female Expatriates' Cross-Cultural Adjustment," *International Journal of Human Resource Management,* vol. 13, no. 5 (2002), pp. 761–772.

35. Caligiuri, P. M.; & Lazarova, M. "Strategic Repartition Policies to Enhance Global Leadership Development," in M. Mendenhall, T. Kuehlmann, & G. Stahl, eds., *Developing Global Business Leaders: Policies, Process, and Innovations* (Westport, Conn.: Quorum Books, 2001).

36. Caligiuri, P. M.; & Tung, R. L. "Male and Female Expatriates' Success in Masculine and Feminine Countries," *International Journal of Human Resource Management,* vol. 10, no. 2 (1999), pp. 763–782.

37. Copeland, L.; & Griggs, L. *Going International* (New York: Random House, 1985).

38. Coyle, W. *On the Move: Minimizing the Stress and Maximising the Benefits of Relocation* (Sydney, Australia: Hampden Press, 1988).

39. Culpan, O.; & Wright, G. H. "Women: Abroad: Getting the Best Results from Women Managers," *International Journal of Human Resource Management,* vol. 13, no. 5 (2002), pp. 784–801.

40. DeCieri, Helen; & Dowling, P. J. "Strategic Human Resource Management in Multinational Enterprises: Theoretical and Empirical Developments," in P. M. Wright, L. D. Dyer, J. W. Boudreau, and G. T. Milkovich, eds., *Research in Personnel and Human Resources Management: Strategic Human Resources Management in the Twenty-First Century,* Supplement 4 (Stamford, Conn.: JAI Press, 1999), pp. 305–327.

41. Derr, C. B.; & Oddou, G. "Are U.S. Multinationals Adequately Preparing Future American Leaders for Global Competition?" *International Journal of Human Resource Management,* vol. 2, no. 2 (1991), pp. 227–244.

42. Dowling, Peter J. "Human Resource Issues in International Business," *Syracuse Journal of International Law and Commerce,* vol. 13, no. 2 (1986), pp. 255–271.

43. Dowling, Peter J.; Welch, D. E.; & Schuler, Randall S. *International Human Resource Management: Managing People in a Multinational Context,* 3d ed. (Cincinnati, Ohio: South-Western, 1998).

44. Elron, E.; & Kark, R. "Women Managers and International Assignments: Some Recommendations for Bridging the Gap," in M. Mendenhall and G. Oddou, eds., *Readings and Cases in*

International Human Resource Management. (Cincinnati, Ohio: South-Western, 2000), pp. 144–154.

45. Fayerweather, John. *The Executive Overseas* (Syracuse, N.Y.: Syracuse University Press, l959).

46. Feldman, D. C.; & Thompson, H. B. "Expatriation, Repatriation, Domestic Geographical Relocation: An Empirical Investigation of Adjustment to New Job Assignments," *Journal of International Business Studies,* vol. 24 (1993), pp. 507–529.

47. Fischlmayr, I. C. "Female Self Perception as Barrier to International Careers?" *International Journal of Human Resource Management,* vol. 13, no. 5 (2002), pp. 773–783.

48. GMAC Global Relocation Services. *Global Relocation Trends 2003/2004 Survey Report* (Oak Brook, Ill.: GMAC Relocation Services, National Foreign Trade Council and SHRM Global Forum, 2004a).

49. GMAC Global Relocation Services. *Ten Years of Global Relocation Trends 1993-2004* (Oak Brook, Ill.: GMAC Relocation Services, National Foreign Trade Council and SHRM Global Forum, 2004b).

50. Gregersen, H. B. "Commitment to a Parent Company and a Local Work Unit During Repatriation," *Personnel Psychology,* vol. 45 (1992), pp. 29–54.

51. Gregersen, H. B.; & Black, J. S. "Keeping High Performers After International Assignments: A Key to Global Executive Development," *Journal of International Management,* vol. 1, no. 1 (1995), pp. 3–31.

52. Gregersen, H. B.; & Black, J. S. "A Multifaceted Approach to Expatriate Retention in International Assignments," *Group and Organization Studies,* vol. 15 (1990), pp. 461–485.

53. Gullahorn, J. T.; & Gullahorn, J. E. "An Extension of the U-Curve Hypothesis," *Journal of Social Sciences,* vol. 19, no. 3 (1963), pp. 33–47.

54. Guthrie, J. P.; Ash, R. A.; & Stevens, C. D. "Are Women Better Than Men? Personality Differences and Expatriate Selection," *Journal of Managerial Psychology,* vol. 18, no. 3 (2003), pp. 229–243.

55. Harris, Hilary. "Think International Manager, Think Male: Why Are Women Not Selected for International Management Assignments?" *Thunderbird International Business Review,* vol. 44, no. 2 (2002), pp. 175–203.

56. Harvey, M. G. "The Other Side of Foreign Assignments: Dealing with the Repatriation Dilemma," *Columbia Journal of World Business,* vol. 17, no. 1 (1982), pp. 53–59.

57. Harvey, M. G. "Repatriation of Corporate Executives: An Empirical Study," *Journal of International Business Studies,* vol. 20 (1989), pp. 131–144.

58. Hazzard, M. S. *Study of the Repatriation of the American International Executive* (New York: Korn/Ferry International, 1981).

59. Howard, C. "The Returning Overseas Executive: Culture Shock in Reverse," *Human Resources Management,* vol. 13, no. 2 (1974), pp. 22–26.

60. Inkson, K.; Arthur, M. B.; Pringle, J.; & Barry, S. "Expatriate Assignment versus Overseas Experience: Contrasting Models of International Human Resource Development," *Journal of World Business,* vol. 32 (1997), pp. 351–368.

61. Kendall, D. W. "Repatriation: An Ending and a Beginning," *Business Horizons* (November–December 1981), pp. 21–25.

62. Kobrin, Steve J. "Expatriate Reduction and Strategic Control in American Multinational Corporations," *Human Resource Management,* vol. 27 (1988), pp. 63–75.

63. Kobrin, Steve J. "Is There a Relationship Between a Geocentric Mind-Set and Multinational Strategy?" *Journal of International Business Studies,* vol. 25 (1994), pp. 493–511.

64. Koretz, Gene. "A Woman's Place Is . . ." *Business Week* (September 28, 1999), p. 13.

65. Lein, Janet D.; & Sisco, Nichole L. "Language and Cross-Cultural Training for Expatriate Employees: A Comparison Between the U.S. and Germany," *Journal of Language of International Business,* vol. 10, no. 2 (1999), pp. 47–59.

66. Linehan, M.; & Scullion H. "Repatriation of European Female Corporate Executives: An Empirical study," *International Journal of Human Resource Management,* vol. 13, no. 2 (2002), pp. 254–267.

67. Linehan, M.; & Scullion H. "Towards an Understanding of the Female Expatriate Experience in Europe," *Human Resource Management Review,* vol. 14 (2004), pp. 433–448.

68. Linehan, M.; & Walsh J. S. "Beyond the Traditional Linear View of International Managerial Careers: A New Model of the Senior Female Career in an International Context," *Journal of European Industrial Training,* vol. 24, no. 2-4 (2000), pp. 178–189.

69. Linehan, M.; & Walsh, J. S. "Key Issues in the Senior Female International Career Move: A Qualitative Study in a European Context," *British Journal of Management,* vol. 12, no. 1 (2001), pp. 85–95.

70. Linehan, M.; & Walsh J. S. "Senior Female International Managers: Breaking the Glass Border," *Women in Management Review,* vol. 14, no. 7 (1999), pp. 264–272.

71. Mathur-Helm, B. "Expatriate Women Managers: At the Crossroads of Success, Challenges and Career Goals," *Women in Management Review,* vol. 17, no. 1 (2002), pp. 18–28.

72. Mendenhall, Mark E.; Dunbar, E.; & Oddou, G. R. "Expatriate Selection, Training and Career-Pathing: A Review and Critique," *Human Resource Management,* vol. 26, no. 3 (1987), pp. 331–345.

73. Mendenhall, Mark E.; & Oddou, G. R. "Acculturation Profiles of Expatriate Managers: Implications for Cross-Cultural Training Programs," *Columbia Journal of World Business* (Winter 1986), pp. 73–79.

74. Mendenhall, Mark E.; & Oddou, G. R. "The Dimensions of Expatriate Acculturation: A Review," *Academy of Management Review,* vol. 10, no. 1 (1985), pp. 39–47.

75. Murray, J. A. "International Personnel Repatriation: Cultural Shock in Reverse," *MSU Business Topic,* vol. 21, no. 2 (1973), pp. 59–66.

76. Napier, Nancy K.; & Taylor, Sully. "Experiences of Women Professionals Abroad: Comparisons Across Japan, China and Turkey," *International Journal of Human Resource Management,* vol. 15, no. 2 (2002), pp. 837–885.

77. Noer, D. M. "Integrating Foreign Service Employees to Home Organization: The Godfather Approach," *Personnel Journal* (January 1974), pp. 45–51.

78. ORC (Organization Resources Counselors). *Dual Careers and International Assignments Survey.* (London: Organization Resources Counselors, Inc., 2002).

79. Osland, J. S. *The Adventure of Working Abroad: Hero Tales from the Global Frontier* (San Francisco: Jossey-Bass, 1995).

80. Paik, Yongsun; & Vance, Charles M. "Evidence of Back-Home Selection Bias Against American Female Expatriates," *Women in Management Review,* vol. 17, no. 2 (2002), pp. 68–79.

81. Ratiu, Indre. "Thinking Internationally: A Comparison of How International Executives Learn," *International Studies of Management and Organization,* vol. 13, nos. 1–2 (1983), pp. 139–150.

82. Selmer, Jan. "Effects of Coping Strategies on Sociocultural and Psychological Adjustment of Western Expatriate Managers in the PRC," *Journal of World Business,* vol. 34, no. 1 (1999), pp. 41–51.

83. Selmer, Jan, ed., *Expatriate Management: New Ideas for International Business* (Westport, Conn.: Quorum Books, 1995).

84. Selmer, Jan; & Leung, A. S. M. "Are Corporate Career Development Activities Less Available to Female than to Male Expatriates?" *Journal of Business Ethics,* vol. 43, no. 1-2 (2003), pp. 125–136.

85. Selmer, Jan; & Leung, A. S. M. "Expatriate Career Intentions of Women on Foreign Assignments and their Adjustment," *Journal of Managerial Psychology,* vol. 18, no. 3 (2003), pp. 244–258.

86. Selmer, Jan; & Leung, A. S. M. "International Adjustment of Female vs. Male Business Expatriates," *The International Journal of*

Human Resource Management, vol. 14, no. 7 (2003), pp. 1117–1131.

87. Selmer, Jan; & Leung, A. S. M. "Personal Characteristics of Female vs. Male Business Expatriates," *International Journal of Cross Cultural Management,* vol. 3, no. 2 (2003d), pp. 195–212.

88. Shaffer, Margaret A.; Harrison, David A; & Gilley, K. Matthew. "Dimensions, Determinants, and Differences in the Expatriate Adjustment Process," *Journal of International Business Studies,* vol. 30, no. 3 (1999), pp. 557–581.

89. Smith, L. "The Hazards of Coming Home," *Dun's Review* (October 1975), pp. 71–73.

90. Stroh, L. K. "Predicting Turnover among Repatriates: Can Organizations Affect Retention Rates?" *International Journal of Human Resource Management,* vol. 6 (1995), pp. 443–456.

91. Stroh, L. K.; & Caligiuri, P. M. "Strategic Human Resources: A New Source for Competitive Advantage in the Global Arena," *International Journal of Human Resource Management,* vol. 9 (1998), pp. 1–17.

92. Stroh, L. K.; Gregersen, H. B.; & Black, J. S. "Closing the Gap: Expectations versus Reality Among Repatriates," *Journal of World Business,* vol. 33 (1998), pp. 111–124.

93. Stroh, L. K.; Varma, A.; & Valy-Durbin, S. J. "Why Are Women Left at Home: Are They Unwilling to Go on International Assignments?" *Journal of World Business,* vol. 35, no. 3 (2000), pp. 241–255.

94. Stroh, L. K.; Varma, A.; & Valy-Durbin, S. J. "Women and Expatriation: Revisiting Adler's Findings" in M. J. Davidson & R. J. Burke, eds., *Women in Management.* (London: Sage, 2000).

95. Taylor, S.; Beechler, S.; Najjar, M.; & Ghosh, B. C. "A Partial Test of a Model of Strategic International Human Resource Management," in J. L. C. Cheng & R. B. Peterson, eds., *Advances in International and Comparative Management,* vol. 12 (Stamford, Conn.: JAI Press, 1998), pp. 207–236.

96. Taylor, Sully; & Napier, Nancy. "An American Woman in Turkey: Adventures Unexpected and Knowledge Unplanned," *Human Resource Management,* vol. 40, no. 4 (2001), pp. 347–364.

97. Thang, L. L.; MacLachlan, E.; & Goda, M. "Expatriates on the Margin—A Study of Japanese Women Working in Singapore," *Geoforum,* vol. 33, no. 4 (2002), pp. 539–551.

98. Theoret, R.; Adler, N. J.; Kealey, D.; & Hawes, F. *Re-entry: A Guide to Returning Home* (Hull, Quebec: Canadian International Development Agency, 1979).

99. Torbiorn, I. *Living Abroad: Personal Adjustment and Personnel Policy in Overseas Setting* (New York: Wiley, 1982).

100. Tung, Rosalie L. "American Expatriates Abroad: From Neophytes to Cosmopolitans," *Journal of World Business*, vol. 33 (1998), pp. 125–144.

101. Tung, Rosalie L. "Career Issues in International Assignments," *Academy of Management Executive*, vol. 2, no. 3 (1988), pp. 241–244.

102. Tung, Rosalie L. "Expatriate Assignments: Enhancing Success and Minimizing Failure," *Academy of Management Executive*, vol. 1, no. 2 (1987), pp. 117–126.

103. Tung, Rosalie L. *The New Expatriates: Managing Human Resources Abroad* (Cambridge, Mass.: Ballinger, 1988).

104. Tung, Rosalie L. "Female Expatriates: The Model Global Manager?" *Organizational Dynamics*, vol. 33, no. 3 (2004), pp. 243–253.

105. Tung, Rosalie L. "Selection and Training Procedures of U.S., European, and Japanese Multinationals," *California Management Review*, vol. 25, no. 1 (1982), pp. 57–71.

106. Van der Boon, Mary. "Women in International Management: An International Perspective on Women's Ways of Leadership," *Women in Management Review*, vol. 18, no. 3 (2003), pp. 132–146.

107. Varma, V.; Stroh, L. K.; & Schmitt, L. B. "Women and International Assignments: The Impact of Supervisor-Subordinate Relationships," *Journal of World Business*, vol. 36, no. 4 (2001), pp. 380–388.

108. Werkman, S. L. "Coming Home: Adjustment of Americans to the United States After Living Abroad," in G. V. Coelho & P. I. Ahmed, eds., *Uprooting and Development: Dilemmas of Coping with Modernization* (New York: Plenum Press, 1980).

109. Windham & NFTC. *Global Relocation Trends 1996 Survey Report* (New York: Windham International & the National Foreign Trade Council, 1997).

110. "Workers Sent Overseas Have Adjustment Problems, a New Study Shows," *Wall Street Journal* (June 19, 1984), p. 1, col. 5.

Chapter 11

A Portable Life:
The Expatriate Spouse

We shall not cease from explorations
And the end of all our exploring
Will be to arrive where we started
And know the place for the first time.

—T. S. Eliot (16)

In global transfers, the spouse has the most difficult role of any family member. Whereas employees have the organization and job structure that continue from the home to the new country, and children have the continuity and routine of school, spouses often leave behind many of the most important aspects of their lives, including friends, relatives, and meaningful activities. More frequently today, spouses must also leave or restructure a job or career in order to follow their partners abroad. Approximately half of expatriate spouses are employed prior to the international transfer, whereas fewer than 20% are employed while abroad (19). Spouses often lose both structure and continuity in their lives (11;32;37). The spouse's dissatisfaction, which leads at times to early return, is the single most frequently reported reason for failure on a global assignment—nearly half of 300 surveyed companies have brought families home early due to the reported unwillingness or inability of the spouse to adapt (19;20). The average cost to a company of repatriating an executive and family ranges from $250,000 to $1.25 million (26;36).

The experience of global managers differs markedly from that of their spouses (3;7;8;9;30;35). The spouse generally becomes more immersed in the new culture than does the employee; the challenges to adjusting successfully are therefore both different and greater. This chapter begins by reviewing the most common situation historically faced by spouses in single-career families: that of a wife following her employee husband abroad without having a job or career of her own outside the family. The reason is not that all spouses are wives; they are not. However, to date, companies have sent few married women abroad and even fewer whose husbands accompanied them (2;4;19;20;22). The chapter then shifts focus and reviews the situation faced by dual-career couples, an increasingly important subset of expatriates. Because the dynamics of single- and dual-career families differ markedly, each is discussed separately.

SINGLE-CAREER COUPLES: THE TRADITIONAL EXPATRIATE'S WIFE

Traditionally, wives have moved from country to country in order to follow their husbands' global careers. What challenges does the wife face in living abroad? How does she adapt to each new culture? How does she create a meaningful, "portable" life for herself—one that proves satisfying in whatever situation she encounters? This section discusses the traditional wife's expatriate cycle: her initial reaction to the global move, her arrival in the foreign country, her approach to creating a new lifestyle, and her return to her home country. Although this cycle takes place concurrently with the employee's global career cycle, its dynamics frequently remain unrecognized by both the couple and the organization.

In a major research study, 197 wives of managers sent abroad by North American corporations and by the Canadian International Development Agency described their experiences of moving and living abroad (1;3). The women accompanied their expatriate husbands to Asia, Africa, Europe, and Latin America. Some lived abroad in urban centers while others lived in rural areas; some in economically developed countries and others in extremely poor regions; some in areas linguistically similar to their home countries and others in areas in which the language spoken was totally new to them. Their ages and family situations also varied. Although the diversity of their backgrounds and the international environments in which they lived are noteworthy, the challenges they faced in managing the expatriate transitions and creating meaningful portable lives abroad are strikingly similar.

MOVING ABROAD: PRE-MADE DECISIONS

Companies' involvement in global operations takes many forms, including exporting, subsidiary management, joint ventures, and strategic alliances. Companies therefore transfer employees for a wide variety of reasons (5;12;13;14;15;19;29;31;39). By contrast, a wife generally moves abroad because the company has transferred her husband (38). Until offered the global assignment, many couples are unaware of the possibility that they might move abroad. Some wives therefore react initially with surprise or shock.

Argentina

"I just didn't have any idea what it would be like. I was thoroughly set-tled in Toronto [Canada]. We were going to live there the rest of our lives. Our family and friends were all around us and everything was very comfortable. . . . I just didn't have any idea of what was ahead of me. I looked South America up on the map and I knew it was an awful long way from Toronto. I remembered a little bit from school about Argentina, that Buenos Aires was the capital. But beyond that, it was just like stepping into oblivion. I had no idea what to expect."

Can a wife turn down an expatriate transfer? Although the company and employee usually believe that the wife has a role in deciding whether to move abroad, she rarely does. By the time the company identifies the employee whom it wants to transfer and announces the decision, it has generally made a large investment in the employee's acceptance. Subtle pressure discourages open discussion of the pros and cons of the international move. The employee often feels he would disappoint the company if he did not accept; his wife feels she would disappoint her husband if she refused to go. The employee often feels he would derail his career by saying no; his wife feels reluctant to disagree. The couple fails to mention concerns they could easily have discussed and resolved prior to departure. At a time when communication is critical, open communication is often absent.

Venezuela

"Bill came home in November and asked me what I thought about moving . . . [abroad]. I was silent. Then he told me about what a big promotion it would be and what it would mean for the rest of his career. I told him that I was delighted. The company told us about the things to take and the name of an international school. And we were made busy with the preparations. We left."

"The Carpenter Case" on the following page presents the conflicting pressures and dilemmas faced by an American couple when offered the opportunity to take a first expatriate assignment. As you read the case, which is based on a true story, ask yourself whether Tom, the manager, should accept the global assignment being offered to him. Should the family move from the United States to Argentina? If the couple chooses to move, what could Tom, his wife Jane, his boss Mr. Abbott, and the company do to increase the chances of the family succeeding?

CROSS-CULTURAL TRANSITIONS

Expatriates not only experience the physical move abroad, they must also adjust to the new culture and create a meaningful life abroad. Companies generally give considerable attention to the logistics of the physical transfer itself: what expatriates should pack, which shipper to use, where to stay upon arrival, and so on. Today, many also pay attention to the skills necessary for adjusting to the new country: good language training; a knowledge of the culture and its people; and an awareness of culturally based differences in values, attitudes, and behaviors. Less attention is paid to assisting the spouse in creating a meaningful portable life abroad. Although rarely recognized as an important issue by either the employee or the children, the structureless role of the spouse demands explicit attention: if she is to have a fulfilling life abroad, she must create it. The following section reviews the transition and initial adjustment issues confronting the spouse; it then discusses the broader and more fundamental issue of creating a meaningful life abroad. The discussion presents the spouse as the wife, because historically, and even today, the spouse is more likely to be a woman than a man.

THE CARPENTER CASE

Tom and Jane Carpenter are a young couple living comfortably in a New England town in the United States. They have three children: Mary, aged eleven, Jerry, aged six, and Ann, aged three.

Tom works at the headquarters of a major manufacturing company as an executive in the engineering department. He has an excellent salary and up until now has been satisfied with his job. A quiet, handsome man about thirty-six years old, he is intelligent, sensitive, ambitious, and known as "a good family man." He has the respect of his colleagues and subordinates. The upper echelons of management regard him as a promising candidate for senior management in this company. They consider Tom a practical man, able to face the changes in life with a basic optimism and adaptability that appear to give him a maturity beyond his years. He likes the material wealth and comfort his years of conscientious work have produced. He enjoys the status of his company, which has an excellent name in its field, being considered one of the most progressive and future-minded global companies.

If Tom is the practical member of the family, Jane is the "dreamer." She is a pretty, energetic woman of thirty, a good wife and mother and an active member of several committees and volunteer groups. She is strongly attached to both her family and her parents, who are in their early sixties and live in a nearby town. She is sincerely interested in many good causes and always finds the time and energy to devote to them. While she is not a very practical woman, her enthusiasm for her projects is admired by her many friends.

Tom and Jane married early and struggled together for several years until they were able to achieve the comfortable life they now enjoy. Their marital life has been happy and more or less undisturbed, and through the struggle of their earlier years they developed a rewarding relationship. Although they have traveled to

THE CARPENTER CASE (continued)

several parts of the United States with and without the children, neither Tom nor Jane had traveled abroad until two years ago. At that time, the company sent Tom, together with three other executives, to Latin America to explore the possibilities of setting up four new plants in four different countries.

Both Tom and Jane have been feeling more and more relaxed in the past years, since they have realized many of their dreams. They have a good family, financial security, and many friends. They feel especially proud of their new home, recently finished. Jane has worked hard to find the furniture and the interior decorations they wanted and now her dream house seems completed. They have both been, so far, generally satisfied with their children, who are well adjusted to their present environment. They have experienced certain problems with Mary, who is a very sensitive and shy girl, and with Jerry, who has had some difficulties adapting in school. But these are very minor problems that have not seriously disturbed the otherwise happy family life. Despite their seemingly very satisfactory family life, there have recently been more occasions when Tom and Jane have felt (each one without admitting it to the other) that something is missing.

Tom believes his life has fallen into a too comfortable routine. The new tasks the company gives him seem to involve less challenge and adventure. For a long while he had been satisfied with the steady development of his career over the years. The time of anxiety and uncertainty has passed, but along with it the sense of excitement and inner feeling of searching and moving. He had begun to feel that he needed a change and it was at that time that the company sent him for four months to Latin America. Tom felt this trip was one of the most interesting and rewarding experiences of his whole life. Being away for the first time from his family for such a long period, he missed them and was disappointed that wives were not allowed to accompany their husbands on that trip. At the same time, Tom found the prospects of building up the company in Latin America attractive. He discovered that he liked to travel, to meet new people, to become acquainted with different ways of living, to be more a part of the world and of events outside his hometown. The three other executives who traveled with him felt about the same as he did. Each seemed to be a little weary of being "a little fish" at headquarters. The possibility of becoming a pioneer in the new expansion into Latin America was an exciting prospect. Tom somehow felt reluctant to communicate to Jane his thoughts about that trip and especially his feelings of satisfaction. He felt particularly reluctant to tell her how much he was hoping the company would choose him from among the four executives to set up the plants in Latin America.

In a different way, but with the same feeling of restlessness and discontent, Jane also feels that their pleasant, well-organized life lacks the excitement of unpredictability. She divides her time among many activities, but finds herself at times dreaming about the world outside her hometown. Like Tom, she sometimes wonders whether their life has not become too settled, an almost unaltered

THE CARPENTER CASE (continued)

routine, but unlike Tom, she checks herself by asking the simple question that, after all, isn't this what life really is?

When Tom came home with the news that Mr. Abbott, the president of the company, had offered him the key position in Latin America, she felt pleased to hear of the high esteem Tom's superiors had for him. Actually, Jane too had been wondering for some time what would be the result of Tom's trip to Latin America.

Although she would have enjoyed traveling with Tom on his first trip to Latin America, the idea that they would have had to leave the children for such a long time forced her to exclude absolutely the possibility of her going, even if the wives of the executives had been allowed to accompany their husbands. After his trip, she used to wonder whether the company would choose Tom, if the decision to establish the plants was made. At that time the idea of having to move to a new environment was not unpleasant.

Now that the offer was firm, with a high salary, cost of living allowance, and opportunity for travel throughout Latin America, she began to have some fears. As Tom talked excitedly about the challenging tasks he would have, her fears grew. She increasingly felt that neither their family nor their life had much to gain from this experience. It would represent a big step forward in Tom's career, to be sure, but Jane felt that Tom would succeed wherever he worked. On his present job, Tom and Jane shared so much time together, while in the new job, as she understood it, Tom would have to travel a great deal. She felt unhappy and ashamed of her fears as opposed to Tom's enthusiasm and obvious willingness to venture ahead.

One evening she tried to sit down by herself and figure out why this new job was not so attractive. There was some urgency for Tom to make up his mind within a week, and she felt the need to understand what this decision to move abroad really meant for her and for her family.

She tried to be honest with herself. She naturally had fears about moving to a strange new environment where people spoke another language. She knew that the climate was very different and she believed that the living conditions were likely to offer fewer comforts. She would live far from her friends and her parents. Their furniture would have to be stored, and their new house rented or sold, since it was not clear how many years Tom would need to establish the four new plants.

She feared she would remain isolated because she believed it would take a long time to enter into close contact with the local people. Everything she had heard so far about the personality of Latin Americans made her fear that close friendships would be difficult for her to achieve, at least for some time, because she had the impression that they were rather temperamental and unstable. Although she admitted to herself that she was basing her impression on hearsay and fiction, she somehow could not avoid believing it. She had also heard that there was a great deal of anti-American sentiment in the country where they would initially live. She also worried that the sanitary conditions would be dangerous to the health of the children. The company had little experience in Latin America, so it

THE CARPENTER CASE (continued)

would be likely that they would have to find their own way and learn, probably through hard experience, how to get along in these countries. She realized that what disturbed her more than anything else was that Tom would have to travel a lot. She would have to face most of the problems of their adaptation alone, whereas up until now they had always shared whatever problems they had to face, and had supported each other in finding solutions. Tom's position also meant that he would see more places, meet more people, and in general enjoy himself more and probably get more satisfaction out of the whole experience than would she and the children. She was distressed to realize that she already resented him for that and felt angry because she could sense that, although he was discussing the decision with her, he had already made up his mind. Jane kept her fears more or less to herself, but she did communicate to Tom her reluctance to go and gave as one of her main reasons her worry about the effect this move would have on the education of their children and their health.

Tom sensed most of Jane's fears and he reacted to her expressed doubts by attempting to reassure her that he thought that the children would adapt after a while and that the experience would be very good for them. They could learn a new language and make new friends. As for themselves, he had the best of memories from his own trip and he believed that they were both going to find this new experience enriching and rewarding. He did not underestimate the difficulties involved, but he expressed his belief that they were capable of overcoming them, while enjoying all the advantages that living abroad would offer. Inwardly Tom felt disappointed with Jane's negative reactions and the difficulties she seemed to be having. He had always believed her to be a woman of courage, endowed with curiosity and interest in the world outside. In previous times of crisis in their life together, she had always proven strong and supportive and had always demonstrated a spirit of adventure and willingness to go ahead. It was a painful surprise for him to realize that this spirit operated only in the security of a familiar environment, and that more profound change seemed to appear to Jane as a great threat to herself and her family. He had hoped that she would back him in this decision that was so important to his career. Nevertheless, he maintained his confidence in her and he believed she would change her mind in time. He called a nearby language school and made plans for both of them to take Spanish lessons.

When Jane's parents came to visit, Jane told them of the company's offer to Tom. Her father, who had been ailing for some time, was visibly depressed by the news. Her mother said that this was going to be a great experience for them, "a chance of a lifetime," as she put it. Jane knew that her mother had always regretted not being able to travel abroad. Now she was thrilled that the children were being given the opportunity and she promised to come and visit them in Latin America if Tom accepted the position.

THE CARPENTER CASE (continued)

Dinner with Mr. Abbott

A few days later, Tom's boss, Mr. Abbott, invited Tom and Jane for dinner, saying that he always talked over a new job abroad with both husband and wife, because he felt that it was very important to take into consideration the wife's feelings. Jane had many fears about this dinner. First, she resented being "looked over" by Mr. Abbott, who until now had not spent much time with them socially. Second, she did not want to reveal her doubts to Tom's boss, who had a reputation for making quick, often unfavorable judgments about people.

This dinner turned out to be a very pleasant one. Mrs. Abbott helped to put everyone at ease throughout the dinner, talking about her pleasant experiences abroad when Mr. Abbott was managing director of a subsidiary in Europe. Mrs. Abbott had enjoyed Paris and Rome, but admitted she knew little about life in cities like Buenos Aires and Rio.

Mr. Abbott finally turned to Jane and said: "Well, we are very glad you are taking the news of this new assignment for Tom so well. I know you realize what an opportunity this job will be for him. It is a real challenge for him, far greater than what he can get here, you know." Tom hurriedly answered for Jane, who was about to reply to Mr. Abbott: "Jane is really a born traveler. I know that she is looking forward to living in Argentina. She has already found out how she can take Spanish lessons." Mr. Abbott seemed pleased. He said: "That is really fine. You know, Tom, that our firm is rapidly becoming a global company. There will be few opportunities at headquarters for executives whose international experience is limited. Our policy is to create a management team that can base its decisions on actual experience abroad. Of course, having the kind of wife who is willing to take the risk of going off to the jungle is quite an asset. You are a lucky man, Tom."

While Jane joined in the laughter, she was inwardly very angry. That night, she and Tom had a quarrel that continued for the next few days. Jane resented that the whole discussion was conducted as though Tom had already accepted the job, as well as the fact that she was not given a chance to talk about Tom's work with Mr. Abbott. Tom insisted that Mr. Abbott was not the kind of man to whom one could reveal any doubts about a company decision. Discussing the move the next day with the children confused Tom and Jane even more, because the children's reactions were not clear. Mary was unwilling to go; Jerry and Ann seemed excited, but it was more because of the thrill they felt than because they really understood the issue. By now Jane was finding it difficult to sleep, and Tom said that the company required a formal decision by the following Monday.

Tom and Jane had a long weekend to think over the decision before giving a final answer to Mr. Abbott on Monday.

Source: Foulie Psalidas-Perlmutter, Ph.D.[1]

It Is Harder for the Spouse As mentioned previously, when the spouse accompanies her husband on an international transfer, she comes into more direct contact with the "foreignness" of the new culture than does her husband. The husband, as an expatriate manager, generally works in the most internationally cosmopolitan strata of society: he meets people who have met foreigners before and speak English. His wife frequently meets people who are much less cosmopolitan. In caring for her family's daily living needs, she often meets people who do not speak English and have rarely encountered foreigners. Whereas a global manager often has a secretary and colleagues to translate the language and explain local customs, his wife must depend on her own skills and ingenuity. Whereas a global manager works in an office filled with other expatriates to answer his questions and share his frustrations, his wife often finds herself isolated in her world at home. She must confront the differences on her own.

Many wives feel unprepared for their move. They know little about the country, culture, or specific location. Their expectations and the foreign reality have little in common. Upon arrival, they often react with surprise and excitement mixed with bewilderment and fear. Below, two expatriate wives describe their arrival in Africa:

> *Africa*
> *"Well, my expectations were . . . very large. For me, Africa was . . . totally unknown . . . except that I could equate it with wild animals, missionaries, nice black people, and a very different way of life than in Canada. . . . I didn't question anything. I was very young, just married, and very happy to discover a new country. I could imagine that they had modern cities, that Conakry would be a modern city with all the amenities; I asked no questions and just left."*

> *"Finally I arrived at . . . this hazy airport. . . . I got off the plane, and there were . . . all of these black faces that I wasn't really used to in such mass. So I said, 'It's so good to be here and I am so looking forward to getting into the house.' . . . [My husband] didn't know how to tell me, but he said, 'But we don't have a house.' So I burst into tears. I guess it was just the whole stress of thinking that finally I was going to be in a house, and the jet lag, and just being in a completely different culture and a completely different color."*

Culture Shock: The Initial Period Abroad Culture shock, as described in Chapter 10, is the reaction of expatriates to entering a new, unpredictable, and therefore uncertain environment. During the first few months in a new culture, expatriates often find that other people's behavior does not make sense, and even more disconcerting, that their own behavior fails to produce expected results. Wives, being in more direct contact with the foreign culture than employees, describe some of their initial reactions as surprise, bewilderment, and disorientation:

Guinea

"Then we went into our building, a very modern building. We were on the ninth floor, and the building had no elevators. So we had to walk up the nine floors. And then we arrived in this beautiful, huge apartment, with three bathrooms and no water."

Argentina

"Everything I was comfortable with in a North American suburban setting, like my shopping, and the schools, and my daily routine, just was drastically different in Argentina. Perhaps the thing that struck me the most was when I set out to do my grocery shopping (which is something that we take for granted with our big supermarkets [in Canada]). I found myself in the biggest supermarket [in Argentina] . . . which was just a filthy little dump really, and as I looked around to fill my grocery cart, the only thing I recognized was a box of Quaker Oats. Everything was packaged differently, everything had Spanish names on it, and I couldn't tell salt from icing sugar."

Hong Kong

"Before I went to Hong Kong, I'd read a lot of books. I expected the Chinese to be dignified and very courteous. The Cantonese in Hong Kong are the opposite of that. They are very noisy and . . . very pushy. In Argentina, I expected the romantic Latin. Instead, I was annoyed at the 'macho-ness' of the men. The reality . . . was disappointing."

Frustration. The first few months in a foreign culture are rarely easy. The constant frustration of not understanding and not being able to get simple things done follows the initial surprise.

"It's the constant minor frustrations . . . the phone never works, the electric power is variable, and, oh yes, filling the water bottles at 4 A.M., just to be sure that we'd have some water."

"I had my new Electrolux vacuum cleaner and I tried to show the help how to use it. . . . The next thing I knew they were vacuuming the patio and the grass. They just had no concept of what this [vacuum] was."

"We were not aware of the fact that everything seems to be done through a bribe. We were insulted when it was suggested. I think we

just didn't understand the culture. So we waited from January until May before our furniture was sprung from customs."

"Things can be very difficult . . . [say] you have to put on a dinner party: dinner parties are very important because there is not very much entertainment, so you have to make your own entertainment. You have ten people coming, and there is no electricity, and you have just put the roast in the oven. Right, what do you do? And it's pouring with rain outside so you can't make a barbecue. So you raid the cupboard and find a tin of ham, and you find some tomatoes, and then you find this and that, and you all have a good giggle. You know, really, there is no other way of doing it. You can't get depressed about these things."

"I like it . . . but things don't work and it's frustrating. I didn't expect things not to work in Europe. In a developing country, yes, but not in Europe."

While the newness of the environment in large part causes the difficulties, insufficient language competence, loneliness, boredom, and a sense of meaninglessness exacerbate the problems.

Foreign Language Illiteracy. Whereas most employees have less immediate need for foreign language competence than do their wives, only 60% of recently surveyed companies offered language training to the spouse (19). They expect the wife to enroll on her own in language courses, if she so desires, and often not at the company's expense. Consequently, many wives never become fluent in the local language and therefore have little possibility of becoming fully comfortable living in the new culture.

Italy
"I think the most difficult thing when you arrive in a country is not being able to communicate. You feel very isolated because you don't speak the language. So everything becomes very difficult; all small details, everyday life is difficult because you don't know how to communicate."

Mexico
"The only foreign language I learned is Spanish . . . and I didn't find it easy. I was embarrassed to speak in case I didn't have it right, and this became a big problem. . . . I would pretend I hadn't been there very long, even when I had been there several months. And I'd have the children speaking for me in the taxi because they could speak far better Spanish than I could."

Argentina

"I think the thing that bothered me the most was just my inability to express myself in Spanish. It was a while before I was able to take lessons, and I never did become fluent in the language. I could get by in English in most situations, but it was a little disappointing to see my husband learning Spanish through the office and my children learning it in school and yet I just could never seem to find the time or the concentration to sit down and master this thing."

Loneliness. The lack of intimate friendships causes a major part of the difficulty during the initial period abroad. Most wives leave their family and friends at home and experience a void upon arrival abroad. The loneliness expresses itself in a number of ways:

"I spent more time alone than anywhere ever. . . . It's hard to spend so much time alone."

"We had a lot of acquaintances, few good friends. . . . You can't make friends until you've learned the language."

"Loneliness is the biggest problem with all the moves. I can remember moving to Mexico from the United States very worried about what we would find there. Looking down at the little family that was in just a shack in Mexico City and envying them because they had the whole family with them. And I thought, they are better off than I am."

". . . In Hong Kong, not long after we arrived, our daughters were going back to school, my husband was going back with them on a business trip, and I felt, well, this is ridiculous. I am the only one here, and the rest of the family is on the other side of the world."

". . . I think that every country and every move has its low point and then you start going up. . . . I think loneliness is probably the low point."

"When you live abroad and you suffer loneliness, you have to . . . be your own best friend. So I was very alone, very lonely, and my husband was not going through the same problems as I. . . . And I felt more lonely because I couldn't share my problems with him. It was very difficult for . . . at least a year or a year and a half."

Boredom and Meaninglessness. Many wives describe themselves as having hours and hours on their hands with nothing to do. They describe themselves as living in a gilded cage: they have nice homes and servants to do the work but they do not have a meaningful role to fulfill. They no longer feel needed to perform many of the duties that they had previously fulfilled for their families. In addition, many are barred, often by legal restrictions, from working or continuing careers outside of the home.

> *"I was like a prisoner in my own apartment. I had nothing to do. I had no books with me, except for one or two and that's very quickly gone through. . . . I had absolutely nothing to do. So I started to write letters. That was my only contact with the outside world; and I don't like writing letters!"*

> *"I felt useless. I was a fifth wheel. There was the maid to do the work and no children who needed my attention."*

> *"I was going to be a nurse, but I had to have a work permit . . . so I threw myself into the women's club . . . bridge and golf, empty activities, but they filled my time."*

> *"Time . . . trying to find things to do with my time. I spent time sewing and I hate to sew. . . . We got together to crochet and talk. Blah!"*

> *"After the novelty wears off, you have to find something to do with your time. I worked in a hospital, cooked, gardened. . . . I want to work again."*

Separation and a Lack of Support   The expatriate employee's frequent absence compounds the difficulties in adjusting to the new environment. Having just started a new job, a global manager often works long hours. Exacerbating the situation further, many global assignments include regional or worldwide responsibilities and a great amount of travel. Whereas the wife has just given up her friends, activities, and in many cases a job or career to follow her husband and family abroad, her husband continues and increases his major involvement in work, often to the near exclusion of his wife. Separation and lack of support cause numerous complaints:

> *"My husband wasn't there to help me. He did nothing on the move. He works and travels."*

> *"My husband was always away; never available. The men are so busy and the women have nothing to do."*

> *"Well, I expected him to travel a little, but I didn't expect it to be so long or so often."*

FIGURE 11-1   Gap: Need Versus Availability

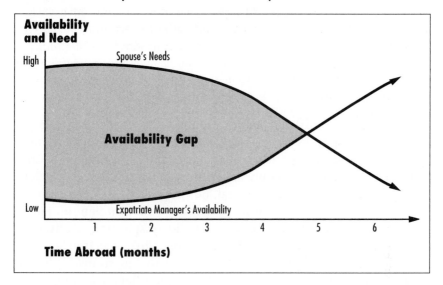

"My husband, as well as most of the men in the company, was away
probably two weeks out of four. We knew before we left that there was
going to be a lot of traveling, but it didn't really make its impact until
he was actually doing it."

As shown in Figure 11-1, the husband's work often leaves him least
available during the first few months abroad, exactly when his wife
needs him the most to help with the logistics of settling in and to provide companionship and support. The pattern of absent husbands and
isolated wives, unfortunately, reinforces itself in a vicious cycle. As
more problems build up at home, many global managers feel less
desire to spend time at home. By their own admission, many spend
more time in their office and traveling than the job actually requires.
As the wife's situation becomes more difficult, her husband, often feeling guilty at the realization that his career caused the situation in the
first place, increasingly avoids home.

CREATING A MEANINGFUL PORTABLE LIFE

Following the initial period of adjustment, the wife faces the hardest
task of all: creating a meaningful life abroad. She must identify what she
wants to do and find a way to do it in the foreign country. For women
who follow their husbands from country to country, it becomes the
search for a meaningful portable life.

"Being a transient, . . . it is very difficult for me to have a career. And
luckily, I am not a particularly career-minded person. I want to take

experiences and opportunities as they come. I want to learn different things, and I want to try different things. I mean, I only have one life. So a career and stepping up the ladder isn't important to me personally, it isn't. But it is important for me to develop skills that are portable because, being a transient, you have to have something that you can grasp hold of, that you can take with you, that can be a certain continuity."

Creating a meaningful portable life remains the most neglected aspect of most spouses' experience abroad. People talk about the initial culture shock, learning a foreign language, and adjusting to the new culture. But adjustment is only half of the challenge; it brings a potentially negative experience to neutral, not to positive. Adjustment only brings the wife to the point where the foreign environment no longer constantly frustrates her; it does not provide inspiration, motivation, direction, and meaning to daily life abroad. Introspection and life planning are necessary for spouses to answer the questions, "What do I really want to do?" "What would I be happiest having accomplished during my years abroad?" "How can I continue doing the things that I find most satisfying and important even while I no longer live at home?" "What do I want to learn from the local culture?" "What do I want to contribute to the local community?" The answers to these questions vary. One woman becomes an artist, another a counselor to expatriate families, a third teaches English to immigrant children, a fourth does extensive volunteer work, and a fifth starts her own business. Most remain very involved in raising their family. One French-Canadian woman, who focused on learning the history, literature, and culture of the country in which she was living, described her growing sense of purpose.

"You start to understand the people around you. . . . They are different, but very often the difference is not so evident. But slowly, you go into knowing these differences, and it is a new world that opens up to you. . . . You discover the arts, and the folklore, and how the folklore is lived in the modern world. It is not so evident but there is always something that stays from these roots. You start to see all the small differences that you wouldn't notice if you were just a tourist for a month or so in the country. When you live there, slowly you get to know the people much more, the civilization, how they are and why they are like that, and then I think it is very enjoyable. You are gaining something, it is not just giving."

More frequently today spouses' questions center on identifying ways to continue a career while living abroad.

RETURNING HOME

Expatriates often remember their home country as a more wonderful and perfect place than it actually is. As things get tough abroad and they experience culture shock and difficulties in adjusting to another culture, they dream about how easy and good life will be when they return home. In reality, however, re-entry often presents more challenges than the initial move abroad. Two women who accompanied their global-manager husbands living in a number of countries capture the difficulty and disillusionment of returning home:

Quebec

"*Coming back was . . . the most difficult move of all. Why was it so difficult? Because . . . you change, the country changes, the people change. You are expecting . . . that you are coming back to your place and that you will feel good right away. . . . It is not true. You come back and you feel like a foreigner in your own country. . . . People deal with you as if . . . you are different. Even your way of speaking the language [is different]. So you feel cut off completely and it is your own country. The roots that you were not really conscious of, but somehow, dreaming with. You know everybody needs some kind of roots and you come back to these roots and you don't feel well [sic] with them.*"

England

"*I was in England recently. I was sitting in the train and I watched two English mums coming from the corner shop, standing and talking. And I said to my husband, 'I know exactly what they are going to do, they are going to go home, have a little lunch, have a little sleep, and then they will watch a little bit of telly [television] and maybe do some ironing, then they will get dinner.' It is a pity that I am not able to do that anymore. I'm wanting more from life. I am pleased that I have changed, that I have matured, that I have developed, but sometimes it would be easier if I had stayed content with that life. We don't feel we can go back to England. We have been gone too long. . . . They have changed and we have changed.*"

RECOMMENDATIONS FOR SINGLE-CAREER COUPLES

Expatriate wives offer a range of suggestions for coping with cross-cultural transitions and creating a meaningful portable life abroad, including knowing yourself and what you want out of life and taking responsibility for creating the type of life you want. They recommend treating the move as permanent, no matter how temporary; persevering and being patient. Whereas some recommendations focus on what wives must do for themselves, most recommendations work best if all three—the organization, employee, and spouse—commit themselves to making the experience abroad successful. Spouses, for example, should ask themselves what they really want out of the time abroad. They should seek out assistance from the wide range and increasingly diverse on-line support groups for expatriate spouses.[2] The company should include the spouse in predeparture site visits and in selecting a home abroad. Expatriate managers, to the extent possible, need to limit their travel during the first three months abroad.

Many companies now interview both the employee and spouse prior to offering the employee a global assignment (18;24;25). They screen out couples with a high probability of failure, including those with excessive alcohol or drug use; indications of rigid and inflexible personalities or lifestyles; lack of communication among the husband, wife, and children; or inappropriate or inadequate coping and stress management mechanisms. Research has shown that the worlds of work and family overlap (10;34). Companies that screen couples recognize that the quality of home life affects the employee's ability to work, and similarly, that the very nature of an expatriate assignment strongly influences the family's daily life.

LIVING GLOBALLY: DUAL-CAREER COUPLES

Over the past decade, the number of couples in which both partners have significant careers outside the home has increased dramatically (19;27;28;33). As discussed in the prior section, most companies, when staffing global assignments, have historically selected men whose wives either did not work outside of the home or who worked in jobs that they were willing to give up in order to follow their husband abroad. This is no longer the case. Companies today select both women and men for global assignments and, in both cases, their spouses often have careers of their own (17;23). By 2000, 13 percent of expatriate managers whom companies sent abroad were women; some are predicting that that the number will soon reach over 20 percent (19). Among women expatriate managers, over 10 percent are married, up from just 5 percent in 1999 (20;23). Given the recent increase in the number of women executives selected for global assignments (many of whom are in dual-career marriages), this section—in a reversal of the prior section—refers to the employee as "she" and to the spouse, her husband, as "he." Needless to say, the pronouns would be reversed for companies offering a man the global assignment and asking his wife to follow him abroad as a *trailing spouse*.

Dual-career couples must decide for themselves the conditions under which they would be willing to accept a global assignment. The couple, and especially the trailing spouse, should consider a number of options:

- Simply **turn down the global assignment,** although this option usually results in negative career consequences.
- Accept the assignment contingent on finding the trailing spouse **a position in the foreign country.** Ideally, both partners would be able to move abroad at the same time, although they more commonly would move at different times—with the timing for each move determined by the separate needs of their two careers.
- Accept the assignment contingent on finding the trailing spouse **a position in the region.** The couple would thus have a shorter distance to commute than they would if the trailing spouse stayed home.
- Decide to have the trailing spouse **remain at home in his current position,** thus becoming a longer-distance commuting couple.
- Decide to have the trailing spouse **take a sabbatical**—a career break that allows him to accompany his wife while she works abroad even though he is unable to continue his own career while abroad.
- Choose to have the trailing spouse accompany his wife on the global assignment while continuing his own career. This is possible if the trailing spouse has a portable career, which the e-business revolution is making increasingly likely.
- **Create other options** that work for the particular couple and family.

REGIONAL COMMUTING
From Beijing to Osaka

A major American manufacturing firm transferred a senior engineer to Beijing for a three-year assignment. When her husband discovered that there were no positions available for his specialty in the Chinese capital, he accepted an excellent position in Osaka, Japan. Although the couple could not live together, their commute between Beijing and Osaka was more reasonable than it would have been if he had remained in Chicago.

The most competitive companies today increase the chances of dual-career couples finding acceptable options by offering them services and benefits that traditional single-career couples neither need nor value. Progressive companies, for example, offer the trailing spouse career counseling and global executive-search services. In so doing, the company shares responsibility with the couple for finding an appropriate solution.

A PLANNED SABBATICAL
A Swedish Husband in Hong Kong

When a New York bank decided to transfer an American woman to a position of vice president in Hong Kong, they told her Swedish economist husband that Hong Kong would not give spouses work permits. After some reflection, the Swedish economist decided to support his wife's career by taking a sabbatical and following her to Hong Kong without a job. As he thought about his upcoming time in Asia, he looked forward to learning about the Chinese culture and economy and having time to improve his tennis game.

One week after arriving in Hong Kong, the Swedish economist began spending his mornings playing tennis with the other expatriate spouses—the wives of the bank's other executives. Suddenly, to the surprise and amusement of the couple, the bank called and told the Swedish economist that they had found him an ideal position and that, based on it, they could obtain a work permit for him.

Whereas the motivation of the bank could certainly be questioned, the outcome benefited all trailing spouses—men and women—who now recognized that the bank could, when motivated, find both appropriate positions and work permits as needed.

The career counselor initially helps the couple determine whether they would find a commuter lifestyle acceptable. Then the counselor helps the trailing spouse decide whether he wants to continue his current career or change careers. After lifestyle flexibility and career aspirations are established, the executive search firm searches for professional positions in the same city or region as the employee's global assignment. They then coach the trailing spouse on effective ways to meet and interview with potential employers in the particular country or countries. Simultaneously, most progressive companies, rather than explaining why it is impossible to secure a work permit for the trailing spouse in the particular country (as has been so common in the past), take responsibility for securing a work permit (often based on the trailing spouse's own newfound position in the foreign country rather than on the expatriate employee's position).[3]

Once the couple identifies an acceptable lifestyle and the trailing spouse selects or creates an appropriate position, progressive companies support the couple's decisions by offering them a flexible expatriate benefits package tailored to their particular needs. The company, for example, might pay for extra airline tickets and telephone calls—"staying connected costs"—for commuting couples (see box "Intercontinental Commuting" on the following page).

Whereas many companies still mistakenly believe that transferring dual-career couples poses great obstacles, even more companies erroneously believe that the challenges of sending dual-career couples with children on global assignments remain insurmountable. They are

INTERCONTINENTAL COMMUTING
Montreal to London

A major telecommunications company transferred a Montreal executive to London for four years. Although her husband, a professor, was able to accompany her to England for the first two years while he wrote his book, he had to return to Montreal to continue teaching at the university for the third and fourth years. To continue spending time with each other during the last two years of the assignment, the couple chose to commute every three weeks between London and Montreal. The telecommunications company supported the decision by allowing the couple to spend less of their expatriate benefits allowance on housing and more on the additional intercontinental airline tickets.

wrong. Many couples report that it is easier, not harder, to maintain the three time-consuming roles of manager, parent, and spouse while abroad on a global assignment than it is at home (see box entitled "Both Careers Transferred to the same city").

Do all dual-career expatriate couples find good solutions? Unfortunately, no. Husbands who decide to accompany their wives on global assignments without having meaningful work of their own, for example, often find that the cultural dynamics of the local community make it almost impossible for them to succeed. Few communities in the world offer social support to a man who chooses to become the primary homemaker or stay-at-home parent in the family (23). In many communities, such men are both disparaged and isolated. To support husbands who accompany their wives on assignments abroad, a group of expatriate husbands in Belgium founded STUDS (Spouses Trailing Under Duress Successfully) (21;23). STUDS offers

BOTH CAREERS TRANSFERRED TO THE SAME CITY
Working in Bangkok with a Husband and Children

When a major oil company transferred a geologist to Bangkok, her husband, a diplomat, arranged a transfer to the same city. In describing their global lifestyle, the geologist explained that the availability of household help—including a driver, a nanny for their two small children, and a housekeeper—made it much easier for her to balance her three extremely time-consuming roles of mother, wife, and geologist in a way that would be financially impossible for her to achieve in the United States. "Even though everyone thought it would be completely impossible, the expatriate assignment has made my life easier, not more difficult. Time is my scarcest resource, and the household help available in Thailand gives me the time I need to be a good mother, a good wife, and a good manager."

both in-person and on-line support groups for male expatriates (23). For most couples, however, acceptable solutions can be found if both the company and the couple actively work to create them, rather than attempting to fit dual-career couples into the lifestyles and constraining arrangements of their single-career predecessors.

"The O'Connors' Story," recounted below, is the true story of a dual-career couple faced with making their fourth international move. If you were the O'Connors, what would you do? If you were the company, what would you offer the couple to make certain that the global assignment succeeded? What could Michael and Kelly each do to increase the chances of success in their move to Hong Kong?

THE O'CONNORS' STORY

Kelly O'Connor sat in her upstairs study of the Southern California home she shared with her husband Michael and their two children, Kate, aged six, and James, aged four. The computer screen in front of her reminded her that she had only four hours to complete a mid-term analysis of downsizing and deliver it to her graduate seminar at UCLA, an hour away. If the return traffic wasn't bad, she would have fifteen minutes to change and straighten the house before Michael arrived for dinner with his law firm's managing partner from New York. She turned away from the computer, reflecting on the decision she and Michael needed to make. Should they move back to Hong Kong?

Early History: The First Seven Years in Hong Kong

Kelly and Michael had begun their global careers in Hong Kong nearly a decade ago, one year after their marriage in New York. After graduating from Harvard Law School, Michael had gone to work for a New York law firm. A few years later, bored with domestic work, he joined Fishbeck, Rhodes and Goncourt (FR&G) to take a position in Hong Kong.

The early years at FR&G in Hong Kong were thrilling and Michael showed real talent both for handling complex cross-border financing and for working with difficult clients. In addition, he enjoyed the family feeling the firm cultivated by celebrating American and local holidays with the entire staff at a partner's home, sharing practices, and pinch-hitting for each other. The firm recognized Michael's talent by electing him partner two months before Kate was born, and by giving him responsibility for managing the Hong Kong office, making him the youngest partner ever to be entrusted with line management in the fifty-year history of the firm. Under Michael's leadership, the office achieved its best financial year ever.

Kelly's career also progressed in Hong Kong. The major British company she had joined as marketing administrator promoted her to vice president before she was thirty.

THE O'CONNORS' STORY (continued)

The Next Two Years in Japan

Recognizing Michael's success at managing the Hong Kong office and concerned about mounting problems in Tokyo, FR&G asked Michael to transfer to Japan. The position they offered him involved responsibility for a start-up operation currently headed by a senior partner whose excesses the firm needed to control. Fortunately, Kelly was able to negotiate a lateral transfer to Tokyo, even though increasing Japanization of her British firm's Tokyo office had created a difficult working climate for expatriates.

As the family prepared to move to Japan, Kelly discovered that she was pregnant again. At the same time, Michael learned that new Japanese regulations would delay his ability to obtain a work permit, thus preventing the rest of the family from accompanying him in dependent status. For the family to continue to live together, Kelly therefore needed to acquire a work permit through her own company and to bring in the children and housekeeper as her dependents. Due to the permit problems, Kelly had to remain in Hong Kong for the first nine months while Michael commuted to Tokyo. Kelly remembers this period as painful and lonely:

> After seven years in Hong Kong, most of my expatriate friends had come and gone. I became a lame duck in the Hong Kong office, since everyone knew I was expected in Tokyo. And shuttling back and forth between Tokyo and Hong Kong satisfied no one.
>
> Fortunately, my second pregnancy was relatively easy, although I almost miscarried on a business trip to Perth and, later, the extra weight made me so clumsy that I tripped and broke a toe coming through immigration at Tokyo's Narita Airport, which left me hobbling around for the week of meetings. All the travel and stress finally resulted in the premature birth of my son.
>
> As soon as we were able to bring the baby home from the hospital, Michael had to return to Japan. James was so tiny he had to be fed every two hours. I became so exhausted I feared I would sleep through his cries, which were only as loud as a kitten mewing. People from the office sent flowers, but no one visited. My parents flew in from the United States to help. Despite my investment in relationships with colleagues, the only people I could count on were family.

The family finally moved to Tokyo. Unfortunately, neither Michael's nor Kelly's professional situation was particularly satisfying, and each day brought new annoyances. For example, after having initiated, designed, and analyzed an important market research study, Kelly discovered that a male Japanese colleague planned to present it. When she suggested that this was unfair, her Japanese colleague told her that she could attend the presentation if she took charge of visual aids.

> At that point, I considered walking out, but I knew I couldn't. Michael still didn't have a residential working permit, so we would have been asked to leave Japan.

THE O'CONNORS' STORY (continued)

Ultimately the Japanese Ministry informed Michael that his visa application had been denied, and that he could accept "trainee" status or leave the country within a year. Although Kelly initially felt disappointed, believing that a longer stay in Japan would have offered them useful international experience, she agreed with Michael that "trainee" status was untenable both for practical reasons and for reasons of "face."

When they had agreed to move to Japan, FR&G had promised Michael that he could return to the U.S. office of his choice. As the situation in Japan deteriorated, Kelly and Michael decided to return to Los Angeles and use it as a base for building a new practice. However, several months later, while dodging the half-full packing boxes on the floor of their Japanese home, Michael received a conference call from the Los Angeles managing partner asking him to either not come to Los Angeles or to delay his arrival. Michael explained that it was too late to change the previously agreed-upon plans. A month later Michael left Tokyo having turned the operating revenue from a loss to a profit and having brought in the firm's third largest transaction of the year. As they left, Kelly and Michael felt particularly satisfied that they had helped build office morale in Tokyo by introducing family social events similar to those they pioneered in Hong Kong.

The Los Angeles Years

Soon after returning to the United States, Michael passed the California State Bar Exam. Kelly settled the children into a rental house, supervised the restoration of their new home, and hunted for a job. The North American headquarters of her British company had originally agreed to transfer her to Los Angeles, but the L.A. office now nixed the idea. As a consequence, during the following months, Kelly sent out more than 300 résumés, which resulted in about seventy-five interviews. To her surprise, American firms did not seem to understand or to appreciate her international experience. Few prospective employers had heard of her prior employer—which is one of Britain's largest companies—nor did they seem to understand the British system of titles and responsibility levels used on her résumé. Kelly's salary requirements frequently intimidated potential employers as well. Kelly sought FR&G's help for introductions, but none were forthcoming. In fact, Kelly was rather surprised that after four months in Los Angeles, which included a holiday season, only one couple from the L.A. office had invited them to their home.

> *I guess I shouldn't have been so surprised, but I felt like a foreigner in my own country. I didn't know how things worked. With the exception of my family, it was almost as though we had never existed in the United States. After nine years in Asia, we had no domestic credit record, which even made buying a car difficult. Our Asian credit histories didn't come with us, nor did our driving records. We returned to the U.S. with no debt and tax returns showing more than $400,000 in annual income, and yet no one wanted to issue us a credit card. The language, parochialism, and obsessions with cars and breakfast cereals all made me feel like an alien in disguise.*

THE O'CONNORS' STORY (continued)

For years, Kelly had wanted to return to school for an MBA. Given the dismal employment situation she faced in Southern California, she chose to enter UCLA's Executive MBA (EMBA) Program. The two-year program, designed for executives with ten or more years of experience, met on alternate weekends, allowing the participants to continue their careers while getting their MBAs.

The Offer to Return to Hong Kong

Shortly after Kelly's initial EMBA orientation, FR&G's Hong Kong office offered Michael the managing partner position for Hong Kong, China, and Thailand. Michael's initial instinct was to say no, but he had encountered major political and practice problems in the L.A. office for which he saw no easy solution. The L.A. managing partner, who was very senior within the firm, used a laissez-faire management style that created strong competition and practice fiefdoms within the office. There was evidence, for example, that the banking partner with whom Michael thought he shared a practice was blocking business referral communiqués intended for him. Oddly enough, a *feng shui* expert* hired by Michael to advise him on the disposition of his new L.A. office indicated that his good fortune was being blocked in the west. As it happened, the other banking partner held the western office.

In addition, Michael found the practice in L.A. less intellectually challenging than his work in Asia. A further consideration was the hint of a recession on the economic horizon. Michael recognized that his two most promising L.A. clients no longer offered much potential due to internal restructuring and a bankruptcy.

Kelly became concerned that the firm's actions were seriously eroding Michael's self-confidence.

> *Michael claims that he could have happily stayed in L.A. in a secondary role in the firm, but I am not so sure. He forgets how depressed he had become. After his success in Hong Kong and Tokyo, Michael expected the firm to reward him. Instead, they held his salary steady the first year he was back, while raising others' salaries. He would come home at night with this hangdog look and absolutely anything to do with the office became a taboo subject. This hurt. By contrast, the people who originally asked him to go back to Asia were close friends, godparents to our children, and people who shared our sense that work could be exciting and rewarding without the backbiting and private empire building. I encouraged Michael to seriously consider Hong Kong because I wanted him to enjoy what he was doing again.*

While Michael and Kelly considered the Hong Kong offer, the L.A. managing partner announced his transfer to Sydney. He left a triumvirate in charge, including the banking partner with the western office. Prompted by other partners who

---

Feng shui (Chinese) translates as "wind water" and is a form of ancient Chinese geomancy for determining the proper positioning of buildings, rooms, and furnishings in relation to the four directions, bodies of water, and other topographic criteria, with the ultimate aim of ensuring the inhabitants' good fortune.

lacked confidence in the new management team, Michael put forward his name for managing partner in the L.A. office, but the New York managing partner rejected it because the firm wanted Michael to go to Hong Kong.

That spring, Kelly watched several people in her EMBA class lose their jobs while Michael continued to have limited success developing an independent practice. As the national recession hit Southern California, Michael and Kelly began to seriously consider moving back to Hong Kong. Kelly, however, made three stipulations: she wanted an option to return to the United States in three years, to finish her degree within the normal time frame, and to keep their home. She also encouraged Michael to review the Hong Kong office's finances before making a final decision and to begin by commuting to ensure his involvement in any major decisions that might affect them later.

At this point, in order to graduate with her class, Kelly dropped her outside activities and began doubling up on her course load. Michael began commuting to Hong Kong on a "two weeks on/two weeks off" basis. Kate and James went to a local preschool during the day and stayed with a baby sitter in the evenings until Kelly could get home.

Second Thoughts

After four months of commuting, Michael came home one evening and reported that the firm had told an L.A. partner, whom it had sent to Tokyo for a two-year assignment and who now wished to return, that he was unwelcome back in Los Angeles. Another partner with a young family, who had opened the Moscow office, was told his compensation would be penalized if he returned according to the originally agreed-upon timetable. The firm penalized another expatriate partner at the annual compensation meeting for supposedly treating himself to excessive housing.

> *The more Michael told me about the schism in the firm between international and domestic, the more irritated I became. There is something odd about people's inability to recognize that when you live abroad you still have a right to a private life. Visitors from other offices often expect you to personally pick them up at the airport and to provide personal attention during their entire stay. They seem to expect this as fair recompense for firm-subsidized housing. Perhaps the partners see expatriates' housing as coming directly out of their pockets. Ultimately, as someone who has now lived and worked both abroad and in the United States, I can tell you the lifestyle is better in the United States.*

When Michael finally reviewed the Hong Kong office's financial statements, he discovered that it no longer had a banking practice and that the office would probably earn a mere $1.1 million in operating profits in the current fiscal year, before allocating funds to compensate the five partners. This represented $1 million less than in the prior year. Not surprisingly, morale was very low.

In addition, Michael discovered that the firm's new managing partner had reorganized Asia as the first region to operate with a consolidated P&L. The Asia region would be run jointly by the managing partners in Singapore and Japan, with the prospective managing partner of Hong Kong and China (Michael) thus being relegated to a mere consultative role.

At the same time, FR&G's new executive committee formally decided that the firm was compensating expatriates excessively in both housing and other benefits. As a consequence, the committee lowered both the cost-of-living index and the allowable rent scale for Hong Kong. As part of their cost-cutting, they decided that the Hong Kong office was top-heavy and made contingency plans to lay off two partners.

Kelly became increasingly concerned that not only would the move to Hong Kong entail the usual transition costs in terms of emotions and time, but also that their standard of living would come under heavy pressure from the New York partners who no longer supported FR&G's global expansion in Asia:

> *During our previous time in Hong Kong, FR&G gave partners firm-sponsored club memberships and expense accounts for documentable home business entertaining. These were considered routine costs of doing business, as apartment buildings typically had no recreational facilities and most business entertaining was done at home. When Michael had been managing partner in Hong Kong, we had hosted 6 to 12 people for business-related dinners at least once a week. If anything, FR&G's housing subsidies and expatriate benefits were now less generous than those of most other American law firms operating in Hong Kong.*

Weighing the Evidence

Kelly couldn't concentrate on her EMBA mid-term. Michael had left the final Hong Kong decision up to her, although there was certainly little evidence that he was building a case to stay in Los Angeles.

Both Michael's FR&G experience and her own experience with the British company had convinced Kelly that she had had enough of working for others and of being under their thumbs. She therefore began to think about starting a business, although she wasn't sure what type. She knew she had access to start-up capital and felt confident that over time she could create a business that would serve some of her social goals. The last year had filled her with an almost missionary zeal to make the United States more globally competitive; to enjoin business to help in providing better public education for the communities from which they drew their workers; to discover a way to motivate businesses to see the possible synergies in Southern California's increasing cultural diversity rather than just seeing the problems; and to build something her children might inherit, to give them a cultural and family anchor in this rapidly changing world. She audited a class on entrepreneurship, discussed ideas with her business school classmates, and began investigating franchise possibilities.

THE O'CONNORS' STORY (continued)

The years in Hong Kong and Japan had led her to believe in the importance of family taking care of family. Not only did she want to be able to help Kate and James finance college and graduate school, but she also wanted to live near her parents in their senior years. If she said yes to Hong Kong, would the firm really allow them to return in three years?

How much energy would she have at forty? Enough to start again from scratch? Did it make sense to move away from all her UCLA contacts that might help her get a new business off the ground? Did Hong Kong's relationship to the People's Republic of China pose major political risks for expatriates and foreign businesses in Hong Kong? If she left Los Angeles, what could she build that she could bring back?

Michael was so bright. Couldn't he sidestep the political obstacles at FR&G and build a practice in Los Angeles if he tried? Or find something else? She was tired of the high transition costs of moving: the emotional upheaval, the cultural adjustments, and the long distances from family and friends. She felt weary from trying to build a new life every two or three years, seeing it swept away, and being forced to start over once again.

Kelly worried about moving two small children accustomed to lots of space in their California home back into one of Hong Kong's high rise apartment buildings. Luckily she knew the schools in Hong Kong were good.

Telephone calls poured in nearly every night from friends in Hong Kong and Michael's colleagues trying to convince her to move. Last week, the managing partner in Japan had stopped in L.A. on just such a mission.

"Analysis paralysis," Kelly said aloud, turning back to her computer. She glanced at her watch and resolved to put these thoughts to rest: the mid-term deadline was more imminent. Besides, there was an hour commute to UCLA and at least an hour back to decide on the next three years and the rest of her life.

Source: Copyright © Katherine D'Arcy.[4]

SUMMARY

Companies transfer women and men abroad; they transfer both single-career and dual-career couples. In a single-career couple, the spouse's role is the most difficult of all family members'. The spouse—most often the wife—must adjust to the new culture and create a meaningful life for herself abroad. Her adjustment is made more difficult by the fact that she must interact with the least internationally sophisticated strata of society. Her ability to lead a meaningful life is challenged by the lack of structure in her life abroad, and this difficulty is compounded by all of the activities, friends, and oftentimes a job or career that she has had to leave behind in her home country. Successfully managing the transition and creating a meaningful life abroad demand the involvement of the expatriate manager, the company, and the spouse.

Increasingly today, companies transfer people abroad who are in dual-career marriages. Progressive companies assist such couples in identifying options for the trailing spouse, helping him or her find an appropriate position abroad, and supporting the couple's new lifestyle, especially when it involves global commuting. Assuming joint responsibility and being creative lead dual-career couples to succeed in living and working abroad; the inappropriate application of procedures and benefits packages designed primarily for single-career couples does not lead to dual-career success.

QUESTIONS FOR REFLECTION

1. **Global Human Resource Systems.** What can global firms do to help spouses adapt to a new country and create a meaningful life abroad?

2. **Expatriate Spouses.** If you were asked to move abroad as an expatriate spouse, why would you want to go? Why would you not want to go? What could you do to increase your chances of success? What could your spouse do to increase your chances of success? What could the company do to increase your chances of success?

3. **Communication: Global Decisions.** As a global manager, you have just been offered an interesting assignment in Poland. As you drive home, you consider how to discuss the topic with your spouse. What are the most important issues that you would want to discuss? How would you plan to approach the discussion? What are the pros and cons of your approach?

4. **The Trailing Spouse Is the Husband.** Both women and men face difficult challenges when transferred abroad in the role of spouse. Which challenges would be particularly difficult for a male spouse (the husband of a female expatriate manager)? If you were vice president of human resources for a major global firm and had chosen to send women abroad as global managers for the first time, what would you do to prepare their husbands for their new role?

5. **Discovering What Works.** Interview three couples who have been abroad as expatriates. Discover from each couple their wisdom and suggestions they would give to you as a future expatriate.

FILM NOTE

Material in the section on single-career couples is presented in the video program, *A Portable Life,* which highlights the role of the spouse from the perspectives of four wives of global executives working for the Montreal-based multinational, Alcan Aluminum Ltd. (1). *A Portable*

Life is available from the McGill University McLennan Library A/V collection (web site: *http://www.mcgill.ca/hssl/services/loans/avinfo/*).

NOTES

1. Copyright © by Foulie Psalidas Perlmutter, Ph.D. Reprinted by permission; adapted by Adler, 2007.

2. There has been a recent explosion of on-line expatriate support groups, from the very general to those targeted at very specific groups—for example, see the expatriate support group for Australian expatriate wives living in Sweden (http://www.coolabah.com/ sweden/expatsites.html).

3. The Permits Foundation is a non-profit organization that helps expatriate spouses get work permits in countries around the world (http://www.permitsfoundation.com/home.htm). PartnerJob.com provides similar services (www.partnerjob.com).

4. Reprinted by permission; adapted by Adler, 2007.

REFERENCES

1. Adler, N. J. *Managing International Transitions* (Montreal: Alcan Aluminum Limited, 1980).

2. Adler, N. J. "Pacific Basin Managers: A Gaijin, Not a Woman," *Human Resource Management,* vol. 26, no. 2 (1987), pp. 169–192.

3. Adler, N. J. "Re-entry: A Study of the Dynamic Coping Processes Used by Repatriated Employees to Enhance Effectiveness in the Organization and Personal Learning during the Transition Back into the Home Country." Ph.D. dissertation, University of California, Los Angeles (June 1980).

4. Adler, N. J. "Women in International Management: Where Are They?" *California Management Review,* vol. 26, no. 4 (1984), pp. 122–132.

5. Adler, N. J.; & Ghadar, F. "International Strategy from the Perspective of People and Culture: The North American Context," in A. M. Rugman, ed., *Research in Global Strategic Management: International Business Research for the Twenty-First Century: Canada's New Research Agenda,* vol. 1 (Greenwich, Conn.: JAI Press, 1990), pp. 179–205.

6. Baker, J. C. "An Analysis of How the U.S. Multinational Company Considers the Wives of American Expatriate Managers," *Academy of Management Proceedings,* vol. 35 (1975), pp. 258–260.

7. Black, J. Stuart; & Gregersen, Hal B. "When Yankee Comes Home: Factors Related to Expatriate and Spouse Repatriation Adjustment," *Journal of International Business Studies,* vol. 22, no. 4 (1991), pp. 671–695.

8. Black, J. Stuart; Gregersen, Hal B.; & Mendenhall, Mark E. *Global Assignments: Successfully Expatriating and Repatriating International Managers* (San Francisco: Jossey-Bass, 1992).

9. Black, J. Stuart; & Stephens, G. K. "The Influence of the Spouses on American Expatriate Adjustment in Overseas Assignments," *Journal of Management*, vol. 15 (1989), pp. 529–544.

10. Culbert, Sam; & Renshaw, Jean. "Coping with the Stresses of Travels as an Opportunity for Improving the Quality of Work and Family Life," *Family Process*, vol. 11, no. 3 (1972), pp. 321–337.

11. D'Orazio, N. "Foreign Executives' Wives in Tokyo," *Institute of Comparative Culture Business Series*, Bulletin no. 82 (Tokyo: Sophia University, 1981).

12. Edstrom, A.; & Galbraith, Jay R. "Alternative Policies for International Transfer of Managers," *Management International Review*, vol. 17, no. 2 (1977), pp. 11–22.

13. Edstrom, A.; & Galbraith, Jay R. "International Transfer of Managers: Some Important Policy Considerations," *Columbia Journal of World Business*, vol. 11 (1976), pp. 100–112.

14. Edstrom, A.; & Galbraith, Jay R. "Transfer of Managers as Coordination and Control Strategy in Multinational Organizations," *Administrative Science Quarterly*, vol. 22 (June 1977), pp. 248–263.

15. Edstrom, A.; & Lorange, Peter. "Matching Strategy and Human Resources in Multinational Corporations," *Journal of International Business Studies*, vol. 15 (1984), pp. 125–137.

16. Eliot, T. S. Quote excerpted from "Little Gidding," from *Four Quartets*, copyright 1942 by T. S. Eliot and renewed 1970 by Esme Valerie Eliot, reprinted by permission of Harcourt, Inc.

17. Frazee, Valerie. "Expert Help for Dual-Career Spouses," *Workforce*, vol. 4, no. 2 (1999), pp. 18–20.

18. "Gauging a Family's Suitability for a Stint Overseas," *Business Week* (April 16, 1979), pp. 127–130.

19. GMAC Global Relocation Services. *Global Relocation Trends 2003/ 2004 Survey Report.* (Oak Brook, Ill.: GMAC Relocation Services, National Foreign Trade Council and SHRM Global Forum, 2004).

20. GMAC Global Relocation Services. *Ten Years of Global Relocation Trends 1993–2004.* (Oak Brook, Ill.: GMAC Relocation Services, National Foreign Trade Council and SHRM Global Forum, 2004).

21. Hyde, Rob "Who Wants To Be A Man About It?" *Weekly Telegraph* (December 7, 2004).

22. Jelinek, Mariann; & Adler, N. J. "Women: World Class Managers for Global Competition," *Academy of Management Executive*, vol. 2, no. 1 (1988), pp. 11–19.

23. Jordan, Miriam. "Your Career Matters: Have Husband, Will Travel—World of the Trailing Spouse Isn't Wives-Only Anymore," *The Wall Street Journal* (February 13, 2001) p. B1.

24. Karras, E. J.; & McMillan, R. F. "Interviewing for a Cultural Match," *Personnel Journal* (April 1971), p. 276.

25. Labovitz, G. "Managing the Personal Side of the Personnel Move Abroad," *Advanced Management Journal,* vol. 42, no. 3 (1977), pp. 26–39.

26. Mervosh, E. M.; & McClenanahen, J. S. "The Care and Feeding of Expats," *Industry Week,* vol. 246, no. 22 (1997), pp. 68–72.

27. Moore, M. J. "Same Ticket, Different Trip: Supporting Dual-Career Couples on Global Assignments," *Women in Management Review,* vol. 17 no. 2 (2002), pp. 61–67.

28. ORC (Organization Resources Counselors). *Dual Careers and International Assignments Survey* (London: Organization Resources Counselors, Inc., 2002).

29. Ondrack, Dan A. "International Transfers of Managers in North American and European MNEs," *Journal of International Business Studies,* vol. 16 (1985), pp. 1–19.

30. Osland, Joyce S. *The Adventure of Working Abroad: Hero Tales from the Global Frontier* (San Francisco: Jossey-Bass, 1995).

31. Pazy, A.; & Zeira, Yoram. "Training of Parent-Country Professionals in Host Country Organizations," *Academy of Management Review,* vol. 8, no. 2 (1983), pp. 262–272.

32. Priestoff, N. "The Gaijin Executive's Wife," *The Conference Board Record,* vol. 13, no. 5 (1976), pp. 51–64.

33. Punnett, B. J.; Crocker, O.; & Stevens, M. A. "The Challenge for Women Expatriates and Spouses: Some Empirical Evidence," *International Journal of Human Resource Management,* vol. 3, no. 3, (1992), pp. 585–592.

34. Renshaw, Jean R. "An Exploration of the Dynamics of the Overlapping Worlds of Work and Family," *Family Process,* vol. 15, no. 1 (1976), pp. 143–165.

35. Selmer, Jan, ed., *Expatriate Management: New Ideas for International Business* (Westport, Conn.: Quorum Books, 1995).

36. Takeuchi, Riki; Tesluk, Paul; Yun, Seokhwa; & Lepak, David P. "An Integrative View of International Experience," *Academy of Management Journal,* vol. 48, no. 1 (2005), pp. 85–100.

37. Thompson, A. "Australian Expatriate Wives and Business Success in Southeast Asia," *Euro-Asia Business Review,* vol. 5, no. 2 (1986), pp. 14–18.

38. Wederspahn, Gary M. "The Overseas Wife: Excess Baggage," *The Bridge,* vol. 5, no. 4 (1980), p. 16.

39. Zeira, Yoram; & Harrari, E. "Genuine Multinational Staffing Policy: Expectations and Realities," *Academy of Management Journal,* vol. 20, no. 2 (1979), pp. 327–333.

Chapter 12

Global Careers:
Succeeding in the 21st Century

*Ideally, . . . [global managers] should have the stamina of
an Olympic runner, the mental agility of an Einstein, the
conversational skill of a professor of languages, the detachment
of a judge, the tact of a diplomat, and the perseverance of an
Egyptian pyramid builder. [And] that's not all. If they are going
to measure up to the demands of living and working in a foreign
country, they should also have a feeling for the culture; their
moral judgment should not be too rigid; they should be able to
merge with the local environment with chameleon-like ease; and
they should show no signs of prejudice.[1]*

—Thomas Aitken (21)

As globalization has evolved from a buzzword to a pervasive reality, demand has increased for executives who are sophisticated in managing the complexities of global business. Government and corporate managers need to be able to think globally. They need to be able to work domestically on global projects as well as abroad on expatriate assignments and business travel. Global business has become so important that companies can no longer afford to consider candidates for executive positions unless they have had global experience (29;53;56).

According to Colby Chandler (41), the former CEO of Eastman Kodak Company, "These days there is not a discussion or a decision that does not have an international dimension. We would have to be blind not to see how critically important international experience is." The *Wall Street Journal* claims that "intensifying international competition will make the home-grown chief executive obsolete" (28). Former chief executive Duane Kullberg agrees that future American CEOs "will be . . . [people] with experience outside the borders of the U.S. . . . If you go back 20 years, you could be pretty insular and still survive. Today, that's not possible" (28).

WHAT IT TAKES TO REACH THE TOP

North American companies compete with British, Brazilian, Chinese, German, Korean, and South African companies, among others, for global executives to manage their worldwide operations (see 82). Yet what it takes to reach the top of a company differs from one country to the next; companies view managerial success through their own cultural blinders (39;40;65). American managers, for example, view ambition and drive as the most important characteristics for success; French managers must be labeled as having high potential; German managers view creativity as essential for career success; and the British see creating the right image and getting noticed for what you do as essential (65).

Similarly, whereas Swiss and German companies respect technical creativity and competence, French and British companies often view managers with such qualities as "mere technicians" (39). Likewise, U.S. companies highly value entrepreneurs, while their British and French counterparts often view entrepreneurial behavior as disruptive (39). Similarly, whereas only half of Dutch managers see "skills in interpersonal relations and communication" as critical to career success, almost 90 percent of their British colleagues do so (40).

Global management expert André Laurent (65) describes German, British, and French managers' careers as follows (39:10):

> *German managers, more than others, believe that creativity is essential for career success. In their minds, successful managers must have the right individual characteristics. German managers' outlook is rational: they view the organization as a coordinated network of individuals who make appropriate decisions based on their professional competence and knowledge.*
>
> *British managers hold a more interpersonal and subjective view of the organizational world. According to them, the ability to create the right image and to get noticed for what they do is essential for career success. British managers view organizations primarily as a network of relationships among individuals who get things done by influencing each other using communication and negotiation.*
>
> *French managers look at organizations as an authority network in which the power to organize and control members stems from their position in the hierarchy. French managers focus on the organization as a pyramid of differentiated levels of power to be acquired or dealt with. They perceive the ability to manage power relationships effectively and to "work the system" as critical to their career success.*

As companies integrate their operations globally, these multiple national realities send conflicting messages to success-oriented managers. Affiliates in different countries operate differently and reward different behaviors based on their unique cultural perspectives (40). Regardless of what headquarters desires or designs, no single best way exists to perform or to achieve global career success (40). The challenge for today's global companies is to recognize local differences, while at the same time creating globally integrated career paths for their most senior executives.

Expatriate assignments form a key part of most global managers' careers (70). Traditionally, North American managers were attracted to working abroad by the financial rewards, increased responsibility, challenge, independence, and unique lifestyle it afforded. Yet during the 1970s, a weakened U.S. dollar, inflation, and additional taxes reduced the attractiveness of financial packages. By the 1980s, increasingly frequent dual-career marriages complicated transfer decisions as well as exacerbated the financial drawbacks; expatriate salary increases rarely compensated for reducing a dual-career couple to a single salary. Further complicating the financial picture, recent trends indicate that many companies no long cover expatriate expenses to the extent that they did previously (75;87;90). Stories of prior expatriates whose careers were sidetracked while abroad also made many managers hesitant to follow a global career path (10;51;56;60;76;94).

It is no secret that business today faces an environment radically different from that of even a few years ago, the result of increasingly networked and integrated global competition. The new global environment demands more, not fewer, globally competent managers (14). Rather than sidetracking a manager's career, global experience has rapidly become the only route to the top. According to the *New York Times* (41), hands-on global experience has slowly but surely moved out of the "nice but not necessary" category and into a "must have" priority for those on the corporate fast track. Given the increasing number of opportunities for global assignments and potentially diminishing interest in them, what can we predict for the twenty-first century? Will global organizations remain capable of attracting sufficient numbers of young managers? Are today's young managers interested in global work? What do they see as the advantages and disadvantages of global assignments?

As you read this chapter, ask yourself how prepared you are to work globally. What would be most exciting about working abroad? What do you consider to be your strengths and weaknesses as a global manager? How competitive is your company in offering young managers the right incentives to pursue a global career?

IS THE TRADITIONAL EXPATRIATE MANAGER EXTINCT?

Traditionally, who was the global executive? According to an early study of 1,161 expatriates working in 40 countries (51), the typical American global executive was about 31 years old when he first went abroad, stayed at least three years on each international assignment, and had three such assignments during his career. Expatriate executives were significantly younger than their domestic counterparts; with few exceptions, they were men. Twenty-one percent married foreign women. Global executives came from a higher socioeconomic background than their domestic counterparts. Typically, expatriates stayed longer with one company: 41 percent worked for only one firm during their careers, 25 percent for only two firms, and 87 percent remained with the same firm after accepting their first international assignment. Global executives were better educated than their domestic counterparts: 81 percent graduated from college, compared with less than 70 percent of domestic executives. Global executives' education was less specialized than that of domestic executives, with more graduating in liberal arts and fewer in business and engineering.

Today the portrait of the global executive is changing. First, given the increasing importance of global business, more executives manage global projects and work with people from around the world, even if they never leave home. They work for companies from other countries, buy from suppliers in other countries, sell to clients worldwide, and, most significantly, develop global strategies together with colleagues from many nations. Second, more fast-track managers are using expatriate assignments to gain the global experience necessary to rise to the top of major, global companies (18). The average duration of expatriate assignments, however, has shortened, with fewer assignments planned to exceed one year (49;50). Third, the number of women seeking global assignments, although still small, is rising (13;19;20;61) with women's overwhelming success in breaking down the men-only barrier (9).

To date, female expatriate managers have been fairly junior within their organizations and in their careers. Unlike their male counterparts, their average age when they first go abroad is under 30 years old. Also dissimilar to male expatriates, nearly half of the women expatriates are single; few have children. Similar to male expatriates, the female expatriates are very well educated and quite internationally experienced. Almost all hold graduate degrees, an MBA being the most common. Over three-quarters of the women have had extensive international interests and experience prior to their companies' sending them abroad. For example, more than three-quarters of female expatriates have traveled internationally and almost two-thirds have engaged in studies with an international focus prior to joining the company. Women who become expatriate managers generally speak two or three languages, with some speaking as many as six. In addition, most women selected for global assignments demonstrate excellent interpersonal and social skills (9).

TODAY'S GLOBAL CAREERS

Why would today's young managers accept global assignments: for the job challenge, the adventure, the status, the career-advancement opportunities? Why would they turn down a global assignment? We conducted a survey to discover why young managers might accept or reject international assignments and global careers.[2] More than 1,000 graduating MBAs from seven top business schools in Canada, Europe, and the United States described their level of interest in global careers, their reasons for accepting or rejecting international assignments, and their assessment of global versus domestic opportunities.

WHO ARE THE FUTURE GLOBAL MANAGERS?

The backgrounds of the MBAs from the seven schools showed more similarity than difference.[3] Although 41 percent were focusing on international issues during their MBA programs, few had extensive global work experience. More than 80 percent had traveled abroad; few of their friends, however, were from other countries. As might be expected, European and Canadian MBAs had more international experience than did their American counterparts.

DO FUTURE MANAGERS WANT GLOBAL CAREERS?

The future managers showed strong interest in pursuing the global aspects of their careers.[4] More than four out of five wanted an international assignment at some time during their career. Slightly fewer than half seriously considered pursuing a global career, including accepting a series of international assignments. More than a third of the future managers wanted to travel extensively for their jobs. Yet, only one-third wanted an international assignment as their first job after graduation. Clearly, most young managers show an interest in global management, but many fewer would like an international assignment "right now."

How interested are you in global management and a global career? The *Careers in Global Management Questionnaire: Assessing Your Preparation and Interest* (see box) provides a way for you to assess your own interest in international assignments and a global career.

CAREERS IN GLOBAL MANAGEMENT: ASSESSING YOUR PREPARATION AND INTEREST

Given the substantial increase in global business, it has become increasingly important for managers and companies to understand the global career aspirations of their managers and executives. This questionnaire allows you to reflect on your own career aspirations, as well as those of your colleagues and subordinates.

Background: How Prepared Are You?

1. Including your native language, which languages do you speak fluently?
2. How many years have you studied outside of your country of origin?
3. How many months have you traveled, lived, or worked outside your country of origin?
4. Did either of your parents travel internationally for their work?
5. List your friends who are neither from your country of origin nor citizens of the country in which you are currently living.

What Are Your Career Plans?

In the following section:

Home Country refers to your country of citizenship.

An *International Assignment* refers to an expatriate assignment in which the company sends an employee for a single assignment of a year or more to another country.

A *Global Career* refers to a series of international assignments in various countries.

International Travel refers to a business trip to another country without the employee moving abroad.

An *Expatriate* refers to an employee who is sent by the company to live and work in another country.

Which of the following statements do you agree with? Which do you strongly agree with?

1. I am seriously considering pursuing a global career.
2. I would like my first job after university to be in another country.
3. If offered equivalent positions in my home country and in the foreign country of my choice, I would choose to work at home.
4. While continuing to live in my home country, I would like to travel internationally at least 40 percent of the time (approximately 20 weeks/year).
5. I would like to have an international assignment at some time during my career.

CAREERS IN GLOBAL MANAGEMENT: ASSESSING YOUR PREPARATION AND INTEREST (continued)

6. I would like to follow a global career path in which I have a series of international assignments.
7. I never seriously considered accepting an international assignment until I read this questionnaire.

People choose not to pursue global careers for many reasons. Which of the following reasons would discourage you from pursuing a global career or from accepting an international assignment?

8. I like living in my home country.
9. I do not want to learn another language.
10. I do not want to adjust to another culture.
11. My spouse would not want to move to another country.
12. It is not good to move children abroad.
13. I want my children to be educated in my home country.
14. I do not want to live in:
    a. any country except my home country
    b. Africa
    c. Asia
    d. Europe
    e. Latin or South America
    f. the Middle East
    g. North America
    h. my home country
    i. other (specify)
15. International jobs involve too much travel.
16. If I live in another country, my children will not gain a sense of national identity.
17. My spouse would not want to interrupt his or her career.
18. I would lose my own sense of identity, my roots.
19. International assignments put too much strain on a marriage.
20. When you are on an international assignment you become "invisible" to the company and tend to be forgotten for promotions.
21. It would be difficult to come back home after having lived and worked for a long time in another country.
22. I do not want to be exposed to the political instability experienced by some in different areas of the world.
23. I would be too socially isolated and lonely in another country.
24. I would be exposed to too much personal danger in another country.

CAREERS IN GLOBAL MANAGEMENT: ASSESSING YOUR PREPARATION AND INTEREST (continued)

In comparing potential domestic and global careers, which do you think would give you the greatest professional opportunities?

	Domestic Career	About Same	Global Career
25. I could succeed faster in	_____	_____	_____
26. I could earn a higher salary in	_____	_____	_____
27. I could have greater status in	_____	_____	_____
28. I could be more recognized for my work in	_____	_____	_____
29. I could have a more interesting professional life in	_____	_____	_____
30. I could have a more satisfying personal life in	_____	_____	_____
31. I could contribute more to the company	_____	_____	_____
32. I could contribute more to society	_____	_____	_____

In comparing women and men, who do you think will have the greater chance of being

	Women	Equal Chances	Men
33. Selected for an international assignment?	_____	_____	_____
34. Effective on an international assignment?	_____	_____	_____
35. Successful in advancing in a global career?	_____	_____	_____
36. Effective on domestic assignments?	_____	_____	_____
37. Successful in advancing in a domestic career?	_____	_____	_____
38. Socially isolated and lonely in another country?	_____	_____	_____
39. Exposed to personal danger in another country?	_____	_____	_____

In Your Opinion

1. What are your main reasons for wanting to accept an international assignment?

   a.

   b.

   c.

CAREERS IN GLOBAL MANAGEMENT: ASSESSING YOUR PREPARATION AND INTEREST (continued)

2. What are your main reasons for potentially turning down an international assignment?

   a.

   b.

   c.

3. What barriers might block women, but not men, from succeeding in pursuing global careers that include international assignments?

   a.

   b.

   c.

4. Compared to men, what advantages might women have in working abroad as expatriate managers?

   a.

   b.

   c.

REASONS FUTURE MANAGERS ACCEPT GLOBAL ASSIGNMENTS

Managers accept global assignments for a multitude of reasons (31;98). As shown in Table 12-1, opportunity for cross-cultural and personal growth experiences is the most common reason for accepting a global assignment. More than half of future managers want to see other cultures, travel, learn new languages, and gain a greater understanding of another way of life; that is, they want to expand their horizons. Having a learning orientation has been shown to predict success on a global assignment (85). The second reason for accepting a global assignment is the job itself. Forty percent of future managers see global positions— compared with available domestic positions—as providing more interesting and challenging work, allowing for more autonomy, power, status, and responsibility, and as providing opportunities for more meaningful contributions to the company and society. The third reason is money. More than a quarter of young managers believe they would earn a higher salary and more benefits in a global position than they would in a domestic position. The fourth most commonly cited

TABLE 12-1   Reasons Young Managers Accept
Global Assignments

Percent of Future Managers Citing Reason	Reasons for Accepting a Global Assignment
52	**Cross-Cultural Experience and Personal Growth**
	Seeing other cultures
	Learning new languages
	Gaining greater understanding of another way of life
	Personal growth: expanding horizons, broadening background
40	**The Job Itself**
	More interesting and challenging
	More opportunities, responsibilities, and chances for useful work
	More power, autonomy, and status
28	**Money**
	Higher salary, more benefits, and more savings
21	**Career Advancement**
	Increased exposure
	Increased opportunities
	Higher possibility for a better future position in my home country or headquarters
16	**Good Location**
	Politically stable country
	Good climate
	Good social and living conditions
	Safe
	Local people speak English and/or another language I already speak
11	**Satisfying Life**
	Greater personal freedom
	More fun, excitement, and adventure
	More variety, less routine, a change
	Higher quality of life
4	**Spouse and Family**
	Good job or career opportunities for spouse
	Good situation for family (education, health facilities)
	Spouse willing to go
3	**Short Term; Other**
	No domestic jobs available
	Women managers respected by local nationals
	Personal business opportunities available in foreign country
	Single

Note: For methodological details, see endnote 5.

reason for accepting a global assignment is career advancement. One future manager in five sees an expatriate assignment increasing company-wide exposure and thus the potential for promotion. The fifth reason is a good location. Almost 16 percent of the future managers expressed more willingness to accept a global assignment in a politically stable country with a good climate, good social and living conditions, few threats to personal safety, and with an English-speaking population. Young managers are most attracted to countries that are more similar to their own country and more economically developed. The sixth reason for accepting an assignment in another country is for a potentially more satisfying life abroad. Eleven percent of the future managers looked forward to a change—less routine, more fun, more adventure, more excitement, more variety, more personal freedom, and a higher quality of life than they imagined having in their home country.

When future managers compare the advantages of global versus domestic careers, they see the primary benefits of a global assignment as greater challenge and responsibility, more interesting work, and better financial rewards. By contrast, they see domestic careers offering slightly greater status, a more satisfying personal life, more rapid career advancement, and greater recognition for their work than would a global career.

REASONS WHY FUTURE MANAGERS WOULD REJECT GLOBAL ASSIGNMENTS

The future managers identified seven major reasons for turning down a global assignment. As shown in Table 12-2, the most frequently mentioned reason is a bad location. More than half the young managers would reject an expatriate assignment if the host country appeared too politically unstable, "uncivilized," dangerous, hostile towards expatriates, or to have a high potential for war and public violence. The second reason is the job itself and the potentially negative career impact the assignment might have. One third of the young managers would turn down a global assignment if the job appeared unchallenging or boring. Similarly, one third see global assignments as a bad long-term career strategy. They fear the higher risk of job failure abroad and the possible damage to their careers caused by extended isolation from company headquarters. They fear being "lost" at re-entry and forgotten at times of promotion.

The third reason, also mentioned by one third of the future managers, reflects their concerns about spouses and families. Young managers view problems confronting dual-career couples as major, especially if the spouse cannot find a suitable position abroad. They also fear increased marital strain as well as potentially inadequate educational and medical facilities for children.

The fourth reason for rejecting a global assignment is money. Nearly one quarter of the young managers would reject an assignment if the

**TABLE 12-2   Reasons Young Managers Reject
                Global Assignments**

Percent of Future Managers Citing Reason	Reasons for Rejecting a Global Assignment
59	**Location** Politically unstable "Uncivilized" Dangerous Hostility toward expatriates Extreme poverty High potential for war or violence
35	**Job and Career** Boring, unchallenging, professionally uninteresting job Not good long-term career strategy Higher risk of job failure Isolation from company headquarters Displacement from company's hierarchy: forgotten at promotion time, "lost" at re-entry
33	**Spouse and Family** Inadequate medical or educational facilities Children wrong age to move (especially teenagers) Problems confronting dual-career couples Spouse unwilling to move Spouse unable to find a suitable position abroad
23	**Money** Salary and benefits package inadequate

19	**Unpleasant Life Abroad**
	Unwillingness to learn new language, and/or adjust to
	    new culture
	Isolation, loneliness, fear, uncertainty
	Restrictions on personal life: lack of physical and
	    intellectual freedom, restricted access to people

14	**Disruption to Life in Home Country** Disruption to personal and social life Reneging on commitments to family, parents, friends
6	**Contract Too Long; Other** Women not accepted as managers Good current position at home Opposition to company's global policies, product, or marketing strategy Too much travel

Note: For methodological details, see endnote 6.

salary and benefits package inadequately compensated them for the disruption and additional problems caused by moving and living in another country.

Young managers cite potentially unpleasant cross-cultural differences as their fifth reason for rejecting a global assignment. Nearly 20 percent reject introducing too much change into their lives, learning new languages, adjusting to new cultures, or subjecting themselves to the isolation, loneliness, fear, and uncertainty associated with living abroad. Similarly, one young manager in seven rejects disrupting his or her current, enjoyable home country lifestyle. Other reasons mentioned by some of the young managers include the contract being too long, fear that local nationals would not accept women managers, the assignment requiring too much travel, or unacceptable home company policies toward the host country.

Future managers consistently rate global work assignments as offering greater job satisfaction, while they perceive working in their home country as offering greater organizational recognition and a more satisfying private life. Young managers would accept positions in other countries for the cross-cultural experience and opportunity for personal growth, the job itself, and the higher salary and financial benefits. They would reject global assignments due to the negative impact on spouses and families, the personal danger and inconvenience of living in a "bad" location, and the potentially detrimental effect on career advancement both while abroad and when returning home.

Young managers' perceptions of the advantages and disadvantages of living and working abroad reflect those of many more experienced managers. Experienced expatriates frequently describe such advantages as increased personal growth opportunities and the inherently more interesting, challenging, and responsible work abroad, as well as traditionally generous salaries and benefit packages. Today's young managers show a greater awareness than their predecessors of the detrimental effects of expatriate positions on their private lives and careers. Research has shown that the major cause of failure on global assignments, often leading to early return, is dissatisfaction on the part of the spouse (see Chapter 11). Nearly half of 300 surveyed companies have brought families home early due to the spouse's inability to adapt (24). With the increasing prevalence of dual-career couples, the impact of global assignments on the spouse and family will increase, not decrease (see Chapter 11). Young managers appear well aware of these problems.

Potentially negative impacts of global assignments on employees' careers have also become more widely recognized. In the past, most expatriates believed that global assignments would help their careers; the majority returned to discover the opposite was true (10). Returning employees have all too frequently discovered that home-country jobs held after an assignment abroad were at substantially lower levels of responsibility and authority than their expatriate positions or, more

dramatically, that no jobs at all were available to return to (see Chapter 10).
Meanwhile, returnees found that domestic colleagues had been promoted while their own careers had plateaued.

Today's young managers appear considerably more aware of the
hazards of moving abroad and of re-entry challenges than were managers of five, ten, or fifteen years ago. Future managers consequently
are less likely to accept global assignments that could jeopardize their
careers. Luckily, with increasing globalization and the parallel rise in
the importance of global experience, the risks of derailing one's career
by going abroad are diminishing just as young managers' interest is
increasing.

GLOBAL MANAGERS AND LEADERS: NO LONGER MEN ALONE

Are women and men equally interested in global careers (19;45;58;67;69;93;97)?
Yes. Although less than 15 percent of current expatriate managers are
women (1;13;29;30;98), male and female future managers express an equal
interest in accepting global assignments and pursuing global careers (12).

WOMEN AS GLOBAL MANAGERS

Although equally interested, both young male and female future managers believe that companies offer fewer opportunities to women than
they do to men to pursue careers in global management (33;54;80;92).
Similarly, both men and women believe that companies offer women
fewer global than domestic management opportunities. The young
managers are right. In a survey of sixty major North American companies with operations around the world, more than half expressed reluctance to select women managers for global assignments (1;4;9;37). The two
primary concerns, expressed by three-quarters of the companies, are
their beliefs that foreigners are so prejudiced against women managers
that they could not succeed, and that the difficulties faced by dual-career
couples in moving abroad are insurmountable. But even with the existing barriers and hesitance, almost three-quarters of the companies
believe that the number of women working globally will continue to
increase (4).

Similar to most companies, more than 80 percent of the future managers themselves believe that foreigners' prejudice against women managers poses the primary barrier to women's success (3;12). More than 70
percent label the home company's reluctance to select women for global assignments and the difficulties faced by global dual-career couples as
the second and third most important barriers (12;32;55;81). Whereas young
managers correctly see companies' current selection processes as creating
barriers, neither they nor the companies correctly understand what they

perceive to be "foreigners' prejudice." A major study of North American women working in countries around the world showed that expatriate women managers are highly successful (9;20;61). As one woman expatriate accurately summarized, "The most difficult job is getting sent, not succeeding once sent" (9).

Why do women succeed as global managers (35)? They succeed because they are seen as *foreigners who happen to be women,* not as women who happen to be foreigners. Although the difference may appear subtle, the effect is huge. Countries such as Japan, Korea, and Saudi Arabia, which promote few of their own women into significant managerial positions, treat foreign women with the same respect they accord male expatriate managers. As one woman who works successfully in Hong Kong explained, "It doesn't make any difference if you are blue, green, purple, or a frog; if you have the best product at the best price, the Chinese will buy" (9). In some countries—Japan, for example— being a foreign woman can actually be an advantage (19). In essence, global business pragmatism wins out over prejudice.

Although more barriers may exist for women than for men, today's organizations clearly can select global managers from equally interested groups of young male and female managers. When considering a woman for a global assignment, companies would be wise not to assume (a) that she does not want to go—she probably does; (b) that foreigners are so prejudiced that such an assignment would be bad for both the company and the woman's career; or (c) that dual-career issues are unsolvable. As discussed in Chapter 11, many North American women expatriates actually find it easier to balance the time-consuming and seemingly conflicting roles of professional, wife, and mother while on a global assignment than it is to balance them at home, because global assignments often provide them with the luxury of a higher level of household help than they have access to at home. Luckily, just at the time when the intensity of global competition demands that companies use nothing but their best managers, both companies and women are discovering that success is both possible and probable.

WOMEN AND GLOBAL COMPANIES

Given the increasing importance of global and transnational corporations, it is encouraging that their impact on women in management, to date, has been primarily positive.[7] Global companies include women in ways that domestic, multidomestic, and multinational firms did not and do not.

First, the extremely competitive business environment forces global firms to select the best people available. The opportunity cost of prejudice—of rejecting women and limiting selection to men—is much higher now than it was in previous economic environments. As *Fortune* magazine succinctly reported, "The best reason for believing that more women will be in charge before long is that in a ferociously competitive global economy, no company can afford to waste valuable brainpower simply because it's wearing a skirt" (46:55).

Second, whereas domestic and multidomestic companies hire primarily local nationals and, therefore, must closely adhere to local norms related to hiring—or not hiring—women managers, global companies are not similarly limited. Because the corporate culture of global firms is not coincident with the local culture of any particular country, transnationals have greater flexibility in defining selection and promotion criteria that best fit the firm's needs rather than those that most closely mimic the historical patterns of a particular culture. Put simply, global companies can and do hire local women managers even in countries in which the local companies rarely do so.

U.S.-based global companies, for example, have often hired local women managers when local firms would not. This dynamic has been particularly pronounced in Japan, where non-Japanese companies have had difficulty attracting top-ranked male applicants (64). American firms have led the way in hiring well-qualified Japanese women, whereas Japanese firms are still reluctant to hire them (95). Following the same pattern, Japanese companies operating in the United States hire more women managers in their American affiliates than they do in their home-country operations (88).

By hiring women, global companies act as role models for firms in many countries that have not seriously considered promoting significant numbers of women into managerial positions. The greater the number of expatriates involved in foreign affiliates, the less likely they are to follow local human resource practices, including being less likely to restrict the number of women managers (88). The firm's global character allows it organizational freedoms and imposes competitive demands not present in domestic or multidomestic environments.

Third, as discussed previously, global companies send women abroad as expatriate managers (13). Because global firms use expatriate and local managers, they can benefit from the greater flexibility that many cultures afford foreign women. As has been described, most countries do not hold foreign women to the same professionally limiting roles that restrict local women (9;61). The outstanding success of the initial group of women expatriate managers in all geographical areas—Africa, the Americas, Asia, Europe, and the Middle East—is encouraging firms both to continue sending women abroad (9;79) and to begin promoting more local women into management (61).

Fourth, whereas domestic, multidomestic, and multinational firms have been characterized by structural hierarchies, global companies are increasingly striving to create networks of equals. Recent research suggests that women work particularly well in such networks:

> . . . *women . . . are countering the values of the hierarchy with those of the web . . . when describing their roles in their organizations, women usually refer . . . to themselves as being in the middle of things. . . . Inseparable from their sense of themselves as being in the middle . . . [is] women's notion of being connected to those around them* (57:45–46;56).

Not surprisingly, transnational firms see women managers as bringing needed collaborative and participative skills to the workplace (83).

Fifth, leading management scholars have identified innovation as a key factor in global competitiveness (25;52;86). An inherent source of innovation is well-managed diversity (1). Women bring diversity to global companies that have heretofore primarily hired men.

Global companies thus include more women than their predecessors could (or would) and benefit organizationally from their professional contributions in new ways. They benefit both from women's increased representation at all levels of the organization as well as from their unique ways of contributing to the organization, which complement those of men.[8]

WOMEN IN GLOBAL LEADERSHIP

Are women strictly becoming managers or are they moving up into senior leadership positions (36;99;101)? For the first time in history, countries and companies are selecting women to lead them. More than 60 percent of women who have led their country as president or prime minister have held office in just the last decade. In 2006, for example, Ellen Johnson-Sirleaf was elected president of Liberia, the first woman ever to be elected president of an African country. In her acceptance speech, she said she would end the era of corrupt, male-dominated rule in war-torn Liberia, and urged women in other African countries to lead their countries. Afghanistan, in its first national elections in thirty years, elected sixty-eight women to parliament. One of the new members of the legislature, Safia Siddiqi, explained that "The women in parliament will be a voice for the half of this country who have been silent for so long." Angela Merkel took power in 2005 as Germany's first woman chancellor; she is the country's first leader to have grown up in the former East Germany.

Similarly, the proportion of female CEOs leading major global firms is increasing, although only ten Fortune 500 CEOs in 2006 were women—a mere 2 percent. Even in Saudi Arabia, progress is being made. In 2005, two Saudi businesswomen became the country's first female elected officials, a definite step forward in a country where women cannot travel abroad or drive without a male guardian giving them permission. In Jeddah, after the Trade and Industry Chamber initially rejected the ten women who had been nominated for the board of governors, an avalanche of petitions from Saudi businesswomen encouraged the trade minister to allow women to be candidates for office and to vote.

The box, "Did You Hear? Global Leadership Is No Longer for Men Alone," describes this rapid shift from male-dominated global leadership to leadership that includes both men and women. It tells the story of women who are global leaders through the eyes of Charity Ngilu, the first woman to run for president of Kenya.

DID YOU HEAR?
Global Leadership Is No Longer for Men Alone

Did you hear?

On July 9th, 1997 Charity Ngilu declared her candidacy to run for the presidency of Kenya. If she had succeeded, Ngilu would have become the first woman ever to become president of Kenya.[9]

Ngilu's candidacy puts her in good company. More than half (65%) of the 78 women who have held their country's highest leadership position have come into office in the last decade.[10] Almost 80 percent (72 of 78) of the women are the first women their countries have ever selected for their highest leadership position. Whereas no women became president or prime minister in the 1950s, only three came into office in the 1960s, six in the 1970s, nine in the 1980s, thirty-five in the 1990s, and another twenty-five already have come into office by midway through the first decade of the 21st century. It does not take a statistical genius to notice that there is a trend, and that this trend is toward an increasing number of women in the world's most senior leadership positions (8).

According to leadership scholar Michael Genovese, "Studies of . . . leadership have been remarkably non-gender specific . . . This is due primarily to a tacit assumption . . . that leaders are men! . . . Historically, there is of course a good deal of validity to this assumption—almost all . . . leaders have been men" (48). Referring "to a generic head of state as 'him' may . . . be understandable," even if, as we enter the twenty-first century, it has become wholly inaccurate" (48).

Why might Charity Ngilu have become the world's next woman president? Does she come from a politically prominent family? Did she grow up with wealth and privilege? Is she a lawyer with a degree from one of the world's most prestigious universities? Did she serve for years in increasingly important positions in one of her country's main political parties?

Well, no, not quite.

Did you hear? Charity Ngilu, the daughter of a local Christian minister, the ninth of thirteen children, announced her candidacy to run for president of Kenya. While she did go to high school, after graduation she became a secretary, not a lawyer. And only after she married did her husband send her on to college where she earned her degree in business administration and then became an entrepreneur, not a politician (74).

So how did Ngilu come to be considered a serious candidate for her nation's foremost leadership position? Had Charity dreamed of becoming a national leader from the time she was a child, or at least from the time she was in college? Since her own family comes from a very modest background, did at least her husband come from a politically prominent family? Did her party rally around her and eagerly nominate Ngilu for the presidency of Kenya?

Well, no, not quite.

Did you hear? Charity Ngilu, candidate for the presidency of Kenya, entered politics only five years ago. On that day, a group of women, each with leafy branches in their hands, none with briefcases, came to her backdoor in Kitui, seventy-five miles away from cosmopolitan Nairobi.[11] Charity knew the women; most belonged to a local women's association with which Charity had worked for years to build both health clinics and better water-supply systems. One of the women knocked on Charity's door. Charity came out, drying her hands on her apron. The women asked Charity to run for parliament in Kenya's first multiparty elections. Charity's response? "You are joking! You are crazy, obviously! (74)"

Clearly not the power-hungry response of the all too typical twentieth-century status- and ego-driven aspiring politician.

Is Charity atypical?

Yes. But only if viewed through the career paths of most of history's recognized world leaders.[12] Former U.S. president Bill Clinton is typical. Bill Clinton dreamed of becoming president from the time he was a little boy. At age sixteen, after having just shaken the hand of then-president John F. Kennedy, Clinton announced that he would like Kennedy's job; that he too would like to become president of the United States of America. To date, as children, none of the women presidents or prime ministers have dreamed about becoming their country's leader. You see, for most women who become leaders, it is not the desire for the position nor for power *per se* that motivates them to seek the highest leadership position; rather it is their commitment to a compelling vision of what society could be, of what society must be.[13]

Charity was an outsider to politics. Is Charity atypical?

DID YOU HEAR?
Global Leadership Is No Longer for Men Alone (continued)

Yes again. But only when viewed from the perspective of most men's paths to political and corporate power. Most women who become leaders do not work their way up through the company or political party power hierarchy. Rather, they laterally transfer into the most senior position (5). Ngilu was an entrepreneur; five years later people considered her as possibly the next president of Kenya. Tansu Çiller served as an economics professor in Istanbul; three years later she became prime minister of Turkey. Gro Harlem Brundtland, a medical doctor, became Norway's first woman prime minister just six years after accepting her first government position.

Is the pattern similar among business leaders? To a large extent, yes. Most women who become business leaders do not work their way up through the company to CEO or managing director; rather they laterally transfer into the top position of one company after having built a career in another company (5). As a double outsider, Marjorie Scardino, the only woman CEO to lead a Financial Times (FT-SE) 100 firm, provides a good example. Not only was she brought in from the Economist to assume the leadership of Pearson Plc, but as an American, she was the first non-English executive to hold a senior executive position in this esteemed British firm (84). Similarly, Carly Fiorina built her career at Lucent before assuming the CEO position at Hewlett-Packard; Fiorina became the first woman to lead a *Fortune* Top-30 firm. Laterally transferring into senior leadership calls into question our image of the glass ceiling. Perhaps the route to the top for women is not to follow men's paths and attempt to break through the glass ceiling, but rather to simply go around the glass ceiling. Why else do we see so many more women CEOs in entrepreneurial enterprises than in major publicly held corporations? And one must ask, why should today's senior women follow the same paths to power in the twenty-first century that men followed in the twentieth century? Not surprisingly, such mimicry serves neither society's nor women's best interests.

Charity initially rejected her women friends' suggestion that she run for parliament. Is Charity atypical?

Yes, but once again, only if we believe that women should try to copy men's twentieth-century paths to power. Typical of women, but not of men, many of the world's women leaders decline senior leadership positions when they are originally offered (5). Golda Meir, for example, initially told her party "no" when offered the Israeli prime ministership. Corazon Aquino's first response to running for president of the Philippines was also "no." Maria Liberia Peters told her party "no" when they first offered to nominate her for prime minister of the Netherlands Antilles. Her party then went on to unanimously nominate her, without her consent![14]

Luckily for Kenya, and the world, the group of women at Ngilu's kitchen door convinced Charity to take them seriously. Charity chose to run for parliament. And, with what the press described as unusually strong grass-roots support, she beat the governing party's incumbent (74). Today many of the traditional, male, party-supported legislators—most of whom ignored Ngilu previously—fervently wish that the women at Charity's kitchen door had failed to convince Ngilu to run. For you see, Charity Ngilu did not just win, but rather she went on to become "a stubborn thorn in the side of both President Daniel arap Moi and his ministers, upbraiding them on a regular basis for doing little or nothing for the poor, [and] especially [little for poor] women (74)"

From the perspective of traditional politicians, the "problem" with Charity Ngilu is that she does not want power for power's sake; she really does want to change Kenya; she really does want to make her country a better place.

Years ago, Ngilu had been shocked that Kenyans were dying of treatable diseases while traditional government politicians continued to spend large sums of money on the trappings of power (74). It was Ngilu's outrage at the indignities of poverty that led her to run for Parliament in 1992, and, in 1997, to declare her candidacy for the presidency. Ngilu, along with an increasingly vocal number of Kenyans, had become outraged at President Moi spending the "colossal sum of $60 million to buy himself a presidential jet [and spending] . . . another $70 million to build an airport in his hometown. Then [as Ngilu incredulously observed] Moi has the audacity to go in front of women [and] say, 'Please vote for me.' The women he is telling that to are walking naked . . . carrying sick children on their back[s], and their homes have holes in them that you can see through, because of poverty (74)."

Charity Ngilu has a vision, a vision for the people of Kenya. It is her burning desire to achieve her vision that drove her to seek the presidency. She wanted the office to accomplish her vision; she did not need or want the office itself.

Did you hear? Charity Ngilu became a candidate for president. But how did she get to be a presidential candidate? Yes, she's appalled at the poverty and equally appalled at President Moi's abuses of power. But how did she become a candidate? When did her party nominate her? Why her? Why then?

Good questions. But once again, such traditional questions do not lead us to understand at all how the story has unfolded. Ngilu's party did not nominate her. Ngilu defected from the Kikuyu-dominated Democratic Party when it became clear that it would not nominate her (74). Ngilu did not run as a candidate of the Democratic party: she ran as a candidate of the much smaller Social Democratic Party.

Strange? Well, no, not really.

Hierarchical power structures, whether political or corporate, often fail to support women as candidates for senior leadership positions. Most women draw

DID YOU HEAR?
Global Leadership Is No Longer for Men Alone (continued)

their support directly from the people—whether via the ballot box or the marketplace—rather than from either political or corporate hierarchical power structures (5). Mary Robinson, for example, before becoming president of Ireland, visited more small communities in Ireland than any politician before her. The opposition now admits that they did not take her candidacy seriously until it was too late (44). Similarly, former prime minister Benazir Bhutto visited more communities in Pakistan than any politician before her. She was only taken seriously as a candidate when "far more people [turned out upon her return to Pakistan in 1986] than anyone—politicians, diplomats, and analysts—had foreseen. Many people had doubted that Benazir Bhutto, a woman, could receive the kind of support from the people that her father, a Prominent Former Prime Minister of Pakistan, had enjoyed, but her triumphant return proved them all wrong" (22).

Likewise, former President Corazon Aquino held rallies in more than 1,000 Filipino communities while her opponent, Ferdinand Marcos, campaigned in only 34. Her victory was labeled the People's Revolution (34). Is not this, at its most fundamental level, what we call democracy? Broadly based community support that has not been orchestrated by a political or societal power elite? Is not this what we increasingly recognize as twenty-first-century networked power as opposed to the hierarchic power that dominated the twentieth century? Is not this what management scholars refer to as power-with ("empowerment") rather than power-over?[15]

It certainly does not surprise anyone who has been observing women in organizations that the strongest evidence for a difference in the way women and men lead is in women's tendency to adopt more democratic, inclusive, participative styles, while men tend to use more autocratic, directive styles. In more than 90 percent of the almost 400 studies comparing male and female leaders' behavior, women exhibit more democratic behavior than do men (42).

> *Unlike many political parties in Kenya, the one that Ngilu chose has no particular ethnic allegiance. That she chose this party is not in the least bit surprising. Ngilu ran, in part, on a unity platform. For you see, "Ngilu sees herself not only as a champion of women and the poor, but [also] as someone who can heal the ethnic rifts that have divided Kenya since independence (74)." As Ngilu says,*
>> *"This is a wounded nation. . . . There is open hostility and hatred between different tribes. Some neutral person, somebody with a difference, must sit down and moderate. . . . I don't have a score to settle with anyone (74)."*
> *For many Kenyans, "Ngilu represent[s] a complete break with [the] divisive tribal politics of the past (74)." As one Kenyan observed during the election campaign, "Charity is talking about unity, and this unity will unite both men and women. . . . If we vote for a man, there will be no change. With a woman, there will have to be a [very] big change (74)."*

Is Kenya unique? Is there something particular about Charity Ngilu's personality or behavior that leads Kenyans to believe that both change and unity are possible? From the details of Charity's story, one might be tempted to conclude that her story is unique. Certainly the rich history of behavioral and trait theories of leadership would suggest that there is something special in Charity Ngilu that allows Kenyans to hope for unity and to believe in change.[16] But enlarging our viewpoint beyond that of the male leaders on which almost all leadership theories have been based changes our perception (6). Throughout the world, among political, business, and societal leaders, women bring with them the symbolic possibility of fundamental societal and organizational change. The combination of women being outsiders at senior leadership levels previously completely dominated by men and of women beating the odds to become the first to lead a particular country or company produces powerful public imagery about the possibility of other fundamental changes (5).

If a woman can be chosen to be president, prime minister, or CEO when no other woman has held such an office and when few people thought that she could possibly be selected, then other major changes become believably possible (5). Mary Robinson's presidential acceptance speech captured the coupling of the unique event of a woman being elected president of Ireland with the possibility of national change and unity:

> "I was elected by men and women of all parties and none, by many with great moral courage who stepped out from the faded flags of Civil War and voted for a new Ireland. And above all by the women of Ireland . . . who instead of rocking the cradle rocked the system, and who came out massively to make their mark on the ballot paper, and on a new Ireland."[17]

The pattern of women leaders symbolizing change and unity is overwhelming. Both Nicaragua's Chamorro and the Philippines' Aquino became symbols of national unity in their strife-torn countries. Chamorro claimed "to have no ideology beyond national 'reconciliation'" (27). Chamorro's ability to bring all the members of her family together for Sunday dinner each week achieved near legendary status in Nicaragua. Why? Because, of Chamorro's four adult children, two were prominent Sandanistas while the other two equally prominently opposed the Sandanistas, not an unusual split in war-torn Nicaragua. As the ". . . matriarch who can still hold [her] family together, Chamorro gives symbolic hope to the nation that it too can find a peace, based on a unity, that can bring together all Nicaraguans" (91). Are these isolated examples? No, Corazon Aquino, although widely condemned in the press for supposed naiveté, invited members of both her own party and the opposition party into her cabinet, a conscious strategy to reunify her deeply divided country (34). In an attempt to bring peace and unity to Sri Lanka, Executive President Kumaratunga chose to meet directly with the Tamil separatists, even though her husband is widely believed to have been murdered by the Tamils and such a unity strategy broke directly with the policies of her father and her mother, both of whom had previously served as prime minister of Sri Lanka before Kumaratunga.

Given that women leaders symbolize unity and the possibility for change, it is not surprising that a woman business leader, Rebecca Mark, when she was chief executive of Enron Development Corporation, became the first person to success-fully negotiate a major multinational commercial transaction between Israel and an Arab country following the Middle East peace accords. Mark succeeded in bring-ing the Israelis and the Jordanians together to build a natural gas power generation station.[18]

Perhaps the best-known woman symbolizing hope for the type of significant change that could bring peace is the elected prime minister of Burma, Nobel Peace Prize Laureate Aung San Suu Kyi (11). Even after the military denied her the oppor-tunity to take office and placed her under house arrest for six years, Suu Kyi still chose to meet directly with the military opposition leaders. In 2003, she was again put under house arrest, and in November 2005, in spite of international opposition, her detention was extended for yet another year. Suu Kyi continues to fight for a peaceful future for her people.

Perhaps the least recognized woman symbolizing the potential for change and unity is Rwanda's former prime minister Agatha Uwilingiyimana. Uwilingiyimana was brought in as Rwanda's prime minister only after it was decided that the Civil War that broke out in 1994, and the ensuing genocide that killed over 800,000 Rwandans in less than three months, had to be stopped and that a peace treaty had to be signed. The former prime minister—a man—refused to have anything to do with sign-ing the peace agreement, as did the majority of his male colleagues. Uwilingiyimana became prime minister knowing that she was risking her life to do so. She paid the ultimate price; she was killed, not by the opposition, but by members of her own peo-ple who could not move beyond the tribal animosity of war (59;89).

> *What does the future portend? Did Charity Ngilu stand a chance of winning the election? The odds were against her. President Moi had been in power for nearly two decades. Even the chairwoman of one of the major opposition parties thought that Ngilu did not stand a chance ". . . not because [Charity was] not a good candidate, but because . . . sexism is still too deeply embedded in Kenya. . . . [Kenya] is not stable now, and it will take these men time to accept being ruled by a woman (74)."*
>
> *Some political strategists disagreed, believing that Ngilu had a fighting chance of winning. They observed that "hundreds [of men] in a mostly male audience cheered [Ngilu] . . . when she rose to speak" at political rallies (74). Some men "said [that] they were ready to vote for . . . Ngilu now (74)." They said "they were weary of the usual cast of opposition politicians, many of whom [had] served in Moi's government at one time or another (74)."*

Would she make it? No one knew. No one could predict the next election, let alone the twenty-first century, either for Kenya or for the rest of the world. Change comes at a price, yet continuing on our current path might well extract an even higher price—the extinction of civilization as we know it. Leaders become lightning rods for dissension within society. Charity Ngilu is no exception.

DID YOU HEAR?
Global Leadership Is No Longer for Men Alone (continued)

On Saturday, July 12th, only three days after Charity declared her candidacy
for president, thugs with machetes attacked her after she spoke at a rally.[19] *"The*
government [of course] denies that its agents orchestrated the attack, but [Charity]
. . . , who was wounded, maintains . . . [that her] assailants were from the youth
wing of the governing party (74)*." As Charity explained, ". . . I received a threaten-*
ing telephone call, [then] the man [on the phone] said, 'So, you are still running for
[president,] . . . after what happened [to you] on Saturday (74)*?'"*
*   Her answer was "Yes!"*

Societal change is not a game for cowards. Global leadership is not a game
played by cowards. Charity Ngilu has a vision—a vision for a peaceful, democratic
Kenya in which all citizens, rich and poor, female and male, from all backgrounds
can live in dignity. It is a vision worthy of the world, not just of Kenya. It is a vision
more strongly supported by the people than by the current political and economic
power elite. It is a vision that requires not only a shift in how we see society, but
also a shift in how we act within society: Ngilu's vision is based on unity, rather
than any form of divisive tribalism; on broadly based networked power, rather than
any form of hierarchic centralized power; and on broadly based access to economic
and social well-being, rather than on extreme advantage reserved only for those at
the top of a hierarchic, predominantly male pyramid.

Societal change has never come without powerful symbols of change.
Women leaders symbolize change. But societal change does not come through
symbols alone. To achieve the type of society in the twenty-first century that we
might envision, the women and men who lead must be vision-driven, globally
inclusive, and multiculturally persuasive. Such leaders must exhibit courage and
humility.

What makes these women global leaders, rather than national leaders? In part,
it is the dynamics of twenty-first-century society that challenge us all, women and
men, to think and to act within a global context. But for women, it is also the inter-
secting dynamics of time and place. Because the women who become leaders are
unique, the media chooses to tell their story.[20] The *New York Times* reported Charity
Ngilu's candidacy and spread the story throughout the world on the major wire services. Rightly or wrongly, the world press probably would not have picked up the
story had one of the smaller political parties in Africa nominated a man. Women
leaders are global leaders because society is going global and because the world
press makes them globally visible. And their global visibility allows them to act in
ways that would be much more difficult, if not impossible, for less visible male
leaders. All too many countries have been known to silence or to eliminate opposition politicians. Charity was placed under house arrest in 1992 after running for
parliament. She was attacked with machetes after declaring her candidacy for president. It is much less likely that Charity will "disappear" or be killed in a world that
is watching than she would be in a world oblivious to her struggle. Global visibility supports courageous action.

DID YOU HEAR?
Global Leadership Is No Longer for Men Alone (continued)

Global Leadership

To become leaders, do women need to fit into the predominantly male history of leadership theory? The answer is a resounding no; women neither fit nor do they need to fit. Neither men nor women leaders in the twenty-first century need to fit the patterns of twentieth century leadership.

> *Charity's story is our story, the story of civilization at a crucial transition as it either marks its demise or celebrates its transformation. Charity's story is our story, the story of leadership—whether by women or men—that transcends history to establish new directions worthy of civilization.*

Afterword

In early January 1998, former president Daniel arap Moi was reelected as president of Kenya. All sides claimed fraud in the election (among many others, see 38;68;71;72;73;100). Moi was constitutionally barred from running again in 2002; his elected successor, Mwai Kibaki, who ran on an anti-graft platform, was rapidly embroiled in his own corruption scandals. Kenya is still waiting for change. As of 2007, Charity was Minister of Health in Kenya.[21]

SUMMARY

Do young managers want global careers? Yes, under certain conditions. Whereas some young male and female managers still see more advantages in domestic than in global careers, more than 80 percent would like a global assignment at some time during their careers. Are women as interested as men in pursuing global careers? Yes, and both women and men are highly successful once sent abroad and in leadership positions. Increased competition is forcing global companies to select the most talented employees for managerial and professional positions, without regard to their nationality or to the fact that they are men or women.

QUESTIONS FOR REFLECTION

1. **Global Career Planning.** Why would you personally accept a global assignment? Why would you reject a global assignment?

2. **Global Human Resource Systems.** If you were vice president of human resources for a major global company and wanted to attract the best young managers to accept global assignments, what would you offer them?

3. **Women Expatriate Managers.** What are some of the best ways to attract women to accept global assignments? What should companies

and women do to make certain that women succeed on global assignments?

4. **Recruiting a Dual-Career Manager.** Companies often consider dual-career couples to be a major problem when selecting candidates for global assignments. How would you recruit a top manager for a global assignment if the manager's spouse was a senior executive for another company?

5. **Global Career Planning.** What kinds of global experiences would you like to have in your career? When? Why?

6. **Global Leadership.** If you could lead any global organization, which organization would it be? Why? What types of experiences would you need to include in your career to be prepared for this type of leadership position?

NOTES

1. The pronoun "he" has been changed in the quote to "they" to include male and female managers.

2. This chapter is based, in part, on the study reported in Adler's "Do MBAs Want International Careers?" (3). The research was supported by a grant from the Social Sciences and Humanities Research Council of Canada.

3. The surveyed MBAs were young (average age 27 years), most were single (68%), approximately a third were women (32%), and most were studying for their MBAs in the country in which they were born, held citizenship, and had received their undergraduate education. The most common undergraduate degrees were business and economics (34%) and engineering (11%), while the most common MBA concentrations were finance (44%) and marketing (29%). Although 38 percent had no work experience, the majority had worked for a short time (approximately two years) prior to entering the MBA program. More than one third (36%) had never lived abroad. Few of the MBAs' parents had worked internationally. See Table 1 in Adler (3).

4. See Table 2 in Adler (3).

5. 1,129 graduating MBAs cited 1,867 reasons for accepting global assignments; the most frequently cited reasons are given here. Listed numbers represent the percent of MBAs citing the particular reason. Because each MBA listed more than one reason, the total percentage exceeds 100%.

6. 1,129 graduating MBAs cited 2,308 reasons for rejecting global assignments; the most frequently cited reasons are listed above. Listed numbers represent the percentage of MBAs citing the particular reason. Because each MBA listed more than one reason, the total percentage exceeds 100%.

7. This section is adapted from Adler's "Competitive Frontiers: Women Managing Across Borders" (1:22-23).

8. For a discussion of how one company's CEO chose to increase the number of women from around the world at the highest levels of executive leadership, see references 15;16;17; 73;77;79.

9. Facts about Charity Ngilu's life are as documented in McKinley's *New York Times* article (74).

10. See Adler's "One World: Women Leading & Managing Worldwide" (8) for a complete list of women presidents and prime ministers, 1950 to 2005.

11. In Kenya, carrying and waving leafy branches symbolizes change and peace.

12. See Adler's "Global Leaders: A Dialogue with Future History" (5) for a description of women leaders' aspirations and paths to power.

13. See Adler's "Global Women Political Leaders: An Invisible History, An Increasingly Important Future," (7) for a description of the visions motivating women's leadership. For a broad understanding of leadership, primarily based on men, see Bass (26).

14. Author's personal interview with Maria Liberia-Peters in Curaçao, June 2, 1997.

15. For an excellent discussion of the increasing overlap of the managerial and feminist literatures both of which now refer to "power with," see Fondas (47).

16. For an excellent review of the leadership literature, including, but not limited to, behavioral and trait theories, see Yukl (102).

17. From Mary Robinson's 1990 presidential acceptance speech, as reported by Finlay (44).

18. See "Amman. Joint Jordan-Israeli Energy Project promises a flying start to cooperation" (http://arabia.com/star/951228/bus1.html) and "Enron Joint Venture" (43). The Associated Press heralded the Israeli and Arab businessmen, brought together by Enron, in anticipation of the first large-scale business agreement between Israel and a Gulf State: Qatar had agreed to sell gas to Israel through Enron ("Mideast Summit Offers Hope of Overcoming Stagnation," *Associated Press*, October 31, 1995). Rebecca Mark left Enron before it collapsed and, while questioned (especially about operations in India), she was not indicted in any of the corruption scandals that surrounded Enron's demise.

19. For a description of the attack, see "Attack on Presidential Candidate Motivated" (23). For a description of an earlier attack on Ngilu's home, see "Kenyan Opposition MPs Protest Police Brutality" (63).

20. Ngilu's opposition complains that "she is always covered [by the local and international media] when she speaks" (62).

21. Updated and adapted in 2007 from Adler's "Did you hear? Global leadership in Charity's World" (2). Reprinted with permission of Sage Publications.

REFERENCES

1. Adler, N. J. "Competitive Frontiers: Women Managing Across Borders," in N. J. Adler & D. N. Izraeli, eds., *Competitive Frontiers: Women Managers in a Global Economy* (Cambridge, Mass.: Blackwell, 1994), pp. 22–44.

2. Adler, N. J. "Did You Hear? Global Leadership in Charity's World," in *Journal of Management Inquiry*, vol. 7, no. 2, (1998), pp. 135–143. Copyright © 1998 Sage Publications. Reprinted by permission of Sage Publications.

3. Adler, N. J. "Do MBAs Want International Careers?" *International Journal of Intercultural Relations*, vol. 10, no. 3 (1986), pp. 277–300.

4. Adler, N. J. "Expecting International Success: Female Managers Overseas," *Columbia Journal of World Business*, vol. 19, no. 3 (1984), pp. 79–85.

5. Adler, N. J. "Global Leaders: A Dialogue with Future History," *International Management*, vol. 1, no. 2 (1997), pp. 21–33.

6. Adler, N. J. "Global Leadership: Women Leaders," *Management International Review*, Special Issue 1, vol. 37 (1997), pp. 171–196.

7. Adler, N. J. "Global Women Political Leaders: An Invisible History, An Increasingly Important Future," *Leadership Quarterly*, vol. 7, no. 1 (1996), pp. 133–161.

8. Adler, N. J. "One World: Women Leading & Managing Worldwide" in Diana Bilimoria & Sandy Kristin Piderit, eds., *Handbook on Women in Business and Management* (Cheltenham, U.K.: Edward Elgar Publishing, 2006).

9. Adler, N. J. "Pacific Basin Managers: A Gaijin, Not a Woman," *Human Resource Management*, vol. 26, no. 2 (1987), pp. 169–191.

10. Adler, N. J. "Re-Entry: Managing Cross-Cultural Transitions," *Group and Organization Studies*, vol. 6, no. 3 (1981), pp. 341–356.

11. Adler, N. J. "Societal Leadership: The Wisdom of Peace," in Suresh Srivastva, ed., *Executive Wisdom and Organizational Change* (San Francisco: Jossey-Bass, 1998), pp. 205–221.

12. Adler, N. J. "Women Do Not Want International Careers: And Other Myths About International Management," *Organizational Dynamics*, vol. 13, no. 2 (1984), pp. 66–79.

13. Adler, N. J. "Women in International Management: Where Are They?" *California Management Review*, vol. 26, no. 4 (1984), pp. 78–89.

14. Adler, N. J.; & Bartholomew, Susan. "Managing Globally Competent People," *Academy of Management Executive*, vol. 6, no. 3 (1992), pp. 52–65.

15. Adler, N. J.; with Brody, Laura W.; & Osland, Joyce S. "Advances in Global Leadership: The Women's Global Leadership Forum," in William H. Mobley, ed., *Advances in Global Leadership*, vol. 2 (Greenwich, Conn.: JAI Press, 2001), pp. 351–383.

16. Adler, Nancy J.; Brody, Laura W.; & Osland, Joyce S. "Going Beyond Twentieth Century Leadership: A CEO Develops His Company's Global Competitiveness," *Cross-Cultural Management: An International Journal*, vol. 8, no. 3–4 (2001), pp. 11–34.

17. Adler, N. J.; with Brody, Laura W.; & Osland, Joyce S. "The Women's Global Leadership Forum: Enhancing One Company's Leadership Capability," *Human Resource Management,* vol. 39, no. 2 & 3 (2000), pp. 209–225.

18. Adler, N. J.; & Ghadar, F. "Globalization and Human Resource Management," in Alan M. Rugman, ed., *Research in Global Strategic Management: A Canadian Perspective,* vol. 1 (Greenwich, Conn.: JAI Press, 1989), pp. 179–205.

19. Adler, N. J.; & Izraeli, D. N. *Competitive Frontiers: Women Managers in a Global Economy* (Cambridge, Mass.: Blackwell, 1994).

20. Adler, N. J.; & Izraeli, D. N. *Women in Management Worldwide* (Armonk, N.Y.: M. E. Sharpe, 1988).

21. Aitken, T. "What It Takes to Work Abroad," in T. Aitken, *The Multinational Man: The Role of the Manager Abroad* (New York: Halstead Press, 1973).

22. Anderson, Nancy Fix. "Benazir Bhutto and Dynastic Politics: Her Father's Daughter, Her People's Sister," in Michael A. Genovese, ed., *Women as National Leaders* (Newbury Park, Calif.: Sage, 1993), pp. 41–69.

23. "Attack on Presidential Candidate Motivated," *Agence France-Press,* (July 14, 1997).

24. Baker, J. C. "An Analysis of How the U.S. Multinational Company Considers the Wife of American Expatriate Managers," *Academy of Management Proceedings,* vol. 35 (1975), pp. 258–260.

25. Bartlett, Chris A.; & Ghoshal, Sumantra. *Managing Across Borders: The Transnational Solution* (Boston: Harvard Business School Press, 1989).

26. Bass, Bernard. *Bass & Stogdill's Handbook of Leadership,* 3d ed. (New York: The Free Press, 1991).

27. Benn, Melissa. "Women Who Rule the World," *Cosmopolitan* (February 1995).

28. Bennett, A. "Going Global: The Chief Executives in Year 2000 Will Be Experienced Abroad," *Wall Street Journal* (February 27, 1989), pp. A1, A9.

29. Black, J. Stuart; & Gregersen, Hal B. "The Right Way to Manage Expatriates," *Harvard Business Review* (March–April 1999), pp. 52–62.

30. Black, J. Stuart; Gregersen, Hal B.; Mendenhall, Mark E.; & Stroh, L. K. *Global Assignments* (New York: Addison-Wesley 1999).

31. Brett, Jeanne M.; & Stroh, Linda K. "Willingness to Relocate Internationally," *Human Resource Management,* vol. 35, no. 3 (1995), pp. 405–424.

32. Carter, Nancy. "Solve the Dual-Career Challenge," *Workforce,* vol. 2 (Global Workforce Supplement) (1997), pp. 21–22.

33. Chusmir, L. H.; & Frontczak, N. T. "International Management Opportunities for Women: Women and Men Paint Different Pictures," *International Journal of Management*, vol. 7, no. 3 (1990), pp. 295–301.

34. Col, Jeanne-Marie. "Managing Softly in Turbulent Times: Corazon C. Aquino, President of the Philippines," in M. A. Genovese, ed., *Women as National Leaders* (Newbury Park, Calif.: Sage, 1993), pp. 13–40.

35. Culpan, O.; & Wright, G. H. "Women: Abroad: Getting the Best Results from Women Managers," *International Journal of Human Resource Management*, vol. 13, no. 5 (2002), pp. 784–801.

36. Daily, C. M.; Certo, S. T.; & Dalton, D. R. "A Decade of Corporate Women: Some Progress in the Boardroom, None in the Executive Suite," *Strategic Management Journal*, vol. 20 (1999), pp. 3–99.

37. Davidson, E. D.; & Punnett, B. J. "International Assignments: Is There a Role for Gender and Race in Decisions?" *International Journal of Human Resource Management*, vol. 6, no. 2 (1995), pp. 411–438.

38. Davies, Karen. "Delays Extend Kenya Election to 2nd Day," *Chicago Sun-Times* (December 30, 1997), p. 21.

39. Derr, C. Brooke. *Managing the New Careerists* (San Francisco: Jossey-Bass, 1986).

40. Derr, C. Brooke; & Laurent, André. "The Internal and External Careers: A Theoretical and Cross-Cultural Perspective," in M. Arthur, D. T. Hall, & B. S. Lawrence, eds., *The Handbook of Career Theory* (Cambridge, U.K.: Cambridge University Press, 1989).

41. Deutsch, C. H. "Losing Innocence, Abroad," *New York Times* (July 10, 1988), Business section, pp. 1, 26.

42. Eagly, Alice H.; & Johnson, Blair T. "Gender and Leadership Style: A Meta-analysis," *Psychological Bulletin,* vol. 8, no. 2 (1990), pp. 233–256, as cited in Vinnicombe, Susan, & Colwill, Nina. *The Essence of Women in Management* (London: Prentice Hall, 1995), p. 32.

43. "Enron Joint Venture," *New York Times* (May 28, 1996), p. D11.

44. Finlay, Fergus. *Mary Robinson: A President with a Purpose* (Dublin, Ireland: The O'Brien Press, 1990).

45. Fischlmayr, I. C. "Female Self-Perception as Barrier to International Careers?" *International Journal of Human Resource Management*, vol. 13, no. 5 (2002), pp. 773–783.

46. Fisher, Anne B. "When Will Women Get to the Top?" *Fortune* (September 21, 1992), pp. 44–56.

47. Fondas, Nanette. "The Origins of Feminization," *Academy of Management Review*, vol. 22 (1997), pp. 257–282.

48. Genovese, Michael. *Women as National Leaders* (Newbury Park, Calif.: Sage, 1993), p. ix.

49. GMAC Global Relocation Services. *Global Relocation Trends 2003/2004 Survey Report* (Oak Brook, Ill.: GMAC Relocation Services, National Foreign Trade Council and SHRM Global Forum, 2004a).

50. GMAC Global Relocation Services. *Ten Years of Global Relocation Trends 1993–2004.* (Oak Brook, Ill.: GMAC Relocation Services, National Foreign Trade Council and SHRM Global Forum, 2004b).

51. Gonzales, R. F.; & Neghandi, Anatute R. *The United States Overseas Executive: His Orientations and Career Patterns* (East Lansing, Mich.: Graduate School of Business Administration, Michigan State University, 1967).

52. Hammond, Val; & Holton, V. "The Scenario for Women Managers in Britain in the 1990s," in N. J. Adler & D. N. Izraeli, eds., *Competitive Frontiers: Women Managers in a Global Economy* (Cambridge, Mass.: Blackwell, 1994), pp. 224–242.

53. Harris, Hilary. "Organizational Influences on Women's Career Opportunities in International Management," *Women in Management Review*, vol. 10 (1995), pp. 26–31.

54. Harris, Hilary. "Think International Manager, Think Male: Why are Women Not Selected for International Management Assignments?" *Thunderbird International Business Review*, vol. 44, no. 2 (2002), pp. 175–203.

55. Harvey, Michael. "Addressing the Dual-Career Expatriation Dilemma," *Human Resource Planning*, vol. 19 (1996), pp. 18–39.

56. Heenan, D. "The Corporate Expatriate: Assignment to Ambiguity," *Columbia Journal of World Business*, vol. 5 (1970), pp. 49–54.

57. Helgesen, Sally. *The Female Advantage: Women's Ways of Leadership* (New York: Doubleday 1990).

58. Hill, C. J.; & Tillery, K. R. "What Do Male/Female Perceptions of an International Business Career Suggest About Recruitment Policies?" *SAM Advanced Management Journal* (Autumn 1992), pp. 10–14.

59. Hill, K. "Agathe Uwilingiyimana (1953–1994)," in R. Salokar & M. Volcansek, eds., *Women and the Law* (Westport, Conn.: Greenwood Press, 1996).

60. Howard, C. "The Returning Overseas Executive: Culture Shock in Reverse," *Human Resources Management*, vol. 13, no. 2 (1974), pp. 22–26.

61. Jelinek, Mariann; & Adler, N. J. "Women: World Class Managers for Global Competition," *Academy of Management Executive*, vol. 2, no. 1 (1988), pp. 11–19.

62. "Kalonzo Tells Ngilu to Bow Out of Race," *The Nation* (Africa News Service: Africa online, August 12, 1997).

63. "Kenyan Opposition MPs Protest Police Brutality" (Agence France-Press: April 15, 1997).

64. Lansing, P.; & Ready, K. "Hiring Women Managers in Japan: An Alternative for Foreign Employers," *California Management Review,* vol. 30, no. 3 (1988), pp. 112–127.

65. Laurent, André. "The Cross-Cultural Puzzle of International Human Resource Management," *Human Resource Management,* vol. 25, no. 1 (1986), pp. 91–102. Copyright 1986 John Wiley & Sons, Inc.

66. Linehan, M.; & Scullion H. "European Female Expatriates Careers: Critical Success Factors," *Journal of European Industrial Training,* vol. 25, no.8 (2001), pp.392–418.

67. Linehan, M.; & Walsh, J. S. "Key Issues in the Senior Female International Career Move: A Qualitative Study in a European Context," *British Journal of Management,* vol. 12, no. 1 (2001), pp. 85–95.

68. Lovgren, Stephan. "Kenya: No Surprise: The 'Big Man' Wins," *U.S. News & World Report* (January 12, 1998), p. 36.

69. Mathur-Helm, B. "Expatriate Women Managers: At the Crossroads of Success, Challenges and Career Goals," *Women in Management Review,* vol. 17, no. 1 (2002), pp. 18–28.

70. Mayerhofer, H.; Hartmann, L. C.; & Herbert, A. "Career Management Issues for Flexpatriate International Staff," *Thunderbird International Business Review,* vol. 46, no. 6 (2004), pp. 647–66.

71. McKinley, James C. "All Sides in Kenya Cry Fraud in Election," *New York Times* (December 31, 1997), p. A4.

72. McKinley, James C. "Chaos in Kenya Voting Sets Off Accusations of Fraud," *New York Times International* (December 30, 1997), p. A6.

73. McKinley, James C. "Kenya's President Takes Lead as Ballot Counting Drags On," *New York Times* (January 1, 1998), p. A4.

74. McKinley, James C. "A Woman to Run Kenya? One Says, 'Why Not?'" *New York Times* (August 3, 1997); Section 1, page 3, column 1.

75. Mervosh, Edward, M. "Managing Expatriate Compensation," *Industry Week,* vol. 246, no. 14 (1997), pp. 13–16.

76. Murray, Alex. "International Personnel Repatriation: Cultural Shock in Reverse," *MSU Business Topics,* vol. 21, no. 2 (1973), pp. 59–66.

77. Osland, Joyce S.; & Adler, Nancy J. "Women and Global Leadership at Bestfoods," in Paul F. Buller & Randall S. Schuler, eds., *Managing Organizations and People: Cases in Management, Organization, and Human Resource Management* (Cincinnati, Ohio: South-Western, 2006), pp. 1–22.

78. Osland, Joyce S.; Adler, Nancy J.; & Brody, Laura W. "Developing Women As Global Leaders: Lessons and Sense Making From an Organizational Change Effort," in Ronald J. Burke & Debra L. Nelson, eds., *Advancing Women's Careers* (Oxford, U.K: Blackwell, 2002), pp. 15–36.

79. Osland, Joyce S.; Adler, N. J.; & Brody, Laura W. "Women and Global Leadership at Bestfoods," in Joyce S. Osland, David Kolb, & Irwin Rubin, eds., *Organizational Behavior: An Experimental Approach* (Upper Saddle River, N.J.: Prentice Hall, 2001), pp. 533–555.

80. Paik, Yongsun; & Vance, Charles M. "Evidence of Back-Home Selection Bias Against American Female Expatriates," *Women in Management Review*, vol. 17, no. 2 (2002), pp. 68–79.

81. Pellico, M. T.; & Stroh, Linda K. "Spousal Assistance Program: An Integral Component of the International Assignment," *New Approaches to Employee Management*, vol. 4 (1997), pp. 225–241.

82. Perham, J. C. "The Boom in Executive Jobs," *Dun's Review,* vol. 110, no. 5 (1977), pp. 80–81.

83. Perry, N. J. "If You Can't Join 'em, Beat 'em," *Fortune* (September 21, 1992), pp. 58–59.

84. Pogrebin, Robin. "Pearson Picks an American as Executive," *New York Times* (October 18, 1996), p. D7.

85. Porter, Gayle; & Tansky, Judith W. "Expatriate Success May Depend on a "'Learning Orientation': Considerations for Selection and Training," *Human Resource Management,* vol. 38, no. 1 (1999), pp. 47–60.

86. Porter, Michael. *The Competitive Advantage of Nations* (New York: Free Press, 1990).

87. Puccino, Shirley. "The Right Mix of Expatriate Employee Compensation Components," *Benefits and Compensation Digest,* vol. 42, no. 9 (2005), pp. 30–33.

88. Rosenzweig, P. M.; & Nohria, N. "Influences on Human Resource Management Practices in Multinational Corporations," *Journal of International Business Studies,* 2nd quarter (1994), pp. 229–251.

89. "Rwanda: First Woman Premier Dies," *Inter-Press Service Newswire* (April 8, 1994).

90. Rykken, Rolf. "The Whole Expatriate?" *Export Today,* vol. 14, no. 12 (1998), pp. 70–71.

91. Saint-Germain, Michelle A. "Women in Power in Nicaragua: Myth and Reality," in M. A. Genovese, ed., *Women as National Leaders* (Newbury Park, Calif.: Sage, 1993), pp. 70–102.

92. Selmer, Jan; & Leung, A. S. M. "Are Corporate Career Development Activities Less Available to Female than to Male

Expatriates?" *Journal of Business Ethics*, vol. 43, no. 1-2 (2003a), pp. 125–136.

93. Selmer, Jan; & Leung, A. S. M. "International Adjustment of Female vs. Male Business Expatriates," *The International Journal of Human Resource Management*, vol. 14, no. 7 (2003b), pp. 1117–1131.

94. Smith, L. "The Hazards of Coming Home," *Dun's Review* (October 1975), pp. 71–73.

95. Steinhoff, P. G.; & Tanaka, K. "Women Managers in Japan," in N. J. Adler & D. N. Izraeli, eds., *Competitive Frontiers: Women Managers in a Global Economy* (Cambridge, Mass.: Blackwell, 1994), pp. 79–100.

96. Stogdill, R. *Handbook of Leadership* (New York: The Free Press, 1974).

97. Stroh, L. K.; Varma, A.; & Valy-Durbin, S. J. "Why are Women Left at Home: Are They Unwilling to Go on International Assignments?" *Journal of World Business*, vol. 35, no. 3 (2000), pp. 241–255.

98. Tung, Rosalie L. "U.S. Multinationals: A Study of Their Selection and Training for Overseas Assignments," *Academy of Management Proceedings*, vol. 39 (1979), pp. 298–301.

99. Van der Boon, Mary. "Women in International Management: An Inter-national Perspective on Women's Ways of Leadership." *Women in Management Review*, vol. 18, no. 3 (2003), pp. 132–146.

100. "Vote Fraud Charges Fly in Kenya Election," *Chicago Sun-Times* (December 31, 1997), p. 28.

101. "Women in Business: Europe's Top 25," *FTMagazine*, Special Issue, no. 127 (October 15/16, 2005).

102. Yukl, Gary. *Leadership in Organizations*, 4th ed. (Upper Saddle River, N.J.: Prentice Hall, 1998).

Epilogue

There are good reasons for suggesting that the modern age has ended. Many things indicate that we are going through a transitional period, when it seems that something is on the way out and something else is painfully being born. It is as if something were crumbling, decaying and exhausting itself, while something else, still indistinct, were arising from the rubble. . . . This state of affairs has its social and political consequences. The planetary civilization to which we all belong confronts us with global challenges. We stand helpless before them because our civilization has essentially globalized only the surface of our lives. . . . [World leaders] . . . are rightly worried by the problem of finding the key to ensure the survival of a civilization that is global and multicultural. . . . The central . . . task of the final years of this century, then, is the creation of a new model of co-existence among the various cultures, peoples, races, and religious spheres within a single interconnected civilization. . . . Yes, it is clearly necessary to invent organizational structures appropriate to the multicultural age.

—Vaclav Havel, former president of the Czech Republic (2)

Vaclav Havel's appreciation of the transition that the world is now experiencing is certainly important to each of us as human beings. Equally importantly, his appreciation of the world situation challenges us as managers and leaders. The world *has* gotten smaller. Global business now dominates world business. Managers worldwide are becoming more internationally sophisticated. It is only as we recognize the extent to which we are culture bound that we can go beyond the limitations of our own necessarily narrow perspectives. It is only as we work globally that we can recognize and benefit from a world economy. We have entered an era in which global organizations, companies, and alliances determine our economic and social well-being. To the extent that organizations respect individual cultural differences, they allow us to contribute based on our uniqueness. To the extent that they transcend national boundaries, they encourage a world, otherwise fraught with wars and animosities, to collaborate and to cooperate. If we fail to recognize cultural differences and choose to maintain ethnocentric domestic approaches, we condemn the world to divisiveness and ultimately to its own demise.

In the past, multinational corporations have not been celebrated for their contributions to world peace or understanding. Perhaps it is only today, as we recognize that worldwide understanding and cooperation have become critical to our very survival, that the function of global companies has become apparent (1). Governments reflect national boundaries; global companies transcend national boundaries and national definitions. Global companies can use their transnational status, their creative public-private partnerships, and their ever-expanding networks of alliances in ways that benefit and enrich their worldwide constituencies or in ways that impoverish us all. The challenge is immense. The importance is inestimable.

REFERENCES

1. Adler, N. J. "Corporate Global Citizenship: Successfully Partnering with the World," in Gabriele Suder, ed., *Corporate Strategies Under International Terrorism and Adversity* (Cheltenham, U.K.: Edward Elgar Publishing, 2006), pp. 177–195.
2. Havel, Vaclav. "The New Measure of Man," from speech delivered in Independence Hall, Philadelphia, July 4, 1994. See *New York Times,* 8, July 1994, A 27 for the full text.

Index

Page numbers followed by "f" denote figures; those followed by "t" denote tables

Painting on Book Cover

"The Audacity of Beauty and Possibility"

"What we cannot comprehend by analysis,
we become aware of in awe."[1]

In the midst of chaos, how do we see beauty? Surrounded by turbulence, how do we discover simplicity? Living together on one planet, how do we simultaneously celebrate our collective humanity and the unique resonance of our individual visions? Given the power of analytic understanding-driven as it is to claim life as *knowable*—how do we re-recognize the *unknown* and *unknowable*? How do we surrender to the humility it takes to stand in awe of life's mysteries? Where do we stand when we stand in awe?

Allowing a painting to be born is to stand in awe of one of life's most beautiful mysteries. Invited by the blank paper, the best of my intentions and experience enter into a dance with uncontrollable coincidence. Neither the process nor the resulting art are ever completely defined. Which way will the colors run? What surprises will the ink reveal as it, ever so gently, touches the paint? I purposely use water-based media that don't stay put where I place them on the paper. There's never any illusion that I control the process. I only enter the dance; paintings emerge out of the dance. For me, being an artist is about giving birth to the possibilities inherent in mystery. Creation—whether on a canvas of words or visual images—is, in fact, about relearning to dance with God.

Among the many artists who have inspired me, Marc Chagall is among the most important. During his lifetime, many of Chagall's contemporaries wrote him off for having refused the avant-garde's invitation to create art strictly for art's sake. Today, critics no longer write him off, but rather acclaim the striking humanity of his paintings, and offer him their highest praise, "Marc Chagall gave this nihilist century a worthy concept: hope."[2]

---

[1] Abraham Joshua Heschel, in *I Asked for Wonder* (Samuel H. Dresner, ed., New York: Crossroad, 2001).

[2] From Alan Riding's "Anxiety and Hope in a Mystical Fusion: Paris Show Offers Chagall's Intense Humanism Beyond the *Joie de Vivre*" (*New York Times*, April 22, 2003: p. B5).

Nancy J. Adler has been creating watercolors for two decades. She was an artist-in-residence at the Banff Centre for the Arts and a guest at the Emily Carr Institute of Art and Design. Her ink and watercolor paintings have been exhibited in Montreal, Toronto, Vancouver, and Washington D.C. Her paintings are currently held in private collections in Canada, England, Hong Kong, Switzerland and the United States.